EITHER/OR

Volume I

EITHER/OR

Søren Kierkegaard

VOLUME I

Translated by David F. Swenson
and Lillian Marvin Swenson
with revisions and a foreword
by Howard A. Johnson

PRINCETON UNIVERSITY PRESS

PRINCETON, NEW JERSEY

FOREWORD BY THE REVISER

Either/Or is a two-volume work, of which the present book is Volume I, the "Either." The companion volume—the "Or" —is also available in Princeton Paperbacks. It cannot be too strongly emphasized that Volume I, for all its intrinsic merit, makes no sense without Volume II. For what use is an "either" without an "or"—and *vice versa?*

To read the one volume without the other is to miss altogether Kierkegaard's fundamental intention with the work; it is to miss the *aut-aut,* the absolute disjunction, the summons to decide between alternative philosophies of life with which Kierkegaard here confronts us. Ideally and conceptually, the two parts belong together; it is only the accident of their size which, in English as in Danish, has caused them to be bound separately. Different as each volume is —in style, content, mood, and philosophical orientation— Kierkegaard means us to see them together, side by side, so that we may see the differences—and decide between them.

Neither volume represents fully or finally what Kierkegaard himself believes. Each volume is written by a pseudonym, yet each of the respective authors is something more than a nom de plume. Behind each pen name lies "a subjectively actual personality" created by Kierkegaard, to be sure, but created not to be simply a mouthpiece for Kierkegaard's own convictions, but rather to represent the convictions of a young romanticist, in Part I, and those of a mature ethical idealist, in Part II. That is to say, Kierkegaard employs the "mimic-method" of teaching. Instead of *lecturing* about romanticism and ethical idealism from the supposedly neutral standpoint of a professor's chair—showing first the good points and then the weak points of each —he impersonates two different individuals who are passionately committed to these divergent outlooks on life. Each man is "sold" on his own position, and each is out to "sell" the other—and you! Obviously Kierkegaard has sympathies with both, but it is equally obvious—when the whole of Kierkegaard is known—that he personally is critical of both. With this book he intends only that we shall be sharply observant of two contrasted philosophies of life, the aesthetic and the ethical, and then choose between them —or else, perhaps, find ourselves impelled to seek a solution elsewhere. True to his method, Kierkegaard will not dictate the answer. What he does do, relentlessly, is compel us to take note of the question and of the need for decision.

Incomparably the best introduction to *Either/Or* has already been written by the man best qualified to write it— that is, by Kierkegaard himself, but it is a Kierkegaard hiding under the pseudonym of Victor Eremita, the purported editor of *Either/Or*. The Preface written by Victor in his capacity as editor stands at the forefront of the present volume. Reading this is *conditio sine qua non* if one is to be oriented in the several hundred pages which follow. Since Victor has said what he has to say with all desirable clarity, there is no need for me to go over the ground covered there. Nor is there any need to touch upon the points made in the prefatory material supplied by the translators of the first English edition, for all of this has been preserved intact in the present edition.

In this foreword of mine it remains only to explain that what is here offered is not a new translation but rather a revision of a previous translation, published in 1944 by Princeton University Press, Volume I being the work of the Swensons and Volume II the work of Walter Lowrie.

The untimely death in 1940 of that pioneer expositor and impeccable translator of Kierkegaard, Professor David F. Swenson, cut short his work, scarcely begun, of translating the first volume of *Either/Or*. As a labor of love, in tribute to his memory, Mrs. Swenson undertook to complete the work he had left unfinished, and at the same time she appealed to Dr. Lowrie to translate the second volume. In many instances it would be impossible to admire sufficiently the felicity of the words and phrases Mrs. Swenson has found to turn into English many of Kierkegaard's best passages—as well as his worst. It must be said that it is not altogether easy to make Kierkegaard speak English, which is due in part to the differences between the two languages, but is due in larger part to the eccentricities of Kierkegaard's diction. Some of his sentences defy even the Danes. Strange that the Kierkegaard whose artistry with words places him in the first rank of Danish prose writers is also the Kierkegaard who at other times could turn out shockingly bad sentences which not even Danish grammarians and philologists can fathom. In the light of these difficulties, Mrs. Swenson showed great resourcefulness. Yet it was a knowledge of her own limitations which prompted Mrs. Swenson (in her Preface to the earlier Princeton edition) to express regret "that the reader of this first volume will find a certain unevenness of style due to my inability as a translator to attain the high standard demanded by my husband of himself." In addition, since Mrs. Swenson picked up the job of translation *in medias res,* certain errors in translation were inevitable. Most of these have, I hope, been corrected in the present edition.

The translation of the second volume, which is the achievement of Walter Lowrie, stands virtually unchallenged, although occasionally—in order to justify my existence—I have permitted myself a minor alteration or two, always with Lowrie's consent and usually at his insistence.

In short, as editor of this new edition, I have limited myself to the task of correcting what I deemed to be errors in translation. Almost nowhere have I yielded to the recurrent temptation of trying to improve the *style*—a task which still remains to be done, if the English-speaking world is to have in *Either/Or* what the Danish-speaking world has in *Enten-Eller:* a virtuoso performance with words, a premier example of prose poetry. Meanwhile, however, I have good hopes that the revised translation here offered, if oftentimes too literal to be good English, is nonetheless close enough to the Danish to make eminent good sense—by which I mean only that the text has become sufficiently intelligible to give sense to one's agreeing with it or taking issue with it.

To whatever degree intelligibility has been attained, it is due, in no small part, to the six members of the Family Schack of Copenhagen and to Niels and Majka Thulstrup of Søborg who, with incredible patience, taught me Danish and answered ten thousand questions about the text of this maddening and strangely compelling book.

Howard A. Johnson

Cathedral Church of St. John the Divine
New York
May 5, 1958

TRANSLATOR'S PREFACE

This first English printing of Søren Kierkegaard's *Either/ Or* by the Princeton University Press in 1943, is noteworthy in that it marks the centennial anniversary of its first Danish publication in 1843. It was also the first of Kierkegaard's important contributions to Danish literature, and established his fame as a writer. The occasion for its production lay in the unhappy circumstance of his engagement to Regina Olsen and its subsequent breach, and this experience constituted the determining factor which placed Kierkegaard, almost at a stroke, in full possession of his aesthetic and literary powers. During the next twelve years he was responsible for a tremendous output of aesthetic and religious literature, the former, as in the case of *Either/ Or*, being published not under his own name, but under the names of various pseudonyms. As he later explained, he was responsible for the creation of the pseudonymous authors, but not for their thoughts which were their own. Space forbids going into the subject of the pseudonyms in detail, but the interested reader is referred to Dr. Walter Lowrie's *Kierkegaard*, where the subject is discussed at some length. His religious productions were for the most part published in his own name.

Since I am not a Kierkegaard scholar it would be presumptuous for me in my own person to try to speak of the character and significance of *Either/Or*. As some degree of orientation is, however, necessary, or at least helpful to the reader for a proper understanding of the form and purpose of this work, I shall take the liberty of reproducing certain passages from my husband's writings, and also some quotations from Kierkegaard himself which have a particular bearing upon this first volume of *Either/Or*.

An ethical view of life is here contrasted with a purely aesthetic attitude. The aestheticist is the author of the papers that constitute the first volume, and is here designated as A; the ethicist B is responsible for the second volume, consisting of letters written to A, couched in terms of friendly admonition. The title of the work suggests that the reader is confronted with a decisive alternative; he is invited to weigh and choose for himself.

A consciously non-ethical philosophy inspires the varied contents of the first volume. These consist of a group of lyrical aphorisms (Diapsalmata); a study of the spirit of modern tragedy contrasted with the ancient, together with a poetized sketch of a modernized Antigone; a psychological analysis of certain heroines of reflective grief (Shadowgraphs), with a poetic rendering of their inner self-communion; an oration on the subject of who may be regarded as the unhappiest of mortals; a review of Scribe's comedy, *The First Love*, sparkling with wit and buoyed up by an aesthetic enthusiasm which puffs its subject up into a masterpiece; a study of the sensuous-erotic in human nature, in so far as it is present in an unconsciously immediate manner, described through the medium of Mozart's music, particularly of his opera *Don Juan;* and a parallel study of a reflective seducer, who is not so much a personality with a consciousness, as he is the abstract embodiment of a force of nature. This seducer is presented through a section of his diary, copied surreptitiously—a diary which besides sketching brilliantly minor episodes, tells the story of a diabolically clever seduction, so managed that the outward appearance leaves it doubtful who is the seducer and who the seduced. In addition there is a bit of pure theorizing in the essay called the Rotation Method, in which a thoroughly sophisticated enjoyment-philosophy explains by means of what artistry its goal may best be realized, and the devil of boredom be exorcised.

Four years after the appearance of *Either/Or* Kierkegaard published his greatest philosophical work, the mammoth *Concluding Unscientific Postscript,* and in that he took occasion to review and evaluate the entire pseudonymous output. Of *Either/Or* he says in part: "It is an indirect polemic against speculative philosophy, which is indifferent to the existential. The fact that there is no result, and no finite decision, is an indirect expression for the truth as inwardness, and thus perhaps a polemic against the truth as knowl-

edge. . . . The *first* part represents an existential probability which cannot win through to existence, a melancholy
that needs to be ethically worked up. Melancholy is its essential character, and this so deep that though autopathic,
it deceptively occupies itself with the sufferings of others
(Shadowgraphs), and for the rest deceives by concealing
itself under the cloak of pleasure, rationality, demoraliza-
tion, the deception and the concealment being at one and
the same time its strength and its weakness, its strength
in imagination, and its weakness in winning through to existence. It is an imagination-existence in aesthetic passion,
and therefore paradoxical, colliding with time; it is in its
maximum despair; it is therefore not existence but an existential possibility tending toward existence, and brought
so close to it that you feel how every moment is wasted
as long as it has not come to a decision. But the existential
possibility in the existing 'A' refuses to become aware of
this, and keeps existence away by the most subtle of all
deceptions, by thinking; he has thought everything possible,
and yet he has not existed at all. The consequence of this
is that only the Diapsalmata are pure lyrical effusions; the
rest has abundant thought-content, which may easily deceive, as if having thought about something were identical
with existing. . . . The relation is not to be conceived as
that between an immature and a mature thought, but between not existing and existing. 'A' is therefore a developed
thinker, he is far superior to 'B' as a dialectician, he has
been endowed with all the seductive gifts of soul and understanding; thereby it becomes clearer by what characteristic it is that 'B' differs from him. . . . If the book has any
merit, this will essentially consist in not giving any result,
but in transforming everything into inwardness: in the first
part, an imaginative inwardness which evokes the possibilities with intensified passion, with sufficient dialectical power
to transform all into nothing in despair; in the second part,
an ethical pathos, which with a quiet, incorruptible, and
yet infinite passion of resolve embraces the modest ethical
task, and edified thereby stands self-revealed before God
and man.

"There is no didacticism in the book, but from this it does

not follow that there is no thought-content; thus it is one thing to think, and another thing to exist in what has been thought. Existence is in its relation to thought just as little something following of itself as it is something thoughtless. . . . We have here presented to us an existence in thought, and the book or the work has no finite relation to anybody." —*Unscientific Postscript*, 226-228.

I regret very much that the reader of this first volume will find a certain unevenness of style due to my inability as a translator to attain the high standard demanded by my husband of himself. [Note by the reviser: *In a brief passage here omitted, Mrs. Swenson explained that "for greater readability," since "there are at the present time so relatively few students of Greek," she had supplied translations of all quotations from the Greek in the body of the text and had relegated the original Greek to the Notes. In this new edition, it must be explained that, for reasons of economy, the Greek has had to be suppressed altogether.*]

I am indebted to the partial translation of the "Diary of the Seducer" by Knud Fick for light on the translation of certain idiomatic expressions. I am particularly grateful to Mr. Paul T. Martinsen for careful reading of the manuscript with me. I also desire to express my sincere appreciation to Princeton University Press for unfailing courtesy and consideration in the face of the tremendous difficulties and delays incident to wartime shortages and restrictions.

Lillian Marvin Swenson

March 17, 1943

CONTENTS

EITHER/OR

A Fragment of Life

EDITED BY

VICTOR EREMITA

———

PART I

Containing the papers of A

———

Are passions, then, the pagans of the soul?
Reason alone baptized?

YOUNG[1]

———

Copenhagen, 1843

Can be purchased from the
University Bookseller C. A. Reitzel
Printed at Bianco Luno's Press

[Translation of the original title page]

PREFACE

[by Victor Eremita]

Dear Reader: I wonder if you may not sometimes have felt inclined to doubt a little the correctness of the familiar philosophic maxim that the external is the internal, and the internal the external.[2] Perhaps you have cherished in your heart a secret which you felt in all its joy or pain was too precious for you to share with another. Perhaps your life has brought you in contact with some person of whom you suspected something of the kind was true, although you were never able to wrest his secret from him either by force or cunning. Perhaps neither of these presuppositions applies to you and your life, and yet you are not a stranger to this doubt; it flits across your mind now and then like a passing shadow. Such a doubt comes and goes, and no one knows whence it comes, nor whither it goes. For my part I have always been heretically-minded on this point in philosophy, and have therefore early accustomed myself, as far as possible, to institute observations and inquiries concerning it. I have sought guidance from those authors whose views I shared on this matter; in short, I have done everything in my power to remedy the deficiency in the philosophical works.

Gradually the sense of hearing came to be my favorite sense; for just as the voice is the revelation of an inwardness incommensurable with the outer, so the ear is the instrument by which this inwardness is apprehended, hearing the sense by which it is appropriated. Whenever, then, I found a contradiction between what I saw and what I heard, then I found my doubt confirmed, and my enthusiasm for the investigation stimulated. In the confessional the priest is separated from the penitent by a screen; he does not see, he only hears. Gradually as he listens, he constructs an outward appearance which corresponds to the voice he hears. Consequently, he experiences no contradiction. It is otherwise, however, when you hear and see at the same time, and yet perceive a screen between yourself and the speaker. My researches in this direction have met with varying degrees of success. Sometimes I have been favored by fortune, sometimes not, and one needs good fortune to win results along this road. However, I have never lost my desire to continue my investigations. Whenever I have been at the point of regretting my perseverance, an unexpected success has crowned my efforts. It was such an unexpected bit of luck which in a very curious manner put me in possession of the papers which I now have the honor of offering to the reading public. These papers have afforded me an insight into the lives of two men, which has confirmed my hunch that the external is not the internal. This was especially true about one of them. His external mode of life has been in complete contradiction to his inner life. The same was true to a certain extent with the other also, inasmuch as he concealed a more significant inwardness under a somewhat commonplace exterior.

Still, I had best proceed in order and explain how I came into possession of these papers. It is now about seven years since I first noticed at a merchant's shop here in town a secretary which from the very first moment I saw it attracted my attention. It was not of modern workmanship, had been used a good deal, and yet it fascinated me. It is impossible for me to explain the reason for this impression, but most people in the course of their lives have had some similar experience. My daily path took me by this shop, and I never failed a single day to pause and feast my eyes upon it. I gradually made up a history about it; it became a daily necessity for me to see it, and so I did not hesitate to go out of my way for the sake of seeing it, when an unaccustomed route made this necessary. And the more I looked at it, the more I wanted to own it. I realized very well that it was a peculiar desire, since I had no use for such a piece of furniture, and it would be an extravagance for me to buy it. But desire is a very sophisticated passion. I made an excuse for going into the shop, asked about other things, and as I was leaving, I casually made the shopkeeper a very low offer for the secretary. I thought possibly he might accept it; then chance would have played into my hands. It was certainly not for the sake of the money I behaved thus, but to salve my conscience. The plan miscarried, the dealer was uncommonly firm. I continued to pass the place daily, and to look at the secretary with loving eyes. "You must make up your mind," I thought, "for suppose it is sold, then it will be too late. Even if you were lucky enough to get hold of it again, you would never have the same feeling about it." My heart beat violently; then I went into the shop. I bought it and paid for it. "This must be the last time," thought I, "that you are so extravagant; it is really lucky that you bought it, for now every time you look at it, you will reflect on how extravagant you were; a new period of your life must begin with the acquisition of the secretary." Alas, desire is very eloquent, and good resolutions are always at hand.

The secretary was duly set up in my apartment, and as in the first period of my enamorment I had taken pleasure in gazing at it from the street, so now I walked back and forth in front of it at home. Little by little I familiarized myself with its rich economy, its many drawers and recesses, and I was thoroughly pleased with my secretary. Still, things could not continue thus. In the summer of 1836 I arranged my affairs so that I could take a week's trip to the country. The postilion was engaged for five o'clock in the morning. The necessary baggage had been packed the evening before, and everything was in readiness. I awakened at four, but the vision of the beautiful country I was to visit so enchanted me that I again fell asleep, or into a dream. My servant evidently thought he would let me sleep as long as possible, for he did not call me until half-past six. The postilion was already blowing his horn, and although I am not usually inclined to obey the mandates of others, I have always made an exception in the case of the postboy and his musical theme. I was speedily dressed and already at the door, when it occurred to me, Have you enough money in your pocket? There was not much there. I opened the secretary to get at the money drawer to take what money there was. Of course the drawer would not move. Every attempt to open it failed. It was all as bad as it could possibly be. Just at this moment, while my ears were ringing with the postboy's alluring notes, to meet such difficulties! The blood rushed to my head, I became angry. As Xerxes ordered the sea to be lashed, so I resolved to take a terrible revenge.[3] A hatchet was fetched. With it I dealt the secretary a shattering blow, shocking to see. Whether in my anger I struck the wrong place, or the drawer was as stubborn as myself, the result of the blow was not as anticipated. The drawer was closed, and the drawer remained closed. But something else happened. Whether my blow had struck exactly the right spot, or whether the shock to the whole framework of the secretary was responsible, I do not know, but I do know that a secret door sprang open, one which I had never before noticed. This opened a pigeonhole that I naturally had never discovered. Here to my great surprise I found a mass of papers, the papers which form the content of the present work. My intention as to the journey remained unchanged. At the first station we came to I would negotiate a loan. A mahogany case in which I usually kept a pair of pistols was hastily emptied and the papers were placed in it. Pleasure had triumphed, and had become even greater. In my heart I begged the secretary for forgiveness for the harsh treatment, while my mind found its doubt strengthened, that the external is not the internal, as well as my empirical generalization confirmed, that luck is necessary to make such discoveries possible.

I reached Hillerød in the middle of the forenoon, set my finances in order, and got a general impression of the magnificent scenery. The following morning I at once began my excursions, which now took on a very different character from that which I had originally intended. My servant followed me with the mahogany case. I sought out a romantic spot in the forest where I should be as free as possible from surprise, and then took out the documents. Mine host, who noticed these frequent excursions in company with the mahogany case, ventured the remark that I must be trying to improve my marksmanship. For this conjecture I was duly grateful, and left him undisturbed in his belief.

A hasty glance at the papers showed me that they were

made up of two collections whose external differences were strongly marked. One of them was written on a kind of vellum in quarto, with a fairly wide margin. The handwriting was legible, sometimes even a little elegant, in a single place, careless. The other was written on full sheets of foolscap with ruled columns, such as is ordinarily used for legal documents and the like. The handwriting was clear, somewhat spreading, uniform and even, apparently that of a business man. The contents also proved to be very dissimilar. One part consisted of a number of aesthetic essays of varying length, the other was composed of two long inquiries and one shorter one, all with an ethical content, as it seemed, and in the form of letters. This dissimilarity was completely confirmed by a closer examination. The second series consists of letters written to the author of the first series.

But I must try to find some briefer designation to identify the two authors. I have examined the letters very carefully, but I have found little or nothing to the purpose. Concerning the first author, the aesthete, the papers yield absolutely nothing. As for the second, the letter writer, it appears that his name was William, and that he was a magistrate, but of what court is not stated. If I were to confine myself strictly to this data, and decide to call him William, I should lack a corresponding designation for the first author, and should have to give him an arbitrary name. Hence I have preferred to call the first author A, the second B.

In addition to the longer essays, I have found among the papers a number of slips of paper on which were written aphorisms, lyrical effusions, reflections. The handwriting indicated A as the author, and the nature of the contents confirmed my conjecture.

Then I tried to arrange the papers as well as I could. In the case of those written by B this was fairly easy. Each of these letters presupposes the one preceding, and in the second letter there is a quotation from the first; the third letter presupposes the other two.

The arranging of A's papers was not so simple. I have therefore let chance determine the order, that is to say, I have left them in the order in which I found them, without being able to decide whether this order has any chronological value or ideal significance. The slips of paper lay loose in the pigeonhole, and so I have had to allot them a place. I have placed them first because it seemed to me that they might best be regarded as provisional glimpses of what the longer essays develop more connectedly. I have called them *Diapsalmata*,[4] and have added as a sort of motto: *ad se ipsum*.[5] This title and this motto are in a manner mine, and yet not altogether so. They are mine in so far as they are applied to the whole collection, but they also belong to A, for the word *Diapsalmata* was written on one of the slips of paper, and on two of them, the phrase, *ad se ipsum*. A little French verse which was found above one of the aphorisms, I have placed on the inside of the title page, a common practice with A himself. Since many of the aphorisms have a lyric form, it seemed proper to use the word *Diapsalmata* as the principal title. If the reader should consider this choice unfortunate, then I must acknowledge that this was my own device, and that the word was certainly in good taste as used by A himself for the aphorism over which it is found. I have left the arrangement of the individual aphorisms to chance. That these individual expressions often contradict one another seemed quite natural, since each one of them belongs precisely to an essential mood. I did not think it worth while to adopt an arrangement that would make these contradictions less striking. I followed chance, and it is also chance that has directed my attention to the fact that the first and the last aphorisms correspond to one another, as the one is touched by the suffering that lies in being a poet, while the other enjoys the satisfaction which lies in always having the laugh on its side.

As to A's aesthetic essays, I have nothing to emphasize concerning them. They were found all ready for printing, and in so far as they contain any difficulties, they must be permitted to speak for themselves. For my part I may state that I have added a translation of the Greek quotations scattered through the essays, which is taken from one of the better German translations.

The last of A's papers is a story entitled, *Diary of the Seducer*. Here we meet with new difficulties, since A does not acknowledge himself as author, but only as editor. This is an old trick of the novelist, and I should not object to it, if it did not make my own position so complicated, as one author seems to be enclosed in another, like the parts in a Chinese puzzle box. Here is not the place to explain in greater detail the reasons for my opinion. I shall only note that the dominant mood in A's preface in a manner betrays the poet. It seems as if A had actually become afraid of his poem, as if it continued to terrify him, like a troubled dream when it is told. If it were an actual occurrence which he had become privy to, then it seems strange that the preface shows no trace of A's joy in seeing the realization of the idea which had so often floated before his mind. The idea of the seducer is suggested in the essay on the *Immediate-Erotic* as well as in the *Shadowgraphs*, namely, the idea that the analogue to Don Juan must be a reflective seducer who comes under the category of the interesting, where the question is not about how many he seduces, but about how he does it. I find no trace of such joy in the preface, but rather, as was said, a certain horror and trembling, which might well have its cause in his poetical relationship to this idea. Nor am I surprised that it affected A thus; for I, who have simply nothing to do with this narrative, I who am twice removed from the original author, I, too, have sometimes felt quite strange when, in the silence of the night, I have busied myself with these papers. It was as if the Seducer came like a shadow over the floor, as if he fixed his demoniac eye upon me, and said: "Well, so you are going to publish my papers! It is quite unjustifiable in you; you arouse anxiety in the dear little lassies. Yet obviously, in return you would make me and my kind harmless. There you are mistaken; for I need only change the method, and my circumstances become more favorable than before. What a stream of lassies I see running straight into my arms when they hear that seductive name: a seducer! Give me half a year and I shall provide a story which will be more interesting than all I have hitherto experienced. I imagine a young, vigorous girl of spirit who

conceives the extraordinary idea of avenging her sex upon
me. She thinks to coerce me, to make me feel the pangs
of unrequited love. That is just the girl for me. If she does
not herself strike deeply enough, then I shall come to her
assistance. I shall writhe like the eel of the Wise Men of
Gotham. And then when I have brought her to the point
I wish, then is she mine!"

But perhaps I have already abused my position as editor
in burdening the reader with my reflections. The occasion
must provide the excuse. It was on account of the awkwardness of my position, occasioned by A's calling himself only
the editor, not the author of this story, that I let myself
be carried away.

What more I have to say about this story shall be exclusively in my role as editor. I think that I have perhaps
found something in it that will determine the time of its
action. The Diary has a date here and there, but the year
is always omitted. This might seem to preclude further inquiry, but by studying the individual dates, I believe I
have found a clue. Of course every year has a seventh of
April, a third of July, a second of August, and so forth;
but it is not true that the seventh of April falls every year
upon Monday. I have therefore made certain calculations,
and have found that this combination fits the year 1834.[6]
I cannot tell whether A had thought of this or not, but
probably not, since then he would not have used so much
caution as he has. Nor does the Diary read, Monday the
seventh of April, and so on, but merely April 7. Even on
the seventh of April, the entry begins thus: "Consequently
on Monday"—whereby the reader's attention is distracted;
but by reading through the entry under this date, one sees
that it must have been written on Monday. As far as this
story is concerned, I now have a definite date. But every
attempt to utilize it in determining the time of the other
essays has failed. I might have made this story the third
in the collection, but, as I said above, I preferred to leave
it to chance, and everything is in the sequence in which
I found it.

As far as B's papers are concerned, these arrange themselves easily and naturally. In their case I have permitted myself an alteration, and have provided them with a title, since their epistolary style prevented the author from using a title. Should the reader, therefore, after having become familiar with the contents, decide that the titles are not well chosen, I shall have to reconcile myself to the disappointment of having done something poorly that I wished to do well.

Here and there I found a remark set down in the margin. These I have made into footnotes, so as not to interrupt the even flow of the text.

As regards B's manuscript, I have allowed myself no alterations, but have scrupulously treated it as a finished document. I might perhaps have easily corrected an occasional carelessness, such as is explicable when one remembers that the author is merely a letter writer. I have not wished to do this because I feared that I might go too far. When B states that out of every hundred young men who go astray, ninety-nine are saved by women, and one by divine grace, it is easy to see that he has not been very rigid in his reckoning, since he provides no place at all for those who are actually lost. I could easily have made a little modification in the reckoning, but there seemed to me something far more beautiful in B's miscalculation. In another place he mentions a Greek wise man by the name of Myson, and says of him that he enjoyed the rare distinction of being reckoned among the Seven Sages, when their number is fixed at fourteen. I wondered at first where B could have got this information, and also what Greek author it was that he cited. My suspicion at once fell on Diogenes Laertius,[7] and by looking up Jøcher and Morèri,[8] I found a reference to him. B's statement might perhaps need correction; the case is not quite as he puts it, since there was some uncertainty among the ancients as to who the Seven Sages were. But I have not thought it worth while to make any corrections, since it seemed to me that while his statement is not quite accurate historically, it might have another value.

The point I have now reached, I had arrived at five years ago. I had arranged the papers as at present, had decided to publish them, but thought best to postpone it for a time. Five years seemed long enough. The five years are now up, and I begin where I left off. I need not assure the reader that I have tried in every conceivable way to find some trace of the authors. The dealer, like most of his kind, kept no books; he did not know from whom he had bought the secretary; he thought it might have been at public auction. I shall not attempt to describe the many fruitless attempts I have made to identify the authors, attempts which have taken so much of my time, since the recollection gives me no pleasure. As to the result, however, I can describe it to the reader very briefly, for the result was simply nil.

As I was about to carry out my decision to have the papers published, one more scruple awakened within me. Perhaps the reader will permit me to speak frankly. It occurred to me that I might be guilty of an indiscretion toward the unknown authors. However, the more familiar I became with the papers, the more these scruples disappeared. The papers were of such a nature that since my most painstaking investigations had failed to throw any light upon them, I was confident that no reader would be able to do so, for I dare compare myself with any such reader, not in taste and sympathy and insight, but in tirelessness and industry. For supposing the anonymous authors were still living, that they lived in this town, that they came unexpectedly upon their own papers, still if they themselves kept silent, there would be no consequences following the publication. For in the strictest sense of the word, these papers do what we sometimes say of all printed matter—they keep their own counsel.

One other scruple that I have had was in itself of less significance and fairly easy to overcome, and has been overcome in even an easier way than I had anticipated. It occurred to me that these papers might be financially lucrative. It seemed proper that I should receive a small honorarium for my editorial services; but an author's royalty would be too much. As the honest Scotch farmers in *The*

White Lady[9] decided to buy and cultivate the family estate, and then restore it to the Counts of Avenel if they should ever return, so I decided to put the entire returns at interest, so that when the authors turned up, I could give them the whole amount with compound interest. If the reader has not already, because of my complete ineptitude, assured himself that I am neither an author nor a professional literary man who makes publishing his profession, then the naïveté of this reasoning must establish it indisputably. My scruples were probably more easily overcome because in Denmark an author's royalty is by no means a country estate, and the authors would have to remain away a long time for their royalties, even at compound interest, to become a financial object.

It remained only to choose a title. I might call them Papers, Posthumous Papers, Found Papers, Lost Papers, and so forth. A number of variants could be found, but none of these titles satisfied me. In selecting a title I have therefore allowed myself a liberty, a deception, for which I shall try to make an accounting. During my constant occupation with the papers, it dawned upon me that they might be looked at from a new point of view, by considering all of them as the work of one man. I know very well everything that can be urged against this view, that it is unhistorical, improbable, unreasonable, that one man should be the author of both parts, although the reader might easily be tempted to the play on words, that he who says A must also say B. However, I have not yet been able to relinquish the idea. Let us imagine a man who had lived through both of these phases, or who had thought upon both. A's papers contain a number of attempts to formulate an aesthetic philosophy of life. A single, coherent, aesthetic view of life can scarcely be carried out. B's papers contain an ethical view of life. As I let this thought sink into my soul, it became clear to me that I might make use of it in choosing a title. The one I have selected precisely expresses this. The reader cannot lose very much because of this title, for while reading the book he may perfectly well forget the title. Then, when he has read the book, he may perhaps reflect upon the title. This will free him from all finite questions as to whether A was really convinced of his error and repented, whether B conquered, or if it perhaps ended by B's going over to A's opinion. In this respect, these papers have no ending. If anyone thinks this is not as it should be, one is not thereby justified in saying that it is a fault, for one must call it a misfortune. For my own part I regard it as fortunate. One sometimes chances upon novels in which certain characters represent opposing views of life. It usually ends by one of them convincing the other. Instead of these views being allowed to speak for themselves, the reader is enriched by being told the historical result, that one has convinced the other. I regard it as fortunate that these papers contain no such information. Whether A wrote his aesthetic essays after having received B's letters, whether his soul continued to be tossed about in wild abandon, or whether it found rest, I cannot say, since the papers indicate nothing. Nor is there any clue as to how things went with B, whether he had strength to hold to his convictions or not. When the book is read, then A and B are forgotten, only their views confront one another, and await no finite decision in particular personalities.

I have nothing further to say except that the honored authors, if they were aware of my project, might possibly wish to accompany their papers with a word to the reader. I shall therefore add a few words with them holding and guiding the pen. A would probably interpose no objection to the publication; he would probably warn the reader: read them or refuse to read them, you will regret both. What B would say is more difficult to decide. He would perhaps reproach me, especially with regard to the publication of A's papers. He would let me feel that he had no part in them, that he washed his hands of responsibility. When he had done this, then he would perhaps turn to the book with these words: "Go out into the world then; escape if possible the attention of critics, seek a single reader in a favorable hour, and should you meet a feminine reader, then would I say: 'My fair reader, you will perhaps find in this book something you ought not to know; other things you might well profit from knowing; may you so read the first that having read it, you may be as one who has not read it; may you read the other so that having read it, you may be as one who cannot forget it.'" I, as editor, only add the wish that the book may meet the reader in an auspicious hour, and that the fair reader may succeed in following B's well meant advice.

The Editor

November 1842

DIAPSALMATA
ad se ipsum

Grandeur, savoir, renommée,
Amitié, plaisir et bien,
   Tout n'est que vent, que fumée:
Pour mieux dire, tout n'est rien.[10]

What is a poet? An unhappy man who in his heart harbors a deep anguish, but whose lips are so fashioned that the moans and cries which pass over them are transformed into ravishing music. His fate is like that of the unfortunate victims whom the tyrant Phalaris imprisoned in a brazen bull, and slowly tortured over a steady fire; their cries could not reach the tyrant's ears so as to strike terror into his heart; when they reached his ears they sounded like sweet music.[11] And men crowd about the poet and say to him, "Sing for us soon again" —which is as much as to say, "May new sufferings torment your soul, but may your lips be fashioned as before; for the cries would only distress us, but the music, the music, is delightful." And the critics come forward and say, "That is perfectly done—just as it should be, according to the rules of aesthetics." Now it is understood that a critic resembles a poet to a hair; he only lacks the anguish in his heart and the music upon his lips. I tell you, I would rather be a swineherd, understood by the swine, than a poet misunderstood by men.

The first question in the earliest and most compendious instruction the child receives is, as everyone knows, this: What will the child have? The answer is: da-da. And with such reflections life begins, and yet men deny original sin. And to whom does the child owe its first drubbings, whom other than the parents?

I prefer to talk with children, for it is still possible to hope that they may become rational beings. But those who have already become so—good Lord!

How absurd men are! They never use the liberties they have, they demand those they do not have. They have freedom of thought, they demand freedom of speech.

I do not care for anything. I do not care to ride, for the exercise is too violent. I do not care to walk, walking is too strenuous. I do not care to lie down, for I should either have to remain lying, and I do not care to do that, or I should have to get up again, and I do not care to do that either. *Summa summarum:* I do not care at all.

There are well-known insects which die in the moment of fecundation. So it is with all joy; life's supreme and richest moment of pleasure is coupled with death.

Tested Advice for Authors: Set down your reflections carelessly, and let them be printed; in correcting the proof sheets a number of good ideas will gradually suggest themselves. Therefore, take courage, all you who have not yet dared to publish anything; even misprints are not to be despised, and an author who becomes witty by the aid of misprints, must be regarded as having become witty in a perfectly lawful manner.

This is the chief imperfection of all things human, that the object of desire is first attainable through its opposite. I shall not speak about the multitude of temperamental types which ought to keep the psychologist busy (the melancholy temperament has the greatest comic sense; the most exuberant is often the most idyllic; the debauched often the most moral; the doubtful often the most religious), I shall merely recall the fact that an eternal happiness is first descried through sin.

In addition to the rest of the numerous circle of my acquaintances, I still have one intimate confidante—my melancholy. In the midst of my joy, in the midst of my work, she beckons to me and calls me aside, even though physically I do not budge. My melancholy is the most faithful mistress I have known; what wonder, then, that I love in return.

There is a gossipy reasoning which in its endlessness bears about the same relation to the result as the interminable line of Egyptian monarchs bears to the historical value of their reigns.

Old age realizes the dreams of youth: look at Dean Swift;[12] in his youth he built an asylum for the insane, in his old age he was himself an inmate.

When you see with what hypochondriac profundity an earlier generation of Englishmen discovered the ambiguity which lies at the root of laughter, it is enough to cause a feeling of anxiety. Dr. Hartley,[13] for example, makes the following remark: "When laughter first manifests itself in the infant, it is an incipient cry, excited by pain, or by a feeling of pain suddenly inhibited, and recurring at brief intervals." What if everything in the world were a misunderstanding, what if laughter were really tears?

There are occasions when it gives one a sense of infinite sadness to see a human being standing all alone in the world. Thus the other day I saw a poor girl walk all alone to church to be confirmed.

Cornelius Nepos tells of a certain commander, who was shut up in a fortress with a considerable force of cavalry, and who ordered the horses to be whipped every day, lest they be injured by so much standing still[14]—so I live these days like one besieged; but lest I take harm from too much sitting still, I cry myself weary.

I say of my sorrow what the Englishman says of his house: my sorrow is my castle. There are many who regard sorrow as one of the conveniences of life.

I feel the way a chessman must, when the opponent says of it: That piece cannot be moved.

The reason why *Aladdin* is so invigorating is that this piece expresses a genial and childlike audacity in the most extravagant desires. How many are there in our age who truly dare to wish, dare to desire, dare to address Nature with anything more than a polite child's please, please, or else with the rage of a lost soul? How many are there who, alive to the feeling that man is made in the image of God, a thing that our age prates so much about, have the true voice of command? Or do we not all stand there like Noureddin, bowing and scraping, fearful lest we ask too much or too little? Does not every magnificent demand little by little get reduced to a sickly reflection over the ego, from the command to the whimper, an art in which we are thoroughly trained?

I am as shrunken as a Hebrew *shewa*, weak and silent as a *daghesh lene*;[15] I feel like a letter printed backward in the line, and yet as ungovernable as a three-tailed Pasha, as jealous for myself and my thoughts as a bank for its notes, and as generally introverted as any *pronomen reflexivum*. If only it were true of misfortunes and sorrows as it is of conscious good works that they who do them have their reward taken away[16]—if this held true of sorrow, then were I the happiest of men: for I take all my troubles in advance, and yet they all remain behind.

The tremendous poetic vigor of folk literature expresses itself, among other ways, in the strength to desire. The desires of our age are in comparison with these both sinful and dull, since we desire what belongs to our neighbor. The characters in folk literature are very well aware that the neighbor as little possesses what they are seeking as they themselves do. And when it indulges in sinful desire, it is so terrible as to cause men to tremble. This desire does not cheapen itself by a cold calculation of probabilities in sober reason. Don Juan still struts across the stage with his 1,003 mistresses. No one dares to smile, out of respect for the venerable tradition. If a poet had ventured the like in our age, he would have been hooted off the stage.

How strangely sad I felt on seeing a poor man shuffling through the streets in a rather worn-out, light yellowish-green coat. I was sorry for him, but the thing that moved me most was that the color of this coat so vividly reminded me of my first childish productions in the noble art of painting. This color was precisely one of my vital hues. Is it not sad that these color mixtures, which I still think of with so much pleasure, are found nowhere in life; the whole world thinks them harsh, bizarre, suitable only for Nüremberg pictures. Or if one sometimes happens on them, there is always something unpleasant about the encounter, as in this present case. It is always some weak-minded person, or one who has been unfortunate, in short, always someone who feels himself an alien in the world, and whom the world will not recognize. And I, who always painted my heroes with this never-to-be-forgotten yellowish-green coloring on their coats! And is it not so with all the mingled colors of childhood? The hues that life once had gradually become too strong, too harsh, for our dim eyes.

Alas, the doors of fortune do not open inward, so that by storming them one can force them open; but they open outward, and therefore nothing can be done.

I have the courage, I believe, to doubt everything; I have the courage, I believe, to fight with everything; but I have not the courage to know anything; not the courage to possess, to own anything. Most people complain that the world is so prosaic, that life is not like romance, where opportunities are always so favorable. I complain that life is not like romance, where one had hard-hearted parents and nixies and trolls to fight, and enchanted princesses to free. What are all such enemies taken together, compared with the pale, bloodless, tenacious, nocturnal shapes with which I fight, and to whom I give life and substance?

How barren is my soul and thought, and yet forever tortured by empty birthpangs, sensual and tormenting! Must my spirit then ever remain tongue-tied, must I always babble? What I need is a voice as penetrating as the eye of Lynceus,[17] as terrifying as the sigh of the giants, as persistent as the sound of nature, as full of derision as a frosty wind-gust, as malicious as Echo's heartless mockeries, of a compass from the deepest bass to the most mellifluous soprano, modulated from the sacred softness of a whisper to the violent fury of rage. This is what I need in order to breathe, to get expression for what is on my mind, to stir the bowels of my compassion and of my wrath.—But my voice is only hoarse like the cry of a gull, or dies away like the blessing upon the lips of the dumb.

What portends? What will the future bring? I do not know, I have no presentiment. When a spider hurls itself down from some fixed point, consistently with its nature, it always sees before it only an empty space wherein it can find no foothold however much it sprawls. And so it is with me: always before me an empty space; what drives me forward is a consistency which lies behind me. This life is topsy-turvy and terrible, not to be endured.

No time of life is so beautiful as the early days of love, when with every meeting, every glance, one fetches something new home to rejoice over.

My view of life is utterly meaningless. I suppose an evil spirit has set a pair of spectacles upon my nose, of which one lens is a tremendously powerful magnifying glass, the other an equally powerful reducing glass.

The doubter is like a whipped top;[18] he stands upright exactly as long as the lashes continue. He can no more stand erect by himself than can a top.

Of all ridiculous things, it seems to me the most ridiculous is to be a busy man of affairs, prompt to meals, and prompt to work. Hence when I see a fly settle down in a crucial moment on the nose of a business man, or see him bespattered by a carriage which passes by him in even greater haste, or a drawbridge opens before him, or a tile from the roof falls down and strikes him dead, then I laugh heartily. And who could help laughing? What do they accomplish, these hustlers? Are they not like the housewife, when her house was on fire, who in her excitement saved the fire-tongs? What more do they save from the great fire of life?

Generally speaking, I lack the patience to live. I cannot see the grass grow, but since I cannot, I do not care to look at it at all. My views are the fleeting observations of a "traveling scholastic," rushing through life in greatest haste. People say that the good Lord fills the stomach before the eyes; I have not noticed it; my eyes are sated and weary of everything, and yet I hunger.

Ask whatever questions you please, but do not ask me for reasons. A young woman may be forgiven for not being able to give reasons, since they say she lives in her feelings. Not so with me. I generally have so many reasons, and most often such mutually contradictory reasons, that for this reason it is impossible for me to give reasons. There seems to be something wrong with cause and effect also, that they do not rightly hang together. Tremendous and powerful causes sometimes produce small and unimpressive effects, sometimes none at all; then again it happens that a brisk little cause produces a colossal effect.

And now the innocent pleasures of life. One must admit that they have but one fault, they are so innocent. Moreover, they must be indulged in moderately. When my doctor prescribes a diet, there is some sense in that; I abstain from certain foods for a certain specified time; but to be dietetic on a diet—that is really asking too much.

Life has become a bitter drink to me, and yet I must take it like medicine, slowly, drop by drop.

No one ever comes back from the dead, no one ever enters the world without weeping; no one is asked when he wishes to enter life, no one is asked when he wishes to leave.

Time flows, life is a stream, people say, and so on. I do not notice it. Time stands still, and I with it. All the plans I make fly right back upon myself; when I would spit, I even spit into my own face.

When I get up in the morning, I go straight back to bed again. I feel best in the evening when I put out the light and pull the eiderdown over my head. Then I sit up again, look about the room with indescribable satisfaction; and so good night, down under the eiderdown.

What am I good for? For nothing or for everything. That is a rare talent; I wonder if the world will appreciate it? God knows whether those servant girls find a place, who seek a position as maid of all work or, failing that, as anything whatsoever.

One ought to be a mystery, not only to others, but also to one's self. I study myself; when I am weary of this, then for a pastime I light a cigar and think: the Lord only knows what He meant by me, or what He would make out of me.

No pregnant woman can have stranger or more impatient desires than I. These desires concern sometimes the most trivial things, sometimes the most exalted, but they are equally imbued with the soul's momentary passion. At this moment I wish a bowl of buckwheat porridge. I remember from my school days that we always had this dish on Wednesdays. I remember how smooth and white it was when served, how the butter smiled at me, how warm the porridge looked, how hungry I was, how impatient to be allowed to begin. Ah, such a dish of buckwheat porridge! I would give more than my birthright for it!

The magician Virgil had himself cut into pieces and put into a kettle to be boiled for a week, in order to renew his youth.[19] He hired a man to stand watch so that no intruder would peep into the caldron. But the watchman could not resist the temptation; it was too early, Virgil vanished with a cry like a little child. I, too, have doubtless peeped too soon into the kettle, the kettle of life and its historical development, and will probably never be able to become anything more than a child.

"A man should never lose his courage; when misfortunes tower most fearfully about him, there appears in the sky a helping hand." Thus spoke the Reverend Jesper Morten last evensong.[20] Now I am in the habit of traveling much under the open sky, but I had never seen anything of the kind. A few days ago, however, while on a walking tour, some such phenomenon took place. It was not exactly a hand, but something like an arm which stretched out of the sky. I began to ponder: it occurred to me that if only Jesper Morten were here, he might be able to decide whether this was the phenomenon he referred to. As I stood there in the midst of my thoughts, I was addressed by a wayfarer. Pointing up to the sky, he said: "Do you see that waterspout? They are very rare in these parts; sometimes they carry whole houses away with them." "The Lord preserve us," thought I, "is that a waterspout?" and took to my heels as fast as I could. I wonder what the Reverend Jesper Morten would have done in my place?

Let others complain that the age is wicked; my complaint is that it is paltry; for it lacks passion. Men's thoughts are thin and flimsy like lace, they are themselves pitiable like the lacemakers. The thoughts of their hearts are too paltry to be sinful. For a worm it might be regarded as a sin to harbor such thoughts, but not for a being made in the image of God. Their lusts are dull and sluggish, their passions sleepy. They do their duty, these shopkeeping souls, but they clip the coin a trifle, like the Jews; they think that even if the Lord keeps ever so careful a set of books, they may still cheat Him a little. Out upon them! This is the reason my soul always turns back to the Old Testament and to Shakespeare. I feel that those who speak there are at least human beings: they hate, they love, they murder their enemies, and curse their descendants throughout all generations, they sin.

I divide my time as follows: half the time I sleep, the other half I dream. I never dream when I sleep, for that would be a pity, for sleeping is the highest accomplishment of genius.

To be a perfect man is after all the highest human ideal. Now I have got corns, which ought to help some.

The result of my life is simply nothing, a mood, a single color. My result is like the painting of the artist who was to paint a picture of the Israelites crossing the Red Sea. To this end, he painted the whole wall red, explaining that the Israelites had already crossed over, and that the Egyptians were drowned.

Nature still recognizes the dignity of humanity; for when you wish to keep the birds away from the trees, you fix up something to resemble a man, and even this faint resemblance to a human being which a scarecrow has is enough to inspire the birds with respect.

For love to have significance, the hour of its birth must be illumined by the moon, just as Apis, in order to be the true Apis, must be moon-illuminated.[21] It was necessary that the moon should shine upon the cow that was to bear Apis, at the moment of impregnation.

The best proof for the wretchedness of existence is the proof that is derived from the contemplation of its glories.

Most men pursue pleasure with such breathless haste that they hurry past it. They fare as did that dwarf who kept guard over a captured princess in his castle. One day he took a midday nap. When he woke up an hour later, the princess was gone. Quickly he pulled on his seven-league boots; with one stride he was far beyond her.

My soul is so heavy that thought can no more sustain it, no wingbeat lift it up into the ether. If it moves, it sweeps along the ground like the low flight of birds when a thunderstorm is approaching. Over my inmost being there broods a depression, an anxiety, that presages an earthquake.

Life is so empty and meaningless.—We bury a man; we follow him to the grave, we throw three spadefuls of earth over him; we ride out to the cemetery in a carriage, we ride home in a carriage; we take comfort in thinking that a long life lies before us. How long is seven times ten years?

Why do we not finish it at once, why do we not stay and step down into the grave with him, and draw lots to see who shall happen to be the last unhappy living being to throw the last three spadefuls of earth over the last of the dead?

The lassies do not please me. Their beauty vanishes like a dream, and like yesterday when it is past. Their constancy—yes, their constancy! Either they are faithless, which no longer concerns me, or they are faithful. If I found such a one, she might please me because of her rarity, but she would not please me in the long run; for she would either always remain constant, and then I should become a victim of my own experimental zeal, since I should have to keep up with her; or she would sometime cease to be faithful, and so I should have the same old story over again.

Wretched Destiny! In vain you paint your furrowed face like an old harlot, in vain you jingle your fool's bells; you weary me; it is always the same, an *idem per idem*.[22] No variety, always a rehash! Come, Sleep and Death, you promise nothing, you keep everything.

These two familiar strains of the violin! These two familiar strains here at this moment, in the middle of the street. Have I lost my senses? Does my ear, which from love of Mozart's music has ceased to hear, create these sounds; have the gods given me, unhappy beggar at the door of the temple—have they given me an ear that makes the sounds it hears? Only two strains, now I hear nothing more. Just as they burst forth from the deep choral tones of the immortal overture,[23] so here they extricate themselves from the noise and confusion of the street, with all the surprise of a revelation.—It must be here in the neighborhood, for now I hear the lighter tones of the dance music.—And so it is to you, unhappy artist pair, I owe this joy.—One of them was about seventeen, he wore a coat of green kalmuck, with large bone buttons. The coat was much too large for him. He held the violin close up under his chin, his hat was pressed down over his eyes, his hand was hidden in a glove without fingers, his fingers were red and blue from cold. The other man was older; he wore a chenille shawl. Both were blind. A little girl, presumably their guide, stood in front of them, her hands tucked under her neckerchief. We gradually gathered around them, some admirers of this music: a letter carrier with his mailbag, a little boy, a servant girl, a couple of roustabouts. The well-appointed carriages rolled noisily by, the heavy wagons drowned out the strains, which by snatches flashed forth. Unhappy artist pair, do you know that these tones are an epitome of all the glories of the world?—How like a tryst it was!

It happened that a fire broke out backstage in a theater. The clown came out to inform the public. They thought it was a jest and applauded. He repeated his warning, they shouted even louder. So I think the world will come to an end amid general applause from all the wits, who believe that it is a joke.

In the last analysis, what is the significance of life? If we divide mankind into two great classes, we may say that one works for a living, the other does not need to. But working for a living cannot be the meaning of life, since it would be a contradiction to say that the perpetual production of the conditions for subsistence is an answer to the question about its significance which, by the help of this, must be conditioned. The lives of the other class have in general no other significance than that they consume the conditions of subsistence. And to say that the significance of life is death, seems again a contradiction.

The essence of pleasure does not lie in the thing enjoyed, but in the accompanying consciousness. If I had a humble spirit in my service who, when I asked for a glass of water, brought me the world's costliest wines blended in a chalice, I should dismiss him, in order to teach him that pleasure consists not in what I enjoy, but in having my own way.

And so I am not the master of my life, I am only one thread among many, which must be woven into the fabric of life! Very well, if I cannot spin, I can at least cut the thread.

Everything is to be acquired in stillness, and in the silence of the divine. It is not only of Psyche's future child it holds, that its future depends on her silence.

Mit einem Kind, das göttlich, wenn Du schweigst—
Doch menschlich, wenn Du das Geheimnis zeigst.[24]

I seem destined to have to suffer every possible mood, to acquire experience in every direction. Every moment I lie like a child, who must learn to swim, out in the middle of the sea. I scream (which I have learned from the Greeks, from whom one can learn everything which is purely human); for I have indeed a harness about my waist, but the pole that holds me up I do not see. It is a fearful way in which to get experience.

It is quite remarkable that one gets a conception of eternity from two of the most appalling contrasts in life. If I think of that unhappy bookkeeper who lost his reason from despair at having involved his firm in bankruptcy by adding 7 and 6 to make 14; if I think of him day after day, oblivious to everything else, repeating to himself: 7 and 6 are 14, then I have an image *of* eternity.—If I imagine a voluptuous feminine beauty in a harem, reclining on a couch in all charming grace, without concern for anything in all the world, then I have a symbol *for* eternity.

What the philosophers say about Reality is often as disappointing as a sign you see in a shop window, which reads: Pressing Done Here. If you brought your clothes to be pressed, you would be fooled; for the sign is only for sale.

There is nothing more dangerous to me than remembering. The moment I have remembered some life-relationship, that moment it ceased to exist. People say that separation tends to revive love. Quite true, but it revives it in a purely poetic manner. The life that is lived wholly in memory is the most perfect conceivable, the satisfactions of memory are richer than any reality, and have a security that no reality possesses. A remembered life-relation has already passed into eternity, and has no more temporal interest.

If any man needs to keep a diary, I do, and that for the purpose of assisting my memory. After a time it frequently happens that I have completely forgotten the reason which led me to do this or that, not only in connection with trifles, but also in connection with the most momentous decisions. And if I do recall my reason, it sometimes seems so strange to me that I can hardly believe it was my reason. This doubt could be resolved if I had something to refer to. A reason is generally a very curious thing; if I apprehend it with the total intensity of my passion, then it grows up into a huge necessity which can move heaven and earth. But if I lack passion, I look down upon it with scorn.—For some time I have been wondering what it was that moved me to resign my position as teacher in a secondary school. As I think it over, it seems to me that such a position was precisely what I wanted. Today a light dawned upon me; the reason was just this, that I had considered myself absolutely fitted for the post. Had I retained it, I should have had everything to lose and nothing to gain. Hence I thought it best to resign, and to seek employment with a traveling troupe of players, since I had no talent for theatricals, and therefore had everything to gain.

One must be very naïve to believe that it will do any good to cry out and shout in the world, as if that would change one's fate. Better take things as they come, and make no fuss. When I was young and went into a restaurant, I would say to the waiter, "A good cut, a very good cut, from the loin, and not too fat." Perhaps the waiter did not even hear me, to say nothing of paying any attention to my request, and still less was it likely that my voice should reach the kitchen and influence the cook, and even if it did, there was perhaps not a good cut on the entire roast. Now I never shout any more.

The social striving and the beautiful sympathy which prompts it spreads more and more. In Leipzig there has recently been formed a society whose members are pledged, out of sympathy for the sad fate of old horses, to eat their flesh.

I have but one friend, Echo; and why is Echo my friend? Because I love my sorrow, and Echo does not take it away from me. I have only one confidant, the silence of the night; and why is it my confidant? Because it is silent.

As it befell Parmeniscus in the legend, who in the cave of Trophonius lost the power to laugh, but got it again on the island of Delos, at the sight of the shapeless block exhibited there as the image of the goddess Leto, so it has befallen me.[25] When I was young, I forgot how to laugh in the cave of Trophonius; when I was older, I opened my eyes and beheld reality, at which I began to laugh, and since then I have not stopped laughing. I saw that the meaning of life was to secure a livelihood, and that its goal was to attain a high position; that love's rich dream was marriage with an heiress; that friendship's blessing was help in financial difficulties; that wisdom was what the majority assumed it to be; that enthusiasm consisted in making a speech; that it was courage to risk the loss of ten dollars; that kindness consisted in saying, "You are welcome," at the dinner table; that piety consisted in going to communion once a year. This I saw, and I laughed.

What is the power that binds me? How was the chain made with which the Fenris wolf was bound? It was wrought from the sound of a cat's paws walking over the ground, from women's beards, from the roots of rocks, from the nerves of bears, from the breath of fishes, and the spittle of birds. And thus I, too, am bound in a chain formed of dark imaginings, of unquiet dreams, of restless thoughts, of dread presentiments, of inexplicable anxieties. This chain is "very supple, soft as silk, elastic under the highest tension, and cannot be broken in two."

Strangely enough, it is always the same thing which at every age engages our attention, and we go only so far, or rather, we go backward. When I was fifteen years old, and a pupil in the classical school, I wrote with much unction about the proofs for the existence of God and the immortality of the soul, about the concept of faith, and on the significance of the miraculous. For my *examen artium* I wrote an essay on the Immortality of the Soul, which was awarded *prae ceteris;* later I won a prize for another essay on this same subject. Who would have believed that I, after having made so substantial and promising a beginning, should now in my twenty-fifth year have come to the pass of not being able to give a single proof for the immortality of the soul? I remember especially from my school days, that an essay of mine on immortality was singled out for extraordinary praise and read to the class by the teacher, both on account of the excellence of the thought and the beauty of the style. Alas, alas, alas! this essay I threw away a long time ago! What a misfortune! By this essay my doubting soul might now perhaps be captivated, both by reason of the style and of the thought. Hence, I advise all parents, guardians, and teachers to caution the children under their care, so that they may preserve the Danish themes they write at the age of fifteen. To give this advice is the only contribution I can make to the welfare of the human race.

Knowledge of the truth I may perhaps have attained to; happiness, certainly not. What shall I do? Accomplish something in the world, men tell me. Shall I then publish my grief to the world, contribute one more proof for the wretchedness and misery of existence, perhaps discover a new flaw in human life, hitherto unnoticed? I might then reap the rare reward of becoming famous, like the man who discovered the spots on Jupiter. I prefer, however, to keep silent.

How true human nature is to itself. With what native genius does not a little child often show us a living image of the greater relation. Today I really enjoyed watching little Louis. He sat in his little chair; he looked about him with apparent pleasure. The nurse Mary went through the room. "Mary," he cried. "Yes, little Louis," she answered with her usual friendliness, and came to him. He tipped his head a little to one side, fastened his immense eyes upon her with a certain gleam of mischief in them, and thereupon said quite phlegmatically, "Not this Mary, another Mary." What about us older folk? We cry out to the whole world, and when it comes smiling to meet us, then we say: "This was not the Mary."

My life is like an eternal night; when at last I die, then I can say with Achilles:
   Du bist vollbracht, Nachtwache meines Daseyns.[26]

My life is absolutely meaningless. When I consider the different periods into which it falls, it seems like the word *Schnur* in the dictionary, which means in the first place a string, in the second, a daughter-in-law. The only thing lacking is that the word *Schnur* should mean in the third place a camel, in the fourth, a dust-brush.

I am like a Lüneburger pig. My thinking is a passion. I can root up truffles excellently for other people, even if I get no pleasure out of them myself. I dig the problems out with my nose, but the only thing I can do with them is to throw them back over my head.

Vainly I strive against it. My foot slips. My life is still a poet's existence. What could be more unhappy? I am predestined; fate laughs at me when suddenly it shows me how everything I do to resist becomes a moment in such an existence. I can describe hope so vividly that every hoping individual will acknowledge my description; and yet it is a deception, for while I picture hope, I think of memory.

There is still another proof for the existence of God, one which has hitherto been overlooked. It is propounded by a servant in Aristophanes' *The Knights:*

Demosthenes: Shrines? shrines? Why surely you don't
             believe in the gods?
Nicias: I do.
Demosthenes: But what's your argument? Where's your
             proof?
Nicias: Because I feel they persecute me and hate
             me, in spite of everything I try to please
             'em.
Demosthenes: Well, well. That's true; you're right about
             that.[27]

How terrible tedium is—terribly tedious; I know no
stronger expression, none truer, for only the like is known
by the like. If only there were some higher, stronger expression, then there would be at least one movement. I lie
stretched out, inactive; the only thing I see is emptiness,
the only thing I move about in is emptiness. I do not even
suffer pain. The vulture constantly devoured Prometheus'
liver; the poison constantly dripped down on Loki; that was
at least an interruption, even though a monotonous one.
Even pain has lost its refreshment for me. If I were offered
all the glories of the world, or all its pain, the one would
move me as little as the other, I would not turn over on
the other side either to obtain them or to escape them. I
die the death.[28] Is there anything that could divert me?
Aye, if I might behold a constancy that could withstand
every trial, an enthusiasm that endured everything, a faith
that could remove mountains, a thought that could unite
the finite and the infinite. But my soul's poisonous doubt
is all-consuming. My soul is like the Dead Sea, over which
no bird can fly; when it has flown midway, then it sinks
down to death and destruction.

Strange, with what equivocal anxiety—for losing and
keeping—man yet clings to this life! Sometimes I have considered taking a decisive step, compared with which all my
preceding ones would be only childish tricks—of setting out
on the great voyage of discovery. As a ship at its launching
is hailed with the roar of cannon, so would I hail myself.
And yet. Is it courage I lack? If a stone fell down and
killed me, that would be a way out.

Tautology is and remains still the supreme principle, the highest law of thought.[29] What wonder then that most men use it? Nor is it so entirely empty but that it may well serve to fill out an entire life. It has its witty, jesting, entertaining form; it is the infinite judgment.[30] This is the paradoxical and transcendental kind of tautology. It has the serious, scientific, edifying form. The formula for this is: when two magnitudes are severally equal to one and the same third magnitude, they are equal to each other. This is a quantitative inference. This kind of tautology is especially useful for rostrums and pulpits, where you are expected to say something profound.

The disproportion in my build is that my forelegs are too short. Like the kangaroo, I have very short forelegs, and tremendously long hind legs. Ordinarily I sit quite still; but if I move, the tremendous leap that follows strikes terror in all to whom I am bound by the tender ties of kinship and friendship.

EITHER/OR

An ecstatic lecture

If you marry, you will regret it; if you do not marry, you will also regret it;[31] if you marry or do not marry, you will regret both; whether you marry or do not marry, you will regret both. Laugh at the world's follies, you will regret it; weep over them, you will also regret that; laugh at the world's follies or weep over them, you will regret both; whether you laugh at the world's follies or weep over them, you will regret both. Believe a woman, you will regret it, believe her not, you will also regret that; believe a woman, or believe her not, you will regret both; whether you believe a woman or believe her not, you will regret both. Hang yourself, you will regret it; do not hang yourself, and you will also regret that; hang yourself or do not hang yourself, you will regret both; whether you hang yourself or do not hang yourself, you will regret both. This, gentlemen, is the sum and substance of all philosophy. It is not only at certain moments that I view everything *aeterno modo,* as Spinoza says, but I live constantly *aeterno modo.*[32] There are many who think that they live thus, because after having done the one or the other, they combine or mediate the opposites. But this is a misunderstanding; for the true eternity does not lie behind either/or, but before it. Hence, their eternity will be a painful succession of temporal moments, for they will be consumed by a two-fold regret. My philosophy is at least easy to understand, for I have only one principle, and I do not even proceed from that. It is necessary to distinguish between the successive dialectic in either/or, and the eternal dialectic here set forth. Thus, when I say that I do not proceed from my principle, this must not be understood in opposition to a proceeding forth from it, but is rather a negative expression for the principle itself, through which it is apprehended in equal opposition to a proceeding or a non-proceeding from it. I do not proceed from my principle; for if I did, I would regret it, and if I did not, I would also regret that. If it seems, therefore, to one or another of my respected hearers that there is anything in what I say, it only proves that he has no talent for philosophy; if my argument seems to have any forward movement, this also proves the same. But for those who can follow me, although I do not make any progress, I shall now unfold the eternal truth, by virtue of which this philosophy remains within itself, and admits of no higher philosophy. For if I proceeded from my principle, I should find it impossible to stop; for if I stopped, I should regret it, and if I did not stop, I should also regret that, and so forth. But since I never start, so can I never stop; my eternal departure is identical with my eternal cessation. Experience has shown that it is by no means difficult for philosophy to begin. Far from it. It begins with nothing, and consequently can always begin. But the difficulty, both for philosophy and for philosophers, is to stop. This difficulty is obviated in my philosophy; for if anyone believes that when I stop now, I really stop, he proves himself lacking in the speculative insight. For I do not stop now, I stopped at the time when I began. Hence my philosophy has the advantage of brevity, and it is also impossible to

refute; for if anyone were to contradict me, I should undoubtedly have the right to call him mad. Thus it is seen
that the philosopher lives continuously *aeterno modo,* and
has not, like Sintenis of blessed memory, only certain hours
which are lived for eternity.[33]

Why was I not born in Nyboder?[34] Why did I not die
in infancy? Then my father would have laid me in a little
box, taken it under his arm, carried me out some Sunday
afternoon to the grave, thrown the earth upon the casket
himself, and softly uttered a few words, intelligible only to
himself. It was only in the happy days when the world was
young, that men could imagine infants weeping in Elysium,
because they had died so early.[35]

Never have I been happy; and yet it has always seemed
as if happiness were in my train, as if glad genii danced
about me, invisible to others but not to me, whose eyes
gleamed with joy. And when I go among men, as happy
and glad as a god, and they envy me my happiness, then
I laugh; for I despise men, and avenge myself upon them.
Never have I wished to wrong any man, but have always
tried to give the impression that everyone who came near
me would be wronged and insulted. And when I hear others praised for their faithfulness and integrity, then I laugh;
for I despise men, and avenge myself upon them. Never
has my heart been hardened against any human being, but
always, just when I was most affected, I made it look as
if my heart were closed and alien to every human feeling.
And when I hear others praised for their goodness of heart,
and see them loved for the depth and wealth of their feeling, then I laugh; for I despise men and avenge myself
upon them. When I see myself cursed, abominated, hated,
for my coldness and heartlessness: then I laugh, then my
wrath is satiated. If these good people could really put me
in the wrong, if they could actually make me do wrong—
well, then I should have lost.

This is my misfortune: at my side there always walks an
angel of death, and I do not besprinkle the door-lintels of

the elect with blood, as a sign that he shall pass by; no, it is just their doors that he enters—for only the love that lives in memory is happy.[36]

Wine can no longer make my heart glad; a little of it makes me sad, much makes me melancholy. My soul is faint and impotent; in vain I prick the spur of pleasure into its flank, its strength is gone, it rises no more to the royal leap. I have lost my illusions. Vainly I seek to plunge myself into the boundless sea of joy; it cannot sustain me, or rather, I cannot sustain myself. Once pleasure had but to beckon me, and I mounted, light of foot, sound, and unafraid. When I rode slowly through the woods, it was as if I flew; now when the horse is covered with lather and ready to drop, it seems to me that I do not move. I am solitary as always; forsaken, not by men, which could not hurt me, but by the happy fairies of joy, who used to encircle me in countless multitudes, who met acquaintances everywhere, everywhere showed me an opportunity for pleasure. As an intoxicated man gathers a wild crowd of youths about him, so they flocked about me, the fairies of joy, and I greeted them with a smile. My soul has lost its potentiality. If I were to wish for anything, I should not wish for wealth and power, but for the passionate sense of the potential, for the eye which, ever young and ardent, sees the possible. Pleasure disappoints, possibility never. And what wine is so sparkling, what so fragrant, what so intoxicating, as possibility!

Music finds its way where the rays of the sun cannot penetrate. My room is dark and dismal, a high wall almost excludes the light of day. The sounds must come from a neighboring yard; it is probably some wandering musician. What is the instrument? A flute? . . . What do I hear— the minuet from *Don Juan!* Carry me then away once more, O tones so rich and powerful, to the company of the maidens, to the pleasures of the dance.—The apothecary pounds his mortar, the kitchen maid scours her kettle, the groom curries the horse, and strikes the comb against the flagstones; these tones appeal to me alone, they beckon only me. O! accept my thanks, whoever you are! My soul is so rich, so sound, so joy-intoxicated!

In itself, salmon is a great delicacy; but too much of it is harmful, since it taxes the digestion. At one time when a very large catch of salmon had been brought to Hamburg, the police ordered that a householder should give his servants only one meal a week of salmon. One could wish for a similar police order against sentimentality.

Carking care is my feudal castle. It is built like an eagle's nest upon the peak of a mountain lost in the clouds. No one can take it by storm. From this abode I dart down into the world of reality to seize my prey; but I do not remain down there, I bear my quarry aloft to my stronghold. My booty is a picture I weave into the tapestries of my palace. There I live as one dead. I immerse everything I have experienced in a baptism of forgetfulness unto an eternal remembrance. Everything temporal and contingent is forgotten and erased. Then I sit like an old man, grey-haired and thoughtful, and explain picture after picture in a voice as soft as a whisper; and at my side a child sits and listens, although he remembers everything before I tell it.

The sun shines into my room bright and beautiful, the window is open in the next room; on the street all is quiet, it is a Sunday afternoon. Outside the window, I clearly hear a lark pour forth its song in a neighbor's garden, where the pretty maiden lives. Far away in a distant street I hear a man crying shrimps. The air is so warm, and yet the whole town seems dead.—Then I think of my youth and of my first love—when the longing of desire was strong. Now I long only for my first longing. What is youth? A dream. What is love? The substance of a dream.

Something wonderful has happened to me. I was caught up into the seventh heaven. There sat all the gods in assembly. By special grace I was granted the privilege of making a wish. "Wilt thou," said Mercury, "have youth or beauty or power or a long life or the most beautiful maiden or any of the other glories we have in the chest? Choose, but only one thing." For a moment I was at a loss. Then I addressed myself to the gods as follows: "Most honorable contemporaries, I choose this one thing, that I may always have the laugh on my side." Not one of the gods said a word; on the contrary, they all began to laugh. From that I concluded that my wish was granted, and found that the gods knew how to express themselves with taste; for it would hardly have been suitable for them to have answered gravely: "Thy wish is granted."

THE IMMEDIATE STAGES

OF THE EROTIC

OR

THE MUSICAL EROTIC

INSIGNIFICANT INTRODUCTION

From the moment that Mozart's music first filled my soul with wonder, and I bowed before it in humble admiration, I have found a dear and grateful occupation in reflecting on how that happy Greek view of the world which calls the world a cosmos, because it manifests itself as a harmonious whole, a transparent and tasteful adornment for the Spirit which works in and through it—how this happy view finds application in a higher realm, in the world of ideals, where there is again an overruling wisdom particularly admirable in joining together those things which belong together: Axel with Valborg, Homer with the Trojan War, Raphael with Catholicism, Mozart with Don Juan. There is a wretched unbelief abroad which seems to contain much healing power. It deems such a connection accidental, and sees in it only a lucky conjunction of the different forces in the game of life. It thinks it an accident that the lovers win one another, accidental that they love one another; there were a hundred other women with whom the hero might have been equally happy, and whom he could have loved as deeply. It thinks that there has been many a poet who might have become as immortal as Homer, if this splendid subject had not already been appropriated by him; many a composer who might have made himself as immortal as Mozart, had the opportunity offered. This wisdom contains much solace and comfort for all mediocre minds, since it lends itself to the delusion with which they deceive themselves and other like-minded souls, that it is a confusion of fate, an error on the part of the world, that they did not become as famous as the famous. It is a very easy optimism that is thus encouraged. But for every high-minded soul, for every optimate[1] who is not so anxious to save himself in this wretched manner as to lose himself in the contemplation of greatness, it is naturally repugnant; while it is a delight to his soul, a sacred joy, to behold the union of those things which belong together. It is this union which is fortunate, but not as if it were merely accidental; and hence, it presupposes two distinct factors, while the accidental involves merely the inarticulate interjections of a blind fate. It is the realization of this union which constitutes the fortunate in the historical process, the divine conjunction of its forces, the high tide of historic time. The accidental has but one factor; it is accidental that Homer found in the Trojan War the most distinguished epic subject conceivable. The fortunate has two factors: it is fortunate that the most distinguished epic subject fell to the lot of Homer; here the accent falls as much on Homer as on the material. It is this profound harmony which reverberates through every work of art we call classic. And so it is with Mozart; it is fortunate that the subject, which is perhaps the only strictly musical subject, in the deeper sense, that life affords, fell to—Mozart.

With his *Don Juan* Mozart enters the little immortal circle of those whose names, whose works, time will not forget, because eternity remembers them. And though it is a matter of indifference, when one has found entrance there, whether one stands highest or lowest, because in a certain sense all stand equally high, since all stand infinitely high, and though it is childish to dispute over the first and the last place here, as it is when children quarrel about the order assigned to them in the church at confirmation, I am still too much of a child, or rather I am like a young girl in love with Mozart, and I must have him in first place, cost what it may. And I will appeal to the parish clerk and to the priest and to the dean and to the bishop and to the whole consistory, and I will implore and adjure them to hear my prayer, and I will invoke the whole congregation on this matter, and if they refuse to hear me, if they refuse to grant my childish wish, I excommunicate myself, and renounce all fellowship with their modes of thought; and I will form a sect which not only gives Mozart first place, but which absolutely refuses to recognize any artist other than Mozart; and I shall beg Mozart to forgive me, because his music did not inspire me to great deeds, but turned me into a fool, who lost through him the little reason I had, and spent most of my time in quiet sadness humming what

I do not understand, haunting like a specter day and night what I am not permitted to enter. Immortal Mozart! Thou, to whom I owe everything; to whom I owe the loss of my reason, the wonder that caused my soul to tremble, the fear that gripped my inmost being; thou, to whom I owe it that I did not pass through life without having been stirred by something. Thou, to whom I offer thanks that I did not die without having loved, even though my love became unhappy. Is it strange then that I should be more concerned for Mozart's glorification than for the happiest moment of my life, more jealous for his immortality than for my own existence? Aye, if he were taken away, if his name were erased from the memory of men, then would the last pillar be overthrown, which for me has kept everything from being hurled together into boundless chaos, into fearful nothingness.

And yet I need not fear that any age will ever deny him his place in the kingdom of the gods, but I am prepared to find that men will consider it childish in me to insist that he must have the first place.[2] And though I am by no means ashamed of my childishness, and though it will always have more significance and more value for me than any exhaustive reflection, just because it is inexhaustible, I shall nevertheless attempt to prove his lawful claim by reasoned consideration.

The happy characteristic that belongs to every classic, that which makes it classic and immortal, is the absolute harmony of the two forces, form and content. This concord is so absolute that a later reflective age will scarcely be able to separate, even for thought, the two constituent elements here so intimately united, without running the risk of entertaining or provoking a misunderstanding. Thus when we say that it was Homer's good fortune that he had the most remarkable epic subject conceivable, we may forget that we always see this epic material through Homer's eyes, and that it seems to us the most perfect subject, is clear to us only in and through the transubstantiation which we owe to Homer. But if, on the other hand, we stress Homer's poetic energy in interpreting the material, we easily run the risk of forgetting that the poem would never have become

the thing it is, if the thought with which Homer has imbued it were not its own thought, if the form were not
precisely the form that belongs to it. The poet wishes for
his subject; but, as we say that wishing is no art, it is quite
rightly and truthfully said about many impotent poetic
wishes. To wish rightly, on the other hand, is a great art,
or, rather, it is a gift. It is the inexplicable and mysterious
quality of genius that, like a divining rod, it never gets the
idea of wishing except when the thing wished for is present.
Here wishing has a more profound significance than it ordinarily does, and to the abstract understanding, it may
even seem ridiculous, since we ordinarily think of a wish
only in relation to that which is not, not in relation to that
which is.

By one-sidedly emphasizing the significance of form, a
certain school of aestheticians has been responsible for pro-
moting the corresponding opposite misunderstanding also.[3]
It has often seemed strange to me that these aestheticians
attached themselves without question to the Hegelian philosophy, since a general knowledge of Hegel, as well as a
special acquaintance with his aesthetics, makes it clear that
he strongly emphasizes, with regard to the aesthetic, the
significance of the content. Both parts belong essentially together, and a single consideration will be sufficient to confirm this, since otherwise such a phenomenon as the following would be unthinkable. It is ordinarily only a single work,
or a single suite of works, which stamps the individual artist
as a classic poet, artist, and so on. The same individual
may have produced a great many different things, none of
which stand in any relation to the classic. Homer has, for
example, written a *Batrachomyomachia*, but this poem has
not made him classic or immortal.[4] To say that this is due
to the insignificance of the subject is foolish, since the classic
depends on the perfect balance. If everything that deter-
mines a production as classic were to be found solely in the
creative artist, then everything produced by him would
have to be classic, in a sense similar to, though higher than,
that in which bees always produce a uniform kind of cells.
To explain this by saying that he was more successful in
the one case than the other, would be to explain exactly

nothing. For, partly, it would be only a pretentious tautology, which only too often in life enjoys the honor of being regarded as an answer; partly, considered as an answer, it lies in another relativity than the one concerning which our question was asked. For it tells us nothing about the relation between form and content, and at best could be taken into account in connection with an inquiry into the formative activity alone.

In Mozart's case it also happens that there is one work, and only one, which makes him a classical composer, and absolutely immortal. That work is *Don Juan*. The other things which Mozart has produced may give us pleasure and delight, awaken the admiration, enrich the soul, satisfy the ear, delight the heart; but it does him and his immortal fame no service to lump them all together, and make them all equally great. *Don Juan* is his reception-piece.[5] Through *Don Juan* he is introduced into that eternity which does not lie outside of time but in the midst of it, which is not veiled from the eyes of men, where the immortals are introduced, not once for all, but constantly, again and again, as the generations pass and turn their gaze upon them, find happiness in beholding them, and go to the grave, and the following generation passes them again in review, and is transfigured in beholding them. Through his *Don Juan*, Mozart becomes one in the order of these immortals, one of these visibly transfigured ones, whom no cloud ever takes away from the sight of men; with his *Don Juan* he stands foremost among them. This last assertion, as I remarked above, I shall attempt to prove.

As has already been noted above, all classic productions stand equally high, because each one stands infinitely high. If, despite this fact, one were to attempt to introduce an order of rank into the classic procession, one would evidently have to choose as a basis for such a distinction, something which was not essential; for if the basis were essential, the difference itself would become an essential difference; from that it would again follow that the word "classic" was wrongly predicated of the group as a whole. A classification based upon the varying character of the subject matter would immediately involve us in a misunderstanding, which in its wider consequences would tend to nullify entirely the very concept of the classical. The subject matter is essential in so far as it is one of the constitutive factors, but it is not the absolute, since it is only one of the factors. We might notice, for example, that certain species of the classic have, in a sense, no subject matter, while, on the other hand, in others the subject matter plays a very significant role. The first holds true of those works which we admire as classic in the realms of architecture, sculpture, music and painting, especially the first three, and even in the case of painting, to the extent that a subject matter is involved, it has hardly more significance than that of having provided an occasion. The second holds true of poetry, taken in its broadest sense, including all artistic productions based upon language and the historical consciousness. This remark is quite correct in itself; but if we made it the basis of a classification, treating the absence or the presence of a subject as a help or a hindrance to the artist's creative energy, we should fall into error. Strictly speaking, we should actually be urging the opposite of what we had really intended, as always happens when dealing abstractly with dialectical concepts; it is not only true that we say one thing and mean another, but that we say the other; we do not say what we think we say, but we say the opposite. Such is the result when we employ the subject matter as the principle of classification. In speaking about the subject matter, it turns out that we really speak about something quite different, namely, the formative process. On the other hand, if we were to start from the formative process and stress it exclusively, the same thing would happen. In the attempt to make a valid distinction here by stressing the fact that in some respects the formative process is creative, in that it creates the subject matter, while in others it receives it, the result would be that while one believed that one was speaking about the formative process, one would really be speaking of the subject matter, and would actually base the classification upon the division of the subject matter. To the formative process as a point of departure for such a classification applies exactly the same law as obtains in the case of the subject matter. Therefore, the one side can never be used alone for the purpose of establishing a distinction in rank; for it is always too essential to be accidental, too accidental to be an adequate basis for an essential distinction.

But this absolutely reciprocal interpenetration, which makes it clearly as proper to say that the subject matter penetrates the form, as that the form penetrates the subject matter—this mutual interpenetration, this like for like in the immortal friendship of the classic, may serve to throw a light upon the classic from a new angle, and to limit it so that it does not become too ample. The aestheticians particularly, who have one-sidedly emphasized poetic activity, have so enlarged this concept that this pantheon became so enriched, aye, so overloaded with classical gimcracks and bagatelles, that the natural conception of a cool hall containing individually distinguished and imposing figures completely disappeared, and this pantheon became rather a lumber-room. Every neat little bit of perfect artistry is, according to this aesthetic verdict, a classical work, assured of absolute immortality; indeed, in this hocus-pocus, such little trifles were admitted most of all. Although otherwise one hated paradoxes, still one did not fear the paradox that the smallest was really the greatest art. The falsity lay in one-sidedly emphasizing the formal. Such an aesthetic could therefore flourish only temporarily, only so long as no one noticed that time made it and its classic works absurd. This tendency in the aesthetic sphere was a form of that radicalism, which, in a corresponding manner, has expressed itself in so many different spheres; it was an expression of the undisciplined subject in its equally undisciplined emptiness.

This endeavor, however, found its master in Hegel. It is, on the whole, a sad fact regarding the Hegelian philosophy that it has by no means received the significance which it would have had, either for the preceding generation or for the present, if the preceding generation had not been so busy intimidating people into it, as to give them little quiet for its appropriation, and if the present generation were not so untiringly active in pushing people beyond it. Hegel reinstated the content, the idea, in its just rights, and thereby banished all these transitory classics, these flimsy beings, the hawk-moths, from the high-arched vaults of the classic pantheon. It is by no means our intention to deny these works their just worth, but, here as elsewhere, it is necessary to take care that the language does not become confused, the concepts emasculated. A certain kind of immortality they may well have, and this is their desert; but this immortality is only the momentary eternity which every true work of art possesses, not that eternal fullness which can withstand all the vicissitudes of time. What these productions lack is ideas, and the greater their formal perfection, the more quickly will they consume themselves; the more their technical performance approximates the highest degree of virtuosity, the more fugitive they become, having neither the courage nor the energy nor the poise to withstand the attacks of time, though all the while they more and more pretentiously claim to be the most rectified of spirits. Only when the idea reposes with transparent clearness in a definite form, can it be called a classic work; but then it will also be able to withstand the attacks of time. This unity, this mutual intensity within itself, is a property of every classical work, and hence it is readily evident that every attempt at a classification of the different classic works, which has for its basis a separation of form and content, or idea and form, is *eo ipso* doomed to failure.

In still another way we might attempt a classification. We might consider the medium through which the idea is made manifest, as an object for contemplation, and, as we have noticed that one medium is richer or poorer than another, make this the basis for a classification wherein the wealth or poverty of the medium would be regarded as a help or a hindrance. But the medium stands in too necessary a relation to the production as a whole, not to make it probable that a classification based upon the medium would sooner or later find itself involved in the difficulties already emphasized.

I believe, on the other hand, that the following considerations may open the way for a classification which will have validity, precisely because it is altogether accidental. The more abstract and hence the more void of content the idea is, and the more abstract and hence the more poverty-stricken the medium is, the greater the probability that a repetition will be impossible, and the greater the probability that when the idea has once obtained its expression, then it has found it once for all. The more concrete and consequently the richer the idea, and similarly the medium, the greater the probability for a repetition. When I now arrange the classics side by side and, without wishing to rank them relatively, find myself wondering at their lofty equality, it nevertheless easily becomes apparent that there are more works in one section than another, or, if this is not the case, that some unequal representation is easily conceivable.

This point I wish to develop a little more in detail. The more abstract the idea is, the smaller the probability of a numerous representation. But how does the idea become concrete? By being permeated with the historical consciousness. The more concrete the idea, the greater the probability. The more abstract the medium, the smaller the probability; the more concrete, the greater. But what does it mean to say that the medium is concrete, other than to say it is language, or is seen in approximation to language; for language is the most concrete of all media. The idea, for example, which comes to expression in sculpture is wholly abstract, and bears no relation to the historical; the medium through which it is expressed is likewise abstract, consequently there is a great probability that the section of the classic works which includes sculpture will contain only a few. In this I have the testimony of time and experience on my side. If, on the other hand, I take a concrete idea and a concrete medium, then it seems otherwise. Homer is indeed a classic epic poet, but just because the epic idea is a concrete idea, and because the medium is language, it so happens that in the section of the classics which contains the epic, there are many epics conceivable, which are all equally classic, because history constantly furnishes us with new epic material. In this, too, I have the testimony of history and the assent of experience.

Now when I propose to base my subdivision wholly on the accidental, one can hardly deny its accidental character. But if, on the other hand, someone should reproach me, my answer would be that the objection is a mistake, since the principle of classification ought to be accidental. It is accidental that one section numbers, or can number, many more works than another. But since this is accidental, it is evident that one might just as well place the class highest which has, or can have, the greatest number. Here I might fall back upon the preceding discussion, and calmly answer that this is quite correct, but that I ought for this very reason to be all the more lauded for my consistency in accidentally setting the opposite class highest. However, I shall not do this, but, on the other hand, I shall appeal to a circumstance that speaks in my favor, the circumstance, namely, that those sections which embrace the more concrete ideas are not yet completed, and do not permit of being completed. Therefore it is quite natural to place the others first, and to keep the double doors wide open for the latter. Should someone say that this is an imperfection, a defect, in the former class, then he plows a furrow outside of my field of thought, and I cannot pay attention to his argument, however thorough it may be; for it is my fixed point of departure, that seen essentially everything is equally perfect.

But which idea is the most abstract? Here the question is naturally concerned only with such ideas as lend themselves to artistic representation, not with ideas appropriate only for scientific treatment. And what medium is the most abstract? The latter question I shall answer first. The most abstract medium is the one farthest removed from language.

But before I pass on to reply to this question, I desire to remind the reader of a circumstance which affects the final solution of my problem. The most abstract medium is not always employed to express the most abstract idea. Thus the medium employed by architecture is doubtless the most abstract medium, but the ideas which receive expression in architecture are by no means the most abstract. Architecture stands in a much closer relation to history than sculpture, for example. Here we are again confronted with a new alternative. I may place in the first class in this arrangement either those works of art which have the most abstract medium, or those whose idea is most abstract. In this respect I shall choose the idea, not the medium.

Now the media employed in architecture and sculpture and painting and music are abstract. Here is not the place to investigate this matter further. The most abstract idea conceivable is sensuous genius.[6] But in what medium is this idea expressible? Solely in music. It cannot be expressed in sculpture, for it is a sort of inner qualification of inwardness; nor in painting, for it cannot be apprehended in precise outlines; it is an energy, a storm, impatience, passion, and so on, in all their lyrical quality, yet so that it does not exist in one moment but in a succession of moments, for if it existed in a single moment, it could be modeled or painted. The fact that it exists in a succession of moments expresses its epic character, but still it is not epic in the stricter sense, for it has not yet advanced to words, but moves always in an immediacy. Hence it cannot be represented in poetry. The only medium which can express it is music. Music has, namely, an element of time in itself, but it does not take place in time except in an unessential sense. The historical process in time it cannot express.

The perfect unity of this idea and the corresponding form we have in Mozart's *Don Juan*. But precisely because the idea is so tremendously abstract, the medium is also abstract, so it is not probable that Mozart will ever have a rival. It was Mozart's good fortune to have found a subject that is absolutely musical, and if some future composer should try to emulate Mozart, there would be nothing else for him to do than to compose *Don Juan* over again. Homer found a perfect epic subject, but many epic poems are conceivable, because history commands more epic material. This is not the case with *Don Juan*. What I really mean will perhaps be best understood if I show the difference in connection with a related idea. Goethe's *Faust* is a genuinely classical production, but the idea is a historical idea, and hence every notable historical era will have its own *Faust*. *Faust* has language as its medium, and since this is a far more concrete medium, it follows on this ground also, that several works of the same kind are conceivable. *Don Juan*, on the other hand, will always stand alone by itself, in the same sense that the Greek sculptures are classics. But since the idea in *Don Juan* is even more abstract than that underlying sculpture, it is easy to see that while sculpture includes several works, in music there can be only one. There can, of course, be a number of classical musical works, but there will never be more than the one work of which it is possible to say that the idea is absolutely musical, so that the music does not appear as an accompaniment, but reveals its own innermost essence in revealing the idea. It is for this reason that Mozart stands highest among the Immortals through his *Don Juan*.

But I abandon this whole inquiry. It is written only for lovers. And as a little can please a child, so it is well known that lovers take pleasure in highly inconsequential things. It is like a heated lovers' quarrel about nothing, and yet it has its meaning—for the lovers.

While the preceding argument has tried in every possible manner, conceivable and inconceivable, to have it recognized that Mozart's *Don Juan* takes the highest place among all classical works, it has made practically no attempt to prove that this work is really a classic; for the suggestions found here and there, precisely as being only suggestions, show that they are not intended to furnish proof, but only to afford an opportunity for enlightenment. This procedure may seem more than peculiar. The proof that *Don Juan* is a classic work is in the strictest sense a problem for thought; while, on the contrary, the other attempt, with regard to the exact sphere of thought, is quite irrelevant. The movement of thought is satisfied with having it recognized that *Don Juan* is a classic, and that every classic production is equally perfect; to desire to do more than that is for thought a thing of evil. In this way the preceding argument involves itself in a self-contradiction and easily dissolves into nothing. This is, however, quite correct, and such a self-contradiction is deeply rooted in human nature. My admiration, my sympathy, my piety, the child in me, the woman in me, demanded more than thought could give. My thought had found repose, rested happy in its knowledge; then I came to it and begged it yet once more to set itself in motion, to venture the utmost. It knew very well that it was in vain; but since I am accustomed to living on good terms with my thought, it did not refuse me. However, its efforts accomplished nothing; incited by me it constantly transcended itself, and constantly fell back into itself. It constantly sought a foothold, but could not find it; constantly sought bottom, but could neither swim nor wade. It was something both to laugh at and to weep over. Hence I did both, and I was very thankful that it had not refused me this service. And although I know perfectly well that it will accomplish nothing, I am still as likely to ask it once more to play the same game, which is to me an inexhaustible source of delight. Any reader who finds the game tiresome is, of course, naturally not of my kind; for him the game has no significance, and it is true here as elsewhere, that like-minded children make the best play-fellows. For him the whole preceding argument is a superfluity, while for me it has such great significance, that I say thereof with Horace: *exilis domus est, ubi non et multa supersunt;*[7] to him it is foolishness, to me wisdom; to him boring, to me a joy and delight.

Consequently such a reader will not be able to sympathize with the lyricism of my thought, which is so elevated that it transcends thought; perhaps he will, however, be good-natured enough to say: "We will not quarrel about that; I skip that part, but now let us see how you approach the far more important problem of proving that *Don Juan* is a classical work; for that, I admit, would be a very suitable introduction to the main inquiry." How far it would be a suitable introduction, I shall leave undecided, but here again I find myself in the unfortunate position of not being able to sympathize with him; for however easy it might be for me to prove it, it would never enter my mind to do so. But while I always presuppose that matter as decided, the following exposition will serve many times and in many ways to shed light upon *Don Juan* in this respect, just as the preceding exposition has already contributed an occasional suggestion.

The task to which this inquiry is committed is to show the significance of the musical-erotic, and again as a means to this end, to point out the different stages which, as they have this in common, that they are all immediately erotic, also agree in being essentially musical. What I have to say on this subject I owe to Mozart alone. Hence, if one or another reader should be polite enough to agree with my exposition, but still be a little doubtful as to whether it was in Mozart's music, or whether I had not myself read it into the music, I can assure him that not only the little which I here present is found there but infinitely more; aye, I can assure him that it is precisely this thought which gives me courage to attempt an explanation of certain features of Mozart's music.

That which you have loved with youthful enthusiasm and admired with youthful ardor, that which you have se-cretly and mysteriously preserved in the innermost recesses of your soul, that which you have hidden in the heart: *that* you always approach with a certain shyness, with mingled emotions, when you know that the purpose is to try to un-derstand it. That which you have learned to know bit by bit, like a bird gathering straws for its nest, happier over each separate little piece than over all the rest of the world; that which the loving ear has absorbed, solitary in the great multitude, unnoticed in the secret hiding-place; that which the greedy ear has snatched up, never sated, the miserly ear has hidden, never secure, whose softest echo has never disappointed the sleepless vigil of the spying ear; that which you have lived with by day, that which you have relived by night, that which has banished sleep and made it rest-less, that which you have dreamed about while sleeping, and have waked up to dream it again while awake, that for which you have leaped out of bed in the middle of the night for fear lest you forget it; that which has been present to your soul in the highest moments of rapture, that which like a woman's work you have kept always at hand; that which has followed you on bright moonlight nights, in lonely forests, by the ocean's shore, in the gloomy streets, in the dead of night, at the break of day; that which has been your companion on horseback, your fellow traveler in the carriage; that which has permeated the home, that to which your chamber has been witness, that with which your ear has re-echoed, that which has resounded through your soul, that which the soul has spun on its finest loom —that now reveals itself to thought. As those mysterious beings in ancient tales rise from the ocean's bed invested with seaweed, so it now rises from the sea of remembrance, interwoven with memories. The soul becomes sad, and the heart softens; for it is as if you were bidding it farewell, as if you were separating yourself from it, never to meet it again either in time or eternity. It seems as if you were false to it, faithless to your trust, you feel that you are no longer the same, neither so young nor so childlike; you fear for yourself, lest you lose what has made you happy and rich and glad; you fear for the object of your love, lest it suffer in this transformation, lest it show itself perhaps less perfect, lest it may not be able to answer the many questions, and then, alas! everything is lost, the magic vanished, never to be evoked again. As far as Mozart's music is concerned, my soul knows no fear, my confidence is boundless. For one thing, I know that what I have hitherto understood is very little, so there will always be enough left behind, hiding in the shadows of the soul's vaguer intimations; and for another, I am convinced that if ever Mozart became wholly comprehensible to me, he would then become fully incomprehensible to me.

To assert that Christianity has brought sensuousness into the world may seem boldly daring. But as we say that a bold venture is half the battle, so also here; and my proposition may be better understood if we consider that in positing one thing, we also indirectly posit the other which we exclude. Since the sensuous generally is that which should be negatived, it is clearly evident that it is posited first through the act which excludes it, in that it posits the opposite positive principle. As principle, as power, as a self-contained system, sensuousness is first posited in Christianity; and in that sense it is true that Christianity brought sensuousness into the world. Rightly to understand this proposition, that Christianity has brought sensuousness into the world, one must apprehend it as identical with the contrary proposition, that it is Christianity which has driven sensuousness out, has excluded it from the world. As principle, as power, as a self-contained system, sensuousness was first posited by Christianity; to add still another qualification, which will, perhaps, show more emphatically what I mean: as a determinant of spirit, sensuousness was first posited by Christianity. This is quite natural, for Christianity is spirit, and spirit is the positive principle which Christianity has brought into the world. But when sensuousness is understood in its relationship to spirit [i.e., as its contrary], it is clearly known as a thing that must be excluded; but precisely because it should be excluded, it is determined as a principle, as a power; for that which spirit—itself a principle—would exclude must be something which is also a principle, although it first reveals itself as a principle in the moment of its exclusion. To say that sensuousness was in the world before Christianity would, of course, be a very stupid objection against me, for it goes without saying that what is to be excluded must have been before that which excludes it, although in another sense it first emerges in being excluded. This means that it begins to exist *in another sense*, and that is why I said at once that a bold venture is only half the battle.

Sensuousness, then, already existed in the world but without being spiritually determined. How then has it existed? Psychically. It was in this manner that it existed in paganism, and, in its most perfect expression, in Greece. But sensuousness psychically determined is not opposition, exclusion, but harmony and accord. But precisely because sensuousness was harmoniously determined, it appeared, not as a principle, but as an enclitic assimilated by assonance.

This consideration will serve to throw light upon the different forms assumed by the erotic in the different stages of the evolution of the world-consciousness, and thereby lead us to determine the immediate-erotic as identical with the musical-erotic. In the Greek consciousness, the sensuous was under control in the beautiful personality, or, more rightly stated, it was not controlled; for it was not an enemy to be subjugated, not a dangerous rebel who should be held in check; it was liberated unto life and joy in the beautiful personality. The sensuous was thus not posited as a principle; the principle of soul which constituted the beautiful personality was unthinkable without the sensuous; the erotic based upon the sensuous was for this reason not posited as a principle. Love was present everywhere as moment, and as such it was momentarily present in the beautiful personality. The gods recognized its power no less than men; the gods, no less than men, knew happy and unhappy love adventures. In none of them, however, was love present as principle; in so far as it was in them, in the individual, it was there as a moment of the universal power of love, which was, however, not present anywhere, and therefore did not even exist for Greek thought nor for the Greek consciousness. The objection might be offered that Eros was the god of love, and that love as principle must be conceived as present in him. But disregarding now the consideration that here again love does not rest upon the erotic, as based upon the sensuous alone, but is a qualification of the soul, there is another circumstance which it is necessary to note, which I shall emphasize more particularly.

Eros was the god of love, but was not himself in love. In so far as the other gods or men felt the power of love in themselves, they ascribed it to Eros, referred it to him, but Eros was not himself in love; and in so far as this happened to him once, this was an exception,[8] and though he was the god of love, he stood far behind the other gods in the number of his love adventures, far behind men. The fact that he did once fall in love, best expresses also the fact that he, too, bowed before the universal power of love, which thus in a certain sense became a force outside of himself, and which, rejected by him, now had no place at all where it might be found. Nor is his love based upon the sensuous, but upon the psychical. It is a genuine Greek thought that the god of love is not himself in love, while all others owe their love to him. If I imagined a god or goddess of longing, it would be a genuinely Greek conception, that while all who knew the sweet unrest of pain or of longing, referred it to this being, this being itself could know nothing of longing. I cannot characterize this remarkable relation better than to say it is the converse of a representative relation. In the representative relation the entire energy is concentrated in a single individual, and the particular individuals participate therein, in so far as they participate in its particular movements. I might almost say that this relation is the opposite of that which lies at the basis of the Incarnation. In the Incarnation, the special individual has the entire fullness of life within himself, and this fullness exists for other individuals only in so far as they behold it in the incarnated individual. The Greek consciousness gives us the converse relation. That which constitutes the power of the god is not in the god, but in all the other individuals, who refer it to him; he is himself, as it were, powerless and impotent, because he communicates his power to the whole world. The incarnated individual, as it were, absorbs the power from all the rest, and the fullness is therefore in him, and only so far in the others as they behold it in him. This consideration will be seen as important in its relation to what follows, as well as significant in itself, with respect to the categories which the universal consciousness makes use of in different periods of the world's history.

As a principle, then, we do not find the sensuous in the Greek consciousness, nor do we find the erotic as principle based upon the principle of the sensuous; and even if we had found this, we still see, what is for this inquiry of the greatest importance, that the Greek consciousness did not have the energy to concentrate the whole in a single individual, but thought of it as emanating from a point which does not possess it, to all the other points, so that this constitutive point is almost identifiable by the fact that it is the only point which does not have that which it gives to all the others.

Hence the sensuous as principle is posited by Christianity, as is also the sensuous-erotic, as principle; the representative idea was introduced into the world by Christianity. If I now imagine the sensuous-erotic as a principle, as a power, as a kingdom qualified spiritually, that is to say, so qualified that the spirit excludes it; if I imagine this principle concentrated in a single individual, then I have the concept of sensuous-erotic genius. This is an idea which the

Greeks did not have, which Christianity first brought into the world, even if only in an indirect sense.

If this sensuous-erotic genius demands expression in all its immediacy, the question arises as to which medium is appropriate for the purpose. Not to be lost sight of here is the fact that it demands expression and representation in its immediacy. In its mediacy and as reflected in something other than itself, it comes under language, and becomes subject to ethical categories. In its immediacy, however, it can only be expressed in music. In this connection I must ask the reader to remember something which was said in the insignificant introduction. Here the significance of music is revealed in its full validity, and it also reveals itself in a stricter sense as a Christian art, or rather as the art which Christianity posits in excluding it from itself, as being a medium for that which Christianity excludes from itself, and thereby posits. In other words, music is the daemonic. In the erotic-sensuous genius, music has its absolute object. It is not of course intended to say by this that music cannot also express other things, but this is its proper object. In the same way the art of sculpture is also capable of producing much else than human beauty, and yet this is its absolute object; painting can express much else than the beauty which is celestially glorified, and yet this is its absolute object. In this respect it is important to be able to see the essential idea in each art, and not to permit oneself to be disturbed by what it is incidentally capable of representing. Man's essential idea is spirit, and we must not permit ourselves to be confused by the fact that he is also able to walk on two legs. The idea in language is thought, and we must not permit ourselves to be disturbed by the opinion of certain sentimental people, that its highest significance is to produce inarticulate sounds.

Here I beg to be allowed a little unmeaning interlude; *praeterea censeo*,[9] that Mozart is the greatest among classic composers, and that his *Don Juan* deserves the highest place among all the classic works of art.

Now regarding the nature of music as a medium, this will naturally always be a very interesting problem. Whether I am capable of saying anything satisfactory about it is another question. I know very well that I do not understand music. I freely admit that I am a layman. I do not conceal the fact that I do not belong to the chosen people who are connoisseurs of music, that I am at most a proselyte at the gate, whom a strangely irresistible impulse carried from far regions to this point, but no farther. And yet it is perhaps possible that the little I have to say might contain some particular remark, which, if it met with a kind and indulgent reception, might be found to contain something true, even if it concealed itself under a shabby coat. I stand outside the realm of music and contemplate it from this standpoint. That this standpoint is very imperfect, I freely admit; that I am in a position to see very little in comparison with the fortunate ones who stand inside, I do not deny; but I still continue to hope that from my standpoint I may be able to throw some light upon the subject, although the initiated could do it much better, aye, to a certain extent, even understand better what I say, than I myself can. If I imagined two kingdoms adjoining one another, with one of which I was fairly well acquainted, and altogether unfamiliar with the other, and I was not allowed to enter the unknown realm, however much I desired to do so, I should still be able to form some conception of its nature. I could go to the limits of the kingdom with which I was acquainted and follow its boundaries, and as I did so, I should in this way describe the boundaries of this unknown country, and thus without ever having set foot in it, obtain a general conception of it. And if this was a task that engrossed my energies, and if I was indefatigable in my desire to be accurate, it would doubtless sometimes happen that, as I stood sadly at my country's boundary and looked longingly into the unknown country, which was so near me and yet so far away, some little revelation might be vouchsafed to me. And though I feel that music is an art which to the highest degree requires experience to justify one in having an opinion about it, still I comfort myself again, as I have so often done before, with the paradox that, even in ignorance and mere intimations, there is also a kind of experience. I comfort myself by remembering that Diana, who had not herself given birth, nevertheless came to the assistance of the child-bearing; moreover, that she had this as a native gift from childhood, so that she came to the assistance of Latona in her labor, when she herself was born.

The kingdom known to me, to whose utmost boundaries I intend to go in order to discover music, is language. If one wished to arrange the different media according to their appointed developmental process, one would have to place music and language next to one another, for which reason it has often been said that music is a language, which is something more than a genial remark. If one enjoyed indulging in clever speeches, one might almost say that sculpture and painting are each a kind of language, in so far as every expression of the idea is necessarily a language, since language is the essence of the idea. Very clever people, therefore, talk about the language of nature, and maudlin clergymen open the book of nature for us now and then to read something which neither they nor their hearers understand. If the remark that music is a language had no better standing than this, I should not trouble about it, but let it go and be valid for what it is. But such, however, is not the case. Not until the spiritual is posited is language invested with its rights; but when the spiritual is posited, all that which is not spirit is thereby excluded. But this exclusion is a determination of spirit, and in so far as the excluded is to assert itself, it requires a medium which is spiritually determined, and this is music. But a medium which is spiritually determined is essentially language; since then music is spiritually determined, it has justly been called a language.

As a medium, language is the one absolutely spiritually qualified medium; therefore it is the proper vehicle for the idea. A more adequate development of this point is not within my competence, nor is it within the scope of this little inquiry. Perhaps I may, however, find room for one remark, which again brings me back to music. In language the sensuous is as medium depressed to the level of a mere instrumentality and constantly negated. Such is not the case with the other media. Neither in sculpture nor in painting is the sensuous a mere instrumentality, but it is an integral part; nor is it constantly negated, for it is constantly taken

into account. It would be a peculiarly preposterous way
of regarding a statue or a painting if I were to contemplate
it in such wise that I took the trouble of abstracting the
sensuous, thereby completely annulling its beauty. In sculpture, architecture, painting, the idea is bound up with the
medium; but this fact that the idea does not depress the
medium to the level of a mere instrumentality, nor constantly negate it, is, as it were, an expression of the fact
that this medium cannot speak. So also with nature. Hence,
we rightly say that nature is dumb, and architecture and
sculpture and painting; we say it correctly, in spite of all
the sensitive and sentimental ears that can hear them speak.
It is in truth as silly to say that nature is a language as it
is inept to say that that which is mute is speaking, since
it is not even a language in the sense in which the manual
alphabet is a language. But it is different in the case of
language. The sensuous is reduced to a mere instrument and
is thus annulled. If a man spoke in such a way that one
heard the movement of his tongue, he would speak badly;
if he heard so that he heard the air vibrations instead of
the words, he would hear badly; if in reading a book he
constantly saw the individual letters, he would read badly.
Language becomes the perfect medium just at the moment
when everything sensuous in it is negatived. So it is also
with music: that which really should be heard, constantly
emancipates itself from the sensuous. That music as a medium stands lower than language has already been pointed
out, and it was, therefore, on this account that I said that
only in a certain sense is music a language.

Language addresses itself to the ear. No other medium
does this. The ear is the most spiritually determined of the
senses. That I believe most men will admit. If anyone wishes
further information on this point, I refer the reader to the
preface of *Karikaturen des Heiligsten* by Steffens.[10] Aside
from language, music is the only medium that addresses
itself to the ear. Herein is again an analogy and a testimony
concerning the sense in which music is a language. There
is much in nature which addresses itself to the ear, but that
which affects the ear is the purely sensuous, and for that
reason nature is dumb; and it is a ridiculous delusion that

one hears something because one hears a cow moo or, that which perhaps makes greater pretensions, a nightingale sing; it is a delusion to think that one hears something, a delusion to think that one is worth more than the other, since it is all a case of tweedledum and tweedledee.

Language has time as its element; all other media have space as their element. Music is the only other one that takes place in time. But the fact that it does take place in time is again a negation of the sensuous. What the other arts produce indicates their sensuousness precisely by reason of the fact that it has its continuance in space. Now there is, of course, much in nature that takes place in time. Thus when a brook ripples and continues to ripple, there seems to be in it a qualification of time. However, this is not so, and in so far as one may wish to insist that we have here a qualification of time, one would have to say that time is indeed present, but present as if spatially qualified. Music exists only in the moment of its performance, for if one were ever so skillful in reading notes and had ever so lively an imagination, it cannot be denied that it is only in an unreal sense that music exists when it is read. It really exists only in being performed. This might seem to be an imperfection in this art as compared with the others whose productions remain, because they have their existence in the sensuous. Yet this is not so. It is rather a proof of the fact that music is a higher, a more spiritual art.

Now if I take language for my point of departure, in order by moving through it, as it were, to spy out the land of music, the result appears about as follows. If I assume that prose is the language-form that is farthest removed from music, then I notice even in the oratorical discourse, in the sonorous structure of its periods, a hint of the musical which manifests itself more and more strongly at different levels in the poetic form, in the structure of the verse, in the rhyme, until at last the musical has been developed so strongly that language ceases and everything becomes music. This is a favorite expression which the poets have used to signify that they have, so to speak, renounced the idea, which vanishes from them, and everything ends in music. This might seem to indicate that music is an even more perfect medium than language. However, this is one of those sentimental misunderstandings which originate only in empty heads. That it is a misunderstanding will be shown later; here I desire only to call attention to the remarkable circumstance that, by moving through the language in the opposite direction, I again come up against music, in that I proceed from a prose interpenetrated by the concept, downward until I land in interjections which are again musical, just as the child's first babbling syllables are musical. Here it will hardly be said that music is a more perfect medium than language or that music is a richer medium than language, unless one is willing to assume that saying "uh" is worth more than a complete thought. But what follows from maintaining that wherever language ceases, I encounter the musical? This is probably the most perfect expression of the idea that music everywhere limits language. From this it is easy to see how the misunderstanding arose that music is a richer medium than language. By saying that when language ceases, music begins, and by saying, as people do, that everything becomes musical, we do not advance but go backwards.

This is the reason why I never had any sympathy—and in this perhaps even the experts will agree with me—with that sublime music which believes it can dispense with words. As a rule it thinks itself higher than words, although it is inferior. Now I might perhaps be confronted with the following objection: "If it is true that language is a richer medium than music, then it is hard to understand why it should be so hard to give an aesthetic account of the musical; inconceivable that language in this connection should always appear as a poorer medium than music." This is, however, neither inconceivable nor inexplicable. Music always expresses the immediate in its immediacy; it is for this reason, too, that music shows itself first and last in relation to language, but for this reason, also, it is clear that it is a misunderstanding to say that music is a more perfect medium. Language involves reflection, and cannot, therefore, express the immediate. Reflection destroys the immediate, and hence it is impossible to express the musical in language; but this apparent poverty of language is precisely its wealth. The immediate is really the indeterminate, and therefore language cannot apprehend it; but the fact that it is indeterminate is not its perfection but an imperfection. This is indirectly acknowledged in many ways. Thus, to cite but one example, we say: "I cannot really explain why I do this or that so and so, I do it by ear." Here we often use about things which have no relation to music a word derived from music, but we indicate by this the obscure, the unexplained, the immediate.

Now if it is the immediate, qualified spiritually, which receives its precise expression in music, we may again inquire more closely what species of the immediate it is which is essentially the subject of music. The immediate, qualified spiritually, may either be determined so as to fall within the sphere of the spiritual or as falling outside it. When the immediate, spiritually qualified, is determined as falling within the sphere of the spiritual, it may then well find its expression in the musical, but this immediacy cannot be the absolute subject of music, for since it is determined in such a way as to be included under the spiritual, it is thereby indicated that music is in a foreign sphere, it constitutes a prelude which is constantly being annulled. But if the immediate, spiritually qualified, is such that it falls outside the realm of spirit, then music here has its absolute subject. For the first species of the immediate, it is unessential that it be expressed in music, whereas it is essential for it to become spirit and, consequently, to be expressed in language; for the second, on the contrary, it is essential that it be expressed in music, it cannot be expressed otherwise than in music, it cannot be expressed in language, since it is spiritually determined so that it falls outside of the spiritual and, consequently, outside of language. But the immediacy which is thus excluded by the spirit is sensuous immediacy. This belongs to Christianity. In music it has its absolute medium, and from this circumstance it is also possible to explain the fact that music did not really become developed in the ancient world but belongs to the Christian era. Music is, then, the medium for that species of the immediate which, spiritually determined, is determined as lying outside of the spirit. Music can, naturally, express many other things, but this is its absolute subject. It is easy to perceive that music is a more sensuous medium than language, since it stresses the sensuous sound much more strongly than language does.

The genius of sensuousness is hence the absolute subject of music. In its very essence sensuousness is absolutely lyrical, and in music it breaks forth in all its lyrical impatience. It is, namely, spiritually determined, and is, therefore, force, life, movement, constant unrest, perpetual succession; but this unrest, this succession, does not enrich it, it remains always the same, it does not unfold itself, but it storms uninterruptedly forward as if in a single breath. If I desired to characterize this lyrical quality by a single predicate, I should say: it *sounds;* and this brings me back again to sensuous genius as that which in its immediacy manifests itself in music.

That even I might be able to say considerably more in connection with this point, I know; that it would be an easy matter for the experts to clear the matter up quite differently, of that I am convinced. But since no one, as far as I know, has attempted or even pretended to do so, since they all continue to reiterate that Mozart's *Don Juan* is the crown of all operas, but without explaining what they mean by that, although they all say it in a manner which clearly demonstrates that by this statement they intend to say something more than that *Don Juan* is the best opera, that there is a qualitative difference between it and all other operas, which cannot well be sought in anything other than in the absolute relationship between idea, form, subject and medium; since, I say, this is so, it is for this reason that I have broken silence. Perhaps I have been a little too hasty, perhaps I should have been able to say it better had I waited a little longer, perhaps—I do not know; but this I know, I have not hurried in order to enjoy the pleasure of speaking, I have not hurried because I feared someone more capable than myself might anticipate me, but because I feared that if I kept silent, even the stones would cry out in Mozart's honor, and cry shame to every human being to whom it has been given to speak.

What has been said in the preceding will, I assume, be

enough with respect to this little inquiry, since it will essentially serve to clear the way for a discussion of the immediate-erotic stages as we learn to know them through Mozart. Before passing on to that, however, I wish to cite a fact, which, from another side, can direct the thought to the absolute relationship between sensuous genius and the musical. It is well known that music has always been the object of suspicion from the standpoint of religious enthusiasm. Whether this is justifiable or not does not concern us here, since it has only a religious interest; on the other hand, it is not unimportant to consider what brought it about. If I trace back the history of religious fervor in regard to this, then I can generally mark the course of the movement in this way: the stronger the religiosity, the more one renounces music and stresses the importance of words. The different stages in this respect are represented in the periods of world history. The last stage entirely excludes music and insists solely upon speech. I could deck out this statement with a variety of particular observations; however I shall not do that, but cite only a word or two from a Presbyterian who figures in a story by Achim v. Arnim: "We Presbyterians regard the organ as the devil's bagpipe, by which serious reflection is not only lulled to sleep, but its devil's dance bewilders the good intention."[11] This must be regarded as a speech *instar omnium*.[12] What reason can one have for excluding music and making the spoken word the only prevalent means of expression? That the spoken word when wrongly used can confuse the emotions equally with music, all intelligent sects will certainly admit. Hence there must be a qualitative difference between them. But that which religious enthusiasm wishes to have expressed is spirit, therefore it requires language, which is the proper medium of the spirit, and rejects music which for it is a sensuous medium and, as such, always an imperfect medium for expressing the spiritual. Whether, then, religious zeal is really right in rejecting music is, as was said, another question; on the other hand, its conception of the relation of music to language may be perfectly right. Music need not, therefore, be excluded, but we must recognize that in the realm of the spirit it is an imperfect medium, and, hence, that it cannot have its absolute subject in the immediately spiritual, determined as spirit. From this it by no means follows that one needs to regard music as the work of the devil, even if our age does offer many horrible proofs of the daemonic power with which music may lay hold upon an individual, and this individual in turn, grip and capture a multitude, especially women, in the seductive snare of fear, by means of the all-disturbing power of voluptuousness. It by no means follows that one needs to regard music as the work of the devil, even though one notices with a certain secret horror that this art, more than any other, frequently harrows its votaries in a terrible manner, a phenomenon which strangely enough seems to have escaped the attention of psychologists and the multitude, except at the single moment when they are startled by the wild shriek of some despairing individual. However, it is noticeable enough that in legends, hence in the popular consciousness which finds its expression in legends, the musical is again the daemonic. As an example I may mention the *Irish March of the Elves*.[13]

Now with respect to the immediate-erotic stages, I owe everything I can say about it exclusively to Mozart, to whom I owe altogether everything. Since, however, the classification and comparison I here attempt can only be referred to him indirectly (the classification having been suggested by somebody else), I have, before setting about it seriously, tested myself and the classification lest I might in any way disturb my own pleasure or that of some other reader in admiring the immortal works of Mozart. He who would see Mozart in his true immortal greatness must witness his *Don Juan;* in comparison with that every other work is accidental, unessential. But if we now look at *Don Juan* so that we see individual things from Mozart's other operas from this same point of view, then I am convinced that we shall neither disparage him nor injure ourselves or our neighbor. Then we shall have the opportunity to rejoice over the fact that all the essential potency of music is poured out in the music of Mozart.

As for the rest, when in the preceding I used, and in what follows I continue to use, the expression "stage," it must not be insisted upon as implying that each stage existed independently, the one wholly separate from the other. I might, perhaps, more pertinently have used the word "metamorphosis." The different stages taken together constitute the immediate stage, and from this we may perceive that the individual stages are rather a revelation of a predicate, so that all the predicates rush down into the wealth of the last stage, since this is the real stage. The other stages have no independent existence; in and of themselves they exist only as parts of a conceptual scheme, and from this one may see their accidental character as over against the last stage. Since, however, they have found separate expression in Mozart's music, I shall discuss them separately. Above all, however, one must avoid considering them as different degrees of consciousness, since even the last stage has not yet arrived at consciousness; I have always to do only with the immediate in its sheer immediacy.

The difficulties which are always met with when one would make music the subject for aesthetic consideration, naturally do not fail to appear here. The difficulty in the preceding lay chiefly in the fact that while I would prove by means of thought that sensuous genius is essentially the subject of music, this can actually only be proved by means of music, just as I, too, can only come to an appreciation of music through the music itself. The difficulty the following must contend with is, rather, that since that which the music under discussion expresses is essentially music's proper subject, it expresses it far more perfectly than does language, which makes a mighty poor showing in comparison therewith. To be sure, if I had to do with different degrees of consciousness, then the advantage would naturally be on my side and on the side of language, but here that is not the case. Hence that which remains to be explained here can only have significance for him who has heard the music and who constantly continues to hear it. For him it may perhaps contain a single suggestion which may influence him to hear it again.

FIRST STAGE

The first stage is suggested by the Page in *Figaro*. It is naturally not fair here to see in the Page a single individual, which we are so easily tempted to do, when in imagination or reality we see it presented on the stage by a person. Then it becomes difficult to avoid, as is also partly the case with the Page in the play, having something accidental, something irrelevant to the idea enter, so that he becomes more than he should be; for in a certain sense he becomes this the moment he becomes an individual. But in becoming more, he becomes less, he ceases to be the idea. Therefore, we cannot grant him speech, but music becomes his only adequate means of expression, and for that reason it is noticeable that *Figaro* as well as *Don Juan*, as they issue from the hand of Mozart, belong to *opera seria*.[14] Now if we regard the Page only as a mythical figure, we shall find the characteristic of this first stage expressed in music.

The sensuous awakens, not yet to movement, but to a hushed tranquillity; not to joy and gladness, but to a deep melancholy. Desire is not yet awake, it is only a gloomy foreboding. In desire there is always present the object of desire, which arises out of it and manifests itself in a bewildering half-light of dawn. This relation obtains for the sensuous: by clouds and mists it is kept at a distance; by being reflected in these it is brought nearer. Desire possesses what will become its object, but possesses it without having desired it, and so does not possess it. This is the painful but also, in its sweetness, the delightful and fascinating contradiction which, in its sadness and its melancholy, resounds throughout this stage. Its pain lies not in there being too little, but rather in there being too much. The desire is quiet desire, the longing quiet longing, the ecstasy quiet ecstasy, wherein the object of desire is dawning, and is so near that it is within the desire. The object of desire hovers over the desire, sinks down in it, still without this movement happening through desire's own power to attract or because desire is operative. The object of desire does not fade away, nor does it elude desire's embrace, for then indeed desire would awaken; but it is, without being desired, present to desire, which just because of this becomes melancholy because it cannot come to the point of desiring. As soon as desire awakens, or rather in and with its awakening, desire and its object are separated; now desire breathes freely and soundly, whereas earlier it could not live and breathe for the desired. When desire is not awake, its object charms and inveigles it, aye, almost frightens it. Desire must have air, it must burst forth; thereby it happens that they part company. The object of desire flees shyly, modest as a woman, and they are separated; the object of desire vanishes *et apparet sublimis*[15] or in any case outside of desire. If one paints the ceiling of a room all over with figures from one side to the other, such a ceiling depresses one, as the painters say; if one paints only one light and graceful figure, then the room seems higher. Such is the relation between desire and its object at a first and later stage.

Hence the desire, which in this stage is present only as a presentiment about itself, is without movement, without disquiet, only gently rocked by an unclarified inner emotion. As the life of the plant is bound to the earth, so is desire lost in a present quiet longing, buried in contemplation, and yet cannot evacuate its object, because essentially in a deeper sense, there is no object. And yet this lack of an object is not its object, for then it would immediately be in motion, would be determined, if not in another way, then in sorrow and pain, but sorrow and pain have not the contradiction in them which is characteristic of melancholy and heaviness, nor the ambiguity which is the sweetness in the melancholy. Although desire in this stage is not qualified as desire, although this nascent desire, so far as its object is concerned, is entirely undefined, still it has the characteristic of being infinitely deep. It sucks, like Thor, through a horn whose point is buried in the sea;[16] yet the reason why it cannot draw its object to it is not that it is infinite, but that this infinity cannot become its object. Its sucking, therefore, does not indicate a relation to the object but is identical with its sigh, and this is infinitely deep.

In harmony with the description of the first stage given here, we shall find it very significant that the Page's part is

so arranged musically that it always lies within the range
of a female voice. The contradictory in this stage is, as it
were, suggested by this contradiction, the desire is so indefinite, its object so little separated from it, that the object of
desire rests androgynously within the desire, just as in plant
life the male and female parts are both present in one blossom. Desire and its object are joined in this unity, that they
both are of neuter gender.

Although speech does not belong to the mythical Page
but to the Page in the play, the poetic figure Cherubino,
and although because of this we cannot in this connection
pay attention to it, partly because it does not belong to
Mozart, partly because it expresses something quite different from that of which we are speaking here, I would, however, point to a particular speech, because it gives me occasion to describe this stage in its analogy to a later one.[17]
Susanne mocks Cherubino because he is in a way in love
with Marcellina, and the Page has no answer ready other
than this: she is a woman. With respect to the Page in the
play, it is essential that he should be in love with the Countess, unessential that he should fall in love with Marcellina,
which is only an indirect and paradoxical expression for the
intensity of the passion which binds him to the Countess.
With respect to the mythical Page, it is equally essential
that he should be in love with the Countess and with Marcellina; the eternal feminine is his object, and both the
Countess and Marcellina have this in common. Hence, when
we later hear about Don Juan:[18]

> Coquettes whom sixty years have kissed,
> With joy he adds them to his list,

we have the perfect analogy to this, except that the intensity and determination of the desire is far more strongly
expressed.

Were I now to venture the attempt of indicating by a
single predicate the characteristic of Mozart's music as it
concerns the Page in *Figaro*, I would say: it is drunk with
love. But like all intoxication, the intoxication of love can
also act in two ways, either increasing the transparent joy
of life, or compressing it in unclarified gloom. This latter

is the case with the music here, and rightly so. Music cannot give the reason for it, that is beyond its power; the spoken word cannot express the mood, it is too heavy, too ponderous, for speech to carry; only music can express it. The reason for its melancholy lies in the profound inner contradiction that we attempted to call attention to in the preceding.

We now leave the first stage, which is represented by the mythical Page; we leave him to continue his melancholy dreaming about what he has, his melancholy desiring of what he possesses. He never comes any farther, he never gets going, for his movements are illusory, and hence nothing. It is otherwise with the Page in the play. We feel a true and sincere friendly interest in his future, we congratulate him upon becoming a captain, we permit him to kiss Susanne once more in farewell, we shall not betray him about the mark on his forehead which none can see except the initiated; but nothing more than this, my good Cherubino, or we shall call the Count, and he will shout: "Be off with you, get out of the house, to your regiment! He is certainly no child, as no one knows better than myself."

SECOND STAGE

This stage is represented by Papageno in *The Magic Flute*. Here again, naturally, it is important to separate the essential from the accidental, to conjure up the mythical Papageno and forget the actual person in the play; particularly so here, since the character in the play appears in connection with all sorts of doubtful galimatias. For this reason it might not be without interest to run through the whole opera in order to show that its subject matter, considered as operatic material, profoundly fails of its purpose. Nor would we lack occasion to illuminate the erotic from a new side, as we noticed how the endeavor to invest it with a deeper ethical view, in such wise that this view tries its hand at all sorts of more significant dialectical exercises, is an adventure which has ventured quite beyond the range of music, so that it was impossible for even a Mozart to lend it any deeper interest. This opera definitively tends toward the unmusical, and therefore, it is, in spite of individually perfect concert numbers and individually deeply moving, pathetic utterances, by no means a classic opera. Still all this cannot occupy us in the present little inquiry. We have only to do with Papageno. This is a great advantage to us, if for no other reason than that we are thereby excused from every attempt to explain the significance of Papageno's relation to Tamino, a relationship which, with regard to the plan, looks so profound and thoughtful that it almost becomes unthinkable for sheer thoughtfulness.

Such a treatment of *The Magic Flute* might perhaps seem arbitrary to one or another reader, both because it sees too much in Papageno and too little in the rest of the opera; he will, perhaps, not approve of our procedure. The reason for this is that he does not agree with us as to the point of departure for every consideration of Mozart's music. In our opinion, this is, of course, *Don Juan,* and it is also our conviction that it is in seeing various features of the other operas in relation to this one that one shows the highest devotion to Mozart, although I would not thereby deny the importance of making each individual opera the object of separate consideration.

Desire awakens, and as it always happens that one first realizes he has dreamed in the moment of awakening, so likewise here, the dream is over. This impulse with which desire awakens, this trembling, separates the desire and its object, affords desire an object. This is a dialectical qualification which must be kept sharply in mind—only when the object exists does the desire exist, only when the desire exists does the object exist; desire and its object are twins, neither of which is born a fraction of an instant before the other. But though they are thus born at exactly the same instant, and with no time interval between, as is the case with other twins, the importance of their thus coming into existence is not that they are united but, on the contrary, that they are separated. But this movement of the sensuous, this earthquake, splits the desire and its object infinitely asunder for the moment; but as the moving principle appears a moment separating, so it again reveals itself as wishing to unite the separated. The result of this separation is that desire is pulled out of its substantial repose within itself, and consequently the object no longer falls under the qualifications of substantiality, but disperses itself in a manifold.

As the life of the plant is bound to earth, so is the first stage held captive in substantial longing. Desire awakens, the object flees, manifold in its revelation; the longing breaks away from the earth and starts out wandering; the flower gets wings and flits inconstant and unwearied here and there. Desire is directed toward the object, it is also moved within itself, the heart beats soundly and joyously, the objects swiftly vanish and reappear; but still before every disappearance is a present enjoyment, a moment of contact, short but sweet, evanescent as the gleam of a glowworm, inconstant and fleeting as the touch of a butterfly, and as harmless; countless kisses, but so swiftly enjoyed, that it is as if there were only taken from one object what is given to the next. Only momentarily is a deeper desire suspected, but this suspicion is forgotten. In Papageno the desire aims at discoveries. This craving for discovery is the throbbing in it, is its sprightliness. It does not find the precise object of this search, but it discovers the manifold, as it seeks therein the object it would discover. Desire is thus awakened, but it is not yet qualified as desire. If you remember that desire is present in all three stages, then you can say that in the first stage, desire is defined as *dreaming*, in the second as *seeking*, in the third as *desiring*. The seeking desire is not yet the desiring one; it only seeks that which it can desire, but it does not desire it. Therefore this predicate will perhaps describe it best: it discovers. If from this perspective we compare Papageno with Don Juan, we see that the latter's journey through the world is something more than a journey of discovery; he enjoys not only the adventures of the journey of discovery, but he is a knight who aims at conquest (*veni, vidi, vici*).[19] Discovery and victory are here identical; indeed, in a certain sense one may say that he forgets the discovery in the victory, or that the discovery lies behind him, and he therefore leaves it to his servant and secretary Leporello, who keeps the list in quite a different sense than if I imagined Papageno keeping books. Papageno selects, Don Juan enjoys, Leporello inspects.

The characteristic of this, as of every stage, I can indeed represent to thought, but always only in the moment that it has ceased to be. For even if I could perfectly describe its characteristic and explain the reason for this, there would still always be something left behind, which I cannot express, and which yet would be heard. It is too immediate to be fixed in words. So here with Papageno, it is the same song, the same melody; as soon as he finishes, he begins anew from the beginning, and so continuously. Someone may now offer the objection that it is wholly impossible to express anything which is immediate. In a certain sense this is quite true, but the immediacy of the spirit has, in the first place, its immediate expression in language, and next, in so far as there occurs, through the intervention of language, a change therewith, it yet remains essentially the same, just because it is a qualification of the spirit. Here, however, it is the immediacy of the sensuous which, as such, has quite another medium, where consequently the disproportion between the media makes the impossibility absolute.

If I should now attempt by means of a single predicate to indicate the characteristics of the Mozart music in the part of this play in which we are interested, I should say: it is cheerfully chirping, vigorous, bubbling with love. What I would especially emphasize are the first aria and the chime of bells; the duet with Pamina and later with Papagena falls entirely outside the category of the immediate-musical. If, on the other hand, one considers the first aria, then one will approve of the predicate I have chosen; and if one pays closer attention, there will be an opportunity to see what significance the musical has, how it appears as the absolute expression of the idea, and how this, as a consequence, is the immediate-musical. As you know, Papageno accompanies his light-hearted cheerfulness on the flute. Every ear has certainly felt itself moved in a strange manner by this accompaniment. But the more one considers it, the more one sees in Papageno the mythical Papageno, all the more expressive and characteristic one will find it; one does not tire of hearing it again and again, because it is an absolutely adequate expression of Papageno's life, whose whole life is such an incessant twittering; who, always carefree, chirps on in all idleness, and who is happy and satisfied because this is his life-content, happy in his work and happy in his song. As you know, it is so very profoundly arranged in the opera, that the flutes of Tamino and Papageno harmonize with one another. And yet, what a difference! Tamino's flute, from which the opera takes its name, fails altogether in its effect. And why? Because Tamino is simply not a musical figure. This is due to the mistaken plan of the opera as a whole. Tamino becomes exceedingly tiresome and sentimental on his flute; and when one considers all the rest of his development, his state of consciousness, one cannot help but think, every time he takes up his flute and begins to play on it, of the farmer in Horace (*rusticus exspectat, dum defluat amnis*), except that Horace did not give his farmer a flute for an unprofitable pastime.[20] Tamino as a dramatic figure is entirely outside of the musical, just as the intellectual development the play would realize is, on the whole, a totally unmusical idea. Tamino has really come so far that the musical ceases; therefore his fluteplaying is only a time-killer, brought in to drive away thought. Music can effectively banish thoughts, even evil thoughts, just as we say about David that his playing exorcised Saul's evil spirit.[21] On the other hand, there is a great delusion in this idea, for it is true only in so far as it carries consciousness back into immediacy, and lulls it therein. The individual may therefore feel happy in the moment of intoxication, but he only becomes the more unhappy. Quite in parenthesis I shall now permit myself an observation. We have used music to heal mental aberrations; we have also in a certain sense achieved our purpose, and yet it is an illusion. That is, when madness has a mental cause, it is always the result of the induration of one or another part of the brain. This induration must be overcome, but in order to overcome it, one must go quite the opposite way from that which leads to music. If one employs music, one uses entirely the wrong method, and makes the patient even more unbalanced, even if he seems to be better.

What I have said here about Tamino's flute-playing, I can readily let stand without fear of seeing it misunderstood. It is by no means my intention to deny what several times has been conceded, that music as an accompaniment can have its significance upon entering an alien sphere—that of language. The fault in *The Magic Flute* is, however, that the whole opera tends toward consciousness, and consequently its whole trend is to do away with music, while still remaining an opera; and not even this thought is brought out clearly in the play. Ethically determined love, or married love, is posited as the goal of the development, and therein lies the radical fault of the play; for let marriage be, ecclesiastically or secularly, what it will be; one thing it is not, it is not musical; indeed, it is absolutely unmusical.

The first aria considered musically has, consequently, great significance as the immediate-musical expression for Papageno's whole life, and to the degree that history can find its absolutely adequate expression in music, it is only history in a figurative sense. The chime of bells, on the other hand, is the musical expression for his activity, of which one can only get an understanding through music; it is charming, tempting, entrancing, alluring, like the playing of the man who caused the fish to pause and listen.[22]

The speeches, for which either Schikaneder or the Danish translator is responsible, are in general so crazy and stupid that it is almost inconceivable how Mozart has brought as much out of them as he has. To let Papageno say of himself, "I am a child of Nature," and so in that very moment make himself a liar, may be regarded as an example *instar omnium*. One might make an exception of the words of the text in the first aria, that he puts the maidens he catches in his cage. That is, if one will put a little more into this than the author himself has presumably done, then it will serve nicely to indicate the inoffensive character of Papageno's activity, as we have indicated it above.

We leave now the mythical Papageno. The fate of the actual Papageno need not concern us. We wish him happiness with his little Papagena, and we willingly permit him to seek his happiness in populating a primitive forest or an entire continent with nothing but Papagenos.

THIRD STAGE

This stage is represented by *Don Juan*. Here I am not under the necessity, as in the preceding, of having to pick out a single portion of an opera. Here it is not necessary to separate but to sum up, since the entire opera is essentially an expression of the idea, and with the exception of one or two numbers, is based essentially upon this idea, with dramatic necessity gravitating toward this as its center. Hence one will again have opportunity to see in what sense I may call the preceding stages by that name, when I call the third stage *Don Juan*. I earlier reminded you that they do not have any separate existence, and when one understands this third stage, which is really the whole stage, then one cannot so easily regard them as one-sided abstractions or provisional anticipations, but rather as presentiments of *Don Juan*, except that something always constantly remains behind, which more or less justifies me in using the term *stage*, in that they are one-sided presentiments, each of them suggesting only one phase.

The contradiction in the first stage lay in the fact that desire could acquire no object, but without having desired was in possession of its object, and therefore could not reach the point of desiring. In the second stage, the object appears in its manifold, but as desire seeks its object in this manifold, it still has, in a deeper sense, no object, it is not yet posited as desire. In *Don Juan*, on the other hand, desire is absolutely determined as desire; it is, in an intensive and extensive sense, the immediate synthesis of the two preceding stages. The first stage desired the one ideally, the second stage desired the particular under the qualification of the manifold; the third stage is a synthesis of these two. Desire has its absolute object in the particular, it desires the particular absolutely. Herein lies the seductiveness of which we shall later speak. Hence, desire in this stage is absolutely sound, victorious, triumphant, irresistible and daemonic. We must, therefore, naturally not overlook the fact that we are not here talking about desire in a particular individual, but about desire as principle, spiritually determined as that which the spirit excludes. This is the idea of sensuous genius, as we also indicated above. Don Juan is the expression for this idea, and the expression for Don Juan is again exclusively musical. It is particularly these two considerations which will be continually emphasized from different points of view in what follows, from which also the proof of this opera's classic significance will be indirectly demonstrated. Meantime, to make it easier for the reader to maintain a general viewpoint, I shall attempt to collect the scattered considerations under particular headings.

It is not my intention to say something simple about this music, and I shall, with the assistance of all good spirits, especially guard against scaring together a multitude of insignificant but very noisy predicates. I likewise eschew the linguistic orgy, which would betray the impotence of language, and that so much the more, since I do not regard it as an imperfection in language but as a high power. But therefore I am the more willing to recognize music within its own limits. By contrast, what I wish to do is, in part, to illuminate the idea from as many sides as possible and its relation to language, thereby always circumscribing more and more closely the region where music has its home; I would, as it were, worry it into breaking forth, yet without my being able to say more of something that exists to be heard than: listen! I mean by this that I have tried to do the best of which aesthetics is capable; whether I shall succeed in doing so is another matter. Only in a single place will a predicate, like a warrant for arrest, furnish the description, without my forgetting, or allowing the reader to forget, that he who holds the warrant in his hand has by no means on that account apprehended the one it names. Further, the whole plan of the opera, its inner structure, will in its place become the subject for separate discussion, but once again in such wise that I do not undertake to shout loud enough for two: "O! bravo schwere Noth Gotts Blitz bravissimo," but only so that I persistently tempt the musical forth, and mean thereby to have wished to do the utmost that one in a purely aesthetic sense is capable of doing with the musical.

What I shall give, consequently, is not a running commentary on the music, which essentially cannot contain other than subjective accidentalities and idiosyncrasies, and can only appeal to something corresponding in the reader. Even so able a commentator as Dr. Hotho,[23] so rich in reflection, so manifold in expression, has still not been able to avoid, on the one hand, his exposition's degenerating into mere verbosity, which must form a counterbalance for Mozart's harmony, or sound like a weak echo, a pale impression of Mozart's full-toned, exuberant vigor; and, on the other hand, Don Juan's becoming at times something more than he is in the opera, a reflective individual, and at times becoming less. This last is naturally due to the fact that the profound, absolute point of *Don Juan* has escaped Hotho; to him *Don Juan* is still only the best of operas but not qualitatively different from all other operas. But if one has not perceived this with the omnipresent certainty of the speculative eye, then one cannot worthily and correctly discuss *Don Juan,* even though, if one had perceived it, one might be able to speak more gloriously, more richly, and above all, more truthfully, than he who here ventures to be the spokesman.

On the other hand, I shall constantly ferret out the musical in the idea, the situation, and so on, distilling its very essence, and then when I have made the reader so musically receptive that he seems to hear the music, although he hears nothing, then I shall have completed my task, then I become mute, then I say to the reader as to myself: listen. You friendly genii, who protect all innocent love, to you I commit all endowments of my mind and soul; guard the questing thoughts that they may be found worthy of the subject; fashion my soul into a harmonious instrument, let the soft breezes of eloquence blow over it, send the refreshment and blessings of fruitful moods! You righteous spirits, who guard the boundaries in the realms of the beautiful, watch over me, that I do not in a moment of unclarified enthusiasm and a blind zeal to exalt *Don Juan* above all, do it wrong, disparage it, make it something other than what it is, which is the highest! You powerful spirits, you who know and understand the hearts of men, stand by me that I may catch the reader, not in the net of passion, nor by the artfulness of eloquence, but by the eternal truth of conviction.

1. SENSUOUS GENIUS QUALIFIED AS SEDUCTION

When the idea in *Don Juan* originated is not known; only so much is known, that it belongs to the Christian era, and through Christianity it also belongs to the Middle Ages. Even if one could not with some degree of certainty trace the idea back in the human consciousness to that period of the world's history, still a consideration of the inner nature of the idea would immediately remove every doubt. The Middle Ages are altogether impregnated with the idea of representation, partly conscious, partly unconscious; the total is represented in a single individual, yet in such a way that it is only a single aspect which is determined as totality, and which now appears in a single individual, who is because of this, both more and less than an individual. By the side of this individual there stands another individual who, likewise, totally represents another aspect of life's content, such as the knight and the scholastic, the ecclesiastic and the layman. The grand dialectic of life is here invariably illustrated by representative individuals, who, more often than not, stand in pairs over against each other; life constantly presents itself only *sub una specie,* and the great dialectic unity which in unity possesses life *sub utraque specie* is not suspected.[24] The contrasts usually stand, therefore, indifferent, apart from one another. This the Middle Ages knew nothing about. Thus they themselves instinctively realize the representative idea, while only a later reflection sees the idea contained in it. If the Middle Ages posit for their own consciousness an individual as representative of the idea, then they usually posit at his side another individual in relation to him. This relationship is generally a comic one, where the one individual, as it were, compensates for the disproportionate greatness of the other in actual life. Thus the king has his fool by his side, Faust has his Wagner, Don Quixote Sancho Panza, Don Juan Leporello. This arrangement, too, belongs essentially to the Middle Ages. The idea belongs, accordingly, to the Middle Ages; in the Middle Ages, however, it is not the exclusive property of a single poet; it is one of those conceptions of primal power which spring forth spontaneously out of the popular world-consciousness. The conflict between flesh and spirit which Christianity brought into the world, the Middle Ages had to regard as a subject for its consideration, and to that end, they made the contending forces individually the subject of reflection. Don Juan is, then, if I dare say so, flesh incarnate, or the inspiration of the flesh by the spirit of the flesh. This has already been sufficiently stressed in the preceding; what I would here call attention to, however, is whether one ought to refer Don Juan to the earlier or later period of the Middle Ages. That he stands in an essential relation to this era is evident to everyone. Either he is, then, the rebellious, misunderstood anticipation of the erotic, which appeared in the days of knighthood, or chivalry is yet only in a relative opposition to the spiritual, and only when this contradiction became still sharper did Don Juan appear as the sensuous which opposes the spiritual to the death. The erotic in the age of chivalry had a certain resemblance to that of the Greeks. The latter, like the former, is psychically determined. But the difference is this, that this psychical determination lay within a general spiritual qualification or in a qualification as totality. The idea of the feminine is constantly in movement in many ways, which was not the case among the Greeks, where everyone was only the beautiful individuality, but the feminine was not anticipated. The erotic element of knighthood was present therefore in the consciousness of the Middle Ages in an attitude somewhat conciliatory toward the spiritual, even if the spiritual in its zealous austerity held it suspect.

If we now assume that the spiritual principle is posited in the world, we may either imagine that the most glaring contrasts come first, the most atrocious disjunctions, and that afterward they gradually become milder. Under such an assumption, Don Juan belongs to the earlier Middle Ages. If, on the contrary, we assume that the relationship gradually developed into this absolute contradiction, as is also more natural, the spiritual more and more withdrawing its shares from the united firm, in order to act independently whereupon the essential offense appears, then Don Juan belongs to the later Middle Ages. We are led thus to that point in time where the Middle Ages are about to become important, where we then meet a related idea, namely, Faust, except that Don Juan must be placed a little earlier. As the spirit, qualified exclusively as spirit, renounces the world, it not only feels that this is not its home, but that it is not even its sphere of action; it withdraws into the higher regions, and so leaves the worldly behind as the arena of the power with which it has always been at strife, and to which it now gives place. As the spirit thus frees itself from the earth, the sensuous appears in all its power; it offers no objection to the change; it, too, sees the advantage in being separated, and rejoices that the Church is not able to keep them together, but cuts the bond which united them.

Stronger than ever before, the sensuous now awakens in all its richness, in all its joy and enthusiasm; and like that hermit of nature, the reticent echo, who never speaks first to anyone, nor speaks without being questioned, it finds great satisfaction in the hunting horn of the knights, in their love ballads, in the baying of the hounds, the snorting of the horses, so that it never becomes tired of repeating it again and again, and at last, as it were, of saying it to itself, so as not to forget it; thus did the whole world become a mammoth sounding-board for the worldly spirit of the sensuous, while the spiritual had abandoned the world.

The Middle Ages had much to say about a mountain, not found on any map, which is called the mountain of Venus. There the sensuous has its home, there it has its own wild pleasures, for it is a kingdom, a state. In this kingdom language has no place, nor sober-minded thought, nor the toilsome business of reflection. There sound only the voice of elemental passion, the play of appetites, the wild shouts of intoxication; it exists solely for pleasure in eternal tumult. The first-born of this kingdom is Don Juan. That it is the kingdom of sin is not yet affirmed, for we confine ourselves to the moment at which this kingdom appears in aesthetic indifference.[25] Not until reflection enters does it appear as the kingdom of sin, but by that time Don Juan is slain, the music is silent; one sees only the despairing defiance which in impotence protests, but which can find no consistency, not even in sounds. When sensuousness appears as that which must be excluded, as that which the spirit can have nothing to do with, yet without passing judgment upon it or condemning it, then the sensuous assumes the form of the daemonic in aesthetic indifference. It is only the matter of a moment; soon everything is changed, the music, too, is over. Faust and Don Juan are the Titans and giants of the Middle Ages, who in the supercilious haughtiness of their endeavors are not different from those of olden times, except that they stand in isolation, not forming a union of forces with which unitedly to storm the heavens, but here all the power is concentrated in the single individual.

Don Juan, consequently, is the expression for the daemonic determined as the sensuous; Faust, its expression determined as the intellectual or spiritual, which the Christian spirit excludes. These ideas stand in an essential relation to one another, and have much in common; hence, one might expect to find them both incorporated in sagas. That this is true for Faust, is well known. There is a folk-book whose title is familiar enough, although the book itself is little used; this is especially strange in our time, when men are so occupied with the idea of Faust. But so it goes. While every intending *privatdocent* or professor, as intellectually mature, hopes to establish his reputation among the reading public by publishing a book on Faust, in which he faithfully repeats what all the other licentiates and candidates for academic degrees have already said, he dares to ignore such an insignificant little folk-book. It never occurs to him how beautiful it is that the veritably great is common property for everybody, that a peasant goes to Tribler's Widow, or to a ballad seller in Halmtorvet, and reads it half aloud to himself at the very time Goethe is composing a *Faust*.[26] And indeed this folk-book merits attention, for it has what one appreciates above all as an honorable quality in wine, it has bouquet, it is an excellent bottling from the Middle Ages, and as one opens it, it bubbles forth so spicy, so sparkling, so characteristically fragrant, that one is quite strangely affected. Still, enough of this. I would only call attention to the fact that no such legend is to be found concerning Don Juan. No folk-book, no ballad issued every year, has preserved his memory. Probably a tradition has existed, but this in all likelihood restricted itself to just a few hints; perhaps it was even shorter than the few stanzas which form the basis of Bürger's *Lenore*.[27] Perhaps it contained nothing but the number; for I am greatly mistaken if the present number, 1,003, did not belong to a legend. A legend which does not contain anything else seems somewhat poverty-stricken, and this would suggest that it was not reduced to writing; but still this number has an excellent property, a lyrical foolhardiness, which many perhaps do not notice because they are so accustomed to seeing it. Although this idea has not found expression in a legend, it has been preserved in another manner. It is well known that Don Juan existed in very early times in the form of a farce; this is likely its first existence. But here the idea is conceived comically, just as everywhere it is remarkable that the Middle Ages, so proficient in furnishing ideals, were inerrant in sensing the comical which lay in the supernatural size of the ideal. To make Don Juan a braggart who imagined that he had seduced every girl he met, to let Leporello believe his lies, was not at all an unfortunate basis for the comic. And had this not been the case, had this not even been the conception, still the comic turn could not have failed to appear, since it lies in the contrast between the hero and his scene of action. So one may permit the Middle Ages to describe heroes so powerfully built that their eyes were a foot apart, but if an ordinary man were to come on the stage and pretend to have eyes a foot apart, the comic would be in full swing.

What has been said here regarding the tradition about Don Juan would not have found a place here if it did not have some closer relation to the subject of the investigation, if it did not serve to direct thought to the one definite goal. The reason that this idea, as compared with that of Faust, has so poor a past lay in the fact, I suppose, that there was something mysterious in it as long as no one noticed that music was its proper medium. Faust is idea, but an idea which is also essentially individual. To imagine daemonic intellectuality concentrated in a single individual is the peculiar office of thought, while to imagine the sensuous thus concentrated is unthinkable. Don Juan constantly hovers between being an idea, that is to say, energy, life—and being an individual. But this hovering is the musical trembling. When the sea tosses tempestuously, then the swirling billows form images of strange creatures in this wild upheaval. It is as if these creatures set the waves in motion, and yet it is the conflict of the opposing billows which creates them. So Don Juan is an image which constantly appears, but does not gain form and substance, an individual who is constantly being formed, but is never finished, of whose life history one can form no more definite impression than one can by listening to the tumult of the waves. When Don Juan is conceived in this manner, there is meaning and profound significance in everything. If I imagine a particular individual, if I see him or hear him speak, then it becomes comic to imagine that he has seduced 1,003; for as soon as he is regarded as a particular individual, the accent falls in quite another place; it stresses, in fact, those whom he has seduced and how. The naïveté of ballads and legends can successfully express such things without suspecting the comical; for reflection, that is impossible. When, on the contrary, he is interpreted in music, then I do not have a particular individual, but I have the power of nature, the daemonic, which as little tires of seducing or is done with seducing as the wind is tired of blowing, the sea of billowing, or a waterfall of tumbling downward from the heights. In this respect, the number of the seduced can just as well be any other number far greater. It is often not an easy task, when translating the text of an opera, to do it so exactly that the translation is not only singable but also harmonizes fairly well with the meaning of the text and thus with the music as well. As an example of the fact that sometimes it is altogether unimportant [to be so exact], I shall cite the number in the list in *Don Juan,* without taking the matter as thoughtlessly as people generally do, thinking that such things do not matter. I, on the contrary, consider the matter aesthetically serious to a high degree, and therefore I think the number is unimportant. Yet I would commend one single characteristic of this number 1,003, that it is odd and accidental, which is not at all unimportant, since it gives the impression that the list is by no means closed, but that, on the contrary, Don Juan is in a hurry. One almost begins to pity Leporello, who must not only, as he himself says, stand watch outside the door, but along with that, carry on so complicated a system of book-keeping that it could well keep a registered accountant busy.

Never before in the world has sensuousness been conceived as it is in *Don Juan*—as a principle: for this reason the erotic is here defined by another predicate: the erotic here is *seduction*. Strangely enough, the idea of a seducer was entirely wanting among the Greeks. It is by no means my intention, because of this, to wish to praise the Greeks, for, as everybody knows, gods as well as men were indiscreet in their love affairs; nor do I censure Christianity, for, after all, it has the idea only as something external to itself. The reason that the Greeks lacked this idea lay in the fact that the whole of the Greek life was posited as individuality. The psychical is thus the predominant or is always in harmony with the sensuous. Greek love, therefore, was psychical, not sensuous, and it is this which inspires the modesty which rests over all Greek love. They fell in love with a girl, they set heaven and earth in motion to get her; when they succeeded, then they perhaps tired of her, and sought a new love. In this instability they may, indeed, have had a certain resemblance to Don Juan. To mention only one instance, Hercules might surely produce a goodly list, when one considers that he sometimes took whole families numbering up to fifty daughters, and like a family son-in-law, according to some reports, had his way with all of them in a single night. Nevertheless, he is still essentially different from a Don Juan, he is no seducer. When one considers Greek love, it is, in accordance with its concept, essentially faithful, just because it is psychical; and it is some accidental factor in the particular individual that he loves many, and with regard to the many he loves, it is again accidental every time he loves a new one; when he is in love with one, he does not think of the next one. Don Juan, on the contrary, is a seducer from the ground up. His love is not psychical but sensuous, and sensuous love, in accordance with its concept, is not faithful, but absolutely faithless; it loves not one but all, that is to say, it seduces all. It exists only in the moment, but the moment, in terms of its concept, is the sum of moments, and so we have the seducer.

Chivalrous love is also psychical and, therefore, in accordance with its concept, is essentially faithful; only sensuous love, in terms of its very concept, is essentially faithless. But this, its faithlessness, appears also in another way; it becomes in fact only a constant repetition. Psychical love has the dialectic in it in a double sense. For partly it has the doubt and unrest in it, as to whether it will also be happy, see its desire fulfilled, and be requited. This anxiety sensuous love does not have. Even a Jupiter is doubtful about his victory, and this cannot be otherwise; moreover, he himself cannot desire it otherwise. With Don Juan this is not the case; he makes short work of it and must always be regarded as absolutely victorious. This might seem an advantage to him, but it is precisely poverty. On the other hand, psychical love has also another dialectic, it is in fact different in its relation to every single individual who is the object of love. Therein lies its wealth, its rich content. But such is not the case with Don Juan. For this, indeed, he has not time; everything for him is a matter of the moment only. To see her and to love her, that was one and the same. One may say this in a certain sense about psychical love, but in that there is only suggested a beginning. With regard to Don Juan it is valid in another way. To see her and to love her is the same thing; it is in the moment, in the same moment everything is over, and the same thing repeats itself endlessly. If one imagines a psychical love in Don Juan, it becomes at once ridiculous and a self-contradiction, which is not even in accord with the idea of positing 1,003 in Spain. It becomes an over-emphasis which acts disturbingly, even if one imagined oneself considering him ideally. Now if we had no other medium for describing this love than language, we should be up against it, for as soon as we have abandoned the naïveté which in all simplicity can insist that there were 1,003 in Spain, then we require something more, namely, the psychical individualization. The aesthetic is by no means satisfied that everything should thus be lumped together, and is astonished at the number. Psychical love does not exactly move in the rich manifold of the individual life, where the nuances are really significant. Sensuous love, on the other hand, can lump everything together. The essential for it is woman in the abstract, and at most is a more sensuous difference. Psychical love is a continuance in time, sensuous love a disappearance in time, but the medium which exactly expresses this is music. Music is excellently fitted to accomplish this, since it is far more abstract than language, and therefore does not express the individual but the general in all its generality, and yet it expresses the general not in reflective abstraction, but in the immediate concrete.

As an example of what I mean, I shall discuss a little more carefully the servant's second aria: the List of the Seduced. This number may be regarded as the real epic of Don Juan. Consequently, make this experiment, if you are sceptical about the truth of my assertion! Imagine a poet more happily endowed by nature than anyone before him; give him vigor of expression, give him mastery and authority over the power of language, let everything wherein there is the breath of life be obedient unto him, let his slightest suggestion be deferred to, let everything wait, ready and prepared for his word of command; let him be surrounded by a numerous band of light skirmishers, swift-footed messengers who overtake thought in its most hurried flight; let nothing escape him, not the least movement; let nothing secret, nothing unutterable be left behind him in the whole world—give him, after all this, the task of singing Don Juan as an epic, of unrolling the list of the seduced. What will the result be? He will never finish! The epic has the fault, if one wishes to call it that, of being able to go on as long as you will. His hero, the improviser, Don Juan, can go on indefinitely. The poet may now enter into the manifold, there will always be enough there which will give pleasure, but he will never achieve the effect which Mozart has obtained. For even if he finally finishes, he will still not have said half of what Mozart has expressed in this one number. Mozart has not even attempted the manifold; he deals only with certain great formations which are set in motion. This finds its sufficient explanation in the medium itself, in the music which is too abstract to express the differences. The musical epic thus becomes something comparatively short, and yet it has in an inimitable manner the epic quality that it can go on as long as it will, since one can constantly let it begin again from the beginning, and hear it over and over again, just because it expresses the general in the concreteness of immediacy. Here we do not hear Don Juan as a particular individual, nor his speech, but we hear a voice, the voice of sensuousness, and we hear it through the longing of womanhood. Only in this manner can Don Juan become epic, in that he constantly finishes, and constantly begins again from the beginning, for his life is the sum of repellent moments which have no coherence, his life as moment is the sum of the moments, as the sum of the moments is the moment.

In this generality, in this floating between being an individual and being a force of nature, lies Don Juan; as soon as he becomes individual the aesthetic acquires quite other categories. Therefore it is entirely proper, and it has a profound inner significance, that in the seduction which takes place in the play, Zerlina, the girl, should be a common peasant girl. Hypocritical aestheticists who, under the show of understanding poets and composers, contribute everything to their being misunderstood, will perhaps instruct us that Zerlina is an unusual girl. Anyone who believes this shows that he has totally misunderstood Mozart, and that he is using wrong categories. That he misunderstands Mozart is evident enough; for Mozart has purposely made Zerlina as insignificant as possible, something Hotho has also called attention to, yet without seeing the real reason for it. If, for instance, Don Juan's love were qualified as other than sensuous, if he were a seducer in an intellectual sense (a type which we shall consider presently), then it would have been a radical fault in the play for the heroine in the seduction which dramatically engages our attention

to be only a little peasant girl. Then the aesthetic would require that Don Juan should have been set a more difficult
task. To Don Juan, however, these differences mean nothing. If I could imagine him making such a speech about
himself, he might perhaps say: "You are wrong. I am no
husband who requires an unusual girl to make me happy;
every girl has that which makes me happy, and therefore I
take them all." In some such way we have to understand the
saying I earlier referred to: "even sixty-year coquettes"—or
in another place: *pur chè porti la gonella, voi sapete quel
chè fà.*[28] To Don Juan every girl is an ordinary girl, every
love affair an everyday story. Zerlina is young and pretty,
and she is a woman; this is the uncommon which she has
in common with hundreds of others; but it is not the uncommon that Don Juan desires, but the common, and this
she has in common with every woman. If this is not the
case, then Don Juan ceases to be absolutely musical, and
aesthetics requires speech, dialogue, while now, since it *is*
the case, Don Juan is absolutely musical.

From another point of view I may throw some additional
light upon this by analyzing the inner structure of the play.
Elvira is Don Juan's mortal enemy; in the dialogue for
which the Danish translator is responsible, this is frequently emphasized.[29] That it is an error for Don Juan to
make a speech is certain enough, but because of this it
does not follow that the speech might not contain an occasional good observation. Well then, Don Juan fears Elvira. Now probably some aestheticist or other believes that
he can profoundly explain this by coming forward with a
long disquisition about Elvira's being a very unusual girl
and so on. This altogether misses the mark. She is dangerous to him because she has been seduced. In the same
sense, exactly in the same sense, Zerlina becomes dangerous
to him when she is seduced. As soon as she is seduced, she
is elevated to a higher sphere, to a consciousness which
Don Juan does not have. Therefore, she is dangerous to
him. Hence, it is not by means of the accidental but by
means of the general that she is dangerous to him.

Don Juan, then, is a seducer; in him the erotic takes the
form of seduction. Here much is well said when it is rightly

understood, little when it is understood with a general lack
of clarity. We have already noted that the concept, a seducer, is essentially modified with respect to Don Juan, as
the object of his desire is the sensuous, and that alone. This
is of importance in order to show the musical in Don Juan.
In ancient times the sensuous found its expression in the
silent stillness of plastic art; in the Christian world the sensuous must burst forth in all its impatient passion. Although
one may say with truth that Don Juan is a seducer, this
expression, which can work so disturbingly upon the weak
brains of certain aestheticians, has often given rise to misunderstandings, as they have scraped this and that together
that could be said about such a one, and have at once
applied it to Don Juan. At times they have exposed their
own cunning in tracking down Don Juan's, at times they
talk themselves hoarse in explaining his intrigues and his
subtlety; in short, the word *seducer* has given rise to the
situation that everybody has been against him to the limit
of his power, has contributed his mite to the total misunderstanding. Of Don Juan we must use the word *seducer* with
great caution—assuming, that is, that it is more important
to say something right than simply to say something. This
is not because Don Juan is too good, but because he simply
does not fall under ethical categories. Hence I should rather
not call him a deceiver, since there is always something
more ambiguous in that word. To be a seducer requires a
certain amount of reflection and consciousness, and as soon
as this is present, then it is proper to speak of cunning and
intrigues and crafty plans. This consciousness is lacking in
Don Juan. Therefore, he does not seduce. He desires, and
this desire acts seductively. To that extent he seduces. He
enjoys the satisfaction of desire; as soon as he has enjoyed it,
he seeks a new object, and so on endlessly. Therefore, I
suppose he is a deceiver, but yet not so that he plans his
deceptions in advance; it is the inherent power of sensuousness which deceives the seduced, and it is rather a kind of
Nemesis. He desires, and is constantly desiring, and constantly enjoys the satisfaction of the desire. To be a seducer,
he lacks time in advance in which to lay his plans, and
time afterward in which to become conscious of his act. A

seducer, therefore, ought to be in possession of a power Don Juan does not have, however well equipped he may otherwise be—the power of eloquence. As soon as we grant him eloquence he ceases to be musical, and the aesthetic interest becomes an entirely different matter.

Achim v. Arnim tells somewhere of a seducer of a very different style, a seducer who falls under ethical categories. About him he uses an expression which in truth, boldness, and conciseness is almost equal to Mozart's stroke of the bow. He says he could so talk with a woman that, if the devil caught him, he could wheedle himself out of it if he had a chance to talk with the devil's grandmother.[30] This is the real seducer; the aesthetic interest here is also different, namely: how, the method. There is evidently something very profound here, which has perhaps escaped the attention of most people, in that Faust, who reproduces Don Juan, seduces only one girl, while Don Juan seduces hundreds; but this one girl is also, in an intensive sense, seduced and crushed quite differently from all those Don Juan has deceived, simply because Faust, as reproduction, falls under the category of the intellectual. The power of such a seducer is speech, i.e., the lie. A few days ago I heard one soldier talking to another about a third who had betrayed a girl; he did not give a long-winded description, and yet his expression was very pithy: "He gets away with things like that by lies and things like that." Such a seducer is of quite a different sort from Don Juan, is essentially different from him, as one can see from the fact that he and his activities are extremely unmusical, and from the aesthetic standpoint come within the category of the interesting. The object of his desire is accordingly, when one rightly considers him aesthetically, something more than the merely sensuous.

But what is this force, then, by which Don Juan seduces? It is desire, the energy of sensuous desire. He desires in every woman the whole of womanhood, and therein lies the sensuously idealizing power with which he at once embellishes and overcomes his prey. The reaction to this gigantic passion beautifies and develops the one desired, who flushes in enhanced beauty by its reflection. As the enthusiast's fire with seductive splendor illumines even those who stand in a casual relation to him, so Don Juan transfigures in a far deeper sense every girl, since his relation to her is an essential one. Therefore all finite differences fade away before him in comparison with the main thing: being a woman. He rejuvenates the older woman into the beautiful middle age of womanhood; he matures the child almost instantly; everything which is woman is his prey (*pur chè porti la gonella, voi sapete quel chè fà*). On the other hand, we must by no means understand this as if his sensuousness were blind; instinctively he knows very well how to discriminate and, above all, he idealizes. If for a moment I here think back to the Page in a preceding stage, the reader will perhaps remember that once when we spoke of the Page, I compared a speech of his with one of Don Juan's. The mythical Page I left standing, the real one I sent away to the army. If I now imagined that the mythical Page had liberated himself, was free to move about, then I would recall here a speech of the Page which is appropriate to Don Juan. As Cherubino, light as a bird and daring, springs out of the window, it makes so strong an impression upon Susanne that she almost swoons, and when she recovers, she exclaims: "See how he runs! My, won't he make conquests among the girls!" This is quite correctly said by Susanne, and the reason for her swoon is not only the idea of the daring leap, but rather that he had already "got around her." The Page is really the future Don Juan, though without this being understood in a ridiculous way, as if the Page by becoming older became Don Juan. Now Don Juan can not only have his way with the girls, but he makes them happy and—unhappy, but, curiously enough, in such wise that that's the way they want it, and a foolish girl it would be who would not choose to be unhappy for the sake of having once been happy with Don Juan. If I still continue, therefore, to call him a seducer, I by no means imagine him slyly formulating his plans, craftily calculating the effect of his intrigues. His power to deceive lies in the essential genius of sensuousness, whose incarnation he really is. Shrewd sober-mindedness is lacking in him; his life is as effervescent as the wine with which he stimulates himself; his life is dramatic like the strains which accompany his joyous feast; always he is triumphant. He requires no preparation, no plan, no time; for he is always prepared. Energy is always in him and also desire, and only when he desires is he rightly in his element. He sits feasting, joyous as a god he swings his cup—he rises with his napkin in his hand, ready for attack. If Leporello rouses him in the middle of the night, he awakens, always certain of his victory. But this energy, this power, cannot be expressed in words, only music can give us a conception of it. It is inexpressible for reflection and thought. The cunning of an ethically determined seducer I can clearly set forth in words, and music will try in vain to solve this problem. With Don Juan, the converse holds true. What is this power?—No one can say. Even if I questioned Zerlina about it before she goes to the dance: "What is this power by which he captivates you?"—she would answer: "No one knows," and I would say: "Well said, my child! You speak more wisely than the sages of India; *richtig, das weiss man nicht;* and the unfortunate thing is that I can't tell you either."

This force in Don Juan, this omnipotence, this animation, only music can express, and I know no other predicate to describe it than this: it is exuberant joy of life. When, therefore, Kruse lets his Don Juan say, as he comes upon the scene at Zerlina's wedding: "Cheer up, children, you are all of you dressed as for a wedding," he says something that is quite proper and also perhaps something more than he is aware of. He himself brings the gaiety with him, and no matter whose wedding it is, it is not unimportant that everyone be dressed as for a wedding; for Don Juan is not only husband to Zerlina, but he celebrates with sport and song the wedding of all the young girls in the parish. What wonder, then, that they crowd about him, the happy maidens! Nor are they disappointed, for he has enough for them all. Flattery, sighs, daring glances, soft handclasps, secret whispers, dangerous proximity, alluring withdrawal—and yet these are only the lesser mysteries, the gifts before the wedding.[31] It is a pleasure to Don Juan to look out over so rich a harvest; he takes charge of the whole parish, and yet perhaps it does not cost him as much time as Leporello spends in his office.

By these considerations we are again brought to the main subject of this inquiry, that Don Juan is absolutely musical. He desires sensuously, he seduces with the dae-monic power of sensuousness, he seduces everyone. Speech, dialogue, are not for him, for then he would be at once a reflective individual. Thus he does not have stable existence at all, but he hurries in a perpetual vanishing, precisely like music, about which it is true that it is over as soon as it has ceased to sound, and only comes into being again, when it again sounds.

Were I to raise the question now as to how Don Juan looks—is he handsome, young or old, or about how old—then it is only an accommodation on my part, and anything I may say about it can only expect to find a place here in the same way that a tolerated sect finds a place in the established church. He is handsome, not very young; were I to venture a guess, I should suggest thirty-three, that being the length of a generation. The hesitation in at-tempting such an inquiry is due to the fact that one easily loses sight of the total in dwelling on the details, as if it were by means of his good looks, or whatever else one might mention, that Don Juan seduced. One sees him, then, but no longer hears him, and in that way he is lost. If, as though to contribute my bit toward helping the reader to get a visual image of Don Juan, I were to say: "See, there he stands, see how his eyes blaze, his lips curve in a smile, so sure he is of his victory. Observe his imperial glance, which demands the things that are Caesar's; see how grace-fully he moves in the dance, how proudly he stretches out his hand; who is the fortunate girl he is inviting?"—or were I to say: "There he stands in the shadow of the forest, he leans against a tree, he accompanies himself on a guitar, and look! yonder a young girl, timid as a startled fawn, disappears among the trees, but he does not hurry, he knows that she is seeking him"—or were I to say: "There he rests by the lake shore in the pale night, so beautiful that the moon pauses and lives over again its first young love, so beautiful that the young girls of the village would

give much to dare to steal upon him, and taking advantage
of a moment of darkness while the moon mounted heavenward, bestow a kiss upon him." If I did this the observant
reader would say: "See, now he has spoiled everything, he
has himself forgotten that Don Juan should not be seen
but heard." Therefore I don't do it, but I say: "Hear Don
Juan, that is to say, if you cannot get a conception of him
by hearing him, then you never will. Hear the beginning
of his life; as the lightning flashes forth from the murk of
the thunderclouds, so he bursts forth from the depths of
earnestness, swifter than the lightning's flash, more inconstant and yet as constant; hear how he rushes down into
the manifold of life, how he dashes himself against its solid
dam; hear those light dancing tones of the violin, hear the
signal of gladness, hear the exultation of lust, hear the festive happiness of enjoyment; hear his wild flight, he is transported beyond himself, ever swifter, ever more impetuously;
hear the unbridled demands of passion, hear the sighing of
love, hear the whisper of temptation, hear the whirlpool of
seduction, hear the stillness of the moment—hear, hear, hear
Mozart's *Don Juan!*"

2. OTHER ADAPTATIONS OF DON JUAN, CONSIDERED IN RELATION TO THE MUSICAL INTERPRETATION

It is well known that the idea in Faust has been the object of a variety of interpretations; this, however, has by
no means been the case with Don Juan. This may seem
strange, especially as this latter idea suggests a far more
universal phase in the development of the individual's life
than does the first. However, this is readily explained by
the fact that Faust presupposes such an intellectual maturity as to make an interpretation far more natural. There
is also the fact, of which I reminded you in the preceding
section, with reference to the circumstance that no such
legend exists about Don Juan, that difficulty with respect
to the medium had been vaguely felt until Mozart discovered the medium and the idea. From that moment the
idea first attained its true dignity, and has more than ever

filled a period of time in the individual life, but so satis-
fyingly that the need of distilling off poetically that which
had been experienced in fantasy did not become a poetic
necessity.

This is again an indirect proof of the absolute classic
value of Mozart's opera. The ideal in this direction had already found its perfect artistic expression to such a degree
that it might indeed act temptingly, but it could not tempt
to poetic productivity. Mozart's music has certainly been
tempting; for where can a young man be found who has
not had moments in his life when he would have given
half, or perhaps all of his possessions to be a Don Juan;
when he would have given half a lifetime, aye, perhaps
his whole life, for the sake of being Don Juan for a single
year. But so it goes. The deepest natures, those which were
affected by the idea, found everything, even the softest
breeze, expressed in Mozart's music; they found in its
grandiose passion a full-toned expression for whatever
stirred their own hearts, they felt how every mood strained
forward, responsive to this music, as the brook hastens on
to lose itself in the infinitude of the sea. These natures found
in Mozart's *Don Juan* as much text as commentary, and
while they were thus borne along and down in its music,
they enjoyed the delight of losing themselves, and gained
in addition the richness of wonder. The music of Mozart
was in no sense too restricted; on the contrary, their own
moods were expanded, assumed a supernatural greatness,
as they found them again in Mozart. The lower natures,
who have no idea of infinity, get no infinity; the dabblers,
who imagine themselves to be Don Juans because they had
pinched the cheek of a peasant girl, flung their arms about
a waitress, or made a little maiden blush, they naturally
understand neither the idea nor Mozart; nor do they know
how to produce a Don Juan, other than a ridiculous de-
formity, a family idol, who perhaps to the dim, sentimental
eyes of some cousins, seems a true Don Juan, the essence
of all attractiveness. Faust has never yet found expression
in this sense, and, as above noted, can never find it, because
the idea in Faust is far more concrete. An interpretation of
Faust may deserve to be called perfect, and yet the follow-

ing generation will produce a new *Faust,* while Don Juan, on account of the abstract character of the idea, will live to all eternity, and to hope to produce a new *Don Juan* after Mozart's, is like wishing to write an *Iliad* after Homer's, in an even more profound sense than is true about Homer.

If now this explanation is correct, it by no means follows from this that some particularly gifted nature might not have attempted to interpret Don Juan in another way. Everyone knows that this is so, but everyone may not have noticed that the pattern for all the other interpretations is essentially Molière's *Don Juan;* but again, this is much older than Mozart's and is also a comedy. It is to Mozart's *Don Juan* what a fairy tale interpreted by Musaeus is to an adaptation of Tieck's. For that reason I can really restrict myself to mentioning the *Don Juan* of Molière, and in seeking to appraise it aesthetically, I shall also indirectly be appraising the other interpretations. Still, I shall make an exception of Heiberg's *Don Juan.*[32] He himself explains in the title that it is "partly after Molière." Although this is true, still Heiberg's play has a great advantage over Molière's. This is due to the unerring aesthetic feeling with which Heiberg always interprets his task, his taste in discriminating; yet it is not impossible that in the present case Professor Heiberg was indirectly influenced by Mozart's interpretation to see how Don Juan might be interpreted, when he is not expressed musically or brought under very different aesthetic categories. Professor Hauch has also produced a *Don Juan* which almost falls under the category of the interesting.[33] But now, as I proceed to mention the other types of adaptations of Don Juan, I trust I do not need to remind the reader that this present little inquiry is not carried on for its own sake, but only for the purpose of showing more completely than was possible in the preceding the importance of the musical interpretation.

The crucial point in the interpretation of Don Juan has already been indicated above: as soon as he acquires speech, everything is altered. The reflection which motivates the speech reflects him out of the obscurity wherein he is only musically audible. For this reason it might seem that Don Juan was perhaps best interpreted through the ballet. Everyone knows that he has been interpreted in this way. However, one must praise this form of interpretation for having recognized its own powers, and it has therefore restricted itself to the last scene, where the passion in Don Juan might most easily become visible in the pantomimic display of muscle. The result is that Don Juan is not presented in his essential passion, but only in the accidental, and the playbills for such a performance always contain more than the play itself; they tell, for instance, that it is Don Juan, the seducer Don Juan, while the ballet at most can only represent the pangs of despair, whose expression, since it can only be in pantomime, he can have in common with many other despairing individuals. The essential in Don Juan cannot be brought out in the ballet, and everyone feels instinctively how ridiculous it would be to see him beguile a girl by his dancing-steps and ingenious gestures. Don Juan is in an inward category, and so cannot become visible nor reveal himself through the physical form and its movements or in plastic harmony.

Even if we are unwilling to grant Don Juan speech, yet we can conceive an interpretation which, notwithstanding this, uses words as the medium. Such an interpretation actually exists in Byron. That Byron was in many ways suitably equipped to produce a *Don Juan* is clear enough, and one can therefore be certain that when the project miscarried, the reason for this was not in Byron, but in something more profound. Byron had ventured to bring Don Juan into existence for us, to describe for us his childhood and youth, to reconstruct him from the sum of his finite relationships. But by this Don Juan became a reflective personality, who lost the ideality he had in the traditional conception. I shall at once explain the change which took place in the idea. When Don Juan is interpreted musically, then I hear in him the whole infinitude of passion, but also its infinite power which nothing can withstand; I hear the wild craving of desire, but also the absolute victory of this desire, against which it would be futile for anyone to offer resistance. If thought dwells a single moment on the obstacle, then it is clear that the obstacle has importance as a means merely of exciting passion rather than as presenting much in the way of opposition; enjoyment is increased, victory is certain, and the obstacle only a stimulus. Such a primitively controlled life, powerfully and irresistibly daemonic, I find in Don Juan. This is his ideality, and this I can unperturbed enjoy, because the music does not represent him as person or as individual, but only as power. If Don Juan is interpreted as individual, then is he, *eo ipso,* in conflict with his environment; as an individual he feels the pressure and restraint of his surroundings; as a great individual he perhaps overcomes them, but we feel immediately that the difficulties caused by these obstacles here play a different role. The interest essentially occupies itself with these. But thereby Don Juan is brought under the category of the interesting. If we would present him here as absolutely victorious through the aid of bombast, we feel at once that this is not satisfactory, since essentially it does not belong to an individual as such to be victorious, and we demand conflict and crisis.

The opposition which the individual has to encounter can in part be an external opposition, which lies not so much in the object as in its environment; in part it can lie in the object itself. The former is the one which has occupied most of the interpretations of Don Juan, because the authors have retained that aspect of the idea which demands that as erotic he must be victorious. Not until the other side is emphasized do I believe that there is a prospect of a significant interpretation of Don Juan, which will furnish a contrast to the musical one, while any interpretation which lies between these two will always contain imperfections. In the musical Don Juan we would then have the extensive seducer, in the other the intensive one. This latter Don Juan is shown, then, not as by a single stroke coming into possession of his object; he is not the seducer immediately determined, he is the reflective seducer. That which we are interested in here is the craftiness, the cunning with which he knows how to insinuate himself into a maiden's heart, the mastery he knows how to establish over it, the beguiling, systematic, continuous seduction. Here the number he has seduced becomes a matter of indifference; what concerns us is the art, the thoroughness, the profound cunning, with which he seduces. At last the enjoyment itself becomes so reflective that in comparison with the musical Don Juan's enjoyment it becomes something different. The musical Don Juan enjoys the satisfaction of desire; the reflective Don Juan enjoys the deception, enjoys the cunning. The immediate enjoyment is over, and a greater enjoyment is found in contemplating the enjoyment. On this point there is found a single suggestion in Molière's interpretation, except that this can by no means come into its rights, because all the rest of the interpretation interferes. Desire awakens in Don Juan because he sees a girl happy in her relation to her beloved; he begins to be jealous. This is an interest which in the opera would not at all engage us, just because Don Juan is not a reflective individual. As soon as he is interpreted as being such, we can achieve something corresponding to the musical ideality only by transferring the matter to the psychological sphere. There one attains the ideality of the intensive. For this reason Byron's *Don Juan* must be stamped as a failure, because it extends itself epically. The immediate Don Juan must seduce 1,003; the reflective need only seduce one, and what interests us is how he did it. The reflective Don Juan's seduction is a sleight-of-hand performance, wherein every single little trick has its special importance; the musical Don Juan's seduction is a handspring, a matter of an instant, swifter done than said. I am reminded of a tableau I once saw. A handsome young man, rightly a ladies' man. He played about with a good many young girls, who were all in the dangerous age of being neither grown-up nor children. Among other things they amused themselves by jumping over a ditch. The young man stood on the edge of the ditch, and to help them with the leap, he would take them around the waist, swing them easily into the air, and set them down on the other side. It was a pleasant sight; I enjoyed him as much as I did the young girls. Then I thought about Don Juan. The young girls fling themselves into his arms, swiftly he catches them, and as swiftly sets them down on the other side of the ditch of life.

The musical Don Juan is absolutely victorious and therefore, naturally, in absolute possession of every means that can contribute to this victory, or rather, he is in such absolute possession of the medium that it is as if he did not need to use it, that is, he does not use it as a means. As soon as he becomes a reflective individual, it appears that there is something in existence which is called the means. If the poet grants him this means, but does it in the face of such serious opposition and obstacles that the victory becomes doubtful, then Don Juan comes under the category of the interesting, and on this basis many interpretations of Don Juan are conceivable, even approaching what we have earlier called intensive seduction. If the poet denies him this means, then the interpretation falls under the category of the comic. I have never yet seen a perfect interpretation which brings him under the category of the interesting; on the other hand, it is true of most of the interpretations of Don Juan, that they approach the comic. This is easily explained by the fact that they follow Molière, in whose interpretation the comic is implicit, and it is Heiberg's merit that he was clearly conscious of this, and that he therefore not only called his play a puppet show, but that in many other ways he let the comic shine through. As soon as passion as represented is denied the means for its satisfaction, then it can produce either a tragic or a comic turn. A tragic note cannot well be evoked where the idea appears as wholly unwarranted, and therefore the comic lies very near. Were I to depict addiction to gambling in an individual, and then give him five dollars to bet with, the effect becomes comic. Such is not quite the case with Molière's *Don Juan,* but yet there is a similarity. If I allow Don Juan to be in financial straits, harassed by creditors, he at once loses the ideality he has in the opera, and the effect becomes comic. The famous comedy scene in Molière, which as comedy has great value, and also fits very well into the whole, ought naturally, therefore, never to be introduced into opera, where it would be utterly disturbing.

That Molière's interpretation strives to achieve the comic is shown not only by the aforementioned comic scene (which, if it stood entirely in isolation, would prove nothing at all) but also the whole layout bears the mark of it. Sganarelle's first and last speeches, the beginning and end of the play, afford more than sufficient evidence concerning this. Sganarelle begins with a eulogy over a rare snuff, from which one learns among other things, that he cannot be quite so busy in the service of this Don Juan; he ends by complaining that he is the only one in the whole world who has been wronged. When one considers now that Molière had allowed the statue to come and fetch Don Juan, and that, although Sganarelle had been a witness to this fright-fulness, he still puts these words into his mouth, as if Sganarelle would say that since the statue otherwise med-dled with exercising justice on earth and punishing vice, it ought to have been prepared to pay Sganarelle the wages due him for long and faithful service to Don Juan, which his master, because of his sudden departure, had not been able to do—when one considers this, then everyone must feel the power of the comical in Molière's *Don Juan*. (Heiberg's adaptation, which has the great advantage over Molière's of being more correct, has also evoked a comic effect in a number of ways, by putting a casual learning into Sganarelle's mouth, which lets us see him as a smat-terer, who after having tried many things, finally ends up as Don Juan's servant.) The hero in the piece, Don Juan, is anything but a hero, he is an unsuccessful individual who presumably has failed in his examinations, and now has chosen another means of livelihood. One indeed learns that he is the son of a very distinguished man, who has also attempted to inspire his son to virtue and immortal deeds, by giving him an idea of the great reputation his forefathers enjoyed, but this is so improbable in connection with all the rest of his deportment, that one begins to won-der if the whole matter is not a lie, fabricated by Don Juan himself. His conduct is not very chivalrous; one does not see him with sword in hand, clearing his way through the difficulties of life; he deals out a box on the ear as readily to one as to the other; indeed, he all but beats up the be-trothed of one girl. Hence, if Molière's Don Juan is really a knight, the poet knows excellently how to make us forget it, and strives to show us a bully, an ordinary rake, who is not afraid to use his fists. Whoever has had occasion to make what we call a bully the object of his observations knows, too, that this class of men has a great predilection for the sea, and he will therefore find it quite in order that Don Juan, having got his eye on a pair of skirts, should immediately put out after them in a boat on the Kallebrødstrand, a Sunday adventure upon the sea, and that the boat should capsize. Don Juan and Sganarelle are almost drowned, and at last are saved by Pedro and the tall Lucas, who at first were betting on whether it really was a man or a stone, a wager that cost Lucas two bits, which was almost too much for Lucas and for Don Juan. Now if one finds all this quite proper, the impression becomes confused the next moment, as one comes to know that Don Juan is also a fellow who had seduced Elvira, murdered the Commandant, and so on, something one finds highly unlikely and which, in turn, one must explain as a lie in order to reconcile the situation. If Sganarelle is supposed to give us an idea of the passion which rages in Don Juan, then his explanation is such a travesty that it is impossible to keep from laughing at it, as when Sganarelle says to Gusmann:[34] "In order to get the one he wants, Don Juan would gladly marry her dog or cat, aye, even worse, he would even marry you." Or as when he remarks that his master not only disbelieves in love but also in medicine.

If, now, Molière's interpretation of Don Juan, considered as a comic adaptation, were correct, then I should say nothing more about it here, since in this inquiry I have only to do with the ideal interpretation and the significance of music for it. I might then be content with calling attention to the remarkable circumstance that only in music has anyone interpreted Don Juan ideally in the ideality he had in the traditional conception of the Middle Ages. The absence of an ideal interpretation through the medium of words might furnish an indirect proof for the soundness of my position. Here, however, I can do more, precisely because Molière is not correct, and that which kept him from being so is that he has retained something of the ideal in Don Juan, as this is derived from the traditional conception. In pointing this out, it will again appear that this could only be essentially expressed in music, and so I return to my proper thesis.

In the first act of Molière's *Don Juan*, Sganarelle imme-diately makes a very long speech in which he would give us a conception of his master's boundless passion, and the multiplicity of his love affairs. This speech corresponds ex-actly to tho scrvant's second aria in the opera. The speech produces simply no effect other than the comic, and here again, Heiberg's interpretation has the advantage of the comic being more unalloyed than in Molière. This speech makes an attempt to give us an idea of his power, but the effect fails to appear; only music can unite it, because at the same time it describes Don Juan's behavior the music lets us hear the power of seduction, as the list of the se-duced is unrolled before us.

In Molière, the statue comes in the last act to fetch Don Juan. Even if the poet has attempted to motivate the ap-proach of the statue by sending a warning in advance, this stone would still always constitute a dramatic stumbling block. If Don Juan is interpreted ideally as force, as pas-sion, then must even heaven itself be set in motion. If this is not the case, it is ill-advised to use such strong measures. The Commandant need not in truth have troubled himself, since it is far easier to have Mr. Paaske throw Don Juan into a debtor's prison.[35] This would be quite in the spirit of modern comedy which does not require such great forces for destruction, precisely because the moving forces them-selves are not so grandiose. It would be quite consistent with the spirit of modern comedy for Don Juan to learn to know the tedious barriers of actuality. In the opera it is quite right that the Commandant should return, but there his appearance also has an ideal truth. The music imme-diately makes the Commandant something more than a particular individual, his voice is expanded to the voice of a spirit. As Don Juan is therefore interpreted in the opera with aesthetic seriousness, so also is the Commandant. In Molière he comes with an ethical solemnity and heaviness which almost makes him ridiculous; in the opera he comes with aesthetic lightness, metaphysical truth. No power in the play, no power on earth, has been able to coerce Don Juan, only a spirit, a ghost, can do that. If this be under-stood correctly, then this will again throw light upon the interpretation of Don Juan. A spirit, a ghost, is a reincarnation; this is the mystery which lies in the return, but Don Juan can do everything, can withstand everything, except the reincarnation of life, precisely because he is immediate sensuous life, whose negation the spirit is.

Sganarelle, as interpreted by Molière, becomes an inexplicable person, whose character is extremely confused. What here causes the confusion is that Molière has again retained something of the traditional. Since Don Juan is above all a force, this also appears in his relation to Leporello. Leporello feels himself drawn to him, overwhelmed by him, absorbed in him, and he becomes only an instrument for carrying out his master's will. This obscure, undefined sympathy is exactly what makes Leporello into a musical personality, and we find it quite in order that he should not be able to disengage himself from Don Juan. With Sganarelle it is another matter. In Molière, Don Juan is a particular individual, and Sganarelle consequently appears in relation to him as to an individual. If Sganarelle feels himself indissolubly bound to Don Juan, it is no more than fair that aesthetics should demand enlightenment as to how this is to be accounted for. It is of no use for Molière to let him say that he cannot tear himself loose from Don Juan, for neither reader nor spectator can see any rational ground for this, and a rational ground is here the point in question. The instability in Leporello is well motivated in the opera because in his relation to Don Juan he is nearer to being an individual consciousness, and the Don Juanesque life therefore reflects itself differently in him, still without his being able to penetrate it. In Molière, Sganarelle is sometimes better, sometimes worse than Don Juan, but it is inconceivable that he should not desert him when he does not even get his wages. If someone perhaps imagines a unity in Sganarelle corresponding to the sympathetic musical obscurity Leporello has in the opera, then there is nothing to do except to leave such a one alone in his prejudiced folly. Here again one sees an illustration of how the musical must come to the fore in order for Don Juan to be interpreted in his true ideality. The fault in Molière is not in his having interpreted him comically, but in his not having interpreted him correctly.

Molière's Don Juan is also a seducer, but the play gives us only a poor conception of his being so. That in Molière Elvira should be Don Juan's wife is undoubtedly rightly planned, especially with respect to the comic effect. We see at once that we are dealing with a common person who uses the promise of marriage in order to deceive a girl. Through this Elvira entirely loses the ideal bearing she has in the opera, where she appears with no other weapon than her affronted womanhood, while here one expects her to come with her marriage certificate; and Don Juan loses the seductive ambiguity of being at once a young man and an experienced husband, experienced, that is, by reason of his many essays in this field. How he had seduced Elvira, by what means he had enticed her out of the convent—of this several of Sganarelle's speeches are supposed to enlighten us; but since the seduction scene which takes place in the play gives us no opportunity to admire Don Juan's art, our confidence in Sganarelle's account is naturally weakened. In so far as Molière's Don Juan is comic, this was hardly necessary; but since he still wishes us to understand that his Don Juan is actually the hero Don Juan, who has deceived Elvira and murdered the Commandant, we readily see the error in Molière, but we are then forced to consider whether this was not really because Don Juan can never be presented as a seducer except in a musical setting, unless, as suggested in the preceding, one wishes to go into the psychological phase, which, again, cannot so easily arouse the dramatic interest.

In Molière, one does not hear him deceiving the two young girls, Mathurine and Charlotte. The deception takes place off stage, and Molière again gives us to understand that Don Juan has given them promises of marriage, so here again we get a poor idea of his talent. To deceive a young girl by a promise of marriage is indeed very poor art, and because one is low enough to do this, it by no means follows that he is worthy of being called a Don Juan. The only scene which seems to show us Don Juan in his seducing, though scarcely seductive, activity is the scene with Charlotte. But to tell a young peasant girl that she is pretty, that she has sparkling eyes, to beg her to turn around in order to observe her form, does not exhibit Don Juan as someone exceptional but simply as a lewd fellow who looks over a girl as a dealer does a horse. One may freely concede the scene a comic effect, and if that had been its sole purpose, I would not mention it here. But since this, his famous attempt, stands in no relation to the many affairs he must have had, this scene contributes, directly or indirectly, to showing the imperfection in the comedy. Molière seems to have wished to make something more of Don Juan, seems to have wished to retain the ideal in him, but he lacks the medium, and therefore everything that actually happens falls flat. On the whole we can say that in Molière's Don Juan we get to know only historically that he is a seducer; dramatically we do not see it. The scene where he shows the greatest activity is the scene with Charlotte and Mathurine, where he keeps them both a-twitter by flattery, and constantly makes each one believe that it is she he has promised to marry. But what engages our attention here is not his seductive art, but a very common theatrical device.

In conclusion, I can perhaps elucidate what has been developed here by considering a remark that is often made, that Molière's Don Juan is more moral than Mozart's. Precisely this, however, when it is rightly understood, is an encomium on the opera. In the opera there is not only talk about a seducer, but Don Juan is a seducer, and we cannot deny that in its details the music can often be very seductive. This, however, is as it should be; this is exactly its strength. Therefore to say that the opera is immoral is a foolishness which only originates with people who do not understand interpreting an opera in its totality, but who only grasp at its details. The definitive endeavor in the opera is highly moral, and the impression it produces absolutely salutary, because everything is big, everything has genuine unaffected pathos, the passion of pleasure not less than the passion of seriousness, the passion of enjoyment not less than the passion of wrath.

3. THE INNER MUSICAL STRUCTURE
OF THE OPERA

Although the title of this section may be regarded as sufficiently illuminating, yet for safety's sake I shall point out that it is naturally not my intention to give an aesthetic appraisal of the play *Don Juan* or a demonstration of its dramatic structure in the text. To discriminate thus requires much caution, especially in the case of a classic production. That which I have so frequently emphasized in the preceding, I shall once again repeat: that Don Juan can only be expressed musically. I have learned this myself essentially through music, and I ought therefore to guard in every way against giving the impression that the music arrives on the scene as an import from without. If you propose to treat the matter in this way, then you may, for all of me, admire the music in this opera as much as you wish, you will not have grasped its absolute significance. Hotho has not kept himself free from such a false abstraction, and therefore it follows that his presentation cannot be regarded as satisfactory, however distinguished it otherwise is. His style, his presentation, his reproduction are lively and moving; his categories are undetermined and vague; his interpretation of Don Juan is not impregnated by one thought, but dispersed in many. To him Don Juan is a seducer. But even this category is indefinite, and it must still be decided in what sense he is a seducer, as I have tried to do. Many things true in themselves are said about this seducer, but since ordinary conceptions are given far too much free play, such a seducer easily becomes so reflective that he ceases to be absolutely musical. He goes through the play, scene by scene; his analysis is freshly saturated by his personality, occasionally perhaps a little too much so. When this has happened, then come sympathetic effusions over how beautifully, how richly, how variously, Mozart has expressed all this. But this lyric pleasure in Mozart's music is too little, and however well it becomes the man, and however beautifully it is expressed, Mozart's *Don Juan* is not by this interpretation recognized in its absolute validity. This is the recognition I am working for, because such recognition is identical with the right insight into that which constitutes the object of this inquiry. Therefore, it is not my intention to analyze the whole opera in detail but rather the opera as a whole, not dealing with its particular parts separately, but incorporating these as far as possible in my observations, so as not to see them outside of their connection with the whole, but within it.

In a drama the chief interest quite naturally centers in what one calls the hero of the play; the other characters in relation to him have only a subordinate and relative importance. The more the inward reflection penetrates the drama with its divisive power, however, the more the subordinate characters tend to assume a certain relative absoluteness, if I may say so. This is by no means a fault, but rather a virtue, just as the contemplation of the world which sees only the few eminent individuals and their importance in the world development, but is unaware of the common man, in a certain sense stands higher but is lower than the contemplation which views the lesser man in his equally great validity. The dramatist will succeed in this only to the degree in which nothing of the incommensurable remains, nothing of the mood from which the drama originates, that is to say, nothing of the mood *qua* mood, but in which everything is converted into the sacred dramatic coin: action and situation. In the same degree as the dramatist is successful in this, to that degree the general impression his work produces will be less that of a mood than of a thought, an idea. The more the general impression of a drama is that of a mood, the more certain one can be that the poet himself has anticipated it in the mood, and continually allowed it to become that, instead of seizing upon an idea, and letting this dramatically unfold itself. Such a drama then suffers from an abnormal excess of the lyric. This is a fault in a drama, but by no means such in an opera. That which preserves the unity in the opera is the keynote which dominates the whole production.

What has been said here about the general dramatic effect also applies to the individual parts of the drama. If I were to characterize in a single word the effect of the drama, in so far as this is different from the effect which every other kind of poetry produces, then I should say: drama operates with the contemporary. In drama I see factors which are external to each other together in the situation, a unity of action. The more, then, the discrete factors are separated and the more profoundly the dramatic situation is self-reflective, so much the less will the dramatic unity manifest itself as a mood and so much the more will it become a definite idea. But just as the totality of the opera cannot be self-reflective as it is in drama proper, this is also the case with the musical situation, which is indeed dramatic, but which still has its unity in the mood. The musical situation has the contemporary quality like every dramatic situation, but the activity of the forces is a concord, a harmony, an agreement, and the impression made by the musical situation is the unity achieved by hearing together what sounds together. The more the drama is self-reflective, the more the mood is explained in the action. The less action, the more the lyrical element dominates. This is quite proper in opera. Opera does not so much have character delineation and action as its immanent goal; it is not reflective enough for that. On the other hand, passion, unreflective and substantial, finds its expression in opera. The musical situation depends on maintaining the unity of mood in the diverse plurality of voices. This is exactly the characteristic of music that it can preserve the diversity in the unity of mood. When in ordinary conversation one uses the word *majority*, one commonly means by that a unity which is the final result; this is not the case in music.

The dramatic interest requires a swift forward movement, a quick-step, what one might call the inherent, increasing tempo of the dénouement. The more the drama is interpenetrated by reflection, the more impetuously it hurries forward. On the other hand, if the lyric or the epic element is one-sidedly predominant, this expresses itself in a kind of lethargy which allows the situation to fall asleep, and makes the dramatic process and progress slow and laborious. This haste is not inherent in the nature of the opera, for this is characterized by a certain lingering movement, a certain diffusion of itself in time and space. The action has not the swiftness of the dénouement or its direction, but it moves more horizontally. The mood is not sublimated in character and action. As a result, the action in an opera can only be immediate action.

If we apply this explanation to the opera *Don Juan,* we shall have an opportunity to see it in its true classic validity. Don Juan is the hero of the opera, the chief interest centers in him; not only so, but he lends interest to all the other characters. This must not be understood, however, in a merely superficial sense, for this constitutes the mysterious in this opera, that the hero is also the animating force in the other characters. Don Juan's life is the life-principle within them. His passion sets the passion of all the others in motion; his passion resounds everywhere; it sounds in and sustains the earnestness of the Commandant, Elvira's anger, and Anna's hate, Ottavio's conceit, Zerlina's anxiety, Mazetto's exasperation, and Leporello's confusion. As hero in the play, he gives it his name, as is generally true in the case of the hero, but he is more than a name, he is, so to speak, the common denominator. The existence of all the others is, compared with his, only a derived existence. If we now require of an opera that its unity provide the keynote, then we shall easily see that one could not imagine a more perfect subject for an opera than Don Juan. The keynote can really be, in relation to the forces in the play, a third force which sustains these. As an illustration of such an opera, I might mention *The White Lady,*[36] but such a unity is, with relation to the opera, a more external determination of the lyric. In *Don Juan* the keynote is nothing other than the primitive power in the opera itself; this is Don Juan, but again—just because he is not character but essentially life—he is absolutely musical. Nor are the other persons in the opera characters, but essentially passions, who are posited with Don Juan, and thereby become musical. That is, as Don Juan encircles them all, so do they in turn encircle Don Juan; they are the external consequences his life constantly posits. It is this musical life of Don Juan, absolutely centralized in the opera, which enables it to create a power of illusion such as no other is able to do, so that its life transports one into the life of the play. Because the musical is omnipresent in this music, one may enjoy any snatch of it, and immediately be transported by it. One may enter in the middle of the play and instantly be in the center of it, because this center, which is Don Juan's life, is everywhere.

We know from experience that it is not pleasant to strain two senses at the same time, and it is often very confusing if we have to use our eyes hard when our ears are already occupied. Therefore we have a tendency to close our eyes when hearing music. This is true of all music more or less, and of *Don Juan* in *sensu eminentiori*.[37] As soon as the eyes are engaged, the impression becomes confused; for the dramatic unity which presents itself to the eye is always subordinate and imperfect in comparison with the musical unity which is heard at the same time. This, at least, has been my own experience. I have sat close up, I have sat farther and farther back, I have tried a corner in the theater where I could completely lose myself in the music. The better I understood it, or believed that I understood it, the farther I was away from it, not from coldness, but from love, for it is better understood at a distance. This has had for my life something strangely mysterious in it. There have been times when I would have given anything for a ticket. Now I need no longer spend a single penny for one. I stand outside in the corridor; I lean up against the partition which divides me from the auditorium, and then the impression is most powerful; it is a world by itself, separated from me; I can see nothing, but I am near enough to hear, and yet so infinitely far away.

Since the characters appearing in the opera do not need to be so self-reflective that as characters they become transparent, it also follows from this, as I earlier emphasized, that the situation cannot be perfectly developed or expanded but to a certain extent is carried by mood. The same applies to the action of an opera. What one in a stricter sense calls action, a deed undertaken with consciousness of a purpose, cannot find its expression in music, but only what we might call immediate action. Both are the case in Don Juan. The action is immediate; concerning this I must refer to a previous statement, where I explained in what sense

Don Juan is a seducer. Because the action is immediate action, it is quite proper that irony should so dominate this piece; for irony is and remains the chastener of the immediate life. Thus, to cite only one example, the Commandant's return is prodigious irony; for Don Juan can overcome every obstacle, but a ghost, you know, cannot be killed. The situation throughout is borne by the mood; in this connection I would remind you of Don Juan's significance for the whole and of the relative existence of the other characters in relation to him. I shall, by citing a single situation, show what I mean. I choose for this Elvira's first aria. The orchestra plays the prelude, Elvira enters. The passion which rages in her bosom must find relief, and she finds it in her song. This, however, would be too lyrical really to create a situation; her aria then would be of the same nature as the monologue in a play. The only difference would be that the monologue more nearly expresses the universal individually, the aria the individual universally. But, as was said, this would be too little for a situation. Therefore, it is not that way. In the background we see Don Juan and Leporello awaiting in tense expectation the approach of the lady they have already seen in the window. Now if this were a drama, the situation would not consist in Elvira standing in the foreground and Don Juan in the background, but the situation would lie in the unexpected encounter. The interest would hinge upon how Don Juan would escape from it. In the opera the encounter also has its importance, but a very subordinate one. The encounter is there to be seen; the musical situation, to be heard. The unity in the situation is effected by the harmony wherein Elvira and Don Juan are heard together. It is therefore quite right for Don Juan to remain as far in the background as possible; for he should be unseen, not only by Elvira, but even by the audience. Elvira's aria begins. I do not know how to characterize her passion other than as love's hatred, a mingled, but still sonorous, full-toned passion. Her inmost being is stirred by turbulent emotions, she has aired her grief, she grows faint for a moment, as every passionate outbreak enervates her; there follows a pause in the music. But the turbulence in her inmost being shows clearly that her passion has not yet reached its full expression; the diaphragm of wrath must yet vibrate more intensely. But what is to call forth this agitation, what incitement? There is but one thing that can do this—Don Juan's mockery. Mozart has, therefore—would that I were a Greek, for then I would say, quite divinely—made use of this pause in the music to fling in Don Juan's jeering laughter. Now passion blazes stronger, rages more violently within her, and bursts forth in sound. Once again it repeats itself; then her emotion shakes her to the depths of her soul, and wrath and pain pour forth like a stream of lava in the celebrated run with which the aria ends.

We see here, then, what I mean when I say that Don Juan re-echoes in Elvira and that it is something more than phrase-making. The spectator should not see Don Juan, should not see him with Elvira in the unity of the situation; he should hear him in Elvira, through Elvira, for it is indeed Don Juan who sings, but he sings in such a way that the more the listener's ear is developed, the more it seems to him as if it came from Elvira herself. As love transforms its object, so also does indignation. She is possessed by Don Juan. That pause and Don Juan's voice make the situation dramatic, but the unity in Elvira's passion wherein Don Juan echoes, while her passion is still engaged with him, makes the situation musical.* The situation conceived as a musical

* In my opinion, Elvira's aria and the situation should be interpreted thus: Don Juan's incomparable irony ought not to be something external, but should be concealed in Elvira's essential passion. They must be heard simultaneously. As the speculative eye sees things together, so the speculative ear should hear things together; I shall take an example from a purely physical realm. When a man from a high point of vantage looks out over a flat plain and sees various highways running parallel with one another, then if he lacks intuition, he will see only the highways, and the fields lying between will be practically invisible; or he will see only the fields, and the highways will disappear; he who has the intuitive eye will see them collectively, will see the whole range intersected by the highways. This is also true of the ear. What I have said here applies naturally to the musical situation; the dramatic situation makes it more probable that the spectator knew it was Don Juan standing in the background and Elvira in the foreground. If I assume now that the spectator is conscious of their earlier relationship (something the spectator could not at

situation is matchless. If, however, Don Juan is a personality and Elvira equally so, then the situation is a failure, and it is a mistake to permit Elvira to unburden herself in the foreground while Don Juan jeers in the background; for this demands that I hear them together without having been given the means for this, and in spite of the fact that they both are characters who could not possibly be heard together. If they are characters, then the encounter forms the situation.

It has been noted above that the same dramatic haste, the mounting acceleration, is not demanded in the opera as in the drama, that the situation here is at liberty to extend itself a bit. This must not, however, degenerate into perpetual retardation. As an example of the happy medium, I may single out the situation I just now mentioned, not as if this were the only situation in *Don Juan,* or the most perfect—on the contrary, there are many such, and all perfect—but because the reader will best remember this one. And yet I here approach a precarious point; for I admit that there are two arias that must go, that however perfect they are in themselves, they still cause an interruption, retard the action. I would willingly keep this a secret, but that would not help, the truth must out. If one takes these two away, then all the rest is perfect. One of these is Ottavio's, the other Anna's, and both are really concert numbers rather than dramatic music, since, on the whole, Ottavio and Anna are far too insignificant to justify their retarding the action. When one takes these two away, then the rest of the opera has a perfect musical-dramatic swiftness, perfect as no other is.

It would well repay the trouble to go through each individual situation piecemeal, not to exclaim over it, but to show its significance, its validity as a musical situation. However, this really lies outside the scope of this little investigation. It was of importance to emphasize Don Juan's centrality in the opera. Something similar recurs with reference to the individual situations.

---

first have known about), then the situation gains much, but one will also see that if the accent falls on this relationship, then it is wrong to keep them apart for so long.

The above-mentioned centrality of Don Juan's in the opera can be further elucidated by considering the rest of the persons in the play in their relationship to him. As in a solar system the dark bodies which receive their light from a central sun are never more than half illuminated, namely, on the side which is turned toward the sun, so is this the case with the persons in this play—only that moment in their lives, that side which is turned toward Don Juan, is illuminated, the rest is dark and obscure. This must not be understood in a restricted sense, as if each of these characters were only an abstract passion, as if Anna, for example, represented hate, Zerlina frivolity. Such a lack of taste belongs here least of all. The passion in the individual is concrete, but concrete in itself, not concrete in the personality, or, to express myself more definitely, the rest of the personality is swallowed up in that passion. This is absolutely right, because we are dealing with an opera. This obscurity, this partly sympathetic, partly antipathetic mysterious communication with Don Juan makes them all musical and causes the whole opera to sound simultaneously in Don Juan. The only figure in the play who seems to be an exception is, naturally, the Commandant; but therefore it is also so wisely planned that to a certain extent he lies outside of, or circumscribes the piece; the more the Commandant is pushed forward, the more the opera ceases to be completely musical. He is always, therefore, kept in the background, and as indistinct as possible. The Commandant is the powerful antecedent and the bold consequence between which lies Don Juan's intermediate clause, but the rich content of this intermediate clause constitutes the value of the opera. The Commandant appears only twice. The first time is at night; it is backstage in the theater; one does not see him, but hears him fall before Don Juan's sword. Even there his earnestness, which contrasts only the more strongly with Don Juan's burlesque mockery, is something Mozart has wonderfully expressed in the music; even there his earnestness is too profound to be that of a human being; he is spirit before he dies. The second time he appears as spirit, and the thunders of heaven reverberate in his earnest, solemn voice, but as he himself is transfigured, his voice is changed into something more than a human voice; he speaks no more, he judges.

Next to Don Juan, the most important character in the play is undoubtedly Leporello. His relation to his master becomes quite explicable through the medium of music, inexplicable without it. If Don Juan is a reflective individuality, then Leporello becomes almost a greater scoundrel than he is, and it becomes inexplicable how Don Juan can exercise so much power over him; the only motive back of this seems to be that Don Juan can pay him better than anyone else, a motive even Molière seems not to have wished to use, since he allows Don Juan to be in financial difficulties. If, however, we regard Don Juan as immediate life, then it is easy to understand that he can exercise a decisive influence upon Leporello, that he assimilates him, so that he can almost become a voice for Don Juan. Leporello in a certain sense comes nearer to being a personal consciousness than Don Juan, but to become that, he must himself become clear about his relationship to Don Juan, and he is unable to do that, he cannot break the spell. Here again it holds good, that as soon as Leporello makes a speech, he becomes transparent to us. There is also something erotic in Leporello's relationship to Don Juan; there is a power by which Don Juan captivates him, even against his will. But in this ambiguity he is musical, and Don Juan constantly echoes through him; later I shall suggest something to show that this is more than a phrase.

With the exception of the Commandant, everyone stands in a kind of erotic relation to Don Juan. Over the Commandant he can exercise no power, for the Commandant represents reflective consciousness; the others are in his power. Elvira loves him, her love puts her in his power; Anna hates him, so she is in his power; Zerlina fears him, which puts her in his power; Ottavio and Mazetto go along for the sake of relationship, for the blood bond is strong.

If for a moment we now glance back over the argument, the reader will perhaps see how it has been developed from many sides, in what relation the Don Juan idea stands to the musical, how this relationship really constitutes the whole opera, how it repeats itself in the individual parts.

I might readily stop at this point, but for the sake of completeness I shall explain this by running through some of the individual parts of the opera. The selection will not be arbitrary. I choose for this the overture, which most nearly gives the keynote of the opera in a condensed concentration. I choose next the most epic and the most lyric moments in the production, in order to show how the perfection of the opera is preserved even to its utmost limits, how the musical-dramatic is maintained, how it is Don Juan who musically sustains the opera.

This is not the place to explain what function the overture has for opera in general. Only so much can here be pointed out, that the fact that an opera requires an overture sufficiently proves the preponderance of the lyrical, and that the effect aimed at is the evocation of a mood, something which the drama cannot undertake to do, since there everything must be transparent. It is therefore proper that the overture should be the last part composed, so that the composer himself may be completely permeated with the music. The overture, therefore, generally affords an opportunity to get a deep insight into the composer and his spiritual relation to his music. If he is not successful in apprehending the central idea in it, if he is not in the most profound sympathetic contact with the keynote of the opera, then this will inevitably betray itself in the overture; it then becomes, by virtue of a loose association of ideas, an aggregate of the leading themes slung together, but with no totality which, as it essentially ought to do, contains the most profound illumination of the content of the music. Such an overture is therefore generally entirely arbitrary, that is, it can be as long or as short as it will, and the cohesive element, the continuity, since it is only an association of ideas, can stretch out as long as it will. Therefore, the overture is often a dangerous temptation to minor composers; they are easily seduced into plagiarizing themselves, filching from their own pockets, something which produces much confusion. While it is clear from this that the overture should not have the same content as the opera, neither should it, naturally, contain something absolutely different. It should, in other words, have the same ideas as the opera, but in a different manner; it should contain the central idea, and grip the listener with the whole intensity of this central idea.

In this respect the ever admirable overture to *Don Juan* is and remains a perfect masterpiece, so that if no other proof were forthcoming for *Don Juan's* classicity, it would be sufficient to emphasize this one thing: the absurdity of thinking that he who had the center should not also have the periphery. This overture is no interweaving of themes, it is not a labyrinthine hodgepodge of associated ideas; it is concise, definite, strongly constructed, and, above all, it is impregnated with the essence of the whole opera. It is powerful as the thought of a god, moving as a world's life, trembling in its earnestness, quivering in its passion, crushing in its terrible wrath, inspiring in its joy of life; it is faithful in its judgment, strident in its lust, it is deliberately solemn in its imposing dignity, it is stirring, flaming, dancing in its joy. And it has not attained this by sucking the blood of the opera; on the contrary, it is related to the opera as a prophecy. In the overture the music unfolds its entire compass; with a few mighty wing-strokes it hovers over itself, as it were, hovers over the place where it will alight. It is a conflict, but a conflict in the loftier regions of the air. He who, after having made a closer acquaintance with the opera, hears the overture, to him it will perhaps seem as if he had penetrated into that secret workshop where the wild forces he has learned to know in the opera move in their primitive energy, where in full fury they strive against each other. Still, the struggle is too unequal. Even before the battle the one power is victorious; the other flees and escapes, but this flight is just its passion, its burning unrest in its brief *joie de vivre*, the quickened pulse in its passionate heat. By its flight it sets the other power in motion, and carries it along with itself. That which at first seemed so firmly fixed as to be almost immovable, must now be off, and soon the movement becomes so swift that it seems like actual combat. It is impossible to follow this farther. Here it is a matter of listening to the music, for the conflict is not a strife about words but a raging of elemental forces. I shall only note what I earlier explained, that the interest of the opera centers in Don Juan, not in Don Juan and the

Commandant. This is everywhere apparent in the overture. Mozart seems purposely to have planned it so that the deep voice of the Commandant, so resonant in the beginning, gradually becomes weaker and weaker, almost loses, as it were, its majestic firmness, must hurry to keep pace with the demoniac haste which eludes him, and which almost has the power to degrade him by projecting him into a race in the brevity of an instant. With this, the transition to the opera itself is more and more formed. As a consequence, one must consider the finale in close relation to the first part of the overture. In the finale, earnestness again comes to itself, while in the progress of the overture, it was as if it were beside itself. Now there is no question about running a race with passion; earnestness returns, and thereby has cut away every possibility for a new race.

While the overture therefore is in one sense independent, in another sense it may be regarded as a running start for the opera. I have tried in the preceding passages to remind the reader of this by recalling the successive diminutions in which the one power approaches the beginning of the play. The same thing is apparent when one observes the other power growing in an increasing progression; it begins in the overture, it waxes and increases. This, its beginning, is particularly admirably expressed. One hears it so faintly, so mysteriously shadowed forth, one hears it, but it is so swiftly over, that one gets the impression of having heard something one has not heard. It takes an attentive, an erotic ear to detect the first hint the overture gives us of the light play of this passion which subsequently gets expressed in all its prodigal abundance. I cannot indicate to the dot where this place is, since I am not an expert in music, but then I only write for lovers, and these will readily understand me, some of them better than I understand myself. I, however, am satisfied with my appointed task, with this mysterious thing of being in love, and though otherwise I always thank the gods that I was born a man and not a woman, still Mozart's music has taught me that it is beautiful and refreshing and rich to love like a woman.

I am no friend of figures of speech; modern literature has given me a distaste for them; it has almost reached the point that every time I meet a metaphor, I am seized by an involuntary fright that its true purpose is to conceal an obscurity of the thought. I shall not, therefore, venture on an indiscreet and fruitless attempt to translate the energetic and pithy brevity of the overture into long-winded and meaningless figurative language. There is only one point in the overture I would emphasize, and in order to call the reader's attention to it, I shall employ a figure of speech, the only way I have to put myself in touch with him. This point is naturally no other than Don Juan's first outburst, the premonition about him, about the power with which he later breaks through. The overture begins with certain deep, earnest, uniform notes. Then we hear for the first time, infinitely far away, a hint which yet, as if it had come too early, is instantly recalled, until later one hears again and again, bolder and bolder, louder and louder, that voice, which first subtly and coyly, and not without anxiety slipped in, but could not force its way through. Sometimes in nature one sees the horizon thus heavy and lowering; too heavy to support itself, it rests upon the earth, and hides everything in the blackness of night; a single hollow rumble is heard, not yet in movement, but a deep muttering within itself—then one sees at the farthest limit of the heavens, remote on the horizon, a flash; swiftly it runs along the earth, and is instantly gone. But soon it comes again, it grows stronger; for a moment it lights up the whole heaven with its flame, in the next the horizon seems darker than ever, but more swiftly, even more fiery it blazes up; it is as if the darkness itself had lost its tranquillity and was coming into movement. As the eye in this first flash suspects a conflagration, so the ear in that dying strain of the violin has a foreboding of the whole intensity of passion. There is apprehension in that flash, it is as if it were born in anxiety in the deep darkness—such is Don Juan's life. There is a dread in him, but this dread is his energy. It is not a subjectively reflected dread, it is a substantial dread. We do not have in the overture—what we commonly say without realizing what we say—despair. Don Juan's life is not despair; but it is the whole power of sensuousness, which is born in dread, and Don Juan himself is this dread, but this dread is precisely the daemonic joy of life. When Mozart has thus brought Don Juan into existence, then his life is developed for us in the dancing tones of the violin in which he lightly, casually hastens forward over the abyss. When one skims a stone over the surface of the water, it skips lightly for a time, but as soon as it ceases to skip, it instantly sinks down into the depths; so Don Juan dances over the abyss, jubilant in his brief respite.

But if, as noted above, the overture is to be regarded as a running start for the opera; if in the overture one comes down from these higher regions, then it may be asked where one lands best in the opera, or how does one get the opera to begin? Here Mozart has perceived the only right thing to do, to begin with Leporello. Perhaps it might seem that there was not such great merit in this, inasmuch as nearly all the adaptations of *Don Juan* begin with a monologue by Sganarelle. Yet there is a great difference, and we have again occasion to admire Mozart's mastery. He has placed the first tenor aria in immediate conjunction with the overture. This is something which is rarely done; here it is entirely proper, and it gives us a new light on the construction of the overture. The overture is trying to settle down, to secure a footing in the theatrical effect. The Commandant and Don Juan we have already heard in the overture, next to them Leporello is the most important character. However, he cannot be lifted up to that conflict in the regions of the air, and yet he has a better right than any other. Therefore the play begins with him so that he stands in immediate connection with the overture. One is absolutely correct, therefore, in including Leporello's first aria with the overture. This aria corresponds to the not inglorious monologue of Sganarelle in Molière. Let us examine the situation a little more closely. Sganarelle's monologue is far from being unwitty, and when we read it in Professor Heiberg's graceful and fluent verse, it is very entertaining. On the other hand, the situation itself is deficient. I say this with particular reference to Molière, for with Heiberg it is another matter, and I say it not to disparage Molière, but to show Mozart's talent. A monologue is always more or less of a breach in the dramatic situation, and when the poet for the sake of an effect, attempts to accomplish this by the humor of the monologue itself, instead of through its character, then he has condemned himself, and has surrendered the dramatic interest. It is otherwise in the opera. Here the situation is absolutely musical. I have previously called attention to the difference that exists between a dramatic and a musically dramatic situation. In the drama no palaver is tolerated; there plot and situation are demanded. In opera there is an easing of the situation. But what establishes this as a musical situation? It was earlier stressed that Leporello is a musical figure, and yet he is not the one who sustains the situation. If he were, then his aria would be analogous to Sganarelle's monologue, even though it remains true that such a quasi-situation belongs to opera rather than to drama. That which makes the situation musical is Don Juan, who is indoors. The gist of the situation does not lie in Leporello who approaches, but in Don Juan, whom we do not see—but do hear. Now someone may object that we do not hear Don Juan. To this I would reply: "One does indeed hear him, for he is heard through Leporello." To this end, I shall call attention to the transition (*vuol star dentro colla bella*), where Leporello evidently reproduces Don Juan.[38] But even if this were not the case, still the situation is so arranged that involuntarily we get Don Juan anyway, forgetting Leporello, who stands outside, because of the force of Don Juan who is within. With true genius Mozart has everywhere permitted Leporello to reproduce Don Juan, and has thereby accomplished two things: the musical effect, that one always hears Don Juan when Leporello is alone; and the burlesque effect, that when Don Juan is present, one hears Leporello repeat him, and thereby unconsciously parody him. As an example of this I may cite the conclusion of the ballet.

If anyone asks which is the most epic moment in the opera, the answer is easily and unmistakably that it is the List in Leporello's second aria. It has been previously emphasized by comparing this aria with the corresponding monologue in Molière, what absolute significance the music has and that the music, precisely because it lets us hear Don Juan, lets us hear the variations in him, evokes the

effect which the spoken word or the dialogue is not able
to do. Here it is important to emphasize both the situation
and the musical in it. Let us now take a look at the stage;
there the scenic ensemble consists of Leporello, Elvira, and
the faithful servant. The faithless lover, on the contrary, is
not present; as Leporello pertinently expresses it, "he is
away." This is a virtuosity possessed by Don Juan, he is—
and so he is away, and he is (that is, for himself) just as
opportunely away as a Jeronimus comes opportunely.[39]
Since it is general knowledge that he is away, it might seem
queer that I mention him, and in a way, draw him into
the situation; on second thought we might find this quite
proper and see here an example of how literally the statement must be taken that Don Juan is omnipresent in the
opera. For this can hardly be more strongly indicated than
by calling attention to the fact that even when he is away,
he is present. However, we shall allow him to be away, and
later we shall come to see in what significance he is present.

Meantime we shall observe the three persons in the scene.
That Elvira is present naturally contributes to producing
the situation; for it would not do to let Leporello unroll the
list just to kill time. But her position also tends to make
the situation painful. It certainly cannot be denied that the
mockery which is sometimes made of Elvira's love is almost
cruel. Thus, in the second act, where in the decisive moment when Ottavio has at last got the courage in his heart
and his sword out of the sheath to murder Don Juan, she
throws herself between them, and then discovers it is not
Don Juan but Leporello, a difference Mozart has so strikingly indicated by a certain whimpering bleat. Thus there
is also something painful in our situation, in that she should
be present to learn that the list of Spanish women seduced
stands at 1,003, and what is more, in the German version
she is told that she is one of them. This is a German improvement which is as foolishly indecent as the German
translation, in a no less foolish manner, is ridiculously decent and a total failure.

Leporello gives Elvira an epic survey of his master's life,
and we cannot deny that it is entirely proper that Leporello
should recite it, and that Elvira should listen to him, for

they are both intensely interested in the matter. As we therefore hear Don Juan throughout the whole aria, so in some places we hear Elvira, who is now visibly present on the stage as a witness *instar omnium,* not because of some accidental advantage she has, but because, since the method is essentially the same, one example does for all. If Leporello were character or a self-reflective personality, then it would be difficult to imagine such a monologue, but precisely because he is a musical figure who is submerged in Don Juan, this aria has so much meaning. He is a reproduction of Don Juan's whole life. Leporello is the epic narrator. Such a one should not be cold or indifferent toward what he tells, but still he ought to maintain an objective attitude toward it. This is not the case with Leporello. He is altogether fascinated by the life he describes, he forgets himself in telling about Don Juan. Thus I have another example of what I mean when I say that Don Juan echoes through everything. The situation, therefore, does not lie in the conversation between Leporello and Elvira about Don Juan, but in the mood that sustains the whole, in Don Juan's invisible, spiritual presence. To explain more particularly the transition in this aria, how it begins quietly with a slow movement, but is enkindled more and more, as Don Juan's life increasingly resounds through it; how Leporello is more and more transported by it, carried away and rocked by these erotic breezes; how the nuances, all as dissimilar as were the women who came within Don Juan's range, all became audible in it—this is not the place for that.

If we ask which is the most lyric moment in the opera, the answer might be more doubtful. It can hardly be open to question, however, that the most lyric moment must be conceded to Don Juan, that it would be a breach of dramatic discipline were a subordinate character allowed to engage our attention in this way. Mozart has realized this. The choice is thus considerably restricted, and on closer inspection, it is apparent that the only possibilities are either the banquet in the first part of the grand finale or the familiar champagne aria.[40] As far as the banquet scene is concerned, this may indeed be regarded as a lyric moment, and the feast's intoxicating cordials, the foaming wine, the festal strains of distant music, everything combines to intensify Don Juan's mood, as his own festivity casts an enhanced illumination over the whole enjoyment, an enjoyment so powerful in its effect that even Leporello is transfigured in this opulent moment which marks the last smile of gladness, the last farewell to pleasure. On the other hand, it is more a situation than a sheerly lyrical moment. This, naturally, is not because there is eating and drinking in the scene, for that in itself is very inadequate, regarded as a situation. The situation lies in the fact that Don Juan is keyed up to life's highest tension. Pursued by the whole world, this victorious Don Juan has now no place of abode other than a little secluded room. It is at the highest point of life's seesaw that once again, for lack of lusty companionship, he excites every lust of life in his own breast. If *Don Juan* were a drama, then this inner unrest in the situation would need to be made as brief as possible. On the other hand, it is right in opera that the situation should be prolonged, glorified by every possible exuberance, which only sounds the wilder, because for the spectators it reverberates from the abyss over which Don Juan is hovering.

It is otherwise with the champagne aria. I believe one will look in vain for a dramatic situation here, but it has the more significance as a lyric effusion. Don Juan is wearied by the many intercrossing intrigues; on the other hand, he is by no means spent; his soul is still as vigorous as ever; he stands in no need of convivial society, of seeing and hearing the foaming of the wine, or of fortifying himself with it; the inner vitality breaks forth in him, stronger and richer than ever. He is still interpreted ideally by Mozart as life, as power, but ideally as over against actuality. He is here, as it were, ideally intoxicated in himself. If every girl in the world surrounded him in this moment, he would not be a source of danger to them, for he is, as it were, too strong to wish to deceive them; even the manifold enjoyments of actuality are too little for him in comparison with what he enjoys in himself. Here is the clear indication of what it means to say that the essence of Don Juan is music. He reveals himself to us in music, he expands in a world of sound. Someone has called this the champagne aria, and this is undeniably very descriptive. But that which especially needs to be noted is that it does not stand in an accidental relationship to Don Juan. His life is like this, effervescent as champagne. And just as the bubbles in this wine ascend and continue to ascend, while it seethes in its own heat, harmonious in its own melody, so the lust for enjoyment sounds through the primitive seething which is his life. Therefore, that which gives this aria dramatic significance is not the situation, but the fact that the keynote of the opera here sounds and resounds in itself.

INSIGNIFICANT POSTLUDE

If now this explanation proves to be correct, then I again return to my favorite theme, that among all classic works Mozart's *Don Juan* ought to stand highest; then I shall again rejoice over Mozart's happiness, a happiness which is in truth enviable, both in itself, and because it makes all of those happy who only moderately understand his happiness. I, at least, feel myself indescribably happy in having even remotely understood Mozart and in having suspected his happiness. How much more, then, those who have perfectly understood him, how much more must they not feel themselves happy with the happy.

THE ANCIENT

TRAGICAL MOTIF

AS REFLECTED

IN THE MODERN

An Essay in the Fragmentary

Read before a Meeting
of the
SYMPARANEKROMENOI[1]

Should anyone feel called upon to say that the tragic always remains the tragic, I should in a sense have no objection to make, in so far as every historical evolution always remains within the sphere of the concept. On the supposition that his statement has meaning, and that the two-fold repetition of the word *tragic* is not to be regarded as constituting a meaningless parenthesis enclosing an empty nothing, then the meaning must be this, that the content of a concept does not dethrone the concept but enriches it. On the other hand, it can scarcely have escaped the attention of any observer—and it is something that the reading and theater-going public already believes itself to be in lawful possession of, as its share dividend in the labors of the experts—that there is an essential difference between ancient tragedy and modern tragedy. If, in turn, one were to emphasize this difference absolutely, and by its aid, first stealthily, then perhaps forcibly, to separate the conceptions of the ancient and modern tragical, his procedure would be no less absurd than that of the man who denied any essential difference, since he would forget that the foothold necessary for him was the tragic itself, and that this again was so far from being able to separate, that it really bound the ancient and modern together. And it must be regarded as a warning against every such prejudiced attempt to separate them, that aestheticians still constantly turn back to established Aristotelian determinations and requirements in connection with the tragical, as being exhaustive of the concept; and the warning is needed so much the more, as no one can escape a feeling of sadness in observing that however much the world has changed, the conception of the tragic is still essentially unchanged, just as weeping is still natural to all men alike.

Reassuring as this may seem to him who desires no such separation, least of all a breach, the same difficulty which has just been rejected reappears in another and almost more dangerous form. That we still constantly go back to the Aristotelian aesthetics, not merely from a dutiful sense of respect, or because of old habits, no one will deny who has any knowledge of modern aesthetics, and thus perceives how exactly this latter follows Aristotle in all the main points.[2] But as soon as we view these a little more in detail, the difficulties immediately become evident. The qualifications are very general, and one may in one sense be quite in agreement with Aristotle, and in another sense wholly disagree with him. In order not to anticipate the following essay by mentioning at once the subject which will constitute its content, I prefer to illustrate my meaning by citing the corresponding observation with respect to comedy. If an old aesthetician had said that comedy presupposes character and situation, and has for its purpose the arousal of laughter, one might indeed turn back to this again and again; but when one reflects upon how widely different are the things which can make a human being laugh, then one soon becomes convinced of how tremendously inclusive this requirement was. Whoever has at any time made his own laughter and that of others the subject of his observation; whoever, in this study, has had his eye not so much on the accidental as on the general; whoever has observed with psychological interest how different are the things which in each generation arouse laughter, will readily be convinced that the invariable requirement that comedy ought to arouse laughter contains a high degree of variability relative to the different conceptions of the ridiculous entertained in the world consciousness, without the variability becoming so diffuse that the corresponding somatic expression would be that the laughter expressed itself in tears. So also in relation to the tragic.

That which will here constitute the principal content of this little inquiry is not so much the relation between ancient and modern tragedy as it will be an attempt to show how the characteristic of ancient tragedy is embodied within the modern, so that the true tragedy herein may come to light. But however much I may endeavor to make this evident, I shall still refrain from every prophecy about this being what the age demands, so that its appearance becomes entirely without result, more especially so as the entire tendency of the age is in the direction of the comic.

Existence is more or less undermined by doubt on the part of the subjects; isolation constantly gets more and more the upper hand, something one can best be convinced of by giving attention to the multitudinous social exertions. These movements seek to counteract isolation in ways which are themselves an expression of it. The isolationist idea is alway in evidence where men assert themselves numerically. When one man will assert himself as one, then this is isolation; in this, all friends of association will concur, even if unable or unwilling to see that there is quite the same isolation when hundreds stress themselves simply and solely as hundreds. The number is always a matter of indifference, whether it be one or a thousand, or the population of the whole world determined merely numerically. This spirit of association is, therefore, in principle just as revolutionary as the spirit it would counteract. When David would rightly savor his power and glory, he took a census of the people;[3] in our age, on the other hand, one might say that the people, in order to feel their importance in comparison with a higher power, count themselves. All these associations bear, however, the stamp of the arbitrary and are most frequently created for some accidental purpose, whose master, naturally, is the Association.

The many associations thus prove the disorganization of the age, and themselves contribute toward hastening that dissolution; they are the infusoria in the organism of the state, which indicate that it is disorganized. When was it that political clubs began to be general in Greece, if not at the very moment when the state was in process of dissolution? And has not our own age a remarkable similarity to that one, which not even Aristophanes could make more ludicrous than it actually was? Is not the invisible and spiritual bond lost which held the state together politically; is not the power of religion, which held fast to the invisible, weakened and annihilated; have not the statesmen and clergy this in common, that they, like the augurs of old, can scarcely look at one another without smiling?[4] One characteristic our age certainly has to a greater degree than Greece, this, namely, that it is more melancholy, and hence it is more profoundly in despair. Thus, our age is melan-

choly enough to realize that there is something which is
called responsibility, and that this indicates something significant. While, therefore, everyone wishes to rule, no one
wishes to accept responsibility. It is still fresh in our memory that a French statesman, when a portfolio was offered
to him for a second time, declared that he would accept it,
but only on the condition that the secretary of state be
made responsible.[5] It is well known that the king of France
is not responsible, while his minister is; the minister does
not wish to be responsible, but will be minister with the
proviso that the secretary of state become responsible;
naturally, the final result is that the watchmen or street
commissioners become responsible. Would not this story of
shifted responsibility really be a proper subject for Aristophanes! And on the other hand, why are the government
and rulers so afraid of accepting responsibility, unless because they fear an attack from an opposition party, which
equally seeks to evade responsibility? When, then, one considers these two powers in opposition to one another, but
not able to come to grips with each other, because the one
constantly vanishes from the other, the one only a duplicate
of the other, then such a lay-out is certainly not without its
comic effect. This is sufficient to show that the bond which
essentially holds the state together is disorganized, but the
isolation effected thereby is naturally comic, and the comic
lies in the fact that subjectivity as mere form would assert
itself. Every isolated individual always becomes comic by
stressing his own accidental individuality over against necessary development. It would undoubtedly be most deeply
comic for some accidental individual to get the universal
idea of wishing to be the saviour of the world. On the other
hand, the appearance of Christ is in a certain sense (in another sense it is infinitely more) the deepest tragedy, because Christ came in the fullness of time, and—a point I
would particularly emphasize in connection with what follows—He bore the sins of the world.

It is well known that Aristotle mentions two things,
thought and character, as the source of action in tragedy,
but he notes also that the main thing is the plot, and the
individuals do not act in order to present characters, but

the characters are included for the sake of the action.[6] Here one readily notices a divergence from modern tragedy. The peculiarity of ancient tragedy is that the action does not issue exclusively from character, that the action does not find its sufficient explanation in subjective reflection and decision, but that the action itself has a relative admixture of suffering [passion, *passio*]. Hence ancient tragedy has not developed the dialogue to the point of exhaustive reflection, so that everything is absorbed in it; it has in the monologue and the chorus exactly the factors supplemental to the dialogue. Whether the chorus approaches nearer the epic substantiality or the lyric exaltation, it indicates, as it were, the more which will not be absorbed in individuality; the monologue, for its part, is more the lyric concentration and has the more which will not be absorbed in action and situation. In ancient tragedy the action itself has an epic moment in it; it is as much event as action. The reason for this naturally lies in the fact that the ancient world did not have subjectivity fully self-conscious and reflective. Even if the individual moved freely, he still rested in the substantial categories of state, family, and destiny. This substantial category is exactly the fatalistic element in Greek tragedy, and its exact peculiarity. The hero's destruction is, therefore, not only a result of his own deeds, but is also a suffering, whereas in modern tragedy, the hero's destruction is really not suffering, but is action. In modern times, therefore, situation and character are really predominant. The tragic hero, conscious of himself as a subject, is fully reflective, and this reflection has not only reflected him out of every immediate relation to state, race, and destiny, but has often even reflected him out of his own preceding life. We are interested in a certain definite moment of his life, considered as his own deed. Because of this the tragedy can be exhaustively represented in situation and dialogue, since absolutely nothing of the immediate remains anymore. Hence, modern tragedy has no epic foreground, no epic heritage. The hero stands and falls entirely on his own acts.

This brief but adequate analysis may be useful in illuminating the difference between ancient and modern tragedy, which I regard as having great significance, the difference, namely, in the nature of tragic guilt. It is well known that Aristotle requires the tragic hero to have guilt.[7] But just as the action in Greek tragedy is intermediate between activity and passivity (action and suffering), so is also the hero's guilt, and therein lies the tragic collision. On the other hand, the more the subjectivity becomes reflected, the more one sees the individual left to himself, as Pelagius would have it, all the more does his guilt become ethical.[8] Between these two extremes lies the tragic. If the individual is entirely without guilt, the tragic interest is nullified, for the tragic collision is thereby enervated; if, on the other hand, he is absolutely guilty, he can no longer interest us tragically. Hence, it is certainly a misunderstanding of the tragic, when our age strives to let the whole tragic destiny become transubstantiated in individuality and subjectivity. One would know nothing to say about the hero's past life, one would throw his whole life upon his shoulders, as being the result of his own acts, would make him accountable for everything, but in so doing, one would also transform his aesthetic guilt into an ethical one. The tragic hero thus becomes bad; evil becomes precisely the tragic subject; but evil has no aesthetic interest, and sin is not an aesthetic element. This mistaken endeavor certainly has its cause in the whole tendency of our age toward the comic. The comic lies exactly in isolation; when one would maintain the tragic within this isolation, then one gets evil in all its baseness, not the truly tragic guilt in its ambiguous innocence. It is not difficult, when one looks about in modern literature, to find examples. Thus, the very ingenious work of Grabbe, *Faust und Don Juan,* is precisely constructed around this evil.[9] However, in order not to argue from a single work, I prefer to show it in the whole general consciousness of the age. If one wished to represent an individual whom an unhappy childhood had influenced so disturbingly that these influences occasioned his downfall, such a defense would simply not appeal to the present age, and this naturally not because it was wrongly handled, for I have a right to assume that it would be handled with distinction, but because our age employs another standard. It would know nothing about such coddling; without further ceremony, it holds every individual responsible for his own life. Hence, if he goes to the dogs, it is not tragic, but it is bad. One might now believe that this must be a kingdom of the gods, this generation in which also I have the honor to live. On the contrary, this is by no means the case; the energy, the courage, which would thus be the creator of its own destiny, aye, its own creator, is an illusion, and when the age loses the tragic, it gains despair. There lies a sadness and a healing power in the tragic, which one truly should not despise, and when a man, in the preternatural manner our age affects, would gain himself, he loses himself and becomes comical. Every individual, however original he may be, is still a child of God, of his age, of his nation, of his family and friends. Only thus is he truly himself. If in all this relativity he tries to be the absolute, then he becomes ridiculous. One sometimes finds in languages a word which, because of the construction, has been so often used in a particular case that at last it ends, if you will, by being declared independent as an adverb in this case.[10] For the experts such a word acquires an emphasis and a weakness that it never loses. If, in spite of this, it should seek recognition as a substantive and demand the right to be inflected in all five cases, it would be truly comic. And so it is, too, with the individual, when perhaps with great difficulty he issues from the womb of time, he will in this tremendous relativity be absolute. If, however, he renounces this claim of the absolute in order to become relative, then he has *eo ipso* the tragic, even if he were the happiest of individuals; indeed I might say that an individual does not become happy until he has the tragic.

The tragic has in it an infinite gentleness; it is really in the aesthetic sense with regard to human life, what the divine love and mercy are; it is even milder, and hence I may say that it is like a mother's love, soothing the troubled. The ethical, that is strict and harsh. If a criminal should therefore plead before the judge that his mother had a propensity for stealing, especially at the time she was carrying him, then the judge might secure the opinion of the health commissioner about his mental condition, and decide that he was dealing with a thief and not with a thief's mother. Since we are talking about a crime, the sinner can hardly flee to the temple of aesthetics, but yet the aesthetic will put in an extenuating word for him. However, it would be wrong for him to seek comfort there, for his path leads him not to the aesthetic but to the religious. The aesthetic lies behind him, and it would be a new sin for him now to grasp at the aesthetic. The religious is the expression of a paternal love, since it contains the ethical, but it makes it milder; and by what means? Precisely by that which gives the tragic its mildness: by continuity. But while the aesthetic offers this repose before the profound opposition of sin is pressed home, the religious does not offer it until after this opposition is seen in all its frightfulness. Just at the moment when the sinner almost sinks under the universal sin that he has taken upon himself, because he felt that the more guilty he became, the more prospect there was of being saved—in that same moment of terror, consolation appears in the fact that it is a universal sinfulness which has asserted itself also in him. But this consolation is a religious consolation, and he who thinks to attain it in some other way, e.g., by aesthetic vaporings, has taken this consolation in vain and possesses it not. In a certain sense, therefore, it is an entirely correct tactic of the age to hold the individual responsible for everything; but the misfortune is that it does not do it deeply and inwardly enough, and hence its vacillation. It is self-complacent enough to disdain the tears of tragedy, but it is also self-complacent enough to dispense with the divine mercy. But what is human life when we take these two things away, what is the human race? Either the sadness of the tragic, or the profound sorrow and profound joy of the religious. Or is that not the characteristic of everything that proceeds from that happy people [the Greeks]—a melancholy, a sadness, in its art, in its poetry, in its life, and in its joy?

In the preceding I have principally attempted to emphasize the difference between ancient and modern tragedy, in so far as this is illustrated in the differing estimates of the tragic hero's guilt. This is precisely the focus from which everything radiates in its peculiar difference. If the hero is unambiguously guilty, the monologue disappears and there is no destiny; the thought is transparent in the dialogue, and the action in the situation. The same thing may also be explained from another side, with regard to the mood which the tragedy evokes in the spectator. It may be remembered that Aristotle requires that tragedy should arouse fear and compassion in the spectator. I recall that Hegel in his *Aesthetics* adopted this view, and indulged in a double reflection about each of these points, which was not, however, particularly exhaustive.[11] When Aristotle separates fear and compassion, then one might interpret fear as the mood which accompanies the individual idea, compassion as the mood which is the definitive impression. This latter mood is the one that engages me most, because it is the one which corresponds to the tragic guilt, and therefore, it has the same dialectic as this concept of guilt. Hegel observes in this connection that there are two kinds of sympathy, the ordinary kind which is concerned with the finite aspect of suffering, and the true tragic pity. This observation is indeed quite correct, but to me it is of less importance, since this common emotion is a misunderstanding which can just as well apply to ancient as to modern tragedy. True and powerful, however, is what Hegel adds regarding true compassion: "Das wahrhafte Mitleiden ist im Gegentheil die Sympathie mit der zugleich sittlichen Berechtigung des Leidenden." While Hegel rather considers sympathy in general and its differences in the variations of the individualities, I prefer to emphasize the different kinds of sympathy in relation to the different kinds of tragic guilt. To make this point promptly, I shall let the thought of "passion" or suffering separate itself from the "com" to which it is joined in the word *compassion*, and shall attribute to each and every man the sympathy expressed by the "com" —yet in such a way that I affirm nothing about the mood of the spectator which could be indicative of his arbitrariness, but in such a way that when I explain the difference in his mood, I also express the difference of the tragic guilt.

In ancient tragedy the sorrow is deeper, the pain less; in modern, the pain is greater, the sorrow less. Sorrow always contains something more substantial than pain. Pain always implies a reflection over suffering which sorrow does not know. From a psychological standpoint it is interesting to watch a child when it sees an older person suffer. The child is not reflective enough to feel pain, and yet its sorrow is infinitely deep. It is not reflective enough to have any conception of sin and guilt; when it sees an older person suffer, it does not occur to it to reflect upon it, and yet when the cause of the suffering is concealed from it, there is a dim suspicion about it in its sorrow. Such, but in complete and profound harmony, is the Greek sorrow, and therefore it is at one and the same time so gentle and so deep. When an older person sees a child suffer, his pain is greater, his sorrow less. The more clearly the conception of guilt stands out, the greater is the pain, the less profound the sorrow. If one now applies this to the relation between ancient and modern tragedy, then must one say: in ancient tragedy, the sorrow is deeper, and in the consciousness which corresponds to this, the sorrow is deeper. It must in fact be constantly remembered that the sorrow does not lie in me, but it lies in the tragedy, and that I, in order to understand the deep sorrow of the Greek tragedy, must myself live in the Greek consciousness. Hence, it is certainly often only an affectation when so many profess to admire the Greek tragedies; for it is obvious that our age, at least, has no great sympathy with the specific character of Greek sorrow. The sorrow is deeper because the guilt has the aesthetic ambiguity. In modern times, the pain is greater. It is a fearful thing to fall into the hands of the living God.[12] One might say this about Greek tragedy. The wrath of the gods is fearful, yet the pain is not so great as in modern tragedy where the hero suffers entirely according to his own desert, is transparent to himself in his suffering of his guilt. Here it is relevant, in conformity with the tragic guilt, to show which sorrow is the true aesthetic sorrow and which the true aesthetic pain. The bitterest pain is manifestly remorse, but remorse has ethical not aesthetic reality. It is the bitterest pain because it has the total transparency of guilt, but just because of this transparency, it does not interest us aesthetically. Remorse has a sacredness which obscures the aesthetic, it may not be seen, least of all by the spectator, and it requires quite a different kind of self-activity. Modern comedy has sometimes presented remorse on the stage, but this only shows a lack of judgment on the part of the author. One may indeed be reminded of the psychological interest it can have to see remorse delineated on the stage, but again the psychological interest is not the aesthetic. This is part of the confusion which in our age asserts itself in so many ways: we look for a thing where we ought not to look for it, and what is worse, we find it where we ought not to find it; we wish to be edified in the theater, aesthetically impressed in church, we would be converted by novels, get enjoyment out of books of devotion, we want philosophy in the pulpit, and the preacher in the professorial chair. This pain of remorse is consequently not the aesthetic pain, and yet it is apparently this which the modern age tends toward as the highest tragic interest. This is also true with regard to the tragic guilt. Our age has lost all the substantial categories of family, state, and race. It must leave the individual entirely to himself, so that in a stricter sense he becomes his own creator, his guilt is consequently sin, his pain remorse; but this nullifies the tragic. Also, that which in a stricter sense is to be called the tragedy of suffering has really lost its tragic interest, for the power from which the suffering comes has lost its significance, and the spectators cry: "Heaven helps those who help themselves!" In other words, the spectator has lost his compassion; but compassion is, in a subjective as well as in an objective sense, the precise expression for the tragic.

For the sake of clarity I shall now, before carrying this explanation further, define a little more carefully the true aesthetic sorrow. Sorrow has the opposite movement from that which pain has. When one does not spoil this by means of a wretched consistency—something I, too, shall prevent in another way—one may say: the more innocence, the more profound the sorrow. If one insists on that, then one destroys the tragic. An element of guilt always remains, but this element is never really subjectively reflected; hence the sorrow in the Greek tragedy is so deep. In order to prevent ill-timed consequences, I shall only note that all exaggerations only succeed in carrying the matter over into another sphere. The synthesis of absolute innocence and absolute guilt is not an aesthetic category, but a metaphysical one. This is the real reason why one has always been ashamed to call the life of Christ a tragedy, because one instinctively feels that aesthetic categories do not exhaust the matter. In yet another way it is clear that Christ's life is something more than can be exhausted in aesthetic categories: by the fact that these categories neutralize themselves in this phenomenon, and are stilled in equilibrium.

The tragic action always has an element of suffering in it, and the tragic suffering an element of action, the aesthetic lies in the relativity of these. The identity of an absolute action and an absolute suffering is beyond the powers of aesthetics, and belongs to metaphysics. This identity is exemplified in the life of Christ, for His suffering is absolute because the action is absolutely free, and His action is absolute suffering because it is absolute obedience. Hence the element of guilt which remains is not subjectively reflected, and this makes the sorrow profound. The tragic guilt is something more than merely subjective guilt, it is inherited guilt; but inherited guilt, like inherited sin, is a substantial category, and it is exactly this substantiality which makes the sorrow deeper. The ever admired tragic trilogy of Sophocles, *Oedipus Coloneus, Oedipus Rex,* and *Antigone,* essentially centers on this authentic tragic interest. But inherited guilt contains the self-contradiction of being guilt, and yet not being guilt. The bond which makes the individual guilty is precisely piety, but the guilt which he thus draws down upon himself has every possible aesthetic ambiguity. One might readily conclude that the people who developed profound tragedy must have been the Jews. Thus, when they say about Jehovah that He is a jealous God who visits the sins of the fathers upon the children unto the third and fourth generations, or when one hears those terrible imprecations in the Old Testament, then one might easily be tempted to seek here for tragic material. But Judaism is too ethically developed for this; Jehovah's curses are, even though terrible, still also righteous punishment. This was not the case in Greece; the wrath of the gods had no ethical character, but only aesthetic ambiguity.

In Greek tragedy itself a transition is found from sorrow to pain, and as an example of this I might mention *Philoctetes*.[13] This, in the stricter sense, is a tragedy of suffering. But here too a high degree of objectivity still obtains. The Greek hero rests in his fate; his fate is unchangeable; there is nothing further to be said about it. This factor furnishes the element of sorrow in the pain. The first doubt with which pain really begins is this: why has this befallen me, why can it not be otherwise? There is, indeed, in Philoctetes a high degree of reflection, which has always seemed remarkable to me, and which essentially separates him from that immortal trilogy: I refer to the masterly depicting of the self-contradiction in his pain, which contains so deep a human truth, while yet there is an objectivity which sustains the whole.[14] Philoctetes' reflection is not absorbed in itself, and it is genuinely Greek when he complains that no one understands his pain. There is an extraordinary truth in this, and yet precisely here is manifested the difference between his pain and the reflective pain which always wants to be alone with its pain, which seeks a new pain in this solitude of pain.

The true tragic sorrow consequently requires an element of guilt, the true tragic pain an element of innocence; the true tragic sorrow requires an element of transparency, the true tragic pain an element of obscurity. This I believe best indicates the dialectic wherein the categories of sorrow and pain come in contact with each other, as well as the dialectic which lies in the concept of tragic guilt.

Since it is contrary to the spirit of the Symparanekromenoi to produce closely coherent works or greater wholes, since it is not our purpose to labor upon a Tower of Babel, which God in His righteousness can descend upon and destroy, since we, conscious of the fact that this confusion of tongues happened justly, recognize as a characteristic of all human striving in its truth that it is fragmentary, and that it is precisely this which distinguishes it from Nature's infinite coherence; that the wealth of an individual consists precisely in his proficiency in fragmentary prodigality, and that that which brings enjoyment to the producing individual also brings enjoyment to the receiving in-

dividual, not the troublesome and meticulous execution, nor
the protracted apprehension of this execution, but the
production and enjoyment of the gleaming transitoriness,
which for the producer contains something more than the
thorough execution, since it is the appearance of the Idea,
and which for the recipient contains something more, since
its fulguration awakens his own productivity—since, I say,
all this is contrary to the purpose of our society (and indeed, since even the period just read must almost be regarded as a disquieting attack upon the interjectory style,
in which the idea breaks out without breaking through, a
style which in our society has an official status): then, after
having called attention to the fact that my procedure still
cannot be called rebellious, since the bond which holds this
period together is so loose that the intermediary clauses
stand out aphoristically and arbitrarily enough, I shall
merely call to mind that my style has made an attempt to
appear to be what it is not—revolutionary.

Our society needs at every single meeting a renewal and
rebirth, to the end that its inner activity may be renewed
by a new description of its productivity. Let us then describe our purpose as an attempt in fragmentary pursuits,
or in the art of writing posthumous papers. A completely
finished work has no relation to the poetic personality; in
the case of posthumous papers one constantly feels, because of the incompletion, the desultoriness, a need to romance about the personality. Posthumous papers are like
a ruin, and what haunted place could be more natural for
the interred? The art, then, is artistically to produce the
same effect, the same appearance of carelessness and the accidental, the same anacoluthic flight of thought; the art
consists in producing an enjoyment which never actually
becomes present, but always has an element of the past
in it, so that it is present in the past. This has already been
expressed in the word: posthumous. In a certain sense, everything a poet has produced is posthumous; but one would
never think of calling a completed work posthumous, even
though it had the accidental quality of not having been
published in the poet's lifetime. Also, I assume that this is
the true characteristic of all human productivity, as we

have apprehended it, that it is a heritage, since men are not permitted to live eternally in the sight of the gods. A heritage, then, is what I shall call the effects produced among us, an artistic heritage; negligence, indolence, I shall call the genius we appreciate; *vis inertiae*,[15] the natural law that we worship. By this explanation I have now complied with our sacred customs and rules.

So draw nearer to me, dear brothers of Symparanekromenoi; close around me as I send my tragic heroine out into the world, as I give the daughter of sorrow a dowry of pain as a wedding gift. She is my creation, but still her outline is so vague, her form so nebulous, that each one of you is free to imagine her as you will, and each one of you can love her in your own way. She is my creation, her thoughts are my thoughts, and yet it is as if I had rested with her in a night of love, as if she had entrusted me with her deep secret, breathed it and her soul out in my embrace, and as if in the same moment she changed before me, vanished, so that her actuality could only be traced in the mood that remained, instead of the converse being true, that my mood brought her forth to a greater and greater actuality. I place the words in her mouth, and yet it is as if I abused her confidence; to me, it is as if she stood reproachfully behind me, and yet it is the other way around, in her mystery she becomes ever more and more visible. She is my possession, my lawful possession, and yet sometimes it is as if I had slyly insinuated myself into her confidence, as if I must constantly look behind me to find her; and yet, on the contrary, she lies constantly before me, she constantly comes into existence only as I bring her forth. She is called Antigone. This name I retain from the ancient tragedy, which for the most part I will follow, although, from another point of view, everything will be modern. First, however, a remark. I use a feminine figure because I firmly believe that a feminine nature will be best adapted for showing the difference. As woman she will have substantiality[16] enough for sorrow to show itself, but as belonging in a reflective world, she will have reflection enough to mark the pain. In order to experience sorrow, the tragic guilt must vacillate between guilt and innocence; that whereby the guilt passes over into her consciousness must always be a determination of substantiality. But since in order to experience sorrow, the tragic guilt must have this vagueness, so reflection must not be present in its infinitude, for then it would reflect her out of her guilt, because reflection in its infinite subjectivity cannot let the element of inherited guilt remain, which causes the sorrow. Since, however, her reflection is awake, it will not reflect her out of her sorrow, but into it, each moment transforming her sorrow into pain.

Labdakos' family is, then, the object of the indignation of the angry gods.[17] Oedipus has slain the sphinx, liberated Thebes; he has murdered his father, married his mother, and Antigone is the daughter of this marriage. Thus goes the Greek tragedy. Here I diverge from the Greek. All the relationships are the same in mine, and yet everything is different. That he has slain the sphinx and liberated Thebes is known to everyone, and Oedipus lives honored and admired, happy in his marriage with Jocasta. The rest is concealed from the eyes of men, and no suspicion has ever called this horrible nightmare into actuality. Only Antigone knows it. How she has come to know it lies outside the tragic interest, and everyone is free to work out his own explanation in regard to it. At an early age, before she was fully developed, dim suspicions of this horrible secret had at times gripped her soul, until certainty with a single blow cast her into the arms of anxiety. Right here I discover a definition of the modern idea of the tragical. For anxiety is a reflection, and in this respect is essentially different from sorrow. Anxiety is the organ by which the subject appropriates sorrow and assimilates it. Anxiety is the energy of the movement by which sorrow bores its way into one's heart. But the movement is not swift like the thrust of a dart, it is successive; it is not once for all, but it is constantly continuing. As a passionate, erotic glance desires its object, so anxiety looks upon sorrow to desire it. As the quiet, incorruptible glance of love is preoccupied with the beloved object, so anxiety occupies itself with sorrow. But anxiety has another element in it which makes it cling even more strongly to its object, for it both loves and fears it. Anxiety has a two-fold function. Partly it is the detective instinct which constantly touches, and by means of this probing, discovers sorrow, as it goes round about the sorrow. Or anxiety is sudden, posits the whole sorrow in the present moment, yet so that this present moment instantly dissolves in succession. Anxiety is in this sense a truly tragic category, and the old saying: *quem deus vult perdere, primum dementat*, in truth rightfully applies here.[18] That anxiety is determined by reflection is shown by our use of words; for I always say: to be anxious about something, by which I separate the anxiety from that about which I am anxious, and I can never use anxiety in an objective sense; whereas, on the contrary, when I say "my sorrow," it can just as well express that which I sorrow over, as my sorrow over it. In addition, anxiety always involves a reflection upon time, for I cannot be anxious about the present, but only about the past or the future; but the past and the future, so resisting one another that the present vanishes, are reflective determinations. Greek sorrow, on the other hand, like the whole of Greek life, is in the present tense, and therefore the sorrow is deeper but the pain less. Anxiety therefore belongs essentially to the tragic. Hence, Hamlet is deeply tragic because he suspects his mother's guilt. Robert le Diable asks how on earth it could happen that he caused so much evil.[19] Høgne, whom his mother had begotten by a troll, happens accidentally to see his image in the water, and asks his mother how his body had acquired such a shape.[20]

The difference is now easily perceptible. In the Greek tragedy Antigone is not at all concerned about her father's unhappy destiny. This rests like an impenetrable sorrow over the whole family. Antigone lives as carefree as any other young Grecian maiden, indeed the chorus pities her, since her death is foreordained, because she must quit this life at so early an age, quit it without having tasted its most beautiful joys, evidently forgetting the family's own deep sorrow. However, it should by no means be said that it is thoughtlessness, or that the particular individual stands alone by himself, without worrying about his relationship to the family. But that is genuinely Greek. Life-relationships are once and for all assigned to them, like the heaven under which they live. If this is dark and cloudy, it is also unchangeable. This furnishes the keynote of the Greek soul, and this is sorrow, not pain. In Antigone the tragic guilt concentrates itself about one definite point, that she had buried her brother in defiance of the king's prohibition. If this is seen as an isolated fact, as a collision between sisterly affection and piety and an arbitrary human prohibition, then *Antigone* would cease to be a Greek tragedy, it would be an entirely modern tragic subject. That which in the Greek sense affords the tragic interest is that Oedipus' sorrowful destiny re-echoes in the brother's unhappy death, in the sister's collision with a simple human prohibition; it is, so to say, the after effects, the tragic destiny of Oedipus, ramifying in every branch of his family. This is the totality which makes the sorrow of the spectator so infinitely deep. It is not an individual who goes down, it is a small world, it is the objective sorrow, which, released, now advances in its own terrible consistency, like a force of nature, and Antigone's unhappy fate, an echo of her father's, is an intensified sorrow. When, therefore, Antigone in defiance of the king's prohibition resolves to bury her brother, we do not see in this so much a free action on her part as a fateful necessity, which visits the sins of the fathers upon the children. There is indeed enough freedom of action in this to make us love Antigone for her sisterly affection, but in the necessity of fate there is also, as it were, a higher refrain which envelops not only the life of Oedipus but also his entire family.

While, then, the Greek Antigone lives so carefree that were it not for the disclosure of this new fact, we might imagine her life as very happy in its gradual unfolding, our Antigone's life, on the contrary, is essentially over. I have not endowed her stingily, and as we say that a word fitly spoken is like apples of gold in pictures of silver, so I have placed the fruit of her sorrow in a cup of pain. Her dowry is not a vain magnificence which moth and rust can corrupt, it is an eternal treasure. Thieves cannot break in and steal it; she herself will be too vigilant for that. Her life does not unfold like that of the Greek Antigone; it is not turned outward but inward, the scene is not external but internal; it is an invisible scene. Have I not succeeded, dear Symparanekromenoi, in arousing your interest in such a maiden, or must I resort to a *captatio benevolentiae?*[21] Then, too, she does not belong to the world she lives in; even though she appears flourishing and sound, her real life is concealed. Although she is living, she is in another sense dead; quiet is her life and secretive, the world hears not even a sigh, for her sigh is hidden in the depths of her soul. I need not remind you that she is by no means a weak and sickly woman, rather she is proud and vigorous. There is nothing, perhaps, which ennobles a human being so much as keeping a secret. It gives a man's whole life a meaning which of course it has for himself only. It saves him from every vain regard for his environment; self-contained he rests, blessed in his secret—that we could almost say, even if his secret was most painful.

Such is our Antigone. Proud she is of her secret, proud that she has been selected to be in a peculiar manner the saviour of the honor and renown of the house of Oedipus; and when the grateful people acclaim Oedipus with praise and gratitude, then she feels her own importance, and her secret sinks ever deeper into her soul, still more inaccessible to every living being. She feels how much responsibility is placed in her hands, and this gives her a supernatural greatness, which is necessary if she is to engage our attention as a tragic personality. As an individual figure she must be able to interest us. She is more than a young girl in general, and yet she is a young girl; she is a bride, and yet she is all innocence and purity. As a bride, woman achieves her destiny, and hence a woman can ordinarily interest us only to the degree that she is brought into relation to her destiny. However, there are analogies here. One says of a bride of God that she has the inward faith and spirit in which she rests. Our Antigone I should call a bride in a perhaps even more beautiful sense, indeed she is almost more, she is mother, she is in the purely aesthetic sense *virgo mater*, she carries her secret under her heart, hidden and concealed. She is silence, precisely because she is secretive, but this introversion which lies in silence, gives her a supernatural bearing. She is proud of her sorrow, she is jealous for it, for her sorrow is her love. But still her sorrow is not a dead, immovable possession; it moves constantly, it gives birth to pain, and is born in pain. When a girl resolves to dedicate her life to an idea, when she stands there with the sacrificial wreath upon her brow, she stands as a bride, for the great inspiring idea transforms her, and the votive wreath is like a bridal garland. She knows not any man, and yet she is a bride; she does not even know the idea which inspires her, for that would be unwomanly, and yet she is a bride.

Such is our Antigone, the bride of sorrow. She dedicates her life to sorrow over her father's destiny, over her own. Such a misfortune as has overtaken her father calls for sorrow, and yet there is no one who can grieve over it, because there is no one who knows about it. And as the Greek Antigone cannot bear to have her brother's corpse flung away without the last honors, so she feels how hard it would have been if no one had known this; it worries her that no tears should be shed; she almost thanks the gods because she is selected as this instrument. Thus is Antigone great in her pain. Here again I can show a difference between Greek and modern tragedy. It is genuinely Greek for Philoctetes to complain that there is no one who knows what he suffers; it is a deep human need to wish that others should realize this; reflective grief, however, does not desire this. It does not occur to Antigone to wish that anyone should understand her pain, but on the other hand, in relation to her father, she feels the justice of having to suffer grief, for this is just as right aesthetically as that a man should suffer punishment when he has done wrong. While, therefore, the very conception that it is predestined that the living should be buried alive wrings from Antigone in the Greek tragedy the outburst of sorrow:

> O mockery of my woe!
> I go to the strong mound of yon strange tomb
> All hapless, having neither part nor room
> With those who live or those who die,[22]

our Antigone can say it about herself all her life. The difference is extraordinary; there is a factual truth in her assertion which makes the pain less. If our Antigone were to say the same, it would be unreal, but this unreality is the real pain. The Greeks do not express themselves figuratively, just because the reflection which goes with this was not present in their lives. So when Philoctetes complains that he lives solitary and forsaken on a desert island, his assertion corresponds to an external truth; when, on the other hand, our Antigone feels pain in her solitude, it is, after all, only in a figurative sense that she is alone, but just because of this, her pain is real pain.

As far as tragic guilt is concerned, it consists partly in the fact that she buries her brother, partly in the context of her father's sorry fate, which is presupposed from the two preceding tragedies. Here again I come to the peculiar dialectic which sets the guilt of the race in relation to the individual. This is the hereditary guilt. Dialectics is commonly considered fairly abstract; one thinks generally of logical movement. However, life will soon teach one that there are many kinds of dialectics, that almost every passion has its own. The dialectic, therefore, which sets the guilt of the race or the family in connection with a particular subject, so that he not only suffers under it—for this is a natural consequence against which one would vainly try to harden himself—but bears the guilt, participates in it, this dialectic is foreign to us, has nothing compelling for the modern mind. If a man, however, were to contemplate regeneration in terms of ancient tragedy, then must every individual contemplate his own regeneration, not merely in a spiritual sense, but in the definite sense of rebirth from the matrix of family and race. The dialectic which sets the individual in connection with family and race is no subjective dialectic, for such a dialectic lifts the connection and the individual out of the continuity; it is an objective dialectic. It is essentially piety. To preserve this cannot be regarded as something injurious to the individual. In our age one allows the applicability of something in natural relations which he is unwilling to allow as applicable to spiritual relationships. Still, one would not wish to be so isolated, so unnatural, that one would not regard the family as a whole, of which one must say that when one member suffers, all suffer. One does this involuntarily, otherwise why is a particular individual so afraid that another member of the family may bring disgrace upon it, unless because he feels that he will suffer thereby? This suffering the individual must obviously endure, whether he will or not. But since the point of departure is the individual, not the family, this forced suffering is *maximum;* one feels that man cannot completely become master over his natural relationship, yet desires this as far as possible. On the other hand, if the individual sees the natural relationship as a factor involved in his truth, this expresses itself in the spiritual world thus: the individual participates in guilt. This is a conclusion many, perhaps, fail to understand, but then neither do they understand the tragic. If the individual is isolated, then he is either absolutely the creator of his own destiny, in which case nothing tragic remains, but only the evil—for it is not even tragic that an individual should be blindly engrossed in himself, it is his own fault—or the individuals are only modifications of the eternal substance of existence, and so again the tragic is lost.

With regard to the tragic guilt, the difference in the modern is readily apparent, after this has assimilated the ancient, for only now can we really speak of this. The Greek Antigone participates by filial piety in her father's guilt, as does also our modern one; but for the Greek Antigone her father's guilt and suffering is an external fact, an immovable fact, which her sorrow does not alter (*quod non volvit in pectore*);[23] and in so far as she herself personally, as a natural consequence, suffers under her father's guilt, this again is altogether an external fact. It is otherwise with our Antigone. I assume that Oedipus is dead. Even while he lived Antigone had been aware of this secret, but she had not had courage to confide in her father. By his death she is deprived of the only way by which she could be freed from her secret. To confide it now to any living being would be to disgrace her father; her life acquires meaning for her as she dedicates it, by her inviolable silence, to a daily, almost hourly, showing him the last honors. Of one thing, however, she is ignorant, whether her father himself had known it or not. Here is the modern: unrest in her sorrow, ambiguity in her pain. She loves her father with all her soul, and this love transports her out of herself and into her father's guilt; as the fruit of such a love, she feels herself alienated from mankind; she feels her own guilt the more she loves her father; only with him could she find rest, as equally guilty they would sorrow together. But while her father lived she had not been able to confide her sorrow to him, for she did not know whether he knew about it, and consequently there was a possibility of plunging him into a similar pain. And yet, was his guilt less if he had not known about it? The movement here is constantly relative. If Antigone had not known with certainty the actual relationship, then she would be insignificant, then she would have had nothing more than a suspicion to fight against, and that contains too little of the tragic to interest us. But she does know everything; yet even in this knowledge there is still an ignorance which can always keep sorrow in movement, always transform it into pain. Then, too, she is constantly at odds with her environment. Oedipus lives in the popular estimation as a fortunate king, honored and acclaimed; Antigone herself has admired as well as loved her father. She participates in every celebration and festival in his honor; she is more enthusiastic about him than any other young girl in the realm; her thoughts constantly turn back to him; she is praised throughout the kingdom as a model, loving daughter, and yet this enthusiasm is the only way in which she can give her sorrow any relief. Her father is always in her thoughts, but in what way is her painful secret. And yet she dares not give way to her sorrow, dares not grieve; she feels how much depends on her; she fears if anyone saw her suffering that people would begin to ask questions, and so, on this side too, she knows not sorrow but pain.

Considered in this way, I think that Antigone can really interest us; I think you will not reproach my extravagance nor my paternal partiality when I believe that she might well try her hand at dramatics and venture to appear in a tragedy. So far she is only an epic figure, and the tragic in her has only epic interest.

It is not so difficult to discover a context into which she might fit; in this respect we may readily be content with what the Greek tragedy gives. She has a sister living, who is, I assume, older than herself and married. Her mother might also be living. That these are naturally always subordinate characters is self-evident, as is the fact that the tragedy acquires an epic element at all, such as the Greek has, without its needing to be so conspicuous; still, the monologue will here always play a principal role, even if it must be assisted by the situation. One must imagine everything united about this one chief interest which constitutes Antigone's life content, and when the whole is set in order, then the question arises as to how the dramatic interest is brought about.

Our heroine, as she has been presented in the foregoing, seems bent on overleaping an element in her life; she is about to become wholly spiritual, something nature does not tolerate. With the depth of soul she possesses, she must necessarily love with an extraordinary passion, if she does fall in love. Here, consequently, I encounter the dramatic interest—Antigone is in love, and, I say it with pain, Antigone is mortally in love. Here manifestly is the tragic collision. One ought generally to be a little more particular about what one calls a tragic collision. The more sympathetic the colliding forces are, the deeper but also the more homogeneous they are, the more important the collision. She is, then, in love, and he who is the object of her affections knows that she loves him. My Antigone is no ordinary woman, and consequently her dowry is unusual—it is her pain. She cannot belong to a man without this dowry; she feels that would be very hazardous. To conceal it from such an observer would be impossible, to wish to conceal it would be a betrayal of her love; but can she marry him with it? Dare she confide it to any human being, even to the beloved? Antigone has strength; the question is not whether for her own sake, to relieve her heart, she should reveal something of her pain, for she can indeed bear this without assistance; but the question is, can she justify this to the dead? She herself suffers in a way by confiding her secret to the man she loves, for her own life, too, is sorrowfully interwoven with this. This, however, does not trouble her. The question is only concerning her father. Consequently the collision from this side is of a sympathetic nature. Her life, which was formerly peaceful and quiet, now becomes violent and passionate, always of course within herself, and her speech here begins to be pathetic. She struggles with herself, she has been willing to sacrifice her life to her secret, but now she must sacrifice her love. She conquers, that is to say, the secret conquers, and she loses. Now comes the second collision, for in order that the tragic collision should really be profound, the colliding forces must be homogeneous. The collision just described had not this quality; for the collision is really between her love for her father and for herself, and whether her own love be not too great a sacrifice. The other colliding force is the sympathetic love for her beloved. He knows he is loved, and boldly presses his suit. Her reserve puzzles him; he notices that there must be quite peculiar difficulties, but he thinks they cannot be insurmountable to him. What is all important to him is to convince her of how much he loves her, to persuade her that his life is over if he is obliged to relinquish her love. His passion at last becomes something almost unfair, but only the more ingenious because of her resistance. With every assurance of his love, he increases her pain, with every sigh he sinks the dart of sorrow deeper and deeper into her heart. He leaves no means untried to influence her. He knows, as did everyone, how deeply she loves her father. He meets her at the grave of Oedipus, where she had gone to find relief for her emotion, where she surrenders herself to her longing for her father, even though this very longing is mingled with pain because she does not know what her encounter with him might be, not knowing whether he was aware of his guilt or not. Her lover surprises her, and he adjures her by the love she bears her father; he notes that he makes an unusual impression upon her; he persists, he hopes for everything by this means, and he does not know that in this he has actually worked against himself.

Consequently, the interest centers on his being able to

wrest her secret from her. To allow her to become momentarily deranged and thus to betray her secret, would not
help. The colliding forces are so evenly matched that action
becomes impossible for the tragic individual. Her pain is
now increased by her love, by her sympathetic suffering
with him whom she loves. Only in death can she find peace;
so her whole life is dedicated to sorrow, and she has, as it
were, established a limit, a dam, for the evil destiny, which
might perhaps fatally have transmitted itself to succeeding
generations. Only in the moment of death can she admit
the intensity of her love, admit that she belongs to him only
in the moment that she does not belong to him. When
Epaminondas was wounded in the battle of Mantinea, he
left the arrow sticking in the wound until he heard that
the battle was won, because he knew that the instant it
was drawn out, he would die. Thus does our Antigone bear
her secret in her heart like an arrow which life unrelent-
ingly has driven in deeper and deeper without depriving
her of life, for as long as it remains in her heart she can
live, but in the moment it is drawn out, she must die. The
beloved must constantly strive to wrest her secret from
her, and yet this means her certain death. By whose hand,
then, does she fall? By the hand of the living or the dead?
In a certain sense, the dead, for what had been foretold of
Hercules, that he would not be slain by the living but by
the dead,[24] applies to her, in so far as the memory of her
father is the cause of her death; in another sense, by the
hand of the living, in so far as her unhappy love makes
that memory kill her.

SHADOWGRAPHS

Psychological Pastime

Lecture delivered before
the
SYMPARANEKROMENOI

Abgeschworen mag die Liebe immer sein;
Liebes-Zauber wiegt in dieser Höhle
Die berauschte, überraschte Seele
In Vergessenheit des Schwures ein.

* * *

Gestern liebt' ich,
Heute leid' ich,
Morgen sterb' ich;
Dennoch denk' ich
Heut' und Morgen
Gern an Gestern.[1]

IMPROVISED SALUTATORY

We celebrate in this hour the founding of our society. Again we rejoice in the return of the happy occasion which marks the passing of the year's longest day, and heralds the approaching victory of night. We have waited the livelong day; a moment ago we heaved a sigh over its length, but now is our despair turned into joy. The victory that has been won is indeed but an insignificant beginning, and day will doubtless maintain its rule for some time to come; but its mastery has been challenged, this cannot escape our attention. Therefore we do not wait to rejoice until the victory of night has become manifest to all, until the growing sluggishness of civic life reminds us that the day is waning. No, as a young bride impatiently awaits the coming of night, so we longingly await the first signs of its coming, the first intimations of its final victory; and the more we have felt the pangs of despair, not comprehending how life was to be endured unless the days were shortened, the greater is now our joy and our surprise.

A year has passed, and our society still lives. Shall we rejoice over this fact, dear Symparanekromenoi, shall we rejoice that its continued existence seems to mock our teaching that all things vanish? Or shall we not rather grieve that it still stands, and rejoice that in any event it has but another year to stand; since we have resolved at that time to put an end to its life if it does not pass out of existence before.—We formed no far-reaching plans in connection with its founding; for, knowing the wretchedness of human life, and the treacherousness of all existence, we determined to come to the assistance of nature in the execution of its universal law, and dissolve our society if we were not anticipated. A year has passed, and our membership is still complete. No one has been released from life, and no one has released himself; for since death is for us the greatest happiness, our pride forbids us to take this way of escape.

Shall we rejoice over this, or shall we not rather grieve, and take pleasure only in the hope that the confusion of life will soon separate us, the storms of life soon tear us apart? Such thoughts are indeed more appropriate to our society, more in harmony with this festive occasion, with every feature of our present environment. For is it not ingeniously significant that the floor in this little room, in accordance with the custom of the land, is strewn with green, as if for a funeral; and does not nature voice its approval of our mood in the wild storm that rages outside, in the wind's mighty roaring? Aye, and let us keep silence a moment while we listen to the music of the storm, its bold assault, its daring challenge; while we harken to the defiant bellowing of the sea, the anguished sigh of the forest, the desperate crashing of the trees, the cowardly rustle of the grass. Men say, indeed, that the divine voice is not in the rushing wind, but rather in the soft breeze.[2] Our ears, however, are not attuned to catching soft breezes, but only to devouring the wild fury of the elements. Aye, let the storm break forth in still greater violence, making an end of life, and of the world, and of this brief speech, which has at least the advantage over all things else, that it is soon ended! Let that wild vortex, which is the inmost principle of the world,[3] although this escapes the attention of men, who eat and drink and marry and increase in heedless preoccupation—let it break forth, I say, and in pent-up resentment sweep away the mountains and the nations and the achievements of culture and the cunning inventions of mankind, let it break forth with the last terrible shriek which more surely than the trump of doom proclaims the destruction of everything; let it move, and moving whirl along this naked cliff on which we stand, as lightly as thistledown before the breath of our nostrils!—But night conquers, the day is shortened, our hope grows stronger! Fill then your cups once more, dear drinking brethren. In this toast I hail thee, silent Night, eternal mother from whom all things are! From thee they come, to thee they return. Again have mercy upon the world, open thine arms wide to receive all things in thy embrace, and hide us safe in thy bosom! Dark Night, I hail thee, I hail thee victor! And this is my solace, for thou

dost shorten all things: day and time and life and troublesome memory in an eternal forgetfulness!

Ever since Lessing in his renowned essay, *Laokoon*, defined the disputed boundaries between poetry and art, the
result, unanimously accepted by all aestheticians, has been
to consider that the difference between them is that art lies
in the qualification of space, poetry in that of time, that art
expresses repose, poetry movement. In order, therefore, for
a subject to lend itself to artistic representation, it must have
a quiet transparency, so that its inner essence rests in a corresponding outer form. The less this is true of a subject, the
more difficult becomes the artist's task, until at last the
difference asserts itself, and warns him that there is simply
nothing he can do. If we apply the principle here casually
suggested but not expounded, to the relation between grief
and joy, we shall readily see that joy is far more easily represented artistically than grief. It should by no means be
denied that grief can be artistically represented, but it
should be said that there is a stage in its evolution when
it becomes essential to establish a contrast between the
inner and the outer, which makes its representation impossible for art.

This evolution is rooted in the very nature of grief. It is
of the essence of joy to reveal itself, while grief tries to hide,
sometimes even to deceive. Joy is communicative, social,
open-hearted, and desires expression; grief is secretive, silent, solitary, and seeks to retire into itself. The truth of this
remark will surely not be denied by anyone who has even
a moderate acquaintance with life. There are men so constituted that under the stress of emotion, the blood rushes
to the surface, making the inner emotion outwardly visible;
others are so constituted that the blood flows backward,
seeking the inner parts and the chambers of the heart. A
somewhat similar relation exists as to the mode of expression, between joy and grief. The first type described is
much easier to observe than the latter. In the first you see
the expression, the inner feeling is outwardly visible; in the
case of the second, you suspect the inner emotion. The outward pallor is, as it were, the parting salutation of the inner

excitement; and imagination and thought hasten after the fugitive emotion to where it conceals itself in its secret hiding place. Especially is this true of the type of grief I propose to consider, that which we may call reflective grief. In reflective grief the external contains at most a hint which may furnish a clue, sometimes not even that much. This type does not lend itself to artistic representation, for the equilibrium between the inner and the outer has been destroyed, and thus the emotion is not spatially determinable. Also, in another respect this grief resists artistic representation, since it lacks inner repose, and is constantly in movement; although this motion does not enrich it with any new content, yet the agitation is nevertheless essential. It revolves within itself, like a squirrel in its cage, although not so monotonously, since it is constantly alternating between the different combinations of sorrow's internal factors. What prevents reflective grief from being artistically portrayed is that it lacks repose, that it never comes into harmony with itself, or rests in any single definitive expression. As a sick man throws himself about in his pain, now on one side and then on the other, so is reflective grief tossed about in the effort to find its object and its expression. Whenever grief finds repose, then will its inner essence gradually work its way out, becoming visible externally, and thus also subject to artistic representation. As soon as it finds rest and peace within itself, this movement from within outward invariably sets in; the reflective grief moves in the opposite direction, like blood retreating from the surface of the body, leaving only a hint of its presence in the sudden paleness. Reflective grief is not accompanied by any characteristic outward change; even at its very inception it hastens inward, and only a watchful observer suspects its vanishing; afterwards it keeps careful guard over its outward appearance, so as to make it as unobtrusive as possible.

Retiring thus within, it finds at last an enclosure, an innermost recess, where it hopes it can remain; and now begins its monotonous movement. Back and forth it swings like a pendulum, and cannot come to rest. Ever it begins afresh from the beginning and reconsiders everything, it rehearses the witnesses, it collates and verifies their testimony, as it has done a hundred times before, but the task is never finished. Monotony exercises in the course of time a benumbing influence upon the mind. Like the monotonous sound of water dripping from the roof, like the monotonous whir of a spinning-wheel, like the monotonous sound of a man walking with measured tread back and forth on the floor above, so this movement of reflective grief finally gives to it a certain sense of numb relief, becoming a necessity as affording it an illusion of progress. Finally an equilibrium is established, and the need of obtaining for itself an outward expression, in so far as this need may have once or twice asserted itself, now ceases; outwardly everything is quiet and calm, and far within, in its little secret recess, grief dwells like a prisoner strictly guarded in a subterranean dungeon, who spends year after year in monotonously moving back and forth within his little enclosure, never weary of traversing sorrow's longer or shorter path.

The circumstance which gives rise to grief of this reflective type may lie partly in the subjective nature of the individual, partly in the objective grief, or in the occasion for it. An abnormally reflective individual will transform every sorrow that comes to him into reflective grief, since his individual make-up and the organization of his personality make it impossible for him to assimilate his sorrow in an immediate manner. This is a morbid condition, however, which does not interest us particularly, since in this way every accidental phenomenon can undergo a metamorphosis which transforms it into reflective grief. It is another matter when the objective grief, or its occasion in the individual, itself nourishes the reflection which makes the grief a reflective grief. This is everywhere the case when the objective grief is not complete, when it leaves a doubt behind, whatever be the specific nature of this doubt. Here a great many different varieties of thought at once present themselves, greater in proportion to the scope and depth of one's experience, or one's predilection for such investigations. It is not, however, by any means my intention to work my way through the entire manifold of these varieties; I desire only to bring out a single aspect of reflective grief, as this has revealed itself to my observation.

When the cause of the grief is a deception, then the objective nature of the emotion is itself such as to produce the reflective grief in the individual. That a deception really is a deception is often very hard to prove, and yet everything hinges on placing this beyond all possible doubt; as long as this remains disputable, grief will find no rest, but will be compelled to wander back and forth in the arena of reflection. Moreover, when the supposed deceit touches not some external fact, but the entire inner life of a human being, the inmost kernel of his personality, it becomes increasingly probable that the reflective grief aroused by it will persist and become permanent. But what can with greater truth be called a woman's entire life than her love? When, therefore, the sorrow of an unhappy love is rooted in deceit, it is an inevitable consequence that reflective grief should set in, whether it persists for the rest of the individual's life, or she succeeds in overcoming it. Unhappy love is indeed of itself one of the most profound sorrows which a woman can experience; but it does not follow that unhappy love always generates a reflective grief. When her lover dies, or her love is unrequited, or circumstances make its realization impossible, there is cause for grief to be sure, but not for reflective grief except in so far as the individual is abnormally reflective beforehand, in which case she does not come within the scope of our interest. But if she is not abnormally reflective, her grief will be of an immediate type, and as such it will be capable of artistic representation; contrariwise, it is quite impossible for the artist adequately to portray reflective grief, or to express the essential point in such grief. The immediate grief is the immediate impression and expression of the inner sorrow's impression, as precisely congruent with its original as the image that Veronica retained in her handkerchief; its sacred script is stamped upon the features, beautiful and clear and legible to all.[4]

Reflective grief, consequently, cannot be represented artistically, partly because it never is, but is always in the process of becoming, and partly it is indifferent to and unconcerned with the external and the visible. Hence, unless the artist is satisfied with the naïveté sometimes found in old books, where a figure is drawn that could represent almost anything, which bears on its breast a plate in the form of a heart or the like, to which it points or otherwise calls attention, whereon one may read a description of the picture, an effect the artist could just as well have produced by writing above the picture: Please note—he will have to renounce the idea of portraying reflective grief, leaving it to be dealt with by poets or psychologists.

It is this reflective grief which I now propose to bring before you and, as far as possible, render visible by means of some pictures. I call these sketches Shadowgraphs, partly by the designation to remind you at once that they derive from the darker side of life, partly because like other shadowgraphs they are not directly visible. When I take a shadowgraph in my hand, it makes no impression upon me, and gives me no clear conception of it. Only when I hold it up opposite the wall, and now look not directly at it, but at that which appears on the wall, am I able to see it. So also with the picture which I wish to show here, an inward picture which does not become perceptible until I see it through the external. This external is perhaps quite unobtrusive but not until I look through it, do I discover that inner picture which I desire to show you, an inner picture too delicately drawn to be outwardly visible, woven as it is of the tenderest moods of the soul. If I look at a sheet of paper, there may seem to be nothing remarkable about it, but when I hold it up to the light and look through it, then I discover the delicate inner inscriptions, too ethereal, as it were, to be perceived directly.

Turn your attention then, dear Symparanekromenoi, to this inner picture; do not allow yourselves to be distracted by the external appearance, or rather, do not yourselves summon the external before you, for it shall be my task constantly to draw it aside, in order to afford you a better view of the inner picture. But surely I do not need to encourage this society, of which I have the honor to be a member, to do this; for although young, we are yet old enough not to be deceived by appearances, nor to continue in this deception. Do I flatter myself with a vain hope when I believe that you will do these pictures the honor of granting them your attention? Or must these efforts of mine be regarded as alien, a matter of indifference to you, out of harmony with the purpose of our society, a society that knows but a single passion: a sympathetic interest in the secrets of sorrow? We too form an order, we too venture forth into the world now and then, in the role of knights errant, each taking his own way, not to fight huge monsters, nor for the sake of assisting innocence in distress, nor to seek adventures in love. Nothing of all this interests us, not even the last, for the dart from a woman's eye cannot wound our hardy breasts, and the merry smile of happy lassies cannot move us—but only the secret beckoning of sorrow. Let others boast that no woman near or far has been able to withstand the power of their love, we do not envy them; we will be proud that no secret sorrow can escape our attention, that no hidden grief can be so coy and so proud as to hinder us from penetrating victoriously into its inner-most haunts.

Which conflict is the more dangerous, which presupposes the greater skill, and which promises the greater reward, we do not ask. Our choice is made: we love only grief, grief alone is the object of our search, and everywhere we find its footprints, there we follow after them, intrepidly, immovably, until grief reveals itself. For this conflict we arm ourselves, in this struggle we train ourselves daily. And in truth, grief steals through the world so secretively that only the sympathetic observer even succeeds in suspecting its presence. You walk through the streets, each house looks like its neighbor, and only the experienced observer suspects that here in this house at midnight, all is different: an unhappy person wanders about, unable to find rest; he ascends the stairs, his footsteps echoing in the stillness of the night. We pass one another on the street, and each resembles his neighbor, and his neighbor the common run of mankind. Only the experienced observer divines that within this head there dwells a lodger who has renounced the world, and pursues a solitary life in quiet domesticity. The external appearance presents itself as an object for our inspection, but it does not engage our interest; thus the fisherman sits by the water and gazes fixedly upon the float, but the float does not interest him at all, but only the movements beneath the surface. The outward appearance has significance, it is true, but not as an expression of the inward, but rather as a telegraphic communication which tells us that there is something hidden deep within.

Sometimes when you have scrutinized a face long and persistently, you seem to discover a second face hidden behind the one you see. This is generally an unmistakable sign that this soul harbors an emigrant who has withdrawn from the world in order to watch over secret treasure, and the path for the investigator is indicated by the fact that one face lies beneath the other, as it were, from which he understands that he must attempt to penetrate within if he wishes to discover anything. The face, which ordinarily is the mirror of the soul, here takes on, though it be but for an instant, an ambiguity that resists artistic production. An exceptional eye is needed to see it, and trained powers of observation to follow this infallible index of a secret grief. This eye is eager, and yet so solicitous; anxious and compelling, and yet so sympathetic; persistent and shrewd, and yet sincere and benevolent. It lulls the individual into a certain pleasant languor, in which he finds an almost voluptuous pleasure in pouring forth his grief, like the pleasure said to accompany blood-letting. The present is forgotten, the external is broken through, the past is resurrected, grief breathes easily. The sorrowing soul finds relief, and sorrow's sympathetic knight errant rejoices that he has found the object of his search; for we seek not the present but the past, not joy which is always of the present, but sorrow whose nature it is to pass by. In the present it manifests itself only for a fleeting instant, like the glimpse one may have of a man turning a corner and vanishing from sight.

But sometimes grief succeeds even better in hiding itself, and the outward appearance gives us not even the slightest intimation. This may then escape our attention for a long time, until by chance one day a look, a word, a sigh, a quaver in the voice, a glance of the eye, a trembling of the lips, or a convulsive handclasp, treacherously betrays the carefully guarded secret—then passion for the quest is aroused, the struggle begins. Now we have need of vigilance and cunning and persistence. For what is so inventive as secret grief? But a prisoner for life has ample time to devise ingenious ways of concealment. And what is so swift to hide itself as secret sorrow? For no young girl can cover an exposed bosom in greater haste and with greater anxiety than the secret grief when it has been surprised. In this conflict there is need of unflinching courage, for one strives with a Proteus; but if only one can hold out, the antagonist must surrender. Though it may, like that ancient sea-god, assume every possible form in order to escape: now a serpent winding about the hand, now a lion terrible in its roaring, now a tree with leaves rustling in the wind, or a turbulent waterfall, or a crackling fire—at last it must prophesy, and grief must at last reveal itself.[5]

Lo, these are the adventures in which we find our pleasure and our pastime, in them is the test of our knighthood. For their sake we arise like thieves in the night, for their sake we are willing to risk everything; for no passion is so undisciplined as sympathy. Nor need we fear that opportunities for adventure will be wanting, but only that we may meet an opposition too hard and unyielding for our strength. As scientists say that by blasting open great rocks which have defied the centuries, they have found a living animal inside, which undiscovered has maintained itself in life, so there may be found human beings whose stony exterior conceals an eternal life of secret sorrow. Such a possibility cannot quench our passion nor cool our ardor, but rather must inflame it. For our passion is not mere curiosity, content with the external and the superficial. It is sympathetic dread which searches the reins and the hidden thoughts of the heart; it evokes things secret by means of magic and incantations, even when death has buried them from our view. Saul came in disguise before the battle to the Witch of Endor and demanded that she summon up for him the shade of Samuel.[6] Surely it was not mere curiosity which prompted him, not a wish to behold Samuel's visible image, but he would learn his thoughts; and it was not without anxiety that he waited for the stern judge to pronounce his verdict. And so it cannot be mere curiosity which prompts one and another of you, dear Symparanekromenoi, to give attention to the pictures I am about to display to you. For though I have borrowed the names of certain literary characters for purposes of designation, it does not follow that only these fictitious characters pass in review. The names must be regarded as *nomina appellativa*,[1] and I shall not object if one or another of you should feel inclined to choose for a particular picture some other name, a dearer one, perhaps, or one which seems more natural to him.

I. MARIE BEAUMARCHAIS

This young woman is known to us through the pages of Goethe's *Clavigo*, and we shall take that work as our point of departure, except that we intend to pursue her history a little further, after she has lost the dramatic interest, and the retinue of grief begins to fall away. We, however, keep her company; for as knights of sympathy we have both the native gift and the acquired art to keep pace in the procession of grief. Her story is brief: Clavigo was betrothed to her, Clavigo left her. And this is quite enough for all who are accustomed to viewing the phenomena of life as one inspects curiosities in an art cabinet—the more briefly the better, the more one can see. In the same way one might briefly relate that Tantalus thirsts, and that Sisyphus rolls a stone up the mountain. For one who is in a hurry, it would only delay matters to linger longer over such things, since one can learn no more than one already knew, which is the whole. To claim more attention, a story must be of a different kind. As we cluster familiarly about the tea table, the samovar singing its last refrain, the hostess asks the mysterious stranger to unburden his heart; as she serves the sugared water and the sweetmeats, he begins: It is a long drawn out and complicated story. The novel employs this method, but that is of course a very different thing: a long and complicated story, and such a brief little advertisement. Whether it is a short story for Marie Beaumarchais is another question; so much is certain, it is not a long story, for a long story has a measurable length; a short story, on the contrary, sometimes has the mysterious quality of being longer than the most long-winded, in spite of its brevity.

I have already remarked that reflective grief is not outwardly visible, that is, it does not find a beautiful outward expression in repose. The inner unrest prevents this transparency, the external is rather consumed thereby, and in so far as the inner manifests itself in the outer, it does so rather by a certain morbidity, which never lends itself to artistic representation since it lacks the interest of beauty. Goethe has given us one or two hints about this. But although one might assent to the correctness of this observation, one might still be tempted to regard it as an accident, and only when by considering the purely poetic and aesthetic point of view, one becomes convinced that what observation teaches has aesthetic truth, only then does one gain the deeper consciousness of its meaning. Now if I imagine a reflective grief, and ask myself if it can be represented artistically, it is at once evident that the external appearance is wholly accidental in relation to it; but if this is true, then the idea of artistic beauty is renounced. It is a matter of indifference whether she be large or small, significant or insignificant in appearance, more or less beautiful; to ask whether it would be more correct to let her head bend to one side or the other, or toward the ground, to let her stare in melancholy, or sadly fix her gaze upon the ground, all such things are entirely irrelevant—the one does not express reflective grief any more adequately than the other. The external is, in comparison with the internal, unimportant and indifferent. The point in reflective grief is the fact that sorrow is constantly seeking its object; this search is its life and the secret of its unrest. But this search is a constant fluctuation, and if the external were in each separate moment a perfect expression for the internal, it would be necessary to have an entire series of pictures to represent it; but no single picture could express it, and no single picture would have essential artistic value, since it would not be beautiful but true. The pictures would have to be regarded as one regards the second-hand of a watch; the works themselves are not visible, but the inner movement constantly expresses itself by the constantly changing positions of the second-hand. This change cannot be represented artistically, and yet it is the gist of the whole matter. Thus, when unhappy love has its ground in a deception, its pain and suffering are due to its inability to find its object. If the deception is proved, and if its victim understands that it is a deception, then the grief does not cease, but it becomes an immediate sorrow, not a reflective one. The dialectical difficulty is readily evident, for why does she grieve? If he was a deceiver, then it was just as well that he left her, the sooner the better; in fact, she should be glad that he left her, and mourn only because she had loved him. And yet it is still a profound sorrow that he was a deceiver. But the question whether or not he really was a deceiver is precisely the unrest which gives perpetual motion to her grief. To establish certainty for the external fact that a deception is really a deception, is always very difficult, and even this would by no means settle the matter, or end the movement of reflection. A deception is for love an absolute paradox, and herein lies the necessity for a reflective grief. The different factors constituting love may be combined in very different ways in the individual, so that love as it exists in one may not be the same as in another; the egoistic may predominate more, or the sympathetic; but whatever the love is, for the particular elements as well as for the total, a deception is a paradox which love cannot think, but which it must nevertheless attempt to think. If either the egoistic or the sympathetic factor were absolutely present, the paradox would disappear, that is, the individual by virtue of the absolute is lifted above reflection; he does not abolish the paradox through reason or reflection but is saved from the paradox by not attempting to think it, by not troubling himself about the illuminations or the confusions of a busy reflection; he rests in himself. An egoistically proud love, because of its pride, regards a deception as impossible; it does not trouble to listen to the arguments for or against, defending or excusing the person in question; it is absolutely secure because it is too proud to believe that anyone would dare to deceive it. Sympathetic love has the faith which can remove mountains; and the strongest defense is as nothing to it compared with the immovable certainty it possesses that there was no deception; every accusation is impotent in the face of the advocate, who explains that there was no deception, and explains it not in this way or that, but absolutely. But such a love is rarely or perhaps never seen in life. Ordinarily, both elements are present in love, and this brings it into relation with the paradox. In the two extreme forms described, the paradox exists in a sense, but love refuses to recognize it; in the last case it exists essentially. The paradox is unthinkable, and yet love persistently attempts to think it, and determined by the momentary dominance of one factor or another, it constantly seeks to think the paradox, often in contradictory fashion, in the ever unsuccessful effort to understand it. This process of reflection pursues an endless path, and can come to an end only if the individual arbitrarily breaks it off by bringing something else into play, a resolution of the will, but in so doing the individual brings himself under ethical categories, and loses his aesthetic interest. What he cannot win by reflection, he attains by a resolution of the will: finality and rest.

This holds true of all unhappy love which has its ground in a deception. What further helps to evoke reflective grief in Marie Beaumarchais is the fact that it is only an engagement which has been broken. An engagement is a possibility, not an actuality, but precisely because it was only a possibility, it might seem that the effect of breaking it could not be so great, that the shock would be far easier for the individual to bear. This might sometimes be the case; but, on the other hand, the fact that it is only a possibility that has been destroyed tends to provoke a more intensive reflection. When an actuality is destroyed, its destruction generally involves a far more radical breach with the past; every nerve is cut, and the finality of the breach is far more complete. When a possibility is destroyed, the suffering for the moment may perhaps not be so great, but it often leaves a small ligament or two whole and uninjured, which remains a constant source of continued suffering. The annihilated possibility seems transfigured into a higher possibility, whereas the temptation to conjure up such a new possibility is not so great when it is the actual which has been destroyed, because the actual is higher than the possible.

So then, Clavigo has forsaken her, he has faithlessly ended their engagement. Accustomed to depend on him, when he rejects her she has not sufficient strength to stand; she sinks helpless into the arms of the environment. Thus it seems to have been with Marie. It is possible also to imagine another beginning. It is possible to conceive of her as having sufficient strength immediately to transform her sorrow into reflective grief, so that, either in order to escape the humiliation of hearing others talk about her having been deceived, or because she still cares so much for him that it gives her pain to hear others repeatedly abuse him as a deceiver, she breaks off at once every connection with her environment, in order to feed upon her grief and to consume herself in sorrow. We follow Goethe. Her environment is not unsympathetic, it feels her pain with her, and sympathetically says: it will be the death of her. Aesthetically this is quite correct. An unhappy love affair may be such that suicide is aesthetically indicated, but not when the cause of it is a deception. In that case suicide loses its elevated character, and implies a concession which pride must refuse to yield. But when, on the other hand, she dies as a result of it, this is identical with his having murdered her. This expression completely harmonizes with the intensity of her inner passion, and she finds relief therein. But life does not exactly follow aesthetic categories, nor always obey aesthetic norms, and she does not die. This becomes a source of embarrassment to the environment. It feels it will not do constantly to repeat the assertion that she will die, when she continues to live; moreover, it cannot infuse the same pathetic energy into the assertion as in the beginning, and yet it is only this condition which might be of any comfort to her. Hence the environment changes the method. He was a scoundrel, it says, a deceiver, a detestable creature, for whose sake it is not worth while to die; forget him, think no more about the matter, it was only an engagement; blot out the affair from your memory, and you will again be young and full of hope. This inflames her, for this angry pathos harmonizes with other moods within her; her pride finds satisfaction in the revengeful thought that she will transform the whole experience into a mere nothing. She tells herself that it was not because he was such an extraordinary man that she loved him, far from it; she saw his faults clearly enough, but she thought he was a good man, a faithful man, and this was why she loved him; it was only pity, and therefore it will be easy to forget him, since she has never really needed him. The environment and Marie are again in tune, and the duet goes capitally.

For the environment, it is not difficult to think of Clavigo as a deceiver; for it has never loved him, and so there is no paradox; and in so far as it perhaps may have admired him a little (something Goethe suggests in connection with Marie's sister), this interest now arms it against him, and this benevolence, which perhaps was a little more than benevolence, now becomes excellent fuel for feeding the flames of hate. Nor is it difficult for the environment to erase every memory of him, and hence it demands that Marie shall do the same. Her pride breaks forth in hate, the environment fans the flames, she finds a vent for her passion in strong words and powerful energetic resolutions, and intoxicates herself with these. The environment rejoices. It does not perceive, what she will hardly acknowledge to herself, that the next moment she is weak and faint; it does not notice the anxious misgiving that seizes her, as to whether the strength she has in certain moments is an illusion. This she carefully conceals, and will admit to no one. The environment continues the theorizing exercises with vigor, but begins to wish signs of practical results. These do not appear. The environment continues to inflame her; her words reveal an inward strength, and yet the suspicion grows that all is not well. It becomes impatient, and ventures upon extreme measures, it drives the spur of ridicule into her side to incite her. It is too late. Misunderstanding has slipped in. There is nothing humiliating to the community in his having been a deceiver, but it is otherwise with Marie. The revenge offered her, the privilege of despising him, does not mean much; only if he loved her would it have real significance, but he does not love her, and her scorn becomes a draft which no one honors. On the other hand, there is no pain for the environment in Clavigo's being a deceiver, but only for Marie, and yet he is not without a defender in her own heart. She feels that she has gone too far, that she has laid claim to a strength she does not possess, although she will not admit it. And what comfort is there for her in despising him? It is better to grieve. Moreover, she is perhaps in possession of a secret note or two, of great importance in explaining the text, and capable of placing him in a more or less favorable light according to circumstances. She has not shared and will not share this knowledge with anyone, for, if he is not a deceiver, it is conceivable that he might regret the step he has taken and return to her; or—and this would be still more glorious—perhaps he has no need of regretting it, perhaps he will be able to justify himself absolutely and explain everything, and then, if she had made use of it, the fact might become a stumbling-block, preventing the establishment of their old relationship; and that would be her fault, for it was she who had made others privy to his love's secret growth. And if she could really be persuaded that he was a deceiver, then it would make no difference anyway, and at all events, it would be more handsome of her not to make use of it.

In this manner the environment now assists her, against its will, in developing a new passion—jealousy in behalf of her own grief. Her decision is made. The environment lacks on every side the energy to harmonize with her passion—she takes the veil. She does not enter a convent, but she puts on the veil of sorrow which conceals her from every alien glance. Her outward appearance is calm, the past is forgotten; her conversation lets no one suspect; she has taken the vow of sorrow, and now begins her solitary secret life. Everything is at once changed; before, it seemed as if she could unburden herself to others, but now she is not only bound by the vow of silence her pride wrung from her with the consent of her love, or which her love required of her, and her pride assented to; but she simply does not know how or where to begin, not because new elements have entered, but because reflection has conquered. If someone should ask her now why she grieves, she would

have nothing to say, or she would answer in the manner
of that ancient sage who was asked what religion was, and
requested time for consideration, and again more time, and
so the answer was always postponed.[8] Now she is lost to
the world, lost to her environment, immured alive. With
sadness she closes the last aperture; even at this moment
she feels that it would perhaps be possible to reveal herself; another moment and she will be forever isolated. However, it is decided, irrevocably decided, and she does not
need to fear, like others immured alive, that when the meager portion of bread and water which is consumed by her
is used up she will perish, for she has nourishment for a
long time; nor need she fear boredom, for she indeed has
occupation. Her outward appearance is calm and quiet, not
arresting the attention, and yet her inner self is not the incorruptible essence of a quiet spirit[9] but the unfruitful activity of a restless spirit. She seeks solitude or its opposite.
In solitude she rests from the effort it always costs to force
the outer appearance into some definite form. As one who
has been standing or sitting for a long time in a cramped
position stretches himself with pleasure, as a branch which
has long been bent by force joyfully returns to its natural
position when the bond is broken, so she finds refreshment
in solitude. Or she seeks the opposite—noise, distraction—
so that while all the others fix their attention on other things,
she may safely occupy herself with her grief. The things
going on nearest to her—the sound of music, the noisy conversation—sound so far away that it is as if she sat in a little
room by herself, far from the entire world. And if perchance
she cannot keep back the tears, she is certain to be misunderstood—perhaps she is just having a good cry [to get it
out of her system]; for when one lives in an *ecclesia pressa*,[10]
it is rightly a satisfaction that one's worship coincides in
mode of expression with the public form. She fears only
the more quiet intercourse, for here she is less on guard,
here it is so easy to make a mistake, so difficult to prevent
its being noticed.

Thus there is outwardly nothing to attract the attention,
but inwardly there is a ceaseless activity. Here she insti-
tutes an inquiry, one which may with perfect right and

particular emphasis be called a painful inquiry; everything is brought forward and accurately tested: his figure, his mien, his voice, his words. It sometimes happens that a judge in such a painful inquiry, fascinated by the beauty of the accused, has broken off the inquiry, and not been able to continue it. The court expectantly awaits the result of his inquiry, but it is not forthcoming. And yet it is by no means because the magistrate neglects his duty; the turnkey can testify that he comes every night, that the accused is brought before him, that the examination lasts several hours, that in his time there has never been a magistrate who could thus persevere. From all this the court concludes that it must be a very complicated case. And so it goes with Marie, not once only, but again and again. She reviews everything precisely as it happened; precisely, for justice requires it, and—love. The accused is summoned. "There he comes, he turns the corner, he opens the wicket, see how he hastens, he has longed to see me, impatiently he throws everything aside so as to reach me as soon as possible, I hear his swift footsteps, swifter than my own heart beats, he comes, there he is"—and the inquiry—it is postponed.

"Great God, this little word! I have so often repeated it to myself, I have remembered it in the midst of so many other things, but I have never before perceived what it really conceals within it. Aye, it explains everything; he is not serious about leaving me, he turns back to me. What is the whole world against this one little word! People weary of me, I had no friend, but now I have a friend, a confidant, a little word which explains everything—he turns back, but not with downcast eye; he looks at me half reproachfully, and says: O you of little faith! and this little word trembles like an olive leaf upon his lips—he is there" —and the inquiry is postponed.

Under such circumstances, it is natural enough that there should be great difficulty in rendering a verdict. Of course a young woman is not a jurist, but it does not follow that she cannot pass judgment, and yet this young woman's verdict will always be of such a nature that while at first glance it appears to be a verdict, it also contains something more

which shows that it is not a real verdict, and which also
shows that an opposite verdict may be rendered in the very
next moment. "He was no deceiver; for if he had been, he
must have been conscious of being one from the beginning.
But this is not so; my heart tells me that he has loved me."
If one insists upon this conception of a deceiver, then it
follows in all likelihood that a deceiver has never existed.
To acquit him on such grounds shows a partiality for the
accused which is inconsistent with strict justice, and cannot hold against a single objection. "He was a deceiver, a
detestable creature, who cold and heartless has made me
infinitely unhappy. Before I knew him I was content. Aye,
it is true, I had no conception that I could become so happy,
or that there was such a wealth of joy as he revealed to
me; but neither had I any conception that I could become
so unhappy as he has made me. Therefore I will hate him,
despise him, curse him. Yea, I curse you, Clavigo, in my
soul's innermost depths I curse you. But no one must know
it; I cannot permit anyone else to curse you, for no one has
the right to do so except myself. I have loved you as no
other has, but I also hate you, for no one knows your craft
as I do. Ye good gods, to whom vengeance belongs, lend
it to me a little while; I shall not misuse it, I shall not be
cruel. I shall creep into his soul when he is about to love
another, not to slay his love, for that would be no punishment, for I know that he loves her as little as he loves me,
for he does not love human beings at all; he loves only
ideas, thoughts, his mighty influence at court, his intellectual power, things which I cannot understand how he can
love. I shall deprive him of these, and then he will learn
to know my pain. And when he is near to the brink of despair, I shall give them all back to him again, and he will
have me to thank for it—and this shall be my revenge."

"No, he was no deceiver. He did not love me any longer,
and so he left me, but this was no deceit. Had he remained
without loving me, then he would have been a deceiver,
then should I have lived like a pensioner on the love he
had once borne me, lived on his compassion, lived on the
mite he, though rich, might perhaps have cast me, lived a
burden to him and a torment to myself. Wretched, cow-

ardly heart, despise yourself, learn to be great, learn it from him; he has loved me more than I have known how to love myself. And should I be angry with him? No, I shall continue to love him, because his love was stronger, his thought more proud than my weakness and cowardice. And perhaps he even loves me still—aye, it was out of love for me that he left me."

"Ah, now I see the truth, now I doubt no longer; he was a deceiver. I saw him; his air was proud and triumphant, his mocking glance swept superciliously over me. At his side was a Spanish lady, ravishingly beautiful; oh, why was she so beautiful—I could murder her—why am I not as beautiful? And was I not?—I did not know it, but he taught me; and why am I no longer beautiful? Whose fault is it? A curse upon you, Clavigo! Had you remained with me I should have become even more beautiful, for my love was nourished by your words and your assurances, and my beauty grew with my love. Now I am faded, now I thrive no more. What virtue is there in the tenderness of a whole world in comparison with a single word of yours? Oh, that I were again beautiful, that I might again be pleasing to him! For this reason alone would I be beautiful. Oh, that he might no longer love youth and beauty, for then I would grieve more than before, and who can grieve as I can?"

"Aye, he was a deceiver. How otherwise could he have ceased to love me? Have I ceased to love him? Or is there one law for a man's love and another for a woman's? Or should a man be weaker than the weak? Or was it perhaps a mistake, an illusion, that he loved me, an illusion that vanished like a dream; is this proper for a man? Or was it instability? Is it then proper for a man to be unstable? And why in the beginning did he assure me that he loved me so much? If love cannot endure, what then can endure? Aye, Clavigo, you have deprived me of everything; you have taken from me my faith, my faith in love, not only my faith in your love!"

"He was no deceiver. What it was that tore him away from me I do not know; I do not understand this mysterious power. But it has given him pain, deep pain; he did not wish me to share this pain, and therefore he pretended to be a deceiver. True, if he had loved another, then would I call him a deceiver, then nothing in the world could make me believe anything else, but he has not done this. Perhaps he thinks to lessen my suffering by making himself appear like a deceiver, and so arm me against him. This is why he shows himself now and then with young girls, this is why he looked so derisively at me the other day, in order to make me angry, and thus set me free. No, he certainly was no deceiver. How could anyone be a deceiver who had a voice like his? It was so calm and yet so full of feeling; as if it burst forth through solid rock, so it sounded forth from a depth I could not even fathom. Can such a voice deceive? What then is the voice—a mere movement of the tongue, a noise produced at pleasure? Somewhere in the soul it must have a home, a birthplace it must have. And it had that; in his heart's innermost chamber it had its home, there he loved me, there he still loves me. True, he also had another voice, it was cold, icy, it had power to kill every joy in my soul, to smother every happy thought, it could even make my kisses seem cold and distasteful to myself. Which was the true voice? He could deceive in all ways, but I feel sure that this quivering voice wherein his passion trembled, that it was no deception, that would be impossible. The other was a deception. Or some evil power overmastered him. No, he was not a deceiver, this voice which has bound me to him forever, it was no deception. A deceiver he was not, even if I never understood him."

The inquiry is never finished, nor the verdict; the inquiry not, because something constantly intrudes, the verdict not, because it is only a mood. Once begun the movement can continue indefinitely, and it is impossible to envisage any end. It can be made to cease only by a breach, by breaking off this entire course of thought. But this cannot happen; for the will is always in the service of the reflection, which gives energy to the momentary passion.

When she tries at times to tear herself free, it comes to nothing, so this is again only a mood, a momentary passion, and reflection constantly remains victorious. Mediation is impossible. If she tries to make a new beginning, but so that this beginning is in one way or another the result of her previous reflection, she is at once carried away. The will must be wholly indifferent; it must begin in the strength of its own willing before there can be any talk of a beginning. If this happens, she may indeed find a beginning, but she removes herself from the field of our interest, since we turn her over willingly to the moralists, or whoever cares to attend her. We wish her a respectable marriage, and pledge ourselves to dance on her wedding-day, when fortunately the altered name will help us forget that it was the Marie Beaumarchais of whom we have spoken.

But we return to Marie Beaumarchais. The characteristic feature of her grief is, as we remarked above, the restlessness which prevents her from finding the object of her grief. Her suffering cannot attain quietude; she lacks the peace which every life must have in order to assimilate its nourishment and benefit by it. No illusion overshadows her with its quiet coolness while she assimilates the pain. She lost childhood's illusion when she gained that of love, and she lost love's illusion when Clavigo deceived her; if it were possible to win the illusion of sorrow, then she would be helped. Then would her grief grow to man's maturity, and she would have compensation for her loss. But her sorrow does not thrive, for she has not lost Clavigo; he has deceived her. Her grief remains always a puny babe with its tiny wail, a child without father or mother; for if Clavigo had been torn away from her, it would have had a father in the memory of his faithful love, and a mother in Marie's ecstasy. But now she has nothing on which she can nourish it; for the experience was indeed beautiful, but it had no significance in itself, but only as a foretaste of the future. And she cannot hope that this child of pain will become transformed into a child of joy; she cannot hope for Clavigo's return, for she would not have strength to bear a future. She has lost the glad confidence with which she would willingly have followed him to the brink of the bottomless pit, and she has acquired instead a hundred hesitations, and would at most only be able to live over the past with him again. When Clavigo left her, there stretched a future before her, so beautiful, so enchanting, that it almost confused her thoughts. It had already begun dimly to exercise its power, her metamorphosis had already begun, when the development was checked, and her transformation ceased. She had begun vaguely to feel a new life, its energies were already moving within her; then it was crushed, she was thrust back, and there is no compensation for her, neither in this world nor in the world to come. The future smiled upon her, and its riches were reflected in the illusion of her love; and still everything was natural and straightforward. Now an impotent reflection perhaps sometimes paints her an impotent illusion, an illusion which does not even tempt her, but for a moment soothes her. And thus she will pass her time until at last she has consumed the object of her grief which was not identical with her grief, but the occasion through which she always sought an object for her grief.

If a man possessed a letter which he knew, or believed, contained information bearing upon what he must regard as his life's happiness, but the writing was pale and fine, almost illegible—then would he read it with restless anxiety and with all possible passion, in one moment getting one meaning, in the next another, depending on his belief that, having made out one word with certainty, he could interpret the rest thereby; but he would never arrive at anything except the same uncertainty with which he began. He would stare more and more anxiously, but the more he stared, the less he would see. His eyes would sometimes fill with tears; but the oftener this happened the less he would see. In the course of time, the writing would become fainter and more illegible, until at last the paper itself would crumble away, and nothing would be left to him except the tears in his eyes.

II. DONNA ELVIRA

We find this young woman in the opera *Don Juan*, and it will not be without significance in our later inquiry to take notice of the hints concerning her earlier life, which the text of the opera contains. She had been a nun; it was from the peace of the cloister that Don Juan had torn her away.[11] In this is suggested the tremendous intensity of her passion. It was no frivolous girl from a boarding school, who had learned to love at school and to flirt at balls; the seduction of such a girl has no great significance. By contrast, Elvira has been brought up in the discipline of the cloister, but this has not been able to eradicate passion, but has taught her to suppress it, and thereby to make it more violent as soon as it is allowed to break forth. She is certain prey for a Don Juan; he will know how to entice her passion forth, wild, ungovernable, insatiable, satisfied only in his love. In him she has everything, and the past is nothing; if she loses him, she loses everything, including the past. She had renounced the world. Then there appeared a figure she could not renounce, and it is Don Juan. From now on she relinquishes everything in order to live with him. The more significant the past she leaves behind her, the more closely must she cling to him; the more closely she has twined herself about him, the more terrible becomes her despair when he leaves her. Her love is even from the beginning a kind of despair; nothing has any significance for her, either in heaven or on earth, except Don Juan.

In the opera Elvira is of interest to us only in so far as her relationship to Don Juan has significance for him. If I were to attempt briefly to indicate this significance, I should say: she is Don Juan's epic fate, the Commandant is his dramatic fate. There is in her a hatred which will seek Juan in every nook and corner, a flame which will light up the darkest hiding place, and should this still not discover him, there is in her a love which will find him. She shares with the rest in the pursuit of Don Juan; but I imagine that if all the forces of the pursuit were neutralized, if the efforts of the pursuers had destroyed one another so that Elvira was alone with Don Juan and he was in her power, then would her hate arm her to murder him; but her love would forbid it, not from pity, since for that he is too great a figure for her, and so she would continue to keep him alive; for if she killed him, she would also have killed herself. Hence, if the forces active in the opera were restricted to Don Juan and Elvira, it would never end; for Elvira would

prevent the lightning itself, if that were possible, from striking him, in order that she might avenge herself, and yet
she would again be unable to take her revenge. Such is
the interest she has for us in the opera; but here we are
concerned about her relationship to Don Juan only in so far
as it has significance for her. Many are interested in her,
but in very different ways. Don Juan was interested in her
before the opera begins, the spectator grants her his dramatic interest, but we, the friends of sorrow, follow her not
only to the nearest street-crossing, not only in the moment
when she passes across the stage, no, we follow her on her
solitary way.

Well then, Don Juan has seduced Elvira and abandoned
her. It was quickly done, as quickly as a "tiger breaks a
lily";[12] when Spain alone reckons 1,003, it is easy to see
that Don Juan is in a hurry, and in some measure to calculate the speed of his movements. Don Juan has abandoned
her, but there is no environment into whose arms she can
fall fainting; she need not fear that the environment will
close too tightly about her, it will rather open wide its ranks
to make her departure easier; she need not fear that anyone will deny her loss, rather perhaps will one or another
take it upon himself to demonstrate it. She stands alone
and abandoned, and there is no doubt to sustain her; it is
clear that he was a deceiver who has deprived her of everything and exposed her to shame and dishonor. This is, however, aesthetically speaking, not the worst for her; it saves
her for a time from the reflective grief which is certainly
more painful than the immediate. The fact is indisputable,
and reflection cannot give it now one meaning, now another.
A Marie Beaumarchais may have loved a Clavigo as intensely, as violently, and as passionately, as regards her own
passion; it may have been entirely an accident that the
worst has not happened, she may almost wish that it had
happened; for then the story would have an end and she
would be far more strongly armed against him, but this
did not happen. The fact in her case is far more ambiguous;
its essential character always remains a secret between her
and Clavigo. When she thinks of the cold craftiness, the
miserable calculation he needed to deceive her so that in

the eyes of the world it takes on a far more innocent aspect, so that she becomes a prey to the sympathy which says: "Well, good Lord, the case is not so terrible, it might have been worse"—it revolts her; she almost loses her mind when she thinks of the proud superiority over against which she has meant absolutely nothing, which set her a limit and said: thus far and no farther. And yet, the whole story can also be explained in another manner, in a more beautiful manner. But as the explanation becomes different, the fact also becomes different. Reflection, therefore, has immediately enough to keep it busy, and the reflective grief is unavoidable.

Don Juan has abandoned Elvira. In the same instant everything is clear to her, and no doubt lures her grief into the discussion room of reflection; she is dumb in her despair. With a single pulse-beat it streams through her, and its current is outward; in a blaze the passion illuminates her, and becomes visible externally. Hate, despair, revenge, love, all break forth, to reveal themselves visibly. In this moment she is picturesque. The imagination therefore also shows us at once a picture of her, and the external is by no means set in indifference; its reflection is not meaningless, and its activity not without significance, as it rejects and chooses.

Whether she is herself in this moment a subject for artistic representation is another question; but so much is certain, in this moment she is visible and can be seen, naturally not in the sense that this or that actual Elvira can be seen, which is most frequently identical with her not being seen, but the Elvira we imagine is essentially visible. Whether art is able to shade her expression to such a degree that the point in her despair becomes visible, I shall not attempt to decide, but she can be described, and the picture which thus appears, becomes not merely a burden for the memory, which neither adds to nor takes away, but has its validity. And who has not seen Elvira!

It was early morning when I undertook a journey by foot in one of the romantic valleys of Spain. Nature awoke, the trees of the forest shook their heads, and the leaves, as it were, rubbed the sleep out of their eyes, one tree bent to the other to see if it was yet awake, and the whole forest billowed in the fresh cool breeze; a light mist rose from the earth, the sun turned it back as if it had been a blanket under which it had rested during the night, and now it looked down like a loving mother upon the flowers and upon everything that had life, and said: Arise, dear children, the sun is already shining. As I swung around a defile, my eye fell on a cloister high up on the peak of the mountain, to which a footpath led up through many turnings. My thoughts dwelt upon the scene; so, I said to myself, it stands there like a house of God fast founded upon a rock. My guide told me that it was a convent, known for its strict discipline. My pace slowed down, like my thought; what is there to hasten for, so near the cloister? I should probably have come altogether to a stop, if I had not been aroused by a quick movement near me. Involuntarily I turned about to look; it was a knight who hurried past. How handsome he was, how light his step, and yet so full of energy; how royal his carriage, and yet so evidently in flight; he turned his head to look back, his aspect so engaging and yet his glance so restless; it was Don Juan. Is he hurrying to some place of assignation, or coming from one? Still, he was soon lost to sight and forgotten by my thought; my eye was fixed upon the cloister. I sank again into a contemplation of the joys of life and the quiet peace of the cloister, when I saw high up on the mountain a feminine figure. In great haste she ran down the path, but the way was steep, and it constantly seemed as if she would tumble down the mountain. She came nearer. Her face was pale, only her eyes blazed terribly, her body was faint, her bosom rose and fell painfully, and yet she ran faster and faster, her disheveled locks streamed loose in the wind, but not even the fresh morning breeze and her own rapid motion was able to redden her pale cheeks; her nun's veil was torn and floated out behind her, her thin white gown would have betrayed much to a profane glance, had not the passion in her countenance turned the attention of even the most depraved of men upon itself. She rushed past me; I dared not address her, her brow was too majestic, her glance too royal, her passion too high-born. Where does this woman belong? In the cloister? Have these passions their home there?—In the world? But this costume?—Why does she hurry so? Is it to conceal her shame and disgrace, or is it to overtake Don Juan? She hastens on to the forest, and it closes about her and hides her, and I see her no more, but hear only the sigh of the forest. Poor Elvira! Have the trees found out something?—and yet, the trees are better than men, for the trees sigh and are silent—men whisper.

In this first moment Elvira can be represented; and even though art cannot really cope with this, because it would be difficult to find a single expression which also includes the whole range of her passions, the soul demands to see her. This I have attempted to suggest by the little picture sketched above; it was not my thought that this picture adequately describes her, but I wished to suggest that description is what belongs to her, that it was not an arbitrary notion of mine, but a valid claim of the idea. However, this is only one moment, and we must follow Elvira farther.

The movement which lies nearest at hand is a movement in time. Through a series of moments she maintains herself at the pitch, previously suggested, of being picturesque. Thereby she achieves a dramatic interest. Through the haste with which she rushed past me, she overtakes Don Juan. This is also quite in order, for he had indeed forsaken her, but he has drawn her into his own life movement, and she must reach him. If she does reach him, her entire attention is again directed outwardly, and we do not yet get a reflective grief. She has lost everything—heaven when she chose the world, the world when she lost Don Juan. She has, therefore, nowhere to seek refuge except with him; only by being in his presence can she keep despair at a distance, either by drowning out the inner voices with the clamor of hate and bitterness, which only sounds with emphasis when Don Juan is personally present, or by hoping. This latter signifies that the elements of a reflective grief are already present, but they have not yet had time to marshal themselves within her. "She must first be cruelly convinced," says Kruse's interpretation, but this requirement completely reveals the inner disposition. If she has not been convinced by what has happened that Don Juan was a deceiver, she never will be. But as long as she requires a further proof, so long can she succeed—by living a restless, wandering life, constantly occupied in pursuing Don Juan—in escaping the inner unrest of a quiet despair. The paradox already exists in her soul, but as long as she can keep her soul in a state of agitation by means of external proofs which do not explain the past, but do throw light upon Don Juan's present condition, so long she escapes the reflective grief. Hate, bitterness, curses, prayers, adjurations alternate, but her soul has not yet turned back upon itself to rest in the reflection that she has been deceived. She looks for an explanation from without. When therefore Kruse makes Don Juan say:

> Have you a mind to hear,
> To believe my words—you who suspect me so;
> Then let me tell you now, strange and improbable
> Must seem the cause which forced, etc.,

one must be careful not to believe that this, which to the spectator's ear sounds like mockery, has the same effect on Elvira. For her this speech is a relief, for she demands the improbable, and she wants to believe it, just because it is improbable.

When we now permit Don Juan and Elvira to meet each other, we have a choice between permitting Don Juan to be the stronger or Elvira. If he is the stronger then her whole appearance will mean nothing. She demands a "proof in order to be cruelly convinced"; he has gallantry enough to furnish it. But she is, naturally enough, not convinced, and demands a new proof; for demanding a proof is an amelioration, and the uncertainty is refreshing. Thus she becomes only one more witness of Don Juan's exploits. But we might also imagine Elvira as the stronger. It rarely happens, but out of gallantry toward the fair sex we shall grant it. She stands, then, still in her full beauty, for though she has wept, the tears have not yet put out the fire in her eyes; and though she has sorrowed, the sorrow has not consumed the vitality of youth; and though she has grieved, her grief has not decimated the vitality of her beauty; and though her cheek has become pale, it has but enhanced the spirituality of her expression; and though she no longer glides with the lightness of childish innocence, she steps forth with the energetic assurance of womanly passion. Thus she confronts Don Juan. She has loved him more than all the world, more than her soul's salvation; she has thrown away everything for him, even her honor, and he was untrue. Now she knows only one passion, hate, only one thought, revenge. Thus she is as great a figure as Don Juan; for the power to seduce all women is the masculine expression which corresponds to the feminine one of being seduced once with her whole soul, and then of hating, or, if you will, of loving her seducer with an energy no wife ever had. Thus she confronts him; she does not lack the courage to dare to meet him, she fights for no moral principles, she fights for her love, a love she does not base on respect; she does not fight to become his wife, she fights for her love, which is not satisfied with a repentant faithfulness, but which demands revenge; out of love for him she has thrown away her eternal happiness, and if it were again offered her, she would cast it away again for the sake of her revenge.

Such a figure cannot fail to make an impression upon Don Juan. He knows the pleasure of inhaling the fragrance of the finest and most fragrant blossoms of first youth, he knows that it lasts but an instant, and he knows what comes later; he has often enough seen these pale figures fade so quickly that it was almost visible to the eyes; but here is indeed a miracle; the laws governing the ordinary course of existence have been broken; it is a young woman he has seduced, but her life is not ruined, her beauty is not faded; she has been transformed, and is more beautiful than ever. He cannot deny that she fascinates him more than any young woman has ever fascinated him before, more than Elvira herself; for the innocent nun was, in spite of her beauty, a girl like many others, his love for her an adventure like many another one; but this woman is alone of her kind. This woman is armed; she does not conceal a dagger in her bosom,[13] but she carries an invisible weapon, for her hate is not to be satisfied with speeches and declamations, but it is unseen, and this weapon is her hate. Don Juan's passion awakens; she must once more be his; but not so. True, if it were a woman who knew his nefariousness, who hated him, although she had not been seduced by him, then would Don Juan be victorious; but this woman he cannot win, all his seductiveness is unavailing. If his voice were more ingratiating than his own voice, his approach more insidious than his own approach, he could not move her; if angels interceded for him, if the Mother of God were willing to be bridesmaid at the wedding, it would be in vain. As Dido, even in the underworld, turns away from Aeneas who was unfaithful to her, so would Elvira not indeed turn away from him, but confront him more coldly than Dido.[14]

But this encounter of Elvira with Don Juan is only a transitional moment; she walks across the stage, the curtain falls, but we, dear Symparanekromenoi, steal away after her; for only now does she really become Elvira. As long as she is in the presence of Don Juan she is beside herself; when she comes to herself then it is time to think the paradox. To think a contradiction is, in spite of all the assurances of modern philosophy and the foolhardy courage of its young adherents, not an easy matter; it is always connected with great difficulties.[15] A young woman may well be forgiven if she finds it difficult, and yet this is the task which is set her, to think that the man she loves is a deceiver. This is something she has in common with Marie Beaumarchais, and yet there is a difference between them, in the manner in which each one comes to the paradox. The fact Marie had to go on was in itself so controversial that reflection with all its exigency could not help seizing it immediately. But with respect to Elvira, the factual proof for Don Juan's deception seems so evident that it is not easy to see how reflection can get hold of it. It therefore attacks the matter from another side. Elvira has lost everything, and yet there lies an entire life before her, and her soul requires a pittance to live on.

Here two possibilities present themselves, either to go on under ethical and religious categories, or to preserve her love for Juan. If she adopts the first, she places herself outside the range of our interest; with pleasure we permit her to retire to an institution for Magdalenes, or wherever she likes. This will probably be difficult for her, however, for to make it possible she must first despair; she has already once known the religious, and the second time it makes greater demands. The religious is in general a dangerous power to have anything to do with; it is jealous for itself, and will not be mocked. When she chose the cloister, it is quite possible that her proud soul found a rich satisfaction in it, for say what you will, no woman makes so brilliant a match as she who becomes the bride of heaven; but now, on the contrary, as a penitent she must go back in penitence and remorse. Moreover it is a question whether she can find a priest who can preach the gospel of repentance and remorse with the same power with which Don Juan had preached the glad gospel of pleasure. Therefore to save herself from that despair, she must hold fast to Don Juan's love, something which she finds so much easier since she still loves him. A third course of action is unthinkable, for that she should seek comfort in the love of another would be still more terrible than the most terrible. For her own sake, consequently, she must love Don Juan; it is self-defense which bids her do it, and this is the spur of reflection which drives her to fix her eyes upon this paradox: can she love him although he has deceived her. Whenever despair would take hold of her, she seeks refuge in the memory of Don Juan's love, and in order to make herself secure in this refuge, she is tempted to think that he is no deceiver, although she thinks this thought in many ways. For a woman's dialectic is remarkable, and only he who has had opportunity to observe, only he can imitate it, whereas even the greatest dialectician who ever lived could speculate himself mad trying to produce it.

I have, however, been so fortunate as to know a couple of excellent examples with whom I have gone through a whole course in dialectics. Strangely enough, though one might expect to find them in the capital, for the noise and multitude of people hide much, this is not so, that is to say, when you wish to find a perfect specimen. In the provinces, in small towns, on country estates, you will find the most beautiful specimens. The one I have particularly in mind was a Swedish lady of noble birth. Her first lover cannot have desired her with greater intensity than I, her

second lover, strove to follow her heart's thoughts. However, I owe it to truth to acknowledge that it was not my
keenness and cunning which put me on the track, but an
accidental circumstance which would take too long to relate
here. She had lived in Stockholm, where she had come to
know a French count, to whose faithless charm she became
a victim. She still stands vividly before me. The first time
I saw her she made no particular impression upon me. She
was still beautiful, with a proud and aristocratic bearing;
she spoke very little, and I should probably have left her
as wise as I had come, if an accident had not initiated me
into her secret. From that moment she became significant
to me; she gave me such a vivid picture of Elvira, that I
was never tired of looking at her. One evening I was present
with her at a large social gathering; I had come before her,
had already waited for some time, when I stepped to the
window to see if she were not coming, and a moment later
her carriage was at the door. She stepped out, and immediately her dress made a singular impression upon me. She
had on a thin light silk coat, almost like the domino in
which Elvira makes her appearance in the ballet. She entered with a stately dignity which was really imposing; she
was attired in a black silk dress; she was in the highest
degree tastefully gowned, and yet very simply; no ornament adorned her, her neck was bare, and as her skin was
whiter than snow, I have rarely seen so beautiful a contrast
as that between her black silk and her white bosom. It is
not rare to see an uncovered neck, but rarely do you see a
young woman who really has a bosom. She curtsied to the
whole company, and when, thereupon, the host stepped
forward to greet her, she curtsied very low to him, but
though her lips parted to form a smile, I heard not a word
from her. To me her deportment was highly perfect; and
I who was a party to her secret mentally applied to her
the words which were spoken of the oracle: It neither
speaks out nor conceals, it hints.[16]

From her I have learned many things, and among others have found the observation confirmed that I have frequently made, that people who hide a sorrow, in the course
of time acquire a special word or thought by which they

are able to indicate everything to themselves and to the individual whom they have initiated therein. Such a word or thought is like a diminutive in comparison with the diffuseness of the grief; it is like a pet name one uses every day. Often it stands in an altogether accidental relation to that which it is supposed to signify, and almost always owes its origin to an accident. After I had won her confidence, after I had succeeded in overcoming her suspicion of me, because an accident had put her in my power, after she had told me everything, I often went through the whole scale of moods with her. If, on the other hand, she did not at times feel inclined to do so, and yet desired to indicate that her soul was occupied with her grief, she would take my hand, look at me and say: "I was more slender than a reed, he more glorious than the cedars of Lebanon." Where she had found these words I do not know; but I am convinced that when Charon comes in his boat to convey her to the underworld, he will find in her mouth not the required obol,[17] but these words upon her lips: "I was more slender than a reed, he more glorious than the cedars of Lebanon!"

Consequently, Elvira cannot discover Don Juan, and now she must find her own way out of her life's labyrinth, she must come to herself. She has changed her surroundings, and so is deprived of the assistance which might perhaps have contributed to directing her grief outward. Her new environment knows nothing of her earlier life, suspects nothing; for her appearance has nothing obtrusive or noteworthy, no marks of grief, no sign which advertises to the public the presence of grief. She can control every expression, for the loss of her honor can indeed teach her this, and even though she does not set a high estimate on the judgment of men, she can at any rate avoid their condolence. And so everything is in order, and she can reckon pretty safely on going through life without awakening any suspicion in the minds of the curious multitude, which is usually as stupid as it is curious. She is in lawful and undisputed possession of her grief, and only if she should be so unfortunate as to come in contact with a professional prowler will she have a more searching examination to fear.

What goes on within her? Does she grieve? Indeed she does! But how shall we designate this grief? I should call it a worry about sustenance; for a man's life consists not alone in meat and drink; the soul also requires nourishment. She is young, and yet her life's supply is exhausted, but it does not follow that she dies. In this respect she is every day anxious for the morrow. She cannot give up her love for him, and yet he deceived her; but if he deceived her then her love has lost its power to nourish her. Aye, had he not deceived her, had a higher power torn him away, then she would have been as well supplied as any woman could wish; for the memory of Don Juan was considerably more than many a living husband. But if she gives up her love, then is she reduced to beggary, then she must return to the cloister in shame and dishonor. Ah, if even this could buy back his love again! So she lives on. The present day, it seems to her, she can still endure, there is still something to live on; but the next day, that she fears for. As she considers over and over again, she seizes every way out, and yet she finds none, and so she can never grieve connectedly and soundly, because she always seeks to discover how she ought to grieve.

"I will forget him, I will tear his image out of my heart, I will search through my soul like a consuming fire, and every thought that belongs to him shall be destroyed; only then can I be saved; it is self-defense, and if I do not tear out every thought of him, even the most remote, I am lost; only in this way can I defend myself. Myself—what is this myself? Wretchedness and misery. To my first love I was faithless, and now shall I try to make up for it by becoming faithless to my second love?"

"No, I will hate him; only so can my soul find satisfaction, only so can I find rest and occupation for my thoughts. I will weave a garland of curses from everything that reminds me of him, and for every kiss I say: Curses upon you! and for every time he has embraced me: Ten times accursed! and for every time he swore he loved me, I shall swear that I hate him. This shall be my work, my task, to which I dedicate myself; in the convent I learned to tell my rosary, and so I become a nun after all, praying early and late. Or should I be content that he has once loved me? Perhaps I ought to be a sensible woman who does not cast him away in proud contempt, now that I know he is a deceiver; perhaps I ought to be a good housewife, thrifty enough to make a little go as far as possible. No, I will hate him, for this is the only way in which I can tear myself away from him, and prove to myself that I do not need him. But do I not owe him something when I hate him? Do I not live on his bounty? for what else is it that feeds my hate, except my love for him?"

"He was not a deceiver, he had no conception of what a woman can suffer. If he had, he would never have forsaken me. He was a man, wholly self-contained. Is that then a comfort to me? Certainly, for my suffering and my torture prove to me how happy I have been, so happy that he can have had no conception of it. Why then do I complain because a man is not like a woman, not as happy as she is when she is happy, not as unhappy as she is when she is infinitely unhappy, because her happiness had no bounds?"

"Did he deceive me? No! Had he promised me anything? No! My Juan was no suitor, he was no wretched poltroon; for such, a nun does not degrade herself. He did not ask for my hand; he stretched out his own, and I seized it; he looked at me, and I was his; he opened his arms, and I belonged to him. I clung to him as a vine clings. I twined myself about him; I reclined my head upon his breast and looked into this omnipotent face, by which he ruled the world, and which nevertheless rested on me as if I were the whole world for him; like a nursing infant, I drank fullness and wealth and blessing. Can I ask for more? Was I not his? Was he not mine? And if he was not, was not I, nonetheless, his? When the gods visited the earth and loved women, did they remain faithful to them? And yet no one thinks of saying that they deceived them! And why not, unless it is that a woman ought to be proud of having been loved by a god. And what are all the gods of Olympus in comparison with my Juan! Ought I not to be proud, should I degrade him, should I insult him in my thoughts, allow myself to place him in the strait-jacket of the miserable laws that hold for ordinary men? No, I will be proud that he loved me, that he was greater than the gods, and I will honor him by making myself nothing. I will love him because he belonged to me, love him because he left me, and I am still his constantly, and I will treasure what he squanders."

"No, I cannot think of him; every time I remember him, every time my thought approaches the hiding place in my heart where his memory dwells, then it is as if I committed a new sin; I feel an anguish, an inexpressible anguish, an anguish like that I felt in the convent when I sat in my solitary cell and waited for him, and the thoughts terrified me: the severe contempt of the prioress, the convent's terrible punishment, my crime against God. And yet did not this anguish form part and parcel of my love for him? What would it have been without it? He was not indeed consecrated to me, we had not received the blessing of the Church, no bells had rung for us, no hymns were sung; and yet, what were all the music and solemnity of the Church, how might it have power over my mood in comparison with this anguish!—But then he came, and the discord of my anguish resolved itself into the harmony of the most blessed safety, and only sweet tremblings moved my soul. Shall I then fear this anguish, does it not remind me of him, is it not a promise of his coming? If I could remember him without the anguish, I would not be remembering him. He comes, he commands stillness, he governs the spirits that desire to tear me away from him. I am his, blessed in him."

If I were to imagine a human being in a wreck at sea, unconcerned for his life, remaining on board because there was something he wanted to save and yet could not save, because he could not decide what it was he should save, then would I have a picture of Elvira; she is in distress at sea, her destruction impends, but this does not worry her, she does not notice it, she is hesitating about what she should save.

III. MARGARET

We know this young woman from Goethe's *Faust*. She was a little girl from the middle class, not, like Elvira, destined for a convent; but yet brought up in the fear of the Lord, although her soul was too childlike to feel the earnestness of it, as Goethe so incomparably says:

> *Halb Kinderspiel,*
> *Halb Gott im Herzen.*[18]

What we especially love in this girl is the charming simplicity and humility of her pure soul. The first time she sees Faust, she feels herself too humble to be loved by him, and it is not out of curiosity to learn whether Faust loves her that she plucks the petals from the daisy, but from humility, because she feels herself too unworthy to make a choice, and therefore bows to the oracular dictum of a mysterious power. Aye, lovely Margaret! Goethe has told us how you plucked the petals and recited the words: he loves me, he loves me not; poor Margaret, you can now continue this occupation, only changing the words: he deceived me, he deceived me not; you can plant a little plot of ground with these flowers, and you will have handiwork for the rest of your life.

Someone has remarked that it is noteworthy that while the folk-tale about Don Juan tells of 1,003 victims in Spain alone, the story of Faust tells of only one woman seduced by him. It will be worth while not to forget this observation, since it will have significance in what follows, and will guide us in determining the characteristic of Margaret's reflective grief. At first sight it might seem that the only difference between Elvira and Margaret was that which exists between two individuals who have had the same experience. The difference is, however, far more essential, not based so much upon the different personalities of the two women, as upon the essential difference between a Don Juan and a Faust. From the very beginning there must be a difference between an Elvira and a Margaret, inasmuch as a woman by whom a Faust is affected must be essentially different from a woman who affects a Don Juan; even if I imagined that it was the same woman who attracted the attention of both, it would still be something different which attracted the one from that which attracted the other. The difference which thus might from the beginning be present only as a possibility would, by being brought into relation with a Faust or a Don Juan, develop into a complete actuality. Faust is indeed a reproduction of Don Juan; but precisely because he is a reproduction, it makes him, even at that stage of his life in which one might call him a Don Juan, essentially different from the other; for to reproduce another stage does not mean merely to become this stage, but to become it with all the elements of the preceding stage within one's self. Even if he desires the same thing as a Don Juan, he still desires it in a different manner. But in order for him to desire it in a different manner, it must also be present in a different manner. There are elements in him which make his method different, just as there are also elements in Margaret which make another method necessary. His method depends upon his inclination, and his inclination is different from Don Juan's, even if there is an essential likeness between them.

It is usually thought to be very clever to say that Faust finally becomes a Don Juan, but this means very little, since the real question is in what sense he becomes one. Faust is a daemonic figure like a Don Juan, but higher. The sensuous first becomes significant for him only after he has lost an entire preceding world, but the consciousness of this loss is not erased, it is constantly present, and he seeks therefore in the sensuous not so much enjoyment as diversion of mind. His doubting soul finds nothing in which it can rest, and now he reaches after love, not because he believes in it, but because it has a present element in which there is rest for a moment, and a striving which distracts and diverts his attention from the nothingness of doubt. Hence his enjoyment does not have the cheerful serenity which distinguishes a Don Juan. His countenance is not wreathed in smiles, his brow is not unclouded, and happiness is not his companion; the young women do not dance into his embrace, but he frightens them to him. What he seeks is not merely the pleasure of the sensuous, but what he desires is the immediacy of the spirit. As the shades of the underworld, when they got hold of a living being, sucked his blood, and lived as long as this blood warmed and nourished them, so Faust seeks an immediate life by which he can be renewed and strengthened. And where can this be found better than in a young woman, and how can he absorb it more perfectly than in the embrace of love? As the Middle Ages tell of sorcerers who understood how to prepare an elixir for the renewal of youth, and used the heart of an innocent child for that purpose, so is this the strengthening potion his starved soul needs, the only thing which is able to satisfy him for a moment. His sick soul needs what I might call a young heart's first green shoots; and with what else shall I compare an innocent feminine soul's first youth? If I were to call it a blossom, I should say too little, for it is more, it is a flowering: the soundness of hope and faith and trust shoots forth and blossoms in rich variety, and soft impulses move the delicate shoots, and dreams shade their fruitfulness. Thus it affects a Faust, it beckons to his restless soul like a peaceful isle in the quiet sea. That it is transient no one knows better than Faust; he does not believe in it any more than he believes in anything else; but that it exists, of that he convinces himself in the embrace of love. Only the fullness of innocence and childlikeness can for a moment refresh him.

In Goethe's *Faust*, Mephistopheles shows him Margaret in a mirror. His eye finds enjoyment in the vision, but it is not her beauty that he desires, although he accepts that also. What he desires is the pure, rich, untroubled, immediate happiness of a woman's soul, but he desires it not spiritually, but sensually. Hence, he desires in a certain sense like Don Juan, but yet quite otherwise. Here perhaps one or another *privatdocent,* who is convinced of having been a Faust, since otherwise he could not possibly have become a *privatdocent,* will remark that Faust requires intellectual culture and breeding in the woman who shall attract him. Perhaps a large number of *privatdocents* would consider this an excellent remark, and their respective wives and sweethearts nod assent. However, it is completely beside the point; for Faust would desire nothing less. A so-called cultured woman would belong within the same relativity as himself, and would have no significance for him, would be simply nothing. By her crumb of culture she might perhaps tempt this old Magister of doubt to take her out on the stream, where she would soon despair. An innocent young girl, however, belongs within another relativity, and is therefore, in a certain sense, nothing over against Faust, and yet, in another sense, tremendously much, since she is immediacy. Only in this immediacy is she the goal of his desire, and therefore I said that he desires immediacy, not spiritually but sensually.

Goethe perfectly perceived all this, and hence we find Margaret an ordinary little maiden, a girl one is almost tempted to call insignificant. Since it is of importance with respect to Margaret's sorrow, we shall consider a little more in detail how Faust must have impressed her. The individual traits that Goethe has emphasized have naturally great value; and yet I believe that for the sake of completeness we must imagine a little modification. In her innocent simplicity Margaret soon notices that all is not as it should be with Faust in respect to his faith. In Goethe this is brought out in a little catechismal scene, which is undeniably an excellent invention by the poet. The question is, what consequences this examination may have on their relation to one another. Faust appears in the role of a doubter, and it seems that Goethe, since he has not suggested anything further in this respect, has wished to let Faust continue to be a doubter also, as over against Margaret. He has attempted to divert her attention from all such inquiries, and to fix it solely and alone on the reality of love. But partly I believe that this would be a difficult task for Faust, after the issue has once been raised, and partly I believe it is not psychologically correct. I would not dwell further on this point for Faust's sake, but for Margaret's sake; for if he has not revealed himself to her as a doubter, her sorrow has an additional moment. Faust is then a doubter, but he is no vain fool, who merely wishes to feel his own significance by doubting what others believe; his doubt has an objective ground in himself. So much must be said in fairness to Faust.

As soon, however, as he would try to involve others in his doubt, there can easily intermingle with it an impure passion. As soon as doubt is urged upon others, an envy may be at work which finds satisfaction in depriving them of that which they regard as sure. But in order that this passion of envy should be aroused in the doubter, there must be some opposition from the individual in question. Where there can either be no opposition, or where it would be impossible to think it, there the temptation ceases. This last is the case with a young girl. Over against her, a doubter finds himself embarrassed. To deprive her of her faith is no task for him; on the contrary he feels that it is only through her faith that she is the great person she is. He feels himself humbled, for there is in her a natural demand that he should protect her, in so far as she has become uncertain. Aye, a poor wretch of a doubter, a half-baked thief, might perhaps find satisfaction in depriving a young girl of her faith, feel a joy in frightening women and children, since he cannot terrify men. But this is not true of Faust, he is too great for that. We may well agree with Goethe, then, that Faust betrays his doubt the first time, but I scarcely think that it will happen a second time. This is of great importance with respect to our conception of Margaret. Faust readily perceives that Margaret's entire significance depends on her innocent simplicity; if this is taken away, then she is nothing in herself, nothing to him. This must therefore be preserved. He is a doubter; but as such he has all the moments of the positive within himself, for otherwise he is a poor doubter. He lacks the final conclusion; herewith all the moments become negative moments. She, on the contrary, has the conclusion; she has childlikeness and innocence. Nothing is therefore easier than for him to endow her. His experience has frequently taught him that what he presented as doubt has affected others as positive truth. Now he finds his happiness in enriching her with the whole wealth of a view of life, he brings forth all the treasures of an immediate faith; he delights in festively adorning her with them, because they are suited to her, and she thereby becomes more beautiful in his eyes. Besides, he also derives from this the advantage that her soul comes to cling to him more and more closely. She does not really understand him; as a child she clings to him, for what is doubt to him is for her irrefragable truth. But while he thus builds up her faith, he at the same time undermines it, for he becomes at last an object of faith to her, a god and not a man.

But here I must seek to forestall a misunderstanding. It might seem that I make Faust a contemptible hypocrite. This is by no means the case. Margaret herself has brought the matter up; with half a glance he surveys the whole glory she thinks she possesses, and perceives that it cannot stand against his doubt; but he has no wish to annihilate it, and his conduct toward her is even dictated by a sort of benevolence. Her love gives her significance for him, and yet she remains almost a child; he descends to her level, and finds his happiness in seeing how she appropriates everything. For Margaret's future, however, this brings sorry consequences. Had Faust stood out before her as a doubter, then she might later perhaps have been able to save her faith; she would then in all humility have acknowledged that his high-flown and daring thoughts were not for her; she would have held fast to what she had. But now, however, she owes to him the content of her faith, and yet she perceives, since he has abandoned her, that he has not believed in it himself. As long as he was with her, she did not discover the doubt; now that he is gone, everything is changed for her, and she sees doubt everywhere, a doubt she cannot control, since she always thinks it with the circumstance that Faust himself had not been able to master it.

The source of Faust's fascination for Margaret, according to Goethe also, is not the seductiveness of a Don Juan, but his tremendous superiority. Hence she simply cannot understand, as she herself says so lovably, what it is that Faust sees in her to love. The first impression she receives of him is altogether overwhelming; she becomes an absolute nothing over against him. She belongs to him, therefore, not in the same sense as Elvira belongs to Don Juan, for this still expresses an independent existence over against him, but Margaret vanishes altogether in him; she does not break with heaven to belong to him, for therein would lie a justification against him; unnoticeably, without the slightest reflection, he becomes her all. But just as from the beginning she is nothing, so, if I may venture to say so, she becomes less and less the more she is convinced of his almost divine superiority; she is nothing, and exists only in him. What Goethe has somewhere said about Hamlet, that in relation to his body his soul was an acorn planted in a flower-pot, which at last breaks the container,[19] is also true of Margaret's love. Faust is too great for her, and her love must finally break her soul in pieces. And the moment for this soon comes, for Faust doubtless feels that she cannot remain in this immediacy; he does not carry her up in the higher regions of the spirit, for it is from these he flees; he desires her sensually—and abandons her.

Faust has accordingly abandoned Margaret. Her loss is so terrible that the environment itself forgets for a moment what it otherwise finds so hard to forget, that she has been dishonored; she sinks back in total impotence, in which she is not even able to think of her loss; even the power to form a conception of her misfortune has been taken from her. If this condition could continue, it would be impossible for reflective grief to gain a foothold. But the grounds of solace afforded by her surroundings will little by little bring her to herself, give her thought an impulse by which it again comes into motion; but as soon as it begins to move, it readily appears that she is not able to hold fast a single one of its considerations. She listens to it as if it were not to her that its words are addressed, and not a word of it halts or advances the disquiet in her train of thought. Her problem is the same as Elvira's, to think that Faust was a deceiver, but it is still more difficult, because she is more deeply impressed by Faust than Elvira is by Don Juan. He was not only a deceiver, but he was a hypocrite; she has not given up anything for him, but she owes him everything, and this everything she still possesses to a certain degree, except that it now reveals itself as a deception. But is then what he said less true because he has not believed it himself? By no means, and yet it is so for her, for she believed it through him.

It might seem that it would be more difficult for reflection to be set in motion in Margaret; that which really tends to stop it is the feeling that she was absolutely nothing. And yet there lies in this a tremendous dialectical elasticity. If she were able to hold the thought fast that she was, in the strictest sense of the word, absolutely nothing, then reflection would be excluded, and then she would not have been deceived; for when you are nothing, then there is no relation, and where there is no relation, there can be no talk of a deception. So far she is at peace. However, this thought cannot be held fast, but instantly changes into its opposite. That she was nothing is merely an expression for the fact that all the finite differences of love are negatived, and is therefore the exact expression for the absolute validity of her love, wherein again lies her absolute justification. His conduct is then not merely a deception, but an absolute deception, because her love was absolute. And herein she will again be unable to find rest; for since he has been her all, she will not even be able to hold this thought fast except through him; but she cannot think it through him, because he was a deceiver.

As her environment becomes more and more alien to her, the inner movement begins. She has not merely loved Faust with all her soul, but he was her vital force, through him she came into being. This has the effect, while her soul is not less moved than Elvira's, of making the individual moods less violent. She is on the way to acquiring a fundamental emotional tone, and the individual mood is like a bubble rising from the deep without strength to maintain itself, which is not so much replaced by a new bubble as it is dissolved in the general mood that she is nothing. This fundamental mood is again a state of mind that is felt, that does not receive expression in any particular outbreak; it is inexpressible, and the attempt that each particular mood makes to give life to it, to raise it up, is in vain. The total mood is therefore constantly present as an undertone in each particular mood, creating for it a resonance of impotence and faintness. The individual mood gives it expression, but it does not soothe, it does not ease, it is—to use an expression of my Swedish Elvira which is certainly very apt, though a man will scarcely feel its full import—like a false sigh which disappoints, and not like a genuine sigh, which is strengthening and beneficial. Nor is the individual mood full-toned and energetic, since her expression is too heavily encumbered.

"Can I forget him? Can the brook, then, however far it continues to flow, forget the spring, forget its source, cut itself off from the fountainhead? Then must it cease to flow! Can the arrow, however swift it flies, forget the bowstring? Then must its motion cease. Can the raindrop, however far it falls, forget the sky from which it fell? Then must it dissolve itself. Can I become another being, can I be born again of a mother who is not my mother? Can I forget him? Then I must cease to be!"

"Can I remember him? Can my memory call him forth, now that he is vanished, I who am myself only a memory of him? This pallid, dim image, is this the Faust I worshipped? I remember his words, but I do not possess the harp in his voice! I remember his speeches, but my breast is too weak to complete them. Meaningless they sound forth on deaf ears!"

"Faust, O Faust! turn back, satisfy the hungry soul, clothe the naked, refresh the faint, visit the solitary! Well do I know that my love had no meaning for you, neither did I demand it. My love laid itself humbly at your feet, my sigh was a prayer, my kiss a thank-offering, my embrace an act of worship. Will you therefore forsake me? Did you not know it from the beginning? Or does it not constitute a ground for loving me that I need you, that my soul dies if you are not with me?"

"God in heaven, forgive me that I have loved a human being more than Thee, and still do so; I know that it is a new sin for me to speak so to Thee. Eternal Love, O may Thy mercy sustain me; do not reject me, give him back to me, incline his heart to me again, have pity upon me, Thou Pity, that I pray thus again!"

"Can I then curse him? What am I, that I should thus dare? Can the earthen vessel presume against the potter?

What was I? Nothing! the clay in his hand, a rib in his side from which he made me! What was I? A lowly plant, and he bent down to me; he caused me to grow; he was my all, my god, the source of my thought, my soul's nourishment!"

"Can I grieve? No, no! Grief settles like a night fog over my soul. O turn back, I will give you up, never demand to belong to you; only sit by my side, look at me, that I may gain strength to sigh; speak to me, speak to me about yourself as if you were a stranger, I will forget that it is you; speak, that the tears may burst forth. Am I then absolutely nothing, unable even to weep without him?"

"Where shall I find rest and peace? The thoughts arise in my soul, the one against the other, the one confounding the other. When you were with me, then they obeyed your least hint, then I played with them like a child, I wove garlands of them and placed them on my head. I let them flutter like my hair loose in the wind. Now they twine themselves terrifyingly about me, like serpents they twist themselves around me and crush my anguished soul."

"And I am a mother! A living creature demands nourishment from me. Can then the hungry satisfy the hungry, the faint slake the thirst of the thirsty? Shall I then become a murderer? O Faust, return, save the child in the womb, even though you do not care to save the mother!"

So she is moved, not by moods, but in her mood; but there is no relief for her in the expression of the individual mood, because it dissolves itself in the total mood which she cannot raise. Aye, if Faust had been taken from her, Margaret would not seek any relief; in her eyes her lot would have been an enviable one; but she is deceived. She lacks what might be called the situation of sorrow, for she cannot grieve alone. Aye, if like poor Florine in the fairy story,[20] she could find access to some cave of echoes, from which she knew that every sigh, every complaint, was wafted to her lover, then she would not only, like Florine, spend three nights there, but she would remain day and night; but in Faust's palace there is no echo-cave, and he has no ear in her heart.

Too long, perhaps, I have already engrossed your attention with these pictures, dear Symparanekromenoi, and
that so much the more, since in spite of all that I have said,
nothing visible has appeared before you. Yet this does not
have its ground in the deceptiveness of my presentation,
but in the matter itself, and in the craftiness of grief.
When a favorable occasion arises, then the hidden reveals
itself. This we have in our power, and we shall now in farewell let these three brides of sorrow come together, let them
embrace one another in the unison of grief, let them form
a group before us, a tabernacle, where the voice of sorrow
is never silenced, where the sigh never ceases, because they
watch more scrupulously and more faithfully than vestal
virgins over the observance of the sacred rites. Should we
interrupt them in this occupation, should we wish them a
restoration of what they have lost, would that be a gain
for them? Have they not already received a higher consecration? And this consecration will unite them, and throw
a beauty over their union, and bring them relief in the
union; for only he who has been bitten by a serpent knows
the suffering of one who has been bitten by a serpent.

THE UNHAPPIEST MAN

An enthusiastic address before
the
SYMPARANEKROMENOI
Peroration presented at the Friday meeting

Somewhere in England there is said to be a grave which is distinguished not by a splendid monument, nor by its melancholy surroundings, but by a brief inscription: The Unhappiest Man.[1] Someone must have opened the grave, but had found no trace of a body. Which is the more astonishing, that no body was found, or that the grave was opened? It is indeed strange that anyone should have taken the trouble to see whether there was a body there or not. Sometimes when you read a name in an epitaph, you wonder what manner of life was his who bore it, and you wish you might step down into the grave to converse with him. But this inscription is so significant! A book may have a title which makes you wish to read the book, but a title can be so richly suggestive of thought, so personally appealing, as to leave you with no desire to read the book. This inscription is indeed so significant—harrowing or comforting according to one's mood—for everyone who has in quietness secretly cherished the thought that he was the unhappiest of men. But I can imagine a man, whose soul has never known such thoughts, to whom it would be a matter of curiosity to find out whether there actually was a body in this grave. And lo, the tomb was empty! Is he perhaps risen from the dead? Has he perhaps wished to mock the poet's word:

> . . . In the grave there is peace,
> Its silent dweller from grief knows release.[2]

Did he find no rest, not even in the grave; does he perhaps wander restlessly about in the world? Has he forsaken his dwelling-place, his home, leaving only his address behind! Or has he not yet been found, he the unhappiest man, who is not even pursued by the furies until he finds the door of the sanctuary and the seat of the humble suppliant, but who is kept alive by sorrow and by sorrow pursued to the grave![3]

If it is true that he has not yet been found, then, dear Symparanekromenoi, let us begin upon a pilgrimage, not as crusaders to seek the sacred tomb in the happy east, but to find this melancholy grave in the unhappy west. At that empty tomb we shall seek for him, the unhappiest man, certain to find him; for as the faithful long to see the sacred tomb, so do the unhappy feel themselves drawn toward that empty tomb in the west, each filled with the thought that it is destined for him.

Or is not such an inquiry worthy of our attention, we whose activities, in conformity with the sacred tradition of our society, are essays devoted to the aphoristical and the accidental, we who do not merely think and speak aphoristically but live aphoristically, we who live *aphorismenoi* and *segregati*,[4] like aphorisms in life, without community of men, without sharing their griefs and their joys; we who are not consonantal sounds in the alarums of life, but solitary birds in the stillness of night, gathering together only occasionally, to be edified by considering the wretchedness of life, the length of the day, and the endless permanence of time; we, dear Symparanekromenoi, who have no faith in the game of happiness or the luck of fools, who believe in nothing save misfortune.

Behold how the unhappy crowd forward in countless multitudes! Many are they who believe themselves called, but few are the chosen. A distinction must be made between them—a word, and the crowd vanishes; excluded are they, the uninvited guests, who think death to be the greatest misfortune, who became unhappy because they fear death; for we, dear Symparanekromenoi, we, like the Roman soldiers, fear not death; we know of greater misfortunes, and first and last and above all—life. If indeed there were some human being who could not die, if the story told of the Wandering Jew be true, then how could we hesitate to declare him the unhappiest of men? Then we could also explain why the tomb was empty, in order to signify, namely, that the unhappiest man was the one who could not die, could not slip down into a grave. The case would then be decided, the answer easy: for the unhappiest man was the one who could not die, the happy, he who could; happy he who died in his old age, happier, whoever died in his youth, happiest he who died at birth, happiest of all he who never was born. But it is not so; death is the common lot of all men, and in so far as the unhappiest man is not yet found, he will have to be sought within this universal limitation.

Behold the crowd vanishes, its number is diminished. I do not now say: grant me your attention, for I know I have it; nor do I say: lend me your ears, for I know they belong to me. Your eyes shine, you rise in your seats. It is a contest for a wager, which it is indeed worth participating in, a struggle even more terrible than one of life and death; for death we do not fear. But the reward, aye, it is more glorious than any other in the world, and more certain; for he who is assured that he is the unhappiest man need fear no good fortune; he will not taste the humiliation in his last hour of having to cry: Solon, Solon, Solon![5]

So we open a free competition, from which no one is excluded by virtue of rank or age. No one is excluded except the happy, and he who fears death—every worthy member of the community of the unhappy is welcome, there is a seat of honor for every really unhappy person, the grave for the unhappiest of all. My voice sounds forth through the world: "Hear you, all you who call yourselves unhappy, and do not fear death." My voice rings back into the past; for we would not be sophistical enough to exclude the dead because they are dead, for they have once lived. "I beseech you, forgive that I disturb your rest for a moment; meet us here by this empty tomb." Thrice I let the call ring forth over the world: "Hear this, you unhappy ones." For it is not our intention to decide this matter among ourselves in a corner. The place is found where it must be decided before all the world.

But before we examine the claimants, let us make ourselves fit to sit here as worthy judges and competitors. Let us reinforce our thought, let us arm it to withstand the seductiveness of words; for what voice is so insinuating as that of the unhappiest, which so beguiling as that of the unhappiest when he speaks of his own unhappiness? Let us make ourselves fit to sit as judges and competitors so that we do not lose the sense of proportion, nor become disturbed by the individual claims; for the eloquence of grief is boundless and infinitely inventive. Let us divide the unhappy into groups, and admit only one spokesman for each group; for this we shall not deny, that it is not some particular individual who is the unhappiest, but it is a class; but, therefore, we shall not hesitate to assign the representative of this class the name: the unhappiest, nor hesitate to assign him the tomb.

In each of Hegel's systematic writings there is a section which treats of the unhappy consciousness.[6] One approaches the reading of such inquiries with an inner restlessness, with a trembling of the heart, with a fear lest one learn too much, or too little. The unhappy consciousness is a term which, when casually introduced, almost makes the blood run cold, and the nerves to quiver; and then to see it so expressly emphasized, like the mysterious sentence in a story of Clemens Brentano's, *tertia nux mors est*[7]—it is enough to make one tremble like a sinner. Ah, happy he who has nothing more to do with it than to write a paragraph on the subject, happier still, he who can write the next. The unhappy person is one who has his ideal, the content of his life, the fullness of his consciousness, the essence of his being, in some manner outside of himself. He is always absent, never present to himself. But it is evident that it is possible to be absent from one's self either in the past or in the future. This, then, at once circumscribes the entire territory of the unhappy consciousness. For this rigid limitation we are grateful to Hegel; and now, since we are not merely philosophers beholding the kingdom from afar, we shall as native inhabitants give our attention in detail to the various types which are implied herein. The unhappy person is consequently absent. But one is absent when living either in the past or in the future. The form of expression must here be carefully noted; for it is clear, as philology also teaches us, that there is a tense which expresses presence in the past, and a tense which expresses presence in the future; but the same science also teaches us that there is a tense which is *plus quam perfectum*, in which there is no present, as well as a *futurum exactum* of an analogous character. Now there are some individuals who live in hope, and others who live in memory. These are indeed in a sense unhappy individuals, in so far, namely, as they live solely in hope or in memory, if ordinarily only he is happy who is present to himself. However, one cannot in a strict sense be called an unhappy individual, who is present in hope or in memory. That which must here be emphasized is that he is present to himself in one or the other of these forms of consciousness. We shall also see from this that a single blow, be it ever so heavy, cannot possibly make a man the unhappiest of all. For one blow can either deprive him of hope, thereby leaving him present in memory, or of memory, thus leaving him present in hope. We now go on to get a more detailed description of the unhappy individual.

First we shall consider the man of hope. When he as a hoping individual (and in so far, of course, unhappy) is not present to himself in his hope, then he becomes in the stricter sense unhappy. An individual who hopes for an eternal life is, indeed, in a certain sense unhappy, since he has renounced the present, but not yet in the strict sense, because he is himself present in this hope, and does not come into conflict with the individual moments of the finite life. But if he does not become present to himself in this hope, but loses his hope and then hopes again and again loses, and so on, he is absent from himself, not only with respect to the present, but also with respect to the future; this gives us one type of the unhappy consciousness. In the case of the man of memory the case is parallel. If he can find himself present in the past, he is not in the strict sense unhappy; but if he cannot, but is constantly absent from himself in the past, then we have another type of unhappiness.

Memory is emphatically the real element of the unhappy, as is natural, because the past has the remarkable characteristic that it is past, the future, that it is yet to come, whence one may say that in a certain sense the future is nearer the present than is the past. In order that the man of hope may be able to find himself in the future, the future must have reality, or, rather, it must have reality for him; in order that the man of memory may find himself in the past, the past must have had reality for him. But when the man of hope would have a future which can have no reality for him, or the man of memory would remember a past which has had no reality, then we have the essentially unhappy individuals. It might seem as if the first supposition were impossible, or sheer lunacy; however, it is not so; for though the hoping individual does not hope for something which has no reality for him, he may nevertheless hope for something which he himself knows cannot be realized. For when an individual loses his hope, and then instead of taking refuge in memory, continues to hope, then we have such a type. When an individual who loses his memory, or who has nothing to remember, will not become a hoping individual, but continues to be a man of memory, then we have one type of unhappiness. If thus an individual buried himself in antiquity, or in the Middle Ages, or in any other period of time so that this had an authentic reality for him, or if he lost himself in his own childhood or youth, so that these things had an authentic reality for him, then he would not in a strict sense be an unhappy individual. On the other hand, if I imagine a man who himself had had no childhood, this age having passed him by without attaining essential significance for him, but who now, perhaps by becoming a teacher of youth, discovered all the beauty that there is in childhood, and who would now remember his own childhood, constantly staring back at it, then I should have an excellent illustration of this type of unhappiness. Too late he would have discovered the significance of that which was past for him but which he still desired to remember in its significance. If I imagined a man who had lived without real appreciation of the pleasures or joy of life, and who now on his deathbed gets his eyes opened to these things, if I imagined that he did not die (which would be the most fortunate thing) but lived on, though without living his life over again—such a man would have to be considered in our quest for the unhappiest man.

The unhappiness of hope is never so painful as the unhappiness of memory. The man of hope always has a more tolerable disappointment to bear. It follows that the unhappiest man will have to be sought among the unhappy individuals of memory.

Let us proceed. Let us imagine a combination of the two stricter types of unhappiness already described. The unhappy man of hope could not find himself present in his hope, just as the unhappy man of memory could not find himself present in his memory. There can be but one combination of these two types, and this happens when it is memory which prevents the unhappy individual from finding himself in his hope, and hope which prevents him from finding himself in his memory. When this happens, it is, on the one hand, due to the fact that he constantly hopes something that should be remembered; his hope constantly disappoints him and, in disappointing him, reveals to him that it is not because the realization of his hope is postponed, but because it is already past and gone, has already been experienced, or should have been experienced, and thus has passed over into memory. On the other hand, it is due to the fact that he always remembers that for which he ought to hope; for the future he has already anticipated in thought, in thought already experienced it, and this experience he now remembers, instead of hoping for it. Consequently, what he hopes for lies behind him, what he remembers lies before him. His life is not so much lived regressively as it suffers a two-fold reversal. He will soon notice his misfortune even if he is not able to understand the reason for it. To make sure, however, that he really shall have opportunity to feel it, misunderstanding puts in its appearance to mock him at each moment in a curious way.

In the ordinary course of things, he enjoys the reputation of being in full possession of his five senses, and yet he knows that if he were to explain to a single person just how it is with him, he would be declared mad. This is quite enough to drive a man mad, and yet he does not become so, and this is precisely his misfortune. His misfortune is that he has come into the world too soon, and therefore he always comes too late. He is constantly quite near his goal, and in the same moment he is far away from it; he finds that what now makes him unhappy because he has it,

or because he is this way, is just what a few years ago
would have made him happy if he had had it then, while
then he was unhappy because he did not have it. His life
is empty, like that of Ancaeus, of whom it is customary to
say that nothing is known about him except that he gave
rise to the proverb: "There's many a slip 'twixt the cup and
the lip"—as if this was not more than enough.[8] His life is
restless and without content; he does not live in the present,
he does not live in the future, for the future has already
been experienced; he does not live in the past, for the past
has not yet come. So like Latona, he is driven about in the
Hyperborean darkness, or to the bright isles of the equator,
and cannot bring to birth though he seems constantly on
the verge.[9] Alone by himself he stands in the wide world.
He has no contemporary time to support him; he has no
past to long for, since his past has not yet come; he has
no future to hope for, since his future is already past.
Alone, he has the whole world over against him as the *alter*
with which he finds himself in conflict; for the rest of the
world is to him only one person, and this person, this
inseparable, importunate friend, is Misunderstanding. He
cannot become old, for he has never been young; he cannot
become young, for he is already old. In one sense of the
word he cannot die, for he has not really lived; in another
sense he cannot live, for he is already dead. He cannot love,
for love is in the present, and he has no present, no future,
and no past; and yet he has a sympathetic nature, and he
hates the world only because he loves it. He has no passion, not because he is destitute of it, but because simultaneously he has the opposite passion. He has no time for
anything, not because his time is taken up with something
else, but because he has no time at all. He is impotent, not
because he has no energy, but because his own energy
makes him impotent.

And now our hearts are indeed sufficiently steeled, our
ears stopped, even if not closed. We have listened to the
cool voice of deliberation; let us now hear the eloquence
of passion—brief, pithy, as all passion is.

There stands a young woman. She complains that her

lover has been faithless. This we cannot take into consideration. But she loved him, and him alone, in all the world. She loved him with all her heart, and with all her soul, and with all her mind—then let her remember and grieve.

Is this a real being, or is it an image, a living person who dies, or a corpse who lives? It is Niobe.[10] She lost all at a single blow; she lost that to which she gave life, she lost that which gave her life. Look up to her, dear Symparanekromenoi, she stands a little higher than the world, on a burial mound, like a monument. No hope allures her, no future moves her, no prospect tempts her, no hope excites her—hopeless she stands, petrified in memory; for a single moment she was unhappy, in that same moment she became happy, and nothing can take her happiness from her; the world changes, but she knows no change; and time flows on, but for her there is no future time.

See yonder, what a beautiful union! The one generation clasps hands with the next! Is it unto blessing, unto loyal fellowship, unto the joy of the dance? It is the outcast house of Oedipus, and the curse is transmitted from one generation to the next, until it crushes the last of the race —Antigone. Yet she is provided for; the sorrow of a family is enough for one human life. She has turned her back on hope, she has exchanged its instability for the faithfulness of memory. Be happy, dear Antigone! We wish you a long life, significant as a deep sigh. May no forgetfulness deprive you of aught, may the daily bitterness of grief be yours in fullest measure!

A powerful figure appears, but he is not alone, he has friends, how comes he here then? It is Job, the patriarch of grief—and his friends. He lost all, but not at a single blow; for the Lord took, and the Lord took, and the Lord took. Friends taught him to feel the bitterness of his loss; for the Lord gave, and the Lord gave, and the Lord also gave him a foolish wife into the bargain.[11] He lost all; for what he retained lies outside the scope of our interest. Respect him, dear Symparanekromenoi, for his gray hairs and his unhappiness. He lost all; but he had possessed it.

His hair is gray, his head bent low, his countenance

downcast, his soul troubled. It is the father of the prodigal son. Like Job he lost his most precious possession. Yet it was not the Lord who took it, but the enemy. He did not lose it, but he is losing it; it is not taken away from him, but it vanishes. He does not sit by the hearth in sackcloth and ashes; he has left his home, forsaken everything to seek the lost. He reaches after him, but his arms do not clasp him; he cries out, but his cries do not overtake him. And yet he hopes even through tears; he sees him from afar, as through a mist; he overtakes him, if only in death. His hope makes him old, and nothing binds him to the world except the hope for which he lives. His feet are weary, his eyes dim, his body yearns for rest, his hope lives. His hair is white, his body decrepit, his feet stumble, his heart breaks, his hope lives. Raise him up, dear Symparanekromenoi, he was unhappy.

Who is this pale figure, unsubstantial as the shadow of the dead? His name has been forgotten, many centuries have passed since his day. He was a youth, he had enthusiasm. He sought martyrdom. In imagination he saw himself nailed to the cross, and the heavens open; but the reality was too heavy for him; enthusiasm vanished, he denied his Master and himself. He wished to lift a world, but he broke down under the strain; his soul was not crushed nor annihilated, but it was broken, and his spirit was enervated, his soul palsied. Congratulate him, dear Symparanekromenoi, for he was unhappy. And yet did he not become happy? He became what he wished, a martyr, even if his martyrdom was not, as he had wished, to be nailed to the cross, nor to be thrown to wild beasts, but to be burned alive, to be slowly consumed by a slow fire.

A young woman sits here of thoughtful mien. Her lover was faithless—but this we cannot take into consideration. Young woman, observe the serious countenances of this society; it has heard of more terrible misfortunes, its daring soul demands something greater still.—Yes, but I loved him and him only in all the world; I loved him with all my soul, and with all my heart, and with all my mind.—You merely repeat what we have already heard before, do not weary our impatient longing; you can remember, and grieve.—No,

I cannot grieve, for he was perhaps not a deceiver, he was perhaps not faithless.—Why, then, can you not grieve? Come nearer, elect among women; forgive the strict censor who sought for a moment to exclude you. You cannot sorrow. Then why not hope?—No, I cannot hope; for he was a riddle.—Well, my girl, I understand you. You stand high in the ranks of the unhappy; behold her, dear Symparanekromenoi, she stands almost at the pinnacle of unhappiness. But you must divide yourself, you must hope by day and grieve by night, or grieve by day and hope by night. Be proud; for happiness is no real ground for pride, but only unhappiness. You are not indeed the unhappiest of all; but it is your opinion, dear Symparanekromenoi, is it not, that we ought to offer her an honorable *accessit*? The tomb we cannot offer her, but the place adjoining shall be hers.

For there he stands, the ambassador from the kingdom of sighs, the chosen favorite of the realm of suffering, the apostle of grief, the silent friend of pain, the unhappy lover of memory, in his memories confounded by the light of hope, in his hope deceived by the shadows of memory.[12] His head hangs heavy, his knees are weak; and yet he seeks no support save in himself. He is faint, and yet how powerful; his eyes seem not to have wept, but to have drunk many tears; and yet there is a fire in them strong enough to destroy a world, but not one splinter of the grief within his breast. He is bent, and yet his youth presages a long life; his lips smile at a world that misunderstands him. Stand up, dear Symparanekromenoi, bow before him, ye witnesses of grief, in this most solemn hour! I hail thee, great unknown, whose name I do not know; I hail thee with thy title of honor: The Unhappiest Man! Welcomed here to your home by the community of the unhappy, greeted here at the entrance to the low and humble dwelling, which is yet prouder than all the palaces of the world. Lo, the stone is rolled away, the grave's shade awaits you with its refreshing coolness. But perhaps your time has not yet come, perhaps the way is long before you; but we promise you to gather here often to envy you your good fortune. Accept then our wish, a good wish: May no one understand you, may all men envy you; may no friend bind himself to you, may no woman love you; may no secret sympathy suspect your lonely pain, may no eye pierce your distant grief; may no ear trace your secret sigh! But perhaps your proud soul spurns such sympathetic wishes, and despises the alleviation, so may the maidens love you; may the pregnant in their anguish seek your aid; may the mothers set their hopes on you, and the dying look to you for comfort; may the youth attach themselves to you; may men depend upon you; may the aged lean upon you as on a staff—may the entire world believe that you are able to make them happy. So live well, then, unhappiest of men! But what do I say: the unhappiest, the happiest, I ought to say, for this is indeed a gift of the gods which no one can give himself. Language fails, and thought is confounded; for who is the happiest, except the unhappiest, and who the unhappiest, except the happiest, and what is life but madness, and faith but folly, and hope but the briefest respite, and love but vinegar in the wound.

He vanished, and we again stand before the empty tomb. Let us then wish him peace and rest and healing, and all possible happiness, and an early death, and an eternal forgetfulness, and no remembrance, lest even the memory of him should make another unhappy.

Arise, dear Symparanekromenoi. The night is spent, and the day begins its unwearied activities, never weary, it seems, of everlastingly repeating itself.

THE FIRST LOVE

A Comedy in One Act by Scribe,
translated by J. L. Heiberg[1]

This article was definitely intended for publication in a periodical which Frederik Unsmann had intended to issue at certain definite intervals. Alas, what are all human intentions!

Anyone who has ever felt an inclination toward literary productivity has certainly noticed that it is a little accidental external circumstance which furnishes the *occasion* for the actual production. Only the authors who in one way or another have been inspired by a definitive purpose will perhaps deny this. This is their own loss, however, for they are thereby deprived of the extreme poles of true and sound productivity. One of these poles is what is traditionally called the invocation of the muse, the other is the occasion. The expression, invocation of the muse, may give rise to a misunderstanding. The call of the muse may partly signify that I call upon the muse, partly that the muse calls upon me. Any author who is naïve enough to believe that everything depends upon honest volition, upon diligence and industry, or who is shameless enough to offer for sale the productions of the spirit, will be sparing neither of zealous invocations nor of audacious importunities. However, not much is accomplished by this, for what Wessel once said regarding the god of taste is still valid: "He whom all call upon, seldom comes."[2] If, however, one understands by this expression that it is the muse who calls, I do not say upon us, but upon the ones concerned, then the saying acquires another significance. While the authors who call upon the muse go on board before she comes, the others, on the contrary, are embarrassed in another way, because—in order that their inward determination may become an outward one—they need one factor more: this is what we call the occasion. When the muse summoned them, she beckoned them away from the world, and they now listen only to her voice, and the wealth of thought lies open before them, but so overpoweringly that although every word stands out clearly and vividly, it seems to them as if it were not their own property. When, then, consciousness has so come to itself that it possesses the entire content, then the moment has arrived which contains the possibility of real creation; and yet something is missing; missing is the occasion, which one might say is

equally necessary, although in another sense, it is infinitely
insignificant. Thus it has pleased the gods to join the greatest contradictions together.[3] This is a mystery in which
reality abounds, a stumbling-block to the Jews, and to the
Greeks foolishness.[4] The occasion is always the accidental,
and this is the tremendous paradox, that the accidental is
just as absolutely necessary as the necessary. The occasion
is not in the ideal sense the accidental, as when I logically
think the accidental; but the occasion is, irrationally regarded, the accidental, and yet in this accidentality, the
necessary.

Regarding what we ordinarily call the occasion, there
rules a great confusion. In part we see too much in it, in
part too little. Every productivity which lies in the category of triviality—and, worse luck, this productivity belongs
especially to the order of the day—overlooks occasion and
inspiration equally. Therefore, too, such a productivity believes, what we may admit, that it is equally suitable at all
times. It entirely overlooks the significance of occasion, that
is to say, it sees an occasion in everything; it is like a garrulous man who sees in the most contradictory things an
occasion to talk about himself and his doings, just as readily
when one has heard it all before as when one has not. But
in this, the salient point is lost. On the other hand, there
is a productivity which falls in love with the occasion. About
the first kind, one may say that it sees an occasion in everything, about the other that it sees everything in the occasion. In this class is included the great body of occasional
authors, the writers of occasional pieces in the more profound sense, as well as those who in a stricter sense see
everything in the occasion, and therefore use the same verse,
the same formulas, and still hope that for the authors concerned, the occasion will be a sufficient occasion for a suitable honorarium.

The occasion which as such is the unessential and accidental can sometimes in our age try its hand at the revolutionary. The occasion quite often plays the master; it decides the matter, it makes the product and the producer
into something or into nothing, whichever it will. The poet
expects the occasion to inspire him, and sees with astonish-

ment that it does not work out that way; or he produces
something which in his heart of hearts he regards as insignificant, and then sees the occasion make it everything, sees
himself honored and distinguished in every possible manner, and knows within himself that he has only the occasion to thank for all this. These become enamored of the
occasion; those we described in the foregoing overlook it,
and therefore always come entirely unbidden. They really
divide themselves into two classes: those who still intimate
that an occasion is necessary, and those who do not even
notice this. Both classes naturally depend on an infinite over-
valuation of their own talents. When a man constantly uses
such phrases as, "on this occasion it occurs to me," "on
this occasion I am reminded," and so on, then one can always be sure that such a man is at fault regarding himself.
Even in the most significant things, he frequently sees only
an occasion for getting his smidgeon of comment noticed.
Those who do not even suspect the necessity for an occasion may be regarded as less vain, but more unbalanced.
They spin assiduously, without looking to the right or to
the left, the thin thread of their small talk, and with their
talk and their writing they produce the same effect in life
as the mill in the fairy story, about which it is said that
whatever happened, the mill went klip klap, klip klap.

And yet even the most complete, the most profound, the
most significant production has an occasion. The occasion
is the delicate, almost invisible, web in which the fruit
hangs. In so far, therefore, as it sometimes seems as if the
occasion were the essential element, this is in general a misunderstanding, for normally it is but a particular side of it.
If someone will not grant that I am right in this, then it
is because he has confused ground and cause with occasion. If such a one should now ask me, "What is the occasion for all these observations," and he was then satisfied
if I answered, "That which follows," then he would make
himself guilty, and allow me to become guilty of such a
confusion. On the other hand, if in his question he used
the word occasion in a very strict sense, it would be exactly
right for me to answer, "It has no occasion." In relation
to a single part of the whole, it would be absurd to de-

mand that which one can rightfully demand of the whole. Should these observations, for instance, demand an occasion, then they must in themselves constitute a well rounded little whole, which would be an egotistic attempt on their part.

Occasion is thus of the greatest importance in regard to every production; indeed, it is this which essentially decides the question regarding its true aesthetic value. Productions without any occasion always lack something, not outside of themselves (for although the occasion belongs to it, yet in another sense it is foreign to it), but they lack something within themselves. A production where the occasion is everything, also lacks something. For the occasion is not positively productive, but negatively productive. A creation is a production from nothing; the occasion is, however, the nothing from which everything comes. The whole wealth of thought, an abundance of ideas can be there and yet lack the occasion. Hence it is not something new that comes with the occasion, but with the occasion everything comes forward. This modest meaning of the occasion is also expressed in the word itself.

There are many men who are not able to understand this, but that is because they have no conception of what an aesthetic production really is. An attorney can write his brief, a merchant his letter, and so on, without suspecting the mystery which hides in the word *occasion*, and that in spite of the fact that he begins thus: "On the occasion of your great favor."

Perhaps, now, one or another may concede my point and admit its significance for poetical productions, but would marvel greatly if I were to make a similar point with respect to reviewers and critics. And yet I believe that just here this is of the greatest importance, and that inattention to the significance of the occasion has been the reason that reviews in general are so bungling, pure hackwork. In the world of criticism, the occasion gets an even potentiated significance. Although one often enough hears talk in critical reviews about the occasion, one still sees with half an eye how little they know the answer as to how the matter stands. The critic does not seem to need to invoke the muse, for it is truly no poetical work he produces; but if he does not need to invoke the muse, neither does he need the occasion. Meanwhile, one should never forget the significance of the old saying: The like is only understood by the like.

The object of the aestheticist's consideration is no doubt something already finished, and he should not, like the poet, himself produce. Notwithstanding this, the occasion has exactly the same significance. The aestheticist who adopts aesthetics as his profession, and in his profession sees the real occasion, is *eo ipso* lost. This is by no means to say that he cannot perform his work skillfully; but the secret of all production he has not understood. He is too much a Pelagian autocrat to be able, in childish wonder, to rejoice over the curious fact that it is as if alien powers had produced that which a human being believes is his own: the inspiration, namely, and the occasion.[5] Inspiration and occasion belong inseparably together; it is a union which one finds often enough in the world, that the great, the elevated, are constantly accompanied by a nimble little person. Such a person is the occasion, a person one otherwise wouldn't tip his hat to, who does not dare to open his mouth in fine society, but who sits silent, with a roguish smile, and enjoys himself by himself, without hinting to anyone why he smiles or that he knows how important, how indispensable he is; even less would he enter into a dispute concerning it; for he knows very well that it would do no good and that the others merely seize every occasion to humiliate him. The occasion is invariably of this ambiguous nature; and it avails a man just as much to wish to deny it, to wish to free himself from this thorn in the flesh, as to wish to set the occasion on the throne; for in purple with a scepter in its hand, it makes a poor showing, and one immediately sees that it was not born to rule. This wrong way, however, lies very near, and it is often the best minds that fall into error. When a man has enough of an eye for life to see how the Eternal Being makes sport of a man, so that something so insignificant and subordinate, something one almost blushes to mention in polite society, belongs absolutely to the whole scheme of things, then he is easily tempted to wish to dabble in the subject, indeed to return the sarcasm, so that he, as well as God, mocks the greatness of man by flinging him headlong into the law of the occasion, thus mocking him again by making the occasion everything and the other moment a foolishness, whereby God then becomes superfluous and the conception of a wise Providence a folly, and the occasion a rogue who ridicules everything, God as well as man, so that the whole of existence ends in a jest, a joke, a charade.

The occasion is at one and the same time the most significant and the most insignificant, the most exalted and the most humble, the most important and the most unimportant. Without the occasion, precisely nothing at all happens, and yet the occasion has no part at all in what does happen. The occasion is the last category, the essential transitional category, from the sphere of the idea to actuality. Logic should consider this. It can be absorbed as much as it wishes in immanent thinking, it can rush down from nothing into the most concrete form; the occasion it never reaches, and, therefore, never reality. The whole of reality can be ready in the idea; without the occasion, it never becomes real. The occasion is a category of the finite, and it is impossible for immanent thinking to lay hold of it; for that it is too paradoxical. This can also be seen from the fact that that which comes out of the occasion is something quite different from the occasion itself, which is an absurdity for all immanent thought. But therefore, the occasion is the most amusing, the most interesting, the wittiest of all categories. Like a wren it is everywhere and nowhere. Like the fairies it goes around in life, invisible to all schoolmasters, whose gestures, therefore, become an inexhaustible source of laughter to one who believes in the occasion. The occasion is, then, in itself nothing, and only something in relation to that which it gives rise to, and in relation to this it is exactly nothing. For as soon as the occasion becomes something other than nothing, then it would stand in a relatively immanent relation to that which it produces, and would then be either ground or cause. Unless one holds on to this firmly, everything again becomes confused.

Thus, if I were to say that the occasion for this little review of a play by Scribe was the masterly performance which fell to its lot, then I should insult the scenic art; for it is indeed true that I might write a review without having seen the play produced, without having seen it expertly performed, aye, even if I had seen it badly performed. In the last case I should rather call the bad performance the occasion. On the other hand, since I have seen it perfectly performed, the stage presentation becomes much more to me than an occasion; it is a very important moment in my interpretation, whether it has served to correct or to confirm and sanction my point of view. My piety will therefore forbid me to call the stage production the occasion, it will oblige me to see something more in it, to confess that without it I should perhaps not quite have understood the play. Therefore, in this case I am not like reviewers in general, who prudently or stupidly enough first mention the play, and later the performance separately. To me the performance itself is the play, and I cannot adequately rejoice over it in a purely aesthetic sense, nor sufficiently rejoice as a patriot. If I wished to show a stranger our theater in its full glory, I would say: Go and see *The First Love*. The Danish stage possesses in Madame Heiberg, Frydendahl, Stage, and Phister, a four-leaf clover which here appears in all its beauty. A four-leaf clover I call this union of artists, and yet I would seem to have said too little, for a four-leaf clover is remarkable only in that four ordinary clover leaves are borne on one stem, but our four-leaf clover has this distinction that each single leaf by itself is just as rare as a four-leaf clover, and yet these four leaves again in their union form a four-leaf clover.

Still, it was on the occasion of the occasion for this little critique that I had wished to say something quite general about the occasion, or about the occasion in general. It happens, however, quite fortunately that I have already said what I wished to say; for the more I consider this matter, the more certain I·am that there is simply nothing to be said about it in general, because there is no occasion in general. So I have come about as far as I was when I began. The reader must not be angry with me; it is not my fault, it is the occasion's. The reader may perhaps think that I ought to have considered the whole thing thoroughly before I started to write, and then not have begun to say something which afterward proved to be nothing. However, I still believe that he ought to do my mode of procedure justice, in so far as he has assured himself far more convincingly that the occasion in general is something which is nothing. Later he will perhaps begin again to reflect on this, when he has ascertained that there is something else in the world about which one can say much, with the idea that it is something, and yet it is of such a nature that when it has been said, then it appears to be nothing. What then is said here must be regarded as unnecessary, like a superfluous title page which is not included when the work is bound. I do not therefore know any way to end it, other than in the incomparable laconic manner in which I see Professor Poul Møller ends the introduction to his excellent review of *The Extremists:* "With this the introduction is finished."

Concerning the special occasion for the present little critique, it has a certain relation to my own insignificant personality, and dares to recommend itself to the reader with the normal quality of being trivial. Scribe's play, *The First Love,* has in numerous ways affected my personal life, and this contact has occasioned the present review, which thus, in the strictest sense, is the child of the occasion. I, too, was once young, was enthusiastic, was in love. The girl who was the object of my longing, I knew from an earlier period, but the different circumstances of our lives made it possible for us to see one another but seldom. On the other hand we thought of each other all the oftener. This mutual preoccupation with each other at the same time drew us closer together, and set us farther apart. When we actually met, we were so shy and bashful that we were farther apart than when we did not see each other. Then when we were again separated, and the unpleasantness of this mutual diffidence was forgotten, our meeting assumed its full significance, we began again in our dreams exactly where we had left off. Such, at least, was the case with me, and I later learned that it was the same with my beloved. I had remote prospects of marriage; our understanding in other respects encountered no obstacles which might

have inflamed us, and so we were in love in the most innocent manner in the world. Before there could be any
thought of declaring my feelings, a rich uncle, whose sole
heir I was, must die. This too seemed the proper thing, for
in all the romances and comedies I knew, the hero was in
a like situation, and I was secretly glad of being a poetical
figure.

So my beautiful, romantic life went on, and then one
day I saw in a newspaper that a play was to be given,
called *The First Love*. I had not known there was such a
play, but the title pleased me, and I resolved to see it. *The
First Love*—thought I—it exactly expresses your own feelings. Have I ever loved anyone else; does not my love go
back to my earliest recollections; could I imagine loving another, or seeing her pledged to another? No, she becomes
my bride, or I never marry. That is why the phrase, *the
first*, is so beautiful. It suggests the primitive in love, for
it is not in a numerical sense that one speaks of first love.
The poet could just as well have said, the true love, or entitled it, "The First Love is the True Love." Now this play
would help me to understand myself; through it I would
get a deep insight into myself; for this reason poets are
called priests, because they explain life, but they will not
be understood by the crowd but only by the natures who
have hearts to feel with. To those the poet is an inspired
singer, who shows beauty everywhere, but first and last
bears witness to the beauty of love. By its poetic power
this play will cause the love in my breast to blossom forth,
its flower to open with a snap like a passion-flower. Ah,
at that time I was very young! I hardly understood what
I said, and yet I found it well said. The flower of love must
open with a snap, the feeling burst its locks with an energy
like that of champagne. It was a bold expression, full of
passion, and I was right pleased with it. And yet what I
said was well said, for I meant that love must open like a
passion-flower. This was the good feature of the remark, for
love really opens with marriage, and in so far as one may
call it a flower, one may appropriately call it a passion-
flower.

Still, back to my youth. The day was approaching when

the play would be presented. I had bought my ticket, my
soul was solemnly attuned, and with a certain unrest and
joyously expectant I hastened to the theater. When I entered the door I glanced up at the first balcony. What did
I see? My beloved, the mistress of my heart, my ideal, she
was sitting there! Involuntarily I stepped back into the dim-
ness of the parquet in order to observe her without being
seen. How had she come here? She must have come to town
this very day, and I did not know it, and now she is here
in the theater. She would see the same play. It was no accident, but a guidance, a benevolence on the part of the
blind god of love. I stepped forward, our eyes met, she
noticed me. There was no question of bowing to her, of
conversing with her; in short, there was nothing to embarrass me. My ardor breathed freely. We were meeting half-
way, like transfigured beings each reached out a hand to
the other, we floated like wraiths, like disembodied spirits,
in a world of fantasy. Her eyes rested longingly upon me;
her breast heaved with a sigh; it was for me, she belonged
to me, I understood that. And yet I did not wish to rush
up to her, nor to throw myself at her feet; that would have
embarrassed me, but thus at a distance I felt the beauty
of loving her and of daring to hope that I was loved. The
overture was over. The chandelier was raised; my eye followed its movement, it cast for the last time its light over
the first balcony and over her. Twilight settled over the
house; this light seemed even more beautiful, even more
infatuating. The curtain went up. Once again it was as if
I gazed in a dream when my eyes sought her. I turned
around. The play began. I would think only of her and of
my love; everything that would be said in honor of first
love, I would apply to her and to my relation to her. There
was perhaps no one else in the whole theater who would
thus understand the divine speech of the poet as well as
I—and perhaps she. Thinking about the powerful impression already made me stronger, I felt courage for the next
day to let my hidden feelings burst forth, they must not
fail of their effect upon her; by a single allusion I would
remind her of what we had this evening heard and seen,
and thus should the poet come to my assistance, and make

her more approachable, make me stronger and more eloquent than ever. I saw and heard—and heard—and the curtain went down. The chandelier again deserted its heavenly
hiding place, the shadows vanished; I looked up—all the
young girls looked so delighted, my beloved also; tears
stood in her eyes, so heartily had she laughed, her bosom
heaved tumultuously, laughter had got the upper hand.
Luckily I was in the same condition.

We met the following day at my aunt's. The shy embarrassment which we had experienced at being in the
same room together had vanished, a certain jubilant gladness had taken its place. We laughed a little at one another,
we had understood each other, and we owed it to the poet.
For this reason a poet is called a prophet, because he pre-
dicts the future.[6] We arrived at an explanation. We still
could not decide to destroy all that had gone before. Then
we bound ourselves by a sacred promise. As Emmeline and
Charles promised one another to look at the moon, so we
promised to see this play every time it was produced. I
have faithfully kept my promise. I have seen it in Danish,
in German, in French, at home and abroad, and never have
tired of its inexhaustible humor, whose truth no one understands better than I. This became the first occasion for
the present little critique. Through having seen it so often,
I finally produced something about the play. However, this
productivity still remained in part unwritten and only a few
observations were recorded. This occasion may then be regarded as an occasion for the ideal possibility of this critique.

I should probably not have carried it any farther, if there
had not arisen a new occasion. For some years past, an
editor of one of our periodicals had solicited me and desired me to furnish him with a little article. He possessed
an uncommon eloquence for ensnaring souls, and me too
he lured into a promise. This promise, then, was also an
occasion, but it was an occasion in general, and therefore
contributed little toward helping me. I found myself in an
embarrassment like that in which a candidate in theology
would find himself, if he were given the whole Bible from
which to choose his own text. I was, however, bound by
my promise. Accompanied by many other thoughts, but

also by the thought of my promise, I started out on a little outing in Zealand. When I reached the station where I intended to spend the night, I had the servant bring all the books the landlord could muster up, a practice I never omit, and from which I have often reaped advantage, because one quite accidentally stumbles on something which otherwise might have escaped one's attention. This was not, however, the case here, for the first book the man brought me was—*The First Love*. It struck me, for one seldom finds a collection of plays in the country. Still, I had really lost faith in first love and no longer believe in the first. In the next town I called upon one of my friends. He was out when I arrived; I was invited to wait, and shown into his study. When I approached his table, I found a book lying open—it was Scribe's *Theater*, and it lay open at *Les premières amours*. Now the lot seemed cast. I resolved to redeem my promise and write a review of this play. To make my resolution unshakeable, it happened strangely enough that my former sweetheart, my first love, who lived there in the country, had come to town, not to the capital, but to the little town where I was. I had not seen her for a long time, and I found her now, engaged, happy, and glad, and it was a pleasure to me to see her. She assured me that she had never loved me, but that her betrothed was her first love, and therewith she told the same story as Emmeline, that only the first love is the true love. Had my resolution not been fixed before, it became so now. I just had to see what "first love" signifies. My theory began to totter, for "my first love" was inexorably insistent that her present love was her first.

There were motives enough; the essay was finished almost to the last point, and there remained only a few intermediate sentences to be introduced here and there. My friend, the editor, pressed me, and held my promise up before me with an obstinacy that would have done honor even to an Emmeline. I explained to him that the essay was ready, that there were lacking only a few trifles, and he expressed his satisfaction. As time went on, however, these gnats changed into elephants, into insurmountable difficulties. Add to this the fact that while I was writing, I had forgotten that it was to be printed. I have written many little essays in this fashion, but have never permitted any of them to be printed. He became tired of this talk about my having finished, when he could not get the manuscript. I became tired of his perpetual demands and wished that the devil might take all promises. Then his periodical folded up for lack of subscribers, and I thanked the gods; I felt easy again, unembarrassed by any promises.

This was the occasion for this criticism coming into the world, as a reality to myself, as a possibility for my friend, the editor, a possibility which later changed into an impossibility. So another year passed, during which I became exactly a year older. There is nothing remarkable about this, for it is with me as it ordinarily is with other people. But one year can sometimes have more significance than another, more significance than that a man becomes a year older. That was the case here. By the end of this year I found myself entering on a new period of my life, into a new world of illusion, something which happens only to a young man. When you belong to the "readers' sect," when in one way or another, you get a reputation for being a diligent and attentive reader, the supposition grows among other people that you probably will become an author of sorts, for, as Hamann says: "Out of children grow people, out of virgins grow brides, out of readers grow writers."[7]

Now there begins a rose-colored life, which has a great similarity to a girl's early youth. Editors and publishers begin to pay court. It is a dangerous period, for editors' talk is very seductive, and one is soon in their power, but they only deceive us poor children, and then, aye, then, it is too late. Watch your step, young men, go not too often to the coffee-houses and restaurants; for there the editors spin their web. And then when they see an innocent young man who freely speaks his mind about all sorts of things, with no idea as to whether what he says is worth while or not, but only for the pleasure of talking freely, of hearing his heart beating as he talks, throbbing at the ideas expressed, then a dark figure approaches him, and this figure is an editor. He has a discriminating ear, he can tell immediately whether what is said would look well in print or not.

Then he tempts the youngster, he shows him how inexcusable it is thus to cast his pearls away; he promises him money, power, influence, even with the fair sex. His courage weakens, the editor's words are attractive, and soon he is caught. Now he haunts no more the solitary places to breathe out his sighs; no more does he hasten joyously to the happy hunting grounds of youth in order to intoxicate himself with talk; he is silent, for he who writes does not talk. He sits pale and cold in his study, his color changes not at the kiss of the idea, nor does he blush like the young rose when the dew falls in its chalice; he neither smiles nor weeps; calmly his eye follows the pen across the paper —for he is an author, and no longer young.

I, too, in my youth had been exposed to temptations of this kind. Still, I believe I dare testify that my courage had been undaunted. What helped me there was the fact that the experience had come when I was much younger. The editor who received my first promise was very friendly toward me, and yet it invariably seemed to me as if it were a favor, an honor conferred upon me, that anyone would accept an article from my hand, as if someone pointed me out among the young men and said: "With time we may be able to make something of him. Let him try it, it encourages him to show him this honor." At that time the temptation was not so great, and yet I learned to know all the harrowing results of a promise. Being uncommonly well-armed against temptation from my early manhood, I therefore dared to frequent coffee-shops and restaurants rather often. The danger must come, then, from another direction, and it was not wanting. It happened that one of my coffee-shop acquaintances decided to become an editor. One will find his name upon the title page of this periodical. He had no sooner formulated this idea and made the necessary arrangements with the publisher, than he sat down at the writing-table one evening, and wrote the whole night through—letters to every possible man about contributions. Such a letter, composed in the most obliging terms and filled with the most glowing prospects, I, too, received. However, I raised stout opposition, but promised, on the other hand, to serve him in every way in editing the articles

submitted. He himself worked assiduously on the first article which was to launch the publication. He was as good
as finished with it, and now was kind enough to show it
to me. We spent a very pleasant forenoon; he seemed satisfied with my suggestions and made several changes. Our
mood was excellent, we ate fruit and confectionery, and
drank champagne; I was pleased with his article, and my
comments seemed to satisfy him, when my unlucky star
willed that just as I bent over to take an apricot, I should
upset the inkhorn over the entire manuscript. My friend was
infuriated. "The whole thing is ruined; the first number of
my periodical will not come out at the appointed time, my
credit is destroyed, the subscribers will fall away; you do
not know how much work it takes to get subscribers, and
when one has got them, they are like all mercenary troops,
faithless, seizing every opportunity to desert. Everything is
lost, there is nothing else to do, you will have to supply
an article. I know you have manuscripts ready, why will
you not print them? You have your critique of *The First
Love*, let me have it, I will get it ready; I beg you, I adjure
you by our friendship, by my honor, by the future of my
periodical!"

He accepted the article, and my inkhorn became the occasion for my little critique's becoming a reality, which now
is—I say it with horror—*publici juris*.[8]

If one would indicate briefly the merit of modern comedies, particularly those of Scribe, in comparison with the
older, one might perhaps express it thus: The personal substance and value of the poetic figure is commensurable with
the dialogue, the outpourings of the monologue are rendered superfluous; the substance and value of the dramatic
action is commensurate with the situation, novelistic expla-
nations are made superfluous; the dialogue finally becomes
audible in the transparency of the situation. Hence, no ex-
planations are necessary to orient the spectator, no retardation of the drama is necessary to give suggestions and state-
ments. That is the way it is in life, where we constantly
need explanatory notes; but it ought not to be so in poetry.
The spectator should be carefree, able to enjoy undisturbed

the dramatic unfolding. But while the modern drama thus seems to require less self-activity on the part of the spectator, it demands more perhaps in another way, or to speak more correctly, it does not demand it, but it avenges the forgetting of it. The more imperfect the dramatic form or construction of a drama is, the more frequently the spectator is stirred up out of his sleep, provided he is sleeping. When one is shaken up on an indifferent country road whenever the wagon strikes against a stone, or the horses are caught in a thicket, there is not much opportunity to sleep. On the other hand, if the road is a leisurely one, then you easily have time and opportunity to look about you, but, also, you may more unconcernedly fall asleep. So it is with the modern drama. Everything moves along so quickly and easily, that the spectator, if he does not pay a little attention, misses much. It is indeed true that a five-act play of the older comedy and a five-act play of the modern are equally long, but the question is always whether as much happens.

To carry this inquiry further could indeed have its own interest, but not for this review; more explicitly to point it out in Scribe's theater might well be important, but I believe that the more detailed report on the little masterpiece, which is the object of the present consideration, will be sufficient. I dwell the more willingly on the present play, since one cannot deny that in some of Scribe's other dramas we sometimes miss the complete perfection, and the situation becomes drowsy, and the dialogue monotonously garrulous. *The First Love,* on the contrary, is a play without a fault, so perfect that it alone should make Scribe immortal.

We shall first examine each of the persons in this play a little more closely, in order to see later how well the poet has known how to let their characters become revealed in speech and situation, and this despite the fact that the whole play is only a sketch.

Dervière, a wealthy iron-founder and widower, has an only daughter, "a little maiden of sixteen years." His every reasonable claim to be regarded as a worthy and honorable man, who is very rich, must no doubt be respected; on the other hand, all his attempts at being a man, at being a father, "who cannot take a joke," must be regarded as a failure. He is also frustrated by his daughter, without whose consent and approval he hardly dares regard himself as a rational being. "She has the run of the house and walks all over him," and he shows an uncommon aptitude for understanding a joke, since her humor incessantly plays blind man's buff with his paternal dignity.

His only daughter Emmeline is now sixteen years old, a nice, fascinating little girl, but a daughter of Dervière, and brought up by Aunt Judith. She has brought her up and educated her on romances, and her father's wealth has made it possible to preserve these refinements undisturbed by the reality of life. Everyone in the house obeys her caprice; and her instability, among other things, one can see in the monologue of Lapierre, the servant, in the third scene. Through Judith's training she has lived in her father's house with no particular knowledge of the world, and has not lacked the opportunity to weave about herself a web of sentimentality. She was brought up with her cousin Charles; he was her playmate, her all, the necessary supplement to the aunt's romances. With him she had read the novels, with him she has associated everything since he parted from her at a very early age. Their ways were separated; they now live at a distance from each other, united only by "a sacred promise."

Being brought up on novels was something Charles had had in common with his cousin; otherwise the circumstances of his life were different. At a very early age he was sent out into the world; he had only 3,000 francs a year, and he soon saw that it was necessary, if possible, to make his education profitable in the world. His efforts in this direction seem not to have been very successful; reality soon reduced him and his theories *in absurdum:* the promising Charles has become a dissolute fellow, a bad lot, an unsuccessful genius. Such a figure in itself is so dramatically effective that it is inconceivable that one so seldom sees it used. A bungling playwright would, however, be easily tempted to interpret it entirely abstractly: a black sheep out and out. It is not so with Scribe, for he is no bungler but a virtuoso. In order that such a figure can arouse interest, we must constantly surmise how it happened; for he has, in a stricter sense than other men, a pre-existence. This, one must discern even in his failure, and thus see the possibility of his depravity. However, it is not so easily done as said, and we cannot sufficiently admire the virtuosity with which Scribe knows how to let it come out, not in an endless monologue, but in the situation. Charles is perhaps on the whole one of the most ingenious characters Scribe has given to the stage; every one of his speeches is worth its weight in gold, and yet the poet has given him no more than a rough sketch. Charles is no abstraction, not a new Charles, but you apprehend immediately how it happened; you see in him the consequences of his life's premises.

The result of an education by novels and romances can be two-fold. Either the individual sinks deeper and deeper into illusion, or he emerges from it and loses faith in the illusion, but gains a belief in mystification. In illusion the individual is hidden from himself; in mystification, he is hidden from others, but both cases are results of a romantic training. In the case of a girl, she will probably sink into illusion; thus the poet has let it happen with Emmeline, and her life in this respect is fortunate. Otherwise with Charles. He has lost the illusion; but although in many ways he has felt the pinch of reality, he has not quite outgrown his romantic training. He believes he can mystify. When therefore Emmeline talks about sympathies, which goes far over her father's head, you hear immediately the fair reader of romances;[9] but you find in Charles's speeches no less accurate reminders of his education. He has great faith in his extraordinary talents for mystifying, but this belief in mystification is just as romantic as Emmeline's ecstasies. "After eight years of wandering, he comes back incognito; he has common sense and is well-read, and he knows that there are five or six ways whereby one can move an uncle's heart; but the principal thing is that one must not be recognized, that is a necessary condition." There we have at once the romantic hero. That Charles should believe himself clever enough to fool such a ninny as his uncle is quite in order; but this is not what Charles means; he is speaking about uncles in general, about five or six methods in general, and about the condition in general for being unrecognized. His faith in mystification is then just as fantastic as Emmeline's illusion, and one recognizes Judith's schooling in both. We get a good idea of Charles's overstraining in this respect from the fact that, in spite of all these excellent theories, he is not able to hit upon the least thing, but must take the advice of the anything but visionary Rinville. His belief in mystification, then, is just as unfruitful as Emmeline's in illusion, and therefore the poet has let them both come to the same result, namely, to the opposite of what they believe they are working for; for Emmeline's sympathy and Charles's mystification effect exactly the opposite of what they believe they will effect. I shall develop this later.

Although Charles, at the cost of his illusion, has gained belief in mystification, he still has left a little of the illusion, and it is in this remnant that one recognizes in the unfortunate Charles, Judith's pupil and Emmeline's playmate. He knows how to apprehend his own life, in spite of its wretchedness and insignificance, in a romantic transfiguration. He contemplates his youth, when he went out into the world as "a highly attractive cavalier, a young man of the best form, full of fire and life and grace, destined for much attention from the fair sex."[10] Even the affair with Pamela had in his eyes a romantic aspect, although the spectator very rightly suspects that Charles had really been made a fool of. One will easily see why I made mystification predominant in Charles; for the illusion he holds is really an illusion about his gift for mystifying. Here again we see the romantic hero. There is an incomparable truth in Charles. In relation to people in general, such an unsuccessful subject possesses something of distinction; he is affected by the idea; his mind is not unacquainted with fantastic conceptions. Such a figure is therefore rightly comic, because his life succumbs to the commonplace, to wretchedness, and yet he believes that he is accomplishing the extraordinary. He believes that the episode with Pamela is an "affair," and yet one entertains a suspicion that it was rather she who had taken him by the nose. One is almost tempted to believe that he is more innocent than he himself thinks, that Pamela had had other reasons than her injured love for terrifying him "with tailor's shears"; indeed, that these reasons even lay outside his relation to her.

Finally, in the unfortunate subject one recognizes the original Charles, because of a low-comic touch, a softness which believes in great emotions and is moved by them. When he hears that his uncle has paid the note, he exclaims: "Aye, the bonds of blood and nature are sacred."* He is really moved, his romantic heart is touched, his feelings are given expression, he becomes enthusiastic: "Aye, I thought as much! Either one has an uncle, or one has not." There is no trace of irony in him, it is the freshest sentimentality; but therefore the comic effect in the play is infinite. When his cousin begs her father for forgiveness for the supposed Charles, he breaks out emotionally, with tears in his eyes, "O, the good cousin!" He has not quite lost faith that there is in life, as in romance, a noble womanly soul whose lofty resignation can only move one to tears. This belief now awakens with its former enthusiasm.

I have purposely given more time to Charles, because as presented by the poet, he is such a perfect character that I believe I could write a whole book about him just by using his speeches. One believes perhaps that Emmeline is sentimental and that Charles, on the contrary, has become worldly-wise. By no means. Therein, precisely, lies Scribe's infinite cleverness, that Charles in his own way is just as sentimental as Emmeline, so that both of them appear equally vividly as pupils of Aunt Judith.

The old Dervière, his daughter, and Charles together make up an entirely fantastic world, even though in another sense they are all figures taken from life. This world must be brought into relation to reality, and this takes place through Mr. Rinville. Rinville is an educated young man

---

* If the reader is very conversant with the play, he will have had the opportunity to rejoice over the poetic chance which wills that Rinville, in the first scene where he is supposed to be Charles, reproduces him with such poetic verisimilitude, that his conversation becomes a sort of ventriloquism, with an infinitely comic effect, because it is as if one saw and heard the sentimentally vapid Charles touchingly proclaiming these words: "Is then the call of blood only imagination? Does it not speak to your heart? Does it not say to you, my dear Uncle . . ." (6th scene)

who has traveled abroad. He is at the age when it might seem suitable through marriage to take a step decisive for his whole life. He has considered the matter by himself, and has fixed his eyes on Emmeline. He is too well acquainted with the world to be sentimental; his marriage is a well-considered step which he decides on for a variety of reasons. In the first place the girl is rich and has a prospect of 50,000 francs in annual interest; in the second place, there is a friendly relation between her father and his own; in the third place, he has said in jest that he would make a conquest of this coy little beauty; finally, she is really a lovable girl. This reason comes last, it is an afterthought.

We have thus surveyed the principal characters in the play, and now pass on to inquire how these must be arranged in relation to one another, in order to arouse a dramatic interest. Here we easily have occasion to admire Scribe. The play must be built up about Emmeline, of that there can be no question. Emmeline is altogether accustomed to dominate; it is therefore proper that in the play she should be the dominating force. She has all possible qualifications for being a heroine, yet not substantially, but in a negative sense. She is comical, and through her the play is a comedy. She is accustomed to rule, as befits a heroine, but that which she rules is a fool of a father, the servants, and so on. She has pathos, but since its content is nonsense, her pathos is essentially nonsense; she has passion, but since its content is unreal, her passion is essentially foolishness; she has enthusiasm, but since its content is nothing, her enthusiasm is essentially prittle-prattle; she will make every sacrifice for her passion, that is, she will sacrifice everything for nothing. As a comic heroine she is incomparable. With her, everything turns upon imagination, and everything external turns about her, and therefore about her imagination. One easily sees how perfectly comical the whole procedure must become; one watches it as one would look down into an abyss of laughter.

Emmeline's imagination terminates in nothing more nor less than that she is in love with her cousin Charles whom she has not seen since she was eight years old. The chief

argument with which she attempts to defend her illusion
is the following: "The first love is the true love, and one
loves only once."

As champion of the absolute validity of first love, Emmeline represents a numerous class of mankind. One thinks
indeed that it may be possible to love more than once; but
the first love is still essentially different from every other.
This cannot be explained in any other way than by assuming that there is a beneficent spirit who has presented mankind with a little gilding with which to embellish life. The
proposition that the first love is the true love is very accom-
modating and can come to the aid of mankind in various
ways. If a man is not fortunate enough to get possession
of what he desires, then he still has the sweetness of the
first love. If a man is so unfortunate as to love many times,
each time is still the first love. The proposition is really a
sophistical one. If a man loves three times, then he says:
"This, my present love, is my first true love, but the true
love is the first, *ergo*, this third love is my first love." The
sophistry lies in the fact that the category, *first*, is at the
same time a qualitative and a numerical category. When a
widower and a widow join fortunes, and each one brings
five children along, then they still assure each other on their
wedding day that this love is their first love. Emmeline in
her romantic orthodoxy would look upon such a connection with aversion; it would be to her a mendacious abomi-
nation, which would be as loathsome to her as a marriage
between a monk and a nun was to the Middle Ages. She
interprets the category numerically and with such con-
scientiousness that she thinks an impression received in her
eighth year is decisive for her whole life. In the same way
she interprets the other proposition: one loves only once.
This proposition is, however, just as sophistical and just as
elastic. One loves many times, and each time one denies
the validity of the preceding times, and thus one still maintains the correctness of the proposition that one loves only
once.

Emmeline, then, holds fast her proposition numerically
understood; no one can refute her; for every one who ventures to do so, she pronounces destitute of sympathy. She

must now acquire experience and the experience refutes her. The question becomes, how one at this point is to understand the poet. It appears that she loves Rinville, not Charles. The answer to that would be decisive in determining whether the play is infinitely comic, or finitely moralizing. As is well known, the play ends by Emmeline's turning away from Charles, and giving her hand to Rinville, saying: "It was a mistake, I confused the past with the future." If then the play in a finite sense is moralizing, as it is generally understood, then it must be the poet's intention to depict Emmeline as a childish, high-strung, romantic girl who has it firmly fixed in her head that she loved only her Charles, but who now comes to a better understanding, is healed of her sickness, makes a suitable match with Mr. Rinville, and leaves the spectators to hope for the best for her future, that she will become an active housewife, and so on. If this is the intention, *The First Love* is thus changed from a masterpiece to a dramatic insignificance, under the presupposition that the poet had in some measure motivated her amelioration. Since this is not the case, then the play, considered as a whole, becomes a mediocre play, and one must complain that the brilliant details in it are wasted.

That Scribe has in no way motivated her improvement, I shall now prove. Rinville decides to pass himself off for Charles. He succeeds in deceiving Emmeline. He adopts the sentimentality of the assumed Charles, and Emmeline is beside herself with joy. Consequently it is not in his own person that Rinville fascinates her, but in Charles's Sunday clothes. Even if he had been the real Charles instead of a false one, even if he had looked exactly the same as Rinville, the approach of this figure would not have provided some new motive for her to love him. On the contrary, she loves him with an objective, mathematical love because he conforms to the picture she had herself created. Rinville has then made simply no impression upon Emmeline. How negligible he is appears also from the fact that when he does not have the ring she does not love him; when he gets the ring she loves him again; thus it appears probable that this ring is to Emmeline a magic ring, and that she would love anyone who came bearing this ring. When Emmeline finally comes to know that Charles is married, she decides to marry Rinville. If this step could in some way indicate a change in her, and what is more, a change for the better, then, on the one hand, Rinville must have succeeded in pleasing her by his own attractiveness, which in the play seems to be of a better quality than that of Charles, and on the other hand, he must have succeeded in dissolving and explaining her theoretical obduracy concerning the absolute validity of first love.

Neither of these alternatives is the case. Rinville enters as Charles, and pleases her only so far as he resembles him. And the picture she has of Charles is not that of a proud, romantic character which a poetic figure is needed to satisfy; no, her ideal Charles is recognizable by a multitude of accidentals, especially by the ring upon his finger. Only by his resemblance to Charles does Rinville please her, and he does not succeed in displaying a single attractive quality peculiar to himself which could make an impression on Emmeline. She simply does not see Rinville at all, but only her own Charles. She is at the point where she loves Charles and loathes Rinville; which of them is the more attractive, she does not decide by looking at them; that was decided long before. When Charles approaches as Rinville, she finds him "loathsome." In this opinion the spectator must agree with her; but it does not seem to be the poet's intention to impute great worth to this; she knows that he is loathsome before she looks at him; she barely looks at him and finds her judgment precisely confirmed. The poet indeed rather wishes to show her judgment on the false Rinville as arbitrary, and therefore lets it constantly be parodied by her father's judgment. The father finds nothing pleasing about the supposed Charles; on the contrary, he finds the supposed Rinville highly attractive, the daughter just the opposite; he finds it so because he wishes it so; she, likewise. That she is right the spectator sees, but her judgment is nevertheless only an arbitrary one, and thereby the situation achieves such a comic power.

Nor does Rinville succeed in overcoming her theory.

Charles is married; consequently, she cannot get him,* unless she would come into conflict with the authorities. She marries Rinville for two reasons, partly to avenge herself upon Charles, partly to obey her father. These reasons do not seem to indicate a change for the better. If she does it to avenge herself upon Charles, it shows that she continues to love him. The motive is quite in accord with the logic of romance, and one can by no means regard her as cured. If she does it in order to obey her father, then either seriousness must have entered her soul, a remorse and repentance over having permitted herself to make fun of a father who had only one weakness, that of being too good to her; but this would be in contradiction with the whole play—or her obedience is due to the fact that his will is in harmony with her own mood, and thus again she is unchanged.

There is, then, not the least thing discernible in the play to indicate that her choice of Rinville might be more reasonable than anything else she has done. Emmeline's nature is infinite nonsense, she is quite as silly at the end as in the beginning, and therefore one can undividedly amuse himself with the whole comic effect of the play, which comes out in the situation's being constantly against her. She is, then, no better at the conclusion of the play, just as little as is Erasmus Montanus in Holberg's play. She is too much a theorist, too good a dialectician (and everyone who has a fixed idea is a virtuoso on one string), to let herself be convinced empirically. Charles has been untrue to her, she marries Rinville; but her romantic conscience does not reproach her. Tranquilly she could approach Aunt Judith, if she were living; she could say to her: "I do not love Rinville, I have never loved him. I love only Charles, and I still say, one loves only once, and the first love is the true love; but I have respect for Rinville, therefore have I mar-

* Another way out might perhaps be found if one let Emmeline get the idea that she would be satisfied with Charles's divided heart. One has indeed seen such things in romances, and it would not be inconceivable that it might dawn on Emmeline in all its clarity. It is altogether remarkable that the whole of European literature lacks a feminine counterpart to *Don Quixote*. May not the time for this be coming, may not the continent of sentimentality yet be discovered?

ried him, and obeyed my father." Then would Judith answer: "Rightly so, my child, the textbook in a note permits this step. It says, 'When the lovers cannot get each other, it is fitting that they live quietly, and although they do not get each other, their relationship should have the same significance as if they had got each other, and their life should be just as beautiful, and be regarded in all respects as a living together.' That I know of my own experience. My first love was a seminarian, but he could get no living. He was my first love and my last. I died unmarried, and he without a living. When on the other hand, one party becomes faithless to the other, then the other has a right to marry, yet so that she does it on the ground of respect."

When one, then, has the choice between reducing Scribe's play to insignificance, by insisting that something is to be found in it which cannot be demonstrated, or taking pleasure in a masterpiece by being able to explain everything, then the choice seems easy. The play is not moralizing in a finite sense, but witty in an infinite sense; it has no definitive purpose, but is an endless jest about Emmeline. For this reason the play has no end. Since the new love for Rinville is only motivated by a mistake of identity, it is quite arbitrary to let the play end. Now, either this is a fault in the play or a merit. Here again the choice is easy. Just as the spectator believes that the play is over, that he has gained a sure foothold, he suddenly discovers that what he steps on is not something firm, but, as it were, the end of a seesaw, and when he steps on it, he raises the whole play up over himself. There appears to be an infinite possibility of confusion, because Emmeline's aspirations, on account of her romantic education, soar above every limit imposed by reality. That the real Charles was not her Charles, she had learned; but soon, when Rinville becomes Rinville, she will convince herself that he isn't her Charles either. Clothes make the man, and the romantic habit is what she looks at. Then perhaps a new figure will appear, who resembles Charles, and so forth. If one understands the play in this way, her closing speech is even profound, while in the other case, it is, at least for me, impossible to find any meaning in it. She indicates, then, change of movement. Previously, her illusion lay behind her in the past, now she will seek it in the world and in the future, for she has not renounced the romantic Charles; but whether she travels forward or backward, her expedition in search of the first love is comparable to the journey one undertakes in search of health, which, as someone has said, is always one station ahead.

One will also find it in order that Emmeline gives no explanation of her theory, which one might otherwise rightfully demand. When a man changes his belief, one requires an explanation; if he is a theorist, one rightly demands it. Emmeline is no common girl; she is well-read, she has a theory; she has loved Charles in the strength of this theory; she has established the proposition that the first love is the true one. How will she extricate herself from that? If she should say that she never had loved Charles, but that Rinville is her first love, she contradicts herself, since she actually believes that Rinville is Charles. If she should say that the first love was a childish fancy, that the other love is the true one, one easily sees that she escapes from this only by a sophism. If she says: "I don't stick at numbers, whether it is number one or number two, the true love is something quite different"; then one must ask what attraction she had found in Rinville, since the attentive observer had not discovered anything other than that he had been so courteous as to put on Charles in order to please her. If the piece is really ended, then one must in fairness require an explanation of all this. If it is, on the contrary, the poet's meaning that the play is endless, then it is unfair to demand an explanation of Emmeline, since she has not yet herself attained clearness about it.

The interest then turns about Emmeline and her illusion. To provide a collision is easy enough. I shall now for a moment place the three persons, omitting Charles, in relation to one another, in order to see how far we can get in this manner. The father wishes to see Emmeline married and provided for. She refuses every proposal. Finally he proposes the young Rinville, recommends him more warmly than any of the others, even appears to have made up his mind. Emmeline confesses that she loves another, namely

Charles. Rinville comes, receives a letter, conceives the idea of passing himself off as Charles.

So far the play might get along with three characters and still not deprive us of one of the most witty situations in the play, the recognition scene. I can here immediately take occasion to show how Scribe lets everything come to light in the situation. Emmeline never gives her sentimentality expression in the form of a monologue but always in dialogue and situation. One does not hear her mooning about Charles in solitude. Only when her father brings strong pressure to bear, must she confess, and this is conducive to bringing out her sentimentality better. One does not hear her in monologue repeating to herself the reminiscences of her love; it comes out first in the situation. Her sympathy tells her at once that Rinville is Charles, and with him she goes over all the old memories. A wittier situation is difficult to imagine. Rinville knows the world, and with the aid of some few details about Emmeline's state of mind, he soon sees that her cousin Charles is a very nebulous and mythical figure. Her fantasy has painted a picture of Charles which can pass for anybody, just as one of the portraits among the many painted by Wehmüller passes for any Hungarian.[11] Charles's portrait is just as abstract as this painter's national face. This portrait and some general formulas, not forgetting a little verse, are the results of her romantic training. A deception is thus made tolerably easy for Rinville and is successful beyond all measure.

One might now from these three persons and their relation to one another create a comedy. Rinville had perceived that although as Rinville he was in good favor with her father, it was of still greater importance to please the daughter, whose wish was law in Dervière's house. He would then continue to masquerade as Charles. Thereby he had gained a foothold in the family and had opportunity to win the girl for himself. He dared reckon on Emmeline's dominance over her father, and then when she had extorted her father's consent, he must know how to captivate the girl so that she would not change her mind again.

One easily sees the imperfection of this plan. In order for Dervière to persuade his daughter to confess her secret,

he must have brought very strong pressure to bear upon
her; for otherwise she could just as well have confessed the
first time he had talked to her at all about marriage. Her
father consequently has had many reasons for wanting Rinville to be his son-in-law. The more eager he is, the more
the relationship is strained, the less likely it is that he will
give his consent to her marrying Charles. On the other
hand, there must be a dramatic probability that Emmeline
can be mistaken. This the poet has accomplished by the
fact that Charles is expected, and he has arranged it so
that Emmeline herself brings the news, and at this same
moment the supposed Charles comes. Her father's embarrassment and his eagerness to conceal Charles's arrival
make her even more certain in believing that it really is
Charles.

Now I shall take up the fourth person in order to show
the excellence of the plan, and how the one situation overshadows the others in cleverness.

Charles hastens home like the prodigal son, in order to
throw himself into his uncle's arms, get rid of his cousin,
and get his debts paid. But to achieve all this, he must be
incognito. As almost every situation is an infinitely witty
mockery of Emmeline's sentimentality, so, too, almost every
situation is likewise a witty mockery of Charles's mystification. He comes home full of confidence in his powers of
mystifying. He believes it is he who contrives intrigues, he
who mystifies, and yet the spectator sees that the mystification was in operation before Charles appears; for Rinville
had already passed himself off for Charles. The intrigue
then carries Charles along with it, Rinville's mystification
forces Charles into his own, and yet Charles believes that
it starts from him. With his entrance the play comes completely to life, manifested by a wantonness, an almost insane crossing of the situations. Altogether four persons
are mutually mystified. Emmeline wants Charles, Charles
wants to be rid of her; Charles the mystifier does not know
that Rinville is passing himself off as Charles and is trying
in this way to captivate the girl. Rinville does not realize
that Charles as Rinville is no recommendation for him;
Dervière backs Rinville, but the Rinville he backs is Charles.

Emmeline backs Charles, but the one she backs is Rinville. So the whole operation dissolves in nonsense. That which the play turns on is nothing, that which comes out of the play is nothing.

Emmeline and Charles work against each other, and yet they both arrive at the opposite of what they wish: she, in getting Rinville; he, who wished to mystify, in giving the whole thing away.

In every theater where *The First Love* is presented, there is no doubt much laughter at the play, but I dare assure the theater-going public that there is never laughter enough. If I, to recall an old story, were to say about a man who laughed very heartily, "Either he is mad, or he has been reading, or perhaps better, he has been seeing *The First Love*," I believe I should not be saying too much.[12] One sometimes laughs at a thing, and regrets it almost in the same moment; but the situations in this play are of the kind that the more one ponders them, the more laughable, the more crazy they appear. As the situation itself is in the highest degree laughable, speeches, which are witty in themselves, appear to even better advantage.

That Scribe can write dialogue is too well known to require mention. One admires him for it, but one admires him even more for the virtuosity by means of which he knows how to adapt it to the situation, so that the speeches grow out of the situation and also illuminate it. If his dialogue is occasionally a little less apt, then he immediately buys an indulgence by its wit. One must remember, however, that I am not speaking about all the plays of Scribe but only about *The First Love*.

This introducing of the fourth person produces a perfect dramatic ferment in the subject matter. One need not fear that the subject will lack animation, but rather that the activity may become too wanton, and indisposed to obey the rein. Every situation must have its time, and yet in it one must feel the play's inner unrest. That Scribe is a master at this, I shall now show, in conclusion, by analyzing the individual situations. The reader must pardon me if I become a little too long-winded; it has its ground in my jealousy for Scribe and my distrust of the reader. My jeal-

ousy for Scribe whispers to me that he can never be well
enough understood; my mistrust of the reader leads me to
believe that he does not see everything there is to see in
the individual passages. One generally believes that the
comic is more transient than the tragic; one laughs at it
and forgets it, while one often returns to the tragic, and
becomes absorbed in it. The comic and the tragic can either
be dialogue or situation. Some men dwell preferably on the
dialogue, preserving it in memory and often turning back
to it. Others prefer the situation, reconstructing it in memory. These latter are the contemplative natures. Nor will
these deny that a comic situation has something just as
satisfying for the intuition, aye, that if in other respects it
is correct, it tempts one to become more absorbed in it than
in the tragic. I have heard and read many tragedies, but
can only remember an occasional speech, and this, too, occupies me less. On the other hand, I can sit quietly and
become absorbed in the situation. I shall cite an example.
When Clärchen in Goethe's *Egmont* learns that Egmont has
been taken prisoner, she appears before the Hollanders to
incite them to raise a rebellion. She is certain her eloquence
will stir them, and yet the Hollanders stand, like true Hollanders, unmoved, only considering how to sneak away
from her. I have never been able to remember a word of
her speech. The situation, on the contrary, has been unfor-
gettable from the very moment I first saw it. As a tragic
situation it is perfect. One would think that the beautiful
young girl, poetic in her love for Egmont, inspired by
Egmont's whole being, would be able to move the whole
world, but no Hollander understands her. The soul broods
in infinite sadness over such a situation; but it rests; contemplation is perfectly at peace. The comic situation doubtless affords a similar quiescent state for contemplation, but
at the same time reflection is moving within it; and the
more it discovers, the more infinitely comic the situation
becomes within itself and all the more dizzy does one become, while yet one cannot refrain from gazing into it.

The situations in *The First Love* are precisely of this kind.
The first impression of them has already produced a comic
effect; yet when we reproduce them for reflection, the

laughter becomes quieter but the smile more explicable. We can hardly tear our thoughts away from it because it is as if something still more laughable might come. This quiet enjoyment of the situation, when one looks at it in the same way that one who smokes tobacco watches the rising smoke, is perhaps unknown to one or another reader. Scribe is not to blame for this; if this be the case, the reader himself is at fault and has sinned against Scribe.

Dervière exerts strong pressure upon Emmeline to make her marry Rinville; she admits her love for Charles, confesses the highly innocent understanding she has had with him; by using affectionate words she persuades her father to write a letter to Rinville conveying a refusal. The servant is sent off with the letter. The family refuses to see him. Rinville shows up. Lapierre, instead of giving orders to the servants downstairs that the family is "not at home," has hurried away. Consequently Rinville is admitted. Here Scribe, instead of allowing Mr. Rinville to enter and announce himself, has directly produced a not unwitty situation, which makes Dervière as ridiculous as it does Emmeline. Rinville has received the letter and read it. Here again is situation. It is not, as is so often the case, a letter which requires the reader's close attention in order to get its meaning. It is in Mr. Dervière's house that the future son-in-law gets his refusal. Rinville lays his plan. Dervière enters. Rinville pretends to be Charles.

Here we have a perfectly witty situation. There could naturally not be any guest more unwelcome to Dervière than Charles. Rinville does not suspect this. This makes his whole intrigue look like a very unfortunate idea. The situation does not lie in the fact that Rinville pretends to be Charles, but in the fact that he has chosen the most unfortunate plan possible, although he necessarily believes that he has chosen the most fortunate. Next to that, the situation lies in the fact that Dervière has the excellent young Rinville in his home without suspecting it. When one comes to notice the dialogue, so poetically correct in itself, then one will repeatedly come to enjoy the situation more intensively, because its ridiculous side becomes clearer and clearer. Rinville begins in a sentimentally pathetic style. Whether this is right or not might seem doubtful. He has no close acquaintance with Charles, consequently he could not know what manner would operate most deceptively. He has, however, some idea of Dervière's household and ventures from this to infer the position of the other members of this family. If one regards the beginning as too incorrect, one cannot deny that Scribe makes up for this weakness by the wittiness of the lines and by the presentiment that is aroused in the spectators about the actual Charles. The incorrectness lies in the fact that Rinville's first speech is so pathetic that it looks as if he feared being unwelcome, whereas Rinville, as a result of the foregoing, ought to believe the exact opposite. Therefore, Rinville resembles a little too much the actual Charles. The uncle seems, in spite of his stupidity in other respects, to have sized Charles up very well; he thinks he may get rid of him with money; he offers him 6,000 francs a year instead of the former 3,000. Here one involuntarily comes to think of the actual Charles. He would have considered himself very lucky and would gladly have accepted this offer. The whole scene would then have ended just as pathetically as it began; he would have thrown himself into his uncle's arms and cried: "Truly the bonds of nature and blood are sacred!" Rinville, however, does not do this; he continues in the way he began, quite as Charles might have done if he had not needed the 6,000 francs. The uncle now decides to use kindness and gain his support; he tells him candidly about the whole matter, eulogizes Rinville, which because of the situation becomes parodical. The situation nears its perfect climax when Dervière confides to Rinville that he has considered devising some stratagem by which he could make Emmeline acquainted with Rinville without her suspecting it.* The ironical contradiction is excellent. Dervière will devise a stratagem; this stratagem Rinville has already adopted. Rinville's stratagem creates the situation,

---

* Here the play might really end, perhaps some attentive reader thinks. For what would be simpler than that Rinville should reveal himself to old Dervière, and thus sail before a twofold wind: with Emmeline, passing for Charles; with Dervière, for what he really was—for Rinville. However, one cannot find

and in this one hears Dervière's speech. Dervière himself admits that he is not inventive; his device is very simple, if only Charles will have the goodness to go. If this stratagem is successful, then Dervière has done about the most stupid thing imaginable.

However, Rinville does not go; on the contrary, Emmeline comes in with the news that a certain Mr. Zacharias[13] wishes to talk with her father about Charles, who is momentarily expected. The father's embarrassment betrays everything; she recognizes Charles. By this plan, the poet has gained much. The first person the alleged Charles stumbles on is the uncle; he must be regarded as the one easiest to deceive. He is stupid, uneasy, too, lest Charles come, and so only too inclined to credit the certainty of this sorry event; he would never dream that anyone would pretend to be Charles. As far as he is concerned, therefore, Rinville can be bold enough. As regards Emmeline, however, it would be too boldly daring, since she is always a lot more clever. Moreover, it would be unbecoming if Rinville should entirely ignore decorum, and not less unbecoming from Emmeline's side. On the other hand, she has now in her father's embarrassment the most convincing proof that it is Charles. The recognition takes place before the father's eyes; Rinville need do nothing; instead of having to be mindful of his role, he can remain quite calm, for now Emmeline has got her eyes open. She practically forces Rinville to be Charles; to this extent he is blameless, and she herself is blameless, since her father is the one who had required her to receive him as such. The poet has then by this plan spread a certain delicacy over the situation, which divests it of all offensiveness, and makes it into an innocent jest.

The situation is not less amusing than the preceding. Dervière is quite perplexed, and still he has himself brought about the whole situation, and helped Rinville over the difficulty, as regards Emmeline, of passing himself off for

---

fault with Rinville for preserving his incognito in the presence of Dervière. For merely a word or two from him is sufficient to show that if one wishes to carry on an intrigue, one should never have Dervière for a confidant.

Charles. The situation also creates a parody on the preceding; the uncle simply could not recognize him immediately. On the contrary, Emmeline can. She explains it by a curious feeling she has for which she cannot account; but it was like a voice which whispered to her: he is there. (This voice is certainly her father's voice, which gave everything away.) She attributes it to sympathies, intuitions, something she cannot explain to her father but can very well explain to her Aunt Judith. Who is now the more clever: Dervière, who did not recognize him, who had no suspicions, but who now recognizes him, or Emmeline who recognized him at once? The more one looks at it, the more laughable it becomes. Here again the dialogue helps the spectator to lose himself in the ridiculous situation. Upon Emmeline's saying that she had such a strange feeling, Dervière replies: "There, I had for my part not the least suspicion, and if he had not told me his name right out . . ." Such a speech is worth its weight in gold. It is so natural and simple, and yet perhaps not one in ten dramatists would have sense enough and enough of an eye for situation to bring it out. An ordinary dramatist would have permitted the whole attention to rest on Emmeline; after all, in the previous scene he had finished with the recognition between Dervière and Charles. This interplay he would not have generated, and yet this contributes to making the whole situation so witty. It is comical that Emmeline immediately recognizes Rinville as Charles, but Dervière's presence tends to make the situation ironic. He stands there like a booby who understands nothing. And yet, which is easier to explain, that Emmeline guessed this, or that Dervière did not?

Now follows the recognition scene, one of the most successful situations imaginable. The humor by no means lies in the fact that she confuses Rinville with Charles. One has frequently seen cases of mistaken identity on the stage. Mistaken identity is based on a real resemblance, whether the individual is unconscious of it or has himself achieved it. If this were the case here, then Rinville after having stood the test must have known fairly well how Charles looked; for Charles must have looked about like himself. This, however, is by no means the case; every such inference would be silly. The humor lies in the fact that Emmeline recognizes in Rinville someone she does not know. The wit does not consist in the fact that she recognizes Rinville, but that it shows that she does not know Charles. As it went with Rinville, so would it go with any man under the same circumstances; she would have taken him for Charles. She then confuses Rinville with someone she does not know, and this is undeniably a very witty kind of confusion. Therefore, the situation has a high degree of probability, which one may readily believe was difficult to attain. Rinville is also a fool, in so far as he believes that he has advanced a step forward; Emmeline's Charles is, in fact, an x, a *desideratur*,[14] and one sees revealed here, what ordinarily takes place in privacy, how such a young maiden behaves in creating an ideal for herself. And yet she has loved Charles for eight years, and she will never love another.

If one stumbles at a particular speech which seems a little faulty, Scribe makes up for it with a witticism. Thus Rinville's speech: "God be praised! I was afraid I had gone further than I wish to."[15]

So then, Emmeline recognizes Charles, or rather she discovers him. For while Rinville does not, as one would have expected, learn to know how Charles looks, Emmeline does come to know it, and this is very wisely arranged, since she did not know it before. The situation is so crazy that it becomes doubtful whether one should say that it is Rinville who deceives Emmeline, or Emmeline who deceives Rinville; for he is in a certain sense deceived, in so far as he had believed that there actually was a Charles. But in the course of all this, the infinite gist of the matter is that the scene is a recognition scene. The situation is as crazy as it would be for a man who had never seen his own picture to say on first looking into a mirror: "I immediately recognize myself."

Emmeline and the pseudo-Charles, in the recognition scene, have reached through reminiscence the precise point at which they were interrupted by Charles's departure, when they are again interrupted by the presence of the uncle. He has received from Mr. Zacharias information

about Charles which is not particularly pleasing. This re-
coils on Rinville. The situation is essentially the same as
earlier; but we shall see what the poet has gained. Charles's
exploits are of such a nature that candidly and correctly
described, they could disturb the total impression of the
play. It is necessary to give them a certain light touch so
that they may not become too serious. This the poet has
accomplished in two ways. The first information we get regarding Charles's life is in the ninth scene. Here it is Rinville, who has pretended to be Charles, upon whom it re-
coils. The spectator's attention is thus diverted from the
explicitness of the narration to the mistaken identity. Instead
of the individual exploits, one thinks only about stupid
antics in general and about Rinville's embarrassment and
of the ludicrousness of demanding more explicit details
from him. The complete information one gets from Charles's
own mouth in the sixteenth scene when Charles passes himself off as Rinville. What would be much too serious or
much too impudent, if Charles told about it in his own person, now gets a comic, almost an exuberant aspect, when
he tells it in the person of Rinville, using his incognito to
make the narrative as fantastic as possible. If he in his own
person had described his life, one would have required from
him a consciousness of his exploits, finding it highly immoral if he did not have it. Now, on the contrary, since he
tells everything in the person of another and for the express
purpose of alarming Emmeline, one finds the fantastic
touches in his narration poetically correct in a two-fold
respect.

Hence, Dervière has got detailed information; the
pseudo-Charles is unable to correct or complete these details. Emmeline discovers that "he is not the same any
more." This is a little hasty after her having been completely sure that he was quite as of old. Emmeline appears
here right in her element; it's all blather, no matter what
she says. The dialogue itself deserves a more careful examination, because it gives occasion for extreme enjoyment
of a situation which in all its comicality is illuminated from
a new angle. The mere sound of the words, "the same,"
works like a new stimulating ingredient on the lunacy of

the situation; one involuntarily has to laugh because one involuntarily begins to ask himself: "the same" as whom? The same as he appeared to be in the testing scene? This leads one to think how inadequate this test was. The same as whom? As Charles, whom she did not know? Moreover, when I say about someone that he is the same or he is not the same, I may use this expression in either an external or an internal sense, with reference to his outer appearance or to his inner nature. The latter, one might believe, would be of especial importance to lovers. Now, however, one discovers that the test had not taken cognizance of this, and yet he was found to be the same. Quite accidentally Emmeline begins to consider whether Charles's character has not changed, and she now discovers that he is not the same. The denial of his moral character's being the same contains also an affirmation that in all other respects he is the same. Still, Emmeline explains herself more exactly. She does not seek the alteration in the fact that Charles has become a spendthrift or possibly something even worse, but in that he has not confided everything to her, as he was accustomed to do. Now this must be one of her romantic ideas, which is probably to be understood as deriving from the fact that she has been accustomed, as in the recognition scene, to chatter about everything to him. That Charles was accustomed to confide everything to her, she simply does not know from experience but from romances wherein one learns that lovers should have no secrets from each other. Even if Charles were an escaped convict, that would not disturb her, if only her erotic curiosity was satisfied by his confiding it to her. The attempt Emmeline makes, by observing Charles's character to convince herself of his identity, must be regarded as sheer nonsense, which throws some light partly on her nature, partly on the rest of her chatter. In the same moment, therefore, she abandons this train of reasoning and gets a new, a far more certain proof that he is not the same, when she discovers that he does not have the ring. Now she needs no further evidence against him. She admits that he might have done what he would, the craziest things, or, in other words, have changed as much as he would, he would still remain the same, but that he did not have the ring bears witness against him. Emmeline distinguishes herself by a special kind of abstract thinking. However, what she has left, after and by abstraction, is not so much Charles's essential nature as the ring. Emmeline is to be regarded as the spirit of the ring, who obeys him "who has the ring in his hand."[16]

Lapierre announces a new stranger. It is agreed that it must be Rinville. Emmeline gets orders to dress herself, and bursts out: "How tiresome it is. Must I go and dress myself up for the sake of a strange man whom I cannot abide; I already know that in advance." By this speech the spectator notices in time the irony in one of the resulting situations. On the whole Emmeline can flatter herself on being irony's darling. It humors her in every way—and later gets the best of her. She wants the supposed Charles to be a handsome young man. Irony indulges her. Dervière cannot see it, he stands like a fool, Emmeline with flying colors, and yet she is most the fool. She wants the supposed Rinville to be a man she cannot bear, although her father assures her that he is an excellent young man. Irony again indulges her, and yet in such wise that she is made a fool of.

The eleventh scene is a monologue by Rinville. It would seem that this monologue might have been omitted, since the effect of it in every way is disturbing. In so far as it was in order to let Rinville remain in possession of the field and be the first to receive Charles, his monologue could have been shortened. Nor would it then have been without effect. He could then proclaim in the poet's words: "Bravo! It goes excellently! Quarrels with the father, quarrels with the daughter; I must certainly admit that it is a plan which promises well." This monologue would then contain a kind of objective reflection on the progress of the play. Should the poet consider it necessary to make the monologue a little longer in order to give Charles time to come, he could allow Rinville to make a little joke with himself over the consideration that in the final analysis he might perhaps have been more clever to have come in his own person and over the drollery involved in his progressing from bad to worse every time new despatches came about Charles. Then it would have been best for him to be interrupted in this deliberation by Charles's speech from the wings. For as Scribe ends the monologue, one feels too strongly that now the monologue is finished and now a new person must appear. If Rinville's monologue were thus interrupted, then a new light would be cast on Charles's fantastic haste, over the importunity in his appearance, by which he always distinguishes himself, *item* over the short-winded imbecility which the poet has so inimitably stamped upon his first speeches.

Still, this is less important. The main fault in this monologue is that the action which Rinville suggests appears entirely as talk, only as imaginary action. Rinville explains that it is no longer for fun that he plays Charles's role. That was never really the case; on the contrary, he himself in the beginning indicated three substantial reasons for it, so that he might be able to bring about a marriage with Emmeline. Next he explains that he will prevent Emmeline from confusing him with Charles; he will convince himself that it is he whom she loves, not the memory of Charles. This is of utmost importance to the whole play, for it is decisive in determining, as developed above, whether the play is, in a finite sense, moralizing or, in an infinite sense, witty. His procedure must then aim at letting his own characteristic attractiveness become visible through the person of Charles. This, however, does not happen, and had it happened, the play would have become something quite different. With Emmeline everything turns on the ring; when, in the fifteenth scene, he appears with it, she takes him into favor, recognizes him as being the same, and so on. Rinville, for the sake of the total effect of the play, must in no way be regarded as a poetic figure, nor could this be demonstrated by the few gleams of light which fall upon him. He is a man who has reached years of discretion, who has sound reasons for what he does. Off and on he is seen in a comic light, because it appears that his sound reasons and his understanding are of little help to him in captivating such a romantic little gazelle as Miss Emmeline. Even if he were a man absolutely attractive and dangerous to a young girl's heart, he would have no power over Emmeline, she is invulnerable; he can effect this only by appealing to her through her fixed idea, that is, through the ring. But since the main interest of the play requires the nullification of his real attractiveness, it would be wrong to accentuate his attractiveness, for which reason the poet has not done it save in this one monologue. In the scene where Rinville has most to do with Emmeline, there can naturally be no talk at all about an opportunity for him to display his personal attractiveness. When a young girl fastens herself upon a man as Emmeline did on Rinville, when by her own willingness, she constantly gives him an opportunity to steal into her heart, then must Rinville be an utter bungler if he cannot come to her assistance. So far from being supposed to display Rinville's attractiveness, this scene seems rather to place him in a somewhat comic light. He is manifestly an intelligent man; he has in the foregoing dialogue been a little self-important, letting the spectators as well as his friends in Paris understand that he is man enough to tame a little maiden like this. It is true he succeeds; but if his friends in Paris could see how it was done, they would have no occasion to admire his talents. His discretion teaches him to pass himself off as Charles. To this extent one must give him his due. Now it has happened; now he must show his attractiveness; now, one thinks, he will have plenty to do. Then it appears that he has simply nothing to do; the swift-footed Emmeline, who is hastening back into her youthful memories, takes Mr. Rinville along; and any man who was not a complete blockhead would be able to imitate this masterpiece.

What has here been developed regarding Rinville's character is, in my opinion, of absolute importance for the whole play. There must not be a single figure in it, not a single dramatic relationship which might make claim to survive the destruction which irony, straight from the beginning, has been preparing for everything and everybody in it. When the curtain falls, then everything is forgotten, only nothing remains, and that is the only thing one gets to see; and the only thing one gets to hear is a laughter, which like a sound in nature, does not issue from a single human being, but is the language of a world force, and this force is irony.

Charles enters and meets Rinville. The wittiness in the situation lies in the fact that Charles, this scheming pate, comes too late, not only with respect to Mr. Zacharias, but especially with respect to the intrigue in the play. His lines are here as everywhere masterly, characteristic of him and, at the same time, in conformity with the situation. Rinville suggests to Charles the scheme of passing himself off for Rinville. He has completely outlined the idea for this, when Charles, who could not possibly take advice from another regarding a mystification, interrupts him and makes it look as if it is he himself who invented the whole plan. Yet it appears immediately thereafter that he is not a man who could hit upon the least thing; he would even have overlooked the ring if Rinville had not called his attention to it. Rinville gets the ring.

Charles presents himself to the family as Mr. Rinville. This guarantees his reception. Dervière finds him younger and handsomer than Charles. Emmeline finds him loathsome. Both judgments are equally unreliable, and one ventures to believe that Emmeline had not even found it worth while to look at him but knew it by virtue of inspiration. It is the same way with her father. The situation holds a profound mockery of Charles, who probably ascribes this favorable reception to his own cleverness and hopes that everything will succeed, if only he continues incognito.

Now comes a monologue in which Emmeline communes with her heart and finds out that she will never forget Charles but will marry Rinville.

Rinville comes to take leave and delivers the ring. They are reconciled again. These situations we are already acquainted with.

Now follows the most brilliant situation in the whole play. There rests a nimbus over it, a transfiguration, which has a solemnity of its own, so that one might almost wish to see Aunt Judith in the background as a spirit looking down upon her two pupils. Emmeline resolves to confide in the assumed Rinville and reveal all. This situation throws a perfect light on Emmeline and Charles. Emmeline's fidelity becomes altogether parodical. For no price will she give him up. She fears neither fire nor water. Charles's embarrassment becomes greater and greater, since he wishes to get rid of her. Such a loyalty is quite in order, for a little maiden like Emmeline always tends to be most loyal when the one loved wishes to be rid of her. Charles who, since he had learned that Mr. Zacharias had not divulged the worst,[17] was certain of being able through his adroitness to get himself out of the whole situation, now becomes the one who betrays everything. The opportunity is too tempting. He can become the troubadour of his own life, and he hopes in that way to get rid of his cousin. We were reminded earlier that this gives the situation a lighter touch so that Charles's aberrations take on a comic aspect. We get a vivid conception of his recklessness and his confusion of mind, but we are not indignant as would be the case if in his own character he had told everything in the same way, and yet we suspect that he probably would do so. We surmise it, but we do not hear it. Charles accomplishes nothing, however, he pleases only himself. Emmeline's loyalty knows no bounds. Finally Charles admits that he is married. It is incredible with what sureness the poet knows how to ironize Emmeline. She hears he is married, and she becomes furious. One or another spectator might perhaps think that the reason she became so enraged with Charles was that she had now learned to know all his bad points. By no means, dear friend! You misunderstand her. She'll take Charles if only she can get him. But he is married. She would indeed find it proper, if in the eight years he had not looked at any other girl but had conscientiously gazed at the moon. Still, she knows how to disregard this. Let him have seduced ten girls, she'll take him, she'll take him *à tout prix;* but if he is married, she cannot have him. *Hinc illae lacrimae.*[18] If this were not the poet's meaning, he would have let Emmeline interrupt Charles somewhat earlier. Charles has explained that he had been subject to many persecutions from the fair sex, that he had had various affairs, that he had perhaps sometimes gone too far in amiability. She does not interrupt him; she promises to do everything possible to reconcile him with her father and get him herself; for it is clear that when she cannot get him (as soon as she hears he is married) she is not one

who forgets to alarm the camp. Charles begins on his story
of Pamela; she listens quietly to it. Then comes the terrible
news that he is married. Down crashed the Kingdom of
Norway.

The profound irony in this situation lies, then, in Emmeline's inviolable loyalty, which will not relinquish Charles
at any price, since it would cost her her life, as well as in
Charles's increasing embarrassment at not being able to get
rid of her. The whole scene is like a letting of public contracts, where the ideal Charles is awarded to Emmeline as
lowest bidder. Finally, the whole thing ends at the point
where it appears that she cannot get Charles, and Charles
cannot escape from his stupid folly.

Emmeline raises an outcry; the father comes in and
promises he will never forgive Charles.

Now the pseudo-Charles comes forward. Emmeline has
begged her father not to lose his temper; she herself will
hear his confession. We must here as always admire the
poet's tactics. For the scene must remain ridiculous and the
situation ironical when we see on the assumed Rinville the
impression the thundering speech is intended to make on
the assumed Charles; the real Charles, in other words, has
the pleasure of being personally present while he is himself
executed in effigy. Had the poet let Dervière make this
speech, it would have been a poetic injustice. The uncle
has been Charles's benefactor and has a lawful right not
to be made a fool of in the presence of Charles. True, the
uncle is not as clever as the girl, but his benefactions over
a period of years place him at an advantage over Charles,
quite different from such a reckless marriage promise as he
has given Emmeline. Since, on the other hand, everything
else that Emmeline says seems to be nonsense, including
the marriage promise, then it is proper that this philippic
should seem so likewise. Her old love for Charles is nonsense, her new love for Rinville is also nonsense; her enthusiasm is nonsense, and likewise her anger; her defiance
is nonsense, as well as her good intentions.

Emmeline then gives vent to her anger, and the pseudo-
Rinville burlesques the effect of her story by behaving and
acting like the pseudo-Charles! It may be regarded as the

crowning feature in this situation that she admits that she really has loved Charles. The confusion here is perfect. For the one that by her own admission she has loved these eight years is Rinville, in whom, by the aid of sympathy, she had immediately recognized Charles, and whom, a little after convincing herself that he was not the same, she again recognized through the ring.

At last the confusion is resolved. It appears that she has got Rinville instead of Charles. Herewith the play is finished, or, more correctly, it is not finished. This I have already explained earlier; here I shall only by a word or two throw some light on the proposition. If it is the intention of the play to show that Emmeline has become a reasonable girl, who, when she chooses Rinville, makes a suitable choice, then the accent of the whole play is laid in the wrong place. For in such a case, it would interest us less to know in what sense Charles has failed. What we do demand, on the contrary, is some illumination about Rinville's attractions. Just because Charles has become a lewd popinjay, it by no means follows that Emmeline must therefore choose Rinville, except in so far as one sets Scribe down for a dramatic bungler who respects the dramatic tradition that every young girl must be married, and if she doesn't want the one, then must she take the other. If, however, one understands the play as I have understood it, then the whole play is a perfect joke, the wit infinite, the comedy a masterpiece.

The curtain falls, the play is over, nothing is left except the great outline in which it appears; only the situation's fantastic shadow-play, which irony directs, remains for contemplation. The immediately real situation is the unreal situation; behind this there appears a new situation which is no less absurd, and so forth. In the situation we hear the dialogue; when it is most reasonable, it appears most crazy; and as the situation recedes, so the dialogue follows along, more and more meaningless in spite of its reasonableness.

In order rightly to enjoy the irony in this play contemplatively, you must not read it but see it; you must see it again and again, and when you have the good fortune to be contemporary with the four dramatic artists who in our theater contribute in every way to showing and suggesting the transparency of the situation, then will the enjoyment become greater and greater every time you see it.

Let the dialogue in this play be ever so witty, you will forget it; the situations you cannot possibly forget, when you have once seen them. When you have become familiar with them, then the next time you see the play you will learn to be thankful for the dramatic presentation. I do not know how to give any greater praise to the performance than by saying that it is so highly perfect that it makes one wholly ungrateful the first times you see it, because what you get is the play, neither more nor less. I know a young philosopher who once expounded a part of the doctrine of being to me. The whole was so easy, so simple, so natural, that when he was finished I almost shrugged my shoulders and said: Is this all? When I came home I wanted to reproduce the logical exercise, and it appeared that I could not even start. Then I observed that there must be something else. I felt how great his virtuosity and his superiority over me were, I felt it almost a mockery that he had done it so well that I became ungrateful. He was a philosophical artist, and as it was with him, so it is with all great artists, our Lord *inclusive*.

As it was with me in the case of my philosophical friend, so it is with me about the performance of *The First Love*. Only when I had seen it performed again and again and on other stages did I become truly grateful to our dramatic artists. If I were therefore to introduce a foreigner to our stage, I should take him to the theater when this play was to be performed, and then, acting on the supposition that he knew the play, I should say to him: "Observe Frydendahl, turn your eyes away from him, shut them; let his image appear before you; these pure noble features, this graceful bearing, how can this be laughable; open your eyes again and see Frydendahl. Observe Madame Heiberg, cast down your eyes, for Emmeline's attraction might become dangerous to you; listen to the sentimentally languishing voice, the childish and whimsical insinuations of the girl, and if you were as dry and stiff as a book-keeper, you would still have to smile. Open your eyes, how is it possible? Repeat these movements so swiftly that they become almost simultaneous in the moment, and you have a conception of what is being presented. Without irony, an artist can never sketch; a dramatic artist can only produce it through contradiction, for the essence of the sketch is superficiality, and where no delineation of character is required, the art is to transform oneself into a surface, which is a paradox for the scenic presentation, and to only a few is it given to resolve it. An unreflective comedian can never play Dervière, for he has no character. Emmeline's whole nature is contradiction and therefore cannot be presented immediately. She must be attractive, for otherwise the effect of the whole play is spoiled; she must not be attractive but affected, for otherwise, in another sense, the whole effect of the play is lost. Behold Phister, you almost become ill when you let your glance rest on the infinitely fresh stupidity that is stamped on his countenance. And yet it is not an immediate dullness; his glance still has an enthusiasm which in its foolishness is reminiscent of the past. No one is born with such a face, it has a history. When I was little I can remember that my nursemaid explained to me that one must not make faces, and as a warning to me and other children, she told a story about a man with a grotesque face, which he himself was to blame for, because he made wry faces. It so happened, curiously enough, that the wind changed, and the man's contorted expression froze on his face. Such an absurd face Phister lets us see; there is even a trace of the romantic grimace, but when the wind changed it became something distorted. Phister's presentation of Charles has less irony but more humor. This is quite correct, for the contradiction in his being is not so evident. He is not to pass for Rinville, except in the eyes of Dervière and Emmeline, who in their own ways are equally biased.

Behold Stage, rejoice over this beautiful manly figure, this refined personality, this easy smile which betrays Rinville's fancied superiority over Dervière's fantastic family, and then see this representative of the intellect whirled along in the confusion which Emmeline's empty passion, like a forward rushing wind, occasions.

THE ROTATION METHOD

An Essay in the Theory of Social Prudence

Chremylos: You get too much at last of everything.
           Of love,
Karion: of bread,
Chremylos: of music,
Karion: and of sweetmeats.
Chremylos: Of honor,
Karion: cakes,
Chremylos: of courage,
Karion: and of figs.
Chremylos: Ambition,
Karion: barley-cakes,
Chremylos: high office,
Karion: lentils.
           (Aristophanes' *Plutus*, v. 189 *ff.*)

S tarting from a principle is affirmed by people of experience to be a very reasonable procedure; I am willing to humor them, and so begin with the principle that all men are bores. Surely no one will prove himself so great a bore as to contradict me in this. This principle possesses the quality of being in the highest degree repellent, an essential requirement in the case of negative principles, which are in the last analysis the principles of all motion.[1] It is not merely repellent, but infinitely forbidding; and whoever has this principle back of him cannot but receive an infinite impetus forward, to help him make new discoveries. For if my principle is true, one need only consider how ruinous boredom is for humanity, and by properly adjusting the intensity of one's concentration upon this fundamental truth, attain any desired degree of momentum. Should one wish to attain the maximum momentum, even to the point of almost endangering the driving power, one need only say to oneself: Boredom is the root of all evil. Strange that boredom, in itself so staid and stolid, should have such power to set in motion. The influence it exerts is altogether magical, except that it is not the influence of attraction, but of repulsion.

In the case of children, the ruinous character of boredom is universally acknowledged. Children are always well-behaved as long as they are enjoying themselves. This is true in the strictest sense; for if they sometimes become unruly in their play, it is because they are already beginning to be bored—boredom is already approaching, though from a different direction. In choosing a governess one, therefore, takes into account not only her sobriety, her faithfulness, and her competence, but also her aesthetic qualifications for amusing the children; and there would be no hesitancy in dismissing a governess who was lacking in this respect, even if she had all the other desirable virtues. Here, then, the principle is clearly acknowledged; but so strange is the way of the world, so pervasive the influence of habit and boredom, that this is practically the only case in which the science of aesthetics receives its just dues. If one were to ask for a divorce because his wife was tiresome, or demand the abdication of a king because he was boring to look at, or the banishment of a preacher because he was tiresome to listen to, or the dismissal of a prime minister, or the execution of a journalist, because he was terribly tiresome, one would find it impossible to force it through. What wonder, then, that the world goes from bad to worse, and that its evils increase more and more, as boredom increases, and boredom is the root of all evil.

The history of this can be traced from the very beginning of the world. The gods were bored, and so they created man. Adam was bored because he was alone, and so Eve was created. Thus boredom entered the world, and increased in proportion to the increase of population. Adam was bored alone; then Adam and Eve were bored together; then Adam and Eve and Cain and Abel were bored *en famille;* then the population of the world increased, and the peoples were bored *en masse.* To divert themselves they conceived the idea of constructing a tower high enough to reach the heavens. This idea is itself as boring as the tower was high, and constitutes a terrible proof of how boredom gained the upper hand. The nations were scattered over the earth, just as people now travel abroad, but they continued to be bored. Consider the consequences of this boredom. Humanity fell from its lofty height, first because of Eve, and then from the Tower of Babel. What was it, on the other hand, that delayed the fall of Rome, was it not *panis* and *circenses?*[2] And is anything being done now? Is anyone concerned about planning some means of diversion? Quite the contrary, the impending ruin is being accelerated. It is proposed to call a constitutional assembly. Can anything more tiresome be imagined, both for the participants themselves, and for those who have to hear and read about it? It is proposed to improve the financial condition of the state by practicing economy. What could be more tiresome? Instead of increasing the national debt, it is proposed to pay it off. As I understand the political situation, it would be an easy matter for Denmark to negotiate a loan of fifteen million dollars. Why not consider this plan? Every once in a while we hear of a man who is a genius, and therefore neglects to pay his debts—why should not a nation do the same, if we were all agreed? Let us then borrow fifteen millions, and let us use the proceeds, not to pay our debts, but for public entertainment. Let us celebrate the millennium in a riot of merriment. Let us place boxes everywhere, not, as at present, for the deposit of money, but for the free distribution of money. Everything would become gratis; theaters gratis, women of easy virtue gratis, one would drive to the park gratis, be buried gratis, one's eulogy would be gratis; I say gratis, for when one always has money at hand, everything is in a certain sense free. No one should be permitted to own any property. Only in my own case would there be an exception. I reserve to myself securities in the Bank of London to the value of one hundred dollars a day, partly because I cannot do with less, partly because the idea is mine, and finally because I may not be able to hit upon a new idea when the fifteen millions are gone.

What would be the consequences of all this prosperity? Everything great would gravitate toward Copenhagen, the greatest artists, the greatest dancers, the greatest actors. Copenhagen would become a second Athens. What then? All rich men would establish their homes in this city. Among others would come the Shah of Persia, and the King of England would also come. Here is my second idea. Let us kidnap the Shah of Persia. Perhaps you say an insurrection might take place in Persia and a new ruler be placed on the throne, as has often happened before, the consequence being a fall in price for the old Shah. Very well then, I propose that we sell him to the Turks; they will doubtless know how to turn him into money. Then there is another circumstance which our politicians seem entirely to have overlooked. Denmark holds the balance of power in Europe. It is impossible to imagine a more fortunate lot. I know that from my own experience; I once held the balance of power in a family and could do as I pleased; the blame never fell on me, but always on the others. O that my words might reach your ears, all you who sit in high places to advise and rule, you king's men and men of the people, wise and understanding citizens of all classes! Consider the crisis! Old Denmark is on the brink of ruin; what a calamity! It will be destroyed by boredom. Of all calamities the most calamitous! In ancient times they made him king who extolled most beautifully the praises of the deceased king;[3] in our times we ought to make him king who utters the best witticism, and make him crown prince who gives occasion for the utterance of the best witticism.

O beautiful, emotional sentimentality, how you carry me away! Should I trouble to speak to my contemporaries, to initiate them into my wisdom? By no means. My wisdom is not exactly *zum Gebrauch für Jedermann*,[4] and it is always more prudent to keep one's maxims of prudence to oneself. I desire no disciples; but if there happened to be someone present at my deathbed, and I was sure that the end had come, then I might in an attack of philanthropic delirium, whisper my theory in his ear, uncertain whether I had done him a service or not. People talk so much about man being a social animal;[5] at bottom, he is a beast of prey, and the evidence for this is not confined to the shape of his teeth. All this talk about society and the social is partly inherited hypocrisy, partly calculated cunning.

All men are bores. The word itself suggests the possibility of a subdivision. It may just as well indicate a man who bores others as one who bores himself. Those who bore others are the mob, the crowd, the infinite multitude of men in general. Those who bore themselves are the elect, the aristocracy; and it is a curious fact that those who do not bore themselves usually bore others, while those who bore themselves entertain others. Those who do not bore themselves are generally people who, in one way or another, keep themselves extremely busy; these people are precisely on this account the most tiresome, the most utterly unendurable. This species of animal life is surely not the fruit of man's desire and woman's lust. Like all lower forms of life, it is marked by a high degree of fertility, and multiplies endlessly. It is inconceivable that nature should require nine months to produce such beings; they ought rather to be turned out by the score. The second class, the aristocrats, are those who bore themselves. As noted above, they generally entertain others—in a certain external sense sometimes the mob, in a deeper sense only their fellow initiates. The more profoundly they bore themselves, the more powerfully do they serve to divert these latter, even when their boredom reaches its zenith, as when they either die of boredom (the passive form) or shoot themselves out of curiosity (the active form).

It is usual to say that idleness is a root of all evil. To prevent this evil one is advised to work. However, it is easy to see, both from the nature of the evil that is feared and the remedy proposed, that this entire view is of a very plebeian extraction. Idleness is by no means as such a root of evil; on the contrary, it is a truly divine life, provided one is not himself bored. Idleness may indeed cause the loss of one's fortune, and so on, but the high-minded man does not fear such dangers; he fears only boredom. The Olympian gods were not bored, they lived happily in happy idleness. A beautiful woman, who neither sews nor spins nor bakes nor reads nor plays the piano, is happy in her idleness, for she is not bored. So far from idleness being the root of all evil, it is rather the only true good. Boredom is the root of all evil, and it is this which must be kept at a distance. Idleness is not an evil; indeed one may say that every human being who lacks a sense for idleness proves that his consciousness has not yet been elevated to the level of the humane. There is a restless activity which excludes a man from the world of the spirit, setting him in a class with the brutes, whose instincts impel them always to be on the move. There are men who have an extraordinary talent for transforming everything into a matter of business, whose whole life is business, who fall in love, marry, listen to a joke, and admire a picture with the same industrious zeal with which they labor during business hours. The Latin proverb, *otium est pulvinar diaboli,* is true enough, but the devil gets no time to lay his head on this pillow when one is not bored.[6] But since some people believe that the end and aim of life is work, the disjunction, idleness-work, is quite correct. I assume that it is the end and aim of every man to enjoy himself, and hence my disjunction is no less correct.

Boredom is the daemonic side of pantheism. If we remain in boredom as such, it becomes the evil principle; if we annul it, we posit it in its truth; but we can only annul boredom by enjoying ourselves—*ergo*, it is our duty to enjoy ourselves. To say that boredom is annulled by work betrays a confusion of thought; for idleness can certainly be annulled by work, since it is its opposite, but not boredom, and experience shows that the busiest workers, whose constant buzzing most resembles an insect's hum, are the most tiresome of creatures; if they do not bore themselves, it is because they have no true conception of what boredom is; but then it can scarcely be said that they have overcome boredom.

Boredom is partly an inborn talent, partly an acquired immediacy. The English are in general the paradigmatic nation. A true talent for indolence is very rare; it is never met with in nature, but belongs to the world of the spirit. Occasionally, however, you meet a traveling Englishman who is, as it were, the incarnation of this talent—a heavy, immovable animal, whose entire language exhausts its riches in a single word of one syllable, an interjection by which he signifies his deepest admiration and his supreme indifference, admiration and indifference having been neutralized in the unity of boredom. No other nation produces such miracles of nature; every other national will always show himself a little more vivacious, not so absolutely stillborn. The only analogy I know of is the apostle of the empty enthusiasm, who also makes his way through life on an interjection. This is the man who everywhere makes a profession of enthusiasm, who cries Ah! or Oh! whether the event be significant or insignificant, the difference having been lost for him in the emptiness of a blind and noisy enthusiasm. The second form of boredom is usually the result of a mistaken effort to find diversion.[7] The fact that the remedy against boredom may also serve to produce boredom, might appear to be a suspicious circumstance; but it has this effect only in so far as it is incorrectly employed. A misdirected search for diversion, one which is eccentric in its direction, conceals boredom within its own depths and gradually works it out toward the surface, thus revealing itself as that which it immediately is. In the case of horses, we distinguish between blind staggers and sleepy staggers, but call both staggers; and so we can also make a distinction between two kinds of boredom, though uniting both under the common designation of being tiresome.

Pantheism is, in general, characterized by fullness; in the case of boredom we find the precise opposite, since it is characterized by emptiness; but it is just this which makes boredom a pantheistic conception.[8] Boredom depends on the nothingness which pervades reality; it causes a dizziness like that produced by looking down into a yawning chasm, and this dizziness is infinite. The eccentric form of diversion noted above sounds forth without producing an echo, which proves it to be based on boredom; for in nothingness not even an echo can be produced.

Now since boredom as shown above is the root of all evil, what can be more natural than the effort to overcome it? Here, as everywhere, however, it is necessary to give the problem calm consideration; otherwise one may find oneself driven by the daemonic spirit of boredom deeper and deeper into the mire in the very effort to escape. Everyone who feels bored cries out for change. With this demand I am in complete sympathy, but it is necessary to act in accordance with some settled principle.

My own dissent from the ordinary view is sufficiently expressed in the use I make of the word, "rotation." This word might seem to conceal an ambiguity, and if I wished to use it so as to find room in it for the ordinary method, I should have to define it as a change of field. But the farmer does not use the word in this sense. I shall, however, adopt this meaning for a moment, in order to speak of the rotation which depends on change in its boundless infinity, its extensive dimension, so to speak.

This is the vulgar and inartistic method, and needs to be supported by illusion. One tires of living in the country, and moves to the city; one tires of one's native land, and travels abroad; one is *europamüde*,[9] and goes to America, and so on; finally one indulges in a sentimental hope of endless journeyings from star to star. Or the movement is different but still extensive. One tires of porcelain dishes and eats on silver; one tires of silver and turns to gold; one burns half of Rome to get an idea of the burning of Troy. This method defeats itself; it is plain endlessness. And what did Nero gain by it? Antonine was wiser; he says: "It is in your power to review your life, to look at things you saw before, from another point of view."[10]

My method does not consist in change of field, but resembles the true rotation method in changing the crop and the mode of cultivation. Here we have at once the principle of limitation, the only saving principle in the world. The more you limit yourself, the more fertile you become in invention. A prisoner in solitary confinement for life becomes very inventive, and a spider may furnish him with much entertainment. One need only hark back to one's schooldays. We were at an age when aesthetic considerations were ignored in the choice of one's instructors, most of whom were for that reason very tiresome; how fertile in invention one then proved to be! How entertaining to catch a fly and hold it imprisoned under a nut shell and to watch how it pushed the shell around; what pleasure from cutting a hole in the desk, putting a fly in it, and then peeping down at it through a piece of paper! How entertaining sometimes to listen to the monotonous drip of water from the roof! How close an observer one becomes under such circumstances, when not the least noise nor movement escapes one's attention! Here we have the extreme application of the method which seeks to achieve results intensively, not extensively.

The more resourceful in changing the mode of cultivation one can be, the better; but every particular change will always come under the general categories of *remembering* and *forgetting*. Life in its entirety moves in these two currents, and hence it is essential to have them under control. It is impossible to live artistically before one has made up one's mind to abandon hope; for hope precludes self-limitation. It is a very beautiful sight to see a man put out to sea with the fair wind of hope, and one may even use the opportunity to be taken in tow; but one should never permit hope to be taken aboard one's own ship, least of all as a pilot; for hope is a faithless shipmaster. Hope was one of the dubious gifts of Prometheus; instead of giving men the foreknowledge of the immortals, he gave them hope.[11]

To forget—all men wish to forget, and when something unpleasant happens, they always say: Oh, that one might forget! But forgetting is an art that must be practiced beforehand. The ability to forget is conditioned upon the method of remembering, but this again depends upon the mode of experiencing reality. Whoever plunges into his experiences with the momentum of hope will remember in such wise that he is unable to forget. *Nil admirari* is therefore the real philosophy.[12] No moment must be permitted so great a significance that it cannot be forgotten when convenient; each moment ought, however, to have so much significance that it can be recollected at will. Childhood, which is the age which remembers best, is at the same time most forgetful. The more poetically one remembers, the more easily one forgets; for remembering poetically is really only another expression for forgetting. In a poetic memory the experience has undergone a transformation, by which it has lost all its painful aspects. To remember in this manner, one must be careful how one lives, how one enjoys. Enjoying an experience to its full intensity to the last minute will make it impossible either to remember or to forget. For there is then nothing to remember except a certain satiety, which one desires to forget, but which now comes back to plague the mind with an involuntary remembrance. Hence, when you begin to notice that a certain pleasure or experience is acquiring too strong a hold upon the mind, you stop a moment for the purpose of remembering. No other method can better create a distaste for continuing the experience too long. From the beginning one should keep the enjoyment under control, never spreading every sail to the wind in any resolve; one ought to devote oneself to pleasure with a certain suspicion, a certain wariness, if one desires to give the lie to the proverb which says that no one can have his cake and eat it too. The carrying of concealed weapons is usually forbidden, but no weapon is so dangerous as the art of remembering. It gives one a very peculiar feeling in the midst of one's enjoyment to look back upon it for the purpose of remembering it.

One who has perfected himself in the twin arts of remembering and forgetting is in a position to play at battledore and shuttlecock with the whole of existence.

The extent of one's power to forget is the final measure of one's elasticity of spirit. If a man cannot forget he will never amount to much. Whether there be somewhere a Lethe gushing forth, I do not know; but this I know, that the art of forgetting can be developed. However, this art does not consist in permitting the impressions to vanish completely; forgetfulness is one thing, and the art of forgetting is something quite different. It is easy to see that most people have a very meager understanding of this art, for they ordinarily wish to forget only what is unpleasant, not what is pleasant. This betrays a complete one-sidedness. Forgetting is the true expression for an ideal process of assimilation by which the experience is reduced to a sounding-board for the soul's own music. Nature is great because it has forgotten that it was chaos; but this thought is subject to revival at any time. As a result of attempting to forget only what is unpleasant, most people have a conception of oblivion as an untamable force which drowns out the past. But forgetting is really a tranquil and quiet occupation, and one which should be exercised quite as much in connection with the pleasant as with the unpleasant. A pleasant experience has as past something unpleasant about it, by which it stirs a sense of privation; this unpleasantness is taken away by an act of forgetfulness. The unpleasant has a sting, as all admit. This, too, can be removed by the art of forgetting. But if one attempts to dismiss the unpleasant absolutely from mind, as many do who dabble in the art of forgetting, one soon learns how little that helps. In an unguarded moment it pays a surprise visit, and it is then invested with all the forcibleness of the unexpected. This is absolutely contrary to every orderly arrangement in a reasonable mind. No misfortune or difficulty is so devoid of affability, so deaf to all appeals, but that it may be flattered a little; even Cerberus accepted bribes of honey-cakes, and it is not only the lassies who are beguiled. The art in dealing with such experiences consists in talking them over, thereby depriving them of their bitterness; not forgetting them absolutely, but forgetting them for the sake of remembering them. Even in the case of memories such that one might suppose an eternal oblivion to be the only safeguard, one need permit oneself only a little trickery, and the deception will succeed for the skillful. Forgetting is tho shears with which you cut away what you cannot use, doing it under the supreme direction of memory. Forgetting and remembering are thus identical arts, and the artistic achievement of this identity is the Archimedean point from which one lifts the whole world. When we say that we *consign* something to oblivion, we suggest simultaneously that it is to be forgotten and yet also remembered.

The art of remembering and forgetting will also insure against sticking fast in some relationship of life, and make possible the realization of a complete freedom.

One must guard against *friendship*. How is a friend defined? He is not what philosophy calls the necessary other, but the superfluous third. What are friendship's ceremonies? You drink each other's health, you open an artery and mingle your blood with that of the friend. It is difficult to say when the proper moment for this arrives, but it announces itself mysteriously; you feel some way that you can no longer address one another formally. When once you have had this feeling, then it can never appear that you have made a mistake, like Geert Vestphaler, who discovered that he had been drinking to friendship with the public hangman.[13] What are the infallible marks of friendship? Let antiquity answer: *idem velle, idem nolle, ea demum firma amicitia,*[14] and also extremely tiresome. What are the infallible marks of friendship? Mutual assistance in word and deed. Two friends form a close association in order to be everything to one another, and that although it is impossible for one human being to be anything to another human being except to be in his way. To be sure one may help him with money, assist him in and out of his coat, be his humble servant, and tender him congratulations on New Year's Day, on the day of his wedding, on the birth of a child, on the occasion of a funeral.

But because you abstain from friendship it does not follow that you abstain from social contacts. On the contrary, these social relationships may at times be permitted to take on a deeper character, provided you always have so much more momentum in yourself that you can sheer off at will, in spite of sharing for a time in the momentum of the common movement. It is believed that such conduct leaves unpleasant memories, the unpleasantness being due to the fact that a relationship which has meant something now vanishes and becomes as nothing. But this is a misunderstanding. The unpleasant is merely a piquant ingredient in the sullenness of life. Besides, it is possible for the same relationship again to play a significant role, though in another manner. The essential thing is never to stick fast, and for this it is necessary to have oblivion back of one. The experienced farmer lets his land lie fallow now and then, and the theory of social prudence recommends the same. Everything will doubtless return, though in a different form; that which has once been present in the rotation will remain in it, but the mode of cultivation will be varied. You therefore quite consistently hope to meet your friends and acquaintances in a better world, but you do not share the fear of the crowd that they will be altered so that you cannot recognize them; your fear is rather lest they be wholly unaltered. It is remarkable how much significance even the most insignificant person can gain from a rational mode of cultivation.

One must never enter into the relation of *marriage*. Husband and wife promise to love one another for eternity. This is all very fine, but it does not mean very much; for if their love comes to an end in time, it will surely be ended in eternity. If, instead of promising forever, the parties would say: until Easter, or until May-day comes, there might be some meaning in what they say; for then they would have said something definite, and also something that they might be able to keep. And how does a marriage usually work out? In a little while one party begins to perceive that there is something wrong, then the other party complains, and cries to heaven: faithless! faithless! A little later the second party reaches the same standpoint, and a neutrality is established in which the mutual faithlessness is mutually canceled, to the satisfaction and contentment of both parties. But it is now too late, for there are great difficulties connected with divorce.

Such being the case with marriage, it is not surprising that the attempt should be made in so many ways to bolster it up with moral supports. When a man seeks separation from his wife, the cry is at once raised that he is depraved, a scoundrel, etc. How silly, and what an indirect attack upon marriage! If marriage has reality, then he is sufficiently punished by forfeiting this happiness; if it has no reality, it is absurd to abuse him because he is wiser than the rest. When a man grows tired of his money and throws it out of the window, we do not call him a scoundrel; for either money has reality, and so he is sufficiently punished by depriving himself of it, or it has none, and then he is, of course, a wise man.

One must always take care not to enter into any relationship in which there is a possibility of many members. For this reason friendship is dangerous, to say nothing of marriage. Husband and wife are indeed said to become one, but this is a very dark and mystic saying. When you are one of several, then you have lost your freedom; you cannot send for your traveling boots whenever you wish, you cannot move aimlessly about in the world. If you have a wife it is difficult; if you have a wife and perhaps a child, it is troublesome; if you have a wife and children, it is impossible. True, it has happened that a gypsy woman has carried her husband through life on her back, but for one thing this is very rare, and for another, it is likely to be tiresome in the long run—for the husband. Marriage brings one into fatal connection with custom and tradition, and traditions and customs are like the wind and weather, altogether incalculable. In Japan, I have been told, it is the custom for husbands to lie in childbed. Who knows but the time will come when the customs of foreign countries will obtain a foothold in Europe?

Friendship is dangerous, marriage still more so; for woman is and ever will be the ruin of a man, as soon as he contracts a permanent relation with her. Take a young man who is fiery as an Arabian courser, let him marry, he is lost. Woman is first proud, then is she weak, then she swoons, then he swoons, then the whole family swoons. A woman's love is nothing but dissimulation and weakness.

But because a man does not marry, it does not follow that his life need be wholly deprived of the erotic element. And the erotic ought also to have infinitude; but poetic infinitude, which can just as well be limited to an hour as to a month. When two beings fall in love with one another and begin to suspect that they were made for each other, it is time to have the courage to break it off; for by going on they have everything to lose and nothing to gain. This seems a paradox, and it is so for the feeling, but not for the understanding. In this sphere it is particularly necessary that one should make use of one's moods; through them one may realize an inexhaustible variety of combinations.

One should never accept appointment to an official position. If you do, you will become a mere Richard Roe, a tiny little cog in the machinery of the body politic; you even cease to be master of your own conduct, and in that case your theories are of little help. You receive a title, and this brings in its train every sin and evil. The law under which you have become a slave is equally tiresome, whether your advancement is fast or slow. A title can never be got rid of except by the commission of some crime which draws down on you a public whipping; even then you are not certain, for you may have it restored to you by royal pardon.

Even if one abstains from involvement in official business, one ought not to be inactive, but should pursue such occupations as are compatible with a sort of leisure; one should engage in all sorts of breadless arts. In this connection the self-development should be intensive rather than extensive, and one should, in spite of mature years, be able to prove the truth of the proverb that children are pleased with a rattle and tickled with a straw.

If one now, according to the theory of social jurisprudence, varies the soil—for if he had contact with one person only, the rotation method would fail as badly as if a farmer had only one acre of land, which would make it impossible for him to fallow, something which is of extreme importance —then one must also constantly vary himself, and this is the essential secret. For this purpose one must necessarily have control over one's moods. To control them in the sense of producing them at will is impossible, but prudence teaches how to utilize the moment. As an experienced sailor always looks out over the water and sees a squall coming from far away, so one ought always to see the mood a little in advance. One should know how the mood affects one's own mind and the mind of others, before putting it on. You first strike a note or two to evoke pure tones, and see what there is in a man; the intermediate tones follow later. The more experience you have, the more readily you will be convinced that there is often much in a man which is not suspected. When sentimental people, who as such are extremely tiresome, become angry, they are often very entertaining. Badgering a man is a particularly effective method of exploration.

The whole secret lies in arbitrariness. People usually think it easy to be arbitrary, but it requires much study to succeed in being arbitrary so as not to lose oneself in it, but so as to derive satisfaction from it. One does not enjoy the immediate but something quite different which he arbitrarily imports into it. You go to see the middle of a play, you read the third part of a book. By this means you insure yourself a very different kind of enjoyment from that which the author has been so kind as to plan for you. You enjoy something entirely accidental; you consider the whole of existence from this standpoint; let its reality be stranded thereon. I will cite an example. There was a man whose chatter certain circumstances made it necessary for me to listen to. At every opportunity he was ready with a little philosophical lecture, a very tiresome harangue. Almost in despair, I suddenly discovered that he perspired copiously when talking. I saw the pearls of sweat gather on his brow, unite to form a stream, glide down his nose, and hang at the extreme point of his nose in a drop-shaped body. From the moment of making this discovery, all was changed. I even took pleasure in inciting him to begin his philosophical instruction, merely to observe the perspiration on his brow and at the end of his nose.

The poet Baggesen says somewhere of someone that he

was doubtless a good man, but that there was one insuper-
able objection against him, that there was no word that
rhymed with his name. It is extremely wholesome thus to
let the realities of life split upon an arbitrary interest. You
transform something accidental into the absolute, and, as
such, into the object of your admiration. This has an excellent effect, especially when one is excited. This method
is an excellent stimulus for many persons. You look at everything in life from the standpoint of a wager, and so forth.
The more rigidly consistent you are in holding fast to your
arbitrariness, the more amusing the ensuing combinations
will be. The degree of consistency shows whether you are
an artist or a bungler; for to a certain extent all men do
the same. The eye with which you look at reality must
constantly be changed. The Neo-Platonists assumed that
human beings who had been less perfect on earth became
after death more or less perfect animals, all according to
their deserts. For example, those who had exercised the
civic virtues on a lower scale (retail dealers) were transformed into busy animals, like bees. Such a view of life,
which here in this world sees all men transformed into animals or plants (Plotinus also thought that some would become plants), suggests rich and varied possibilities. The
painter Tischbein sought to idealize every human being
into an animal. His method has the fault of being too serious, in that it endeavors to discover a real resemblance.

The arbitrariness in oneself corresponds to the accidental
in the external world. One should therefore always have an
eye open for the accidental, always be *expeditus*,[15] if anything should offer. The so-called social pleasures for which
we prepare a week or two in advance amount to so little;
on the other hand, even the most insignificant thing may
accidentally offer rich material for amusement. It is impossible here to go into detail, for no theory can adequately
embrace the concrete. Even the most completely developed
theory is poverty-stricken compared with the fullness which
the man of genius easily discovers in his ubiquity.

DIARY OF
THE SEDUCER

Sua passion' predominante
è la giovin principiante
DON GIOVANNI, ARIA NO. 4[1]

I cannot conceal from myself, scarcely can I master the anxiety which grips me at this moment, when I decide for my own satisfaction to make a clear and accurate copy of the rough transcript which I was able at the time to secure only in the greatest haste and with much disquietude. The situation stands out before me just as alarmingly, but also as reprehensibly, as it did at that time. Contrary to his custom, he had not locked his secretary, so its whole content was at my disposal; but it is futile for me to try to extenuate my behavior by reminding myself that I did not open the drawer. One drawer was pulled out. In it I found a number of loose papers, and on top of them lay a book in broad quarto, tastefully bound. On the upper side was placed a vignette of white paper on which he had written in his own hand: *Commentarius perpetuus No. 4.*[2] Vainly, however, have I tried to make myself believe that if the face of the book had not been turned up, and if the strange title had not tempted me, I should not have fallen into temptation, or I should at least have resisted it. The title was peculiar, not so much in itself as because of its surroundings. From a hasty glance at the loose papers I learned that these contained interpretations of erotic situations, a few hints about one and another relationship, outlines for letters of a very peculiar character, which I later learned to know in their artistically perfected, calculated carelessness. When now, after having looked into the scheming mind of this depraved personality, I recall my situation; when, with my eye alert for every subtlety, I in thought approach that drawer, it makes the same impression upon me as it must make upon a police officer when he enters the room of a forger, opens his belongings, and finds in a drawer a number of loose papers, samples of handwriting; on one there is a piece of tracing, on another a monogram, on a third a line of reversed writing. It clearly proves to him that he is on the right track, and his satisfaction over this is mingled with a certain admiration for the study and industry which is here evidenced.

In my case it might have turned out a little differently, since I am less accustomed to tracking down criminals, and am not armed—with a policeman's badge. I should have felt with double weight the truth that I was following unlawful ways. At that time I was no less deficient in thoughts than in words, as is usually the case. One is overawed by an impression until reflection again reasserts itself and, swift and manifold in its movements, insinuates itself with the unknown stranger and coaxes him around. The more reflective thought is developed, the sooner it knows how to pull itself together; it becomes, like a passport clerk dealing with foreign travelers, so accustomed to seeing eccentric figures that it is not easily disconcerted. But although my reflective thought is certainly now very strongly developed, still at first I was greatly astonished. I remember very well that I turned pale, that I almost fell over, and how alarmed I was about it. Suppose he had come home, had found me swooning, with the drawer in my hand—a bad conscience can still make life interesting.

The title of the book did not strike me in itself; I thought it was a collection of excerpts which seemed quite natural to me since I knew that he had always pursued his studies with enthusiasm. It contained, however, something quite different. It was neither more nor less than a diary, carefully kept; and as I, from what I had formerly known about him, had not found that his life particularly needed a commentary, so now I do not deny, after that first glimpse, that the title was selected with much taste and understanding, with a true, aesthetically objective superiority over himself and over the situation. The title harmonizes perfectly with the whole content of the Diary. His life had been an attempt to realize the task of living poetically. With a keenly developed talent for discovering the interesting in life, he had known how to find it, and after finding it, he constantly reproduced the experience more or less poetically. His Diary is therefore neither historically exact nor simply fiction, not indicative but subjunctive. Although the experience is recorded, naturally, after it has happened —sometimes, perhaps, a long time after—yet it is often described with the dramatic vividness of an action taking

place before one's very eyes. That he should have done this
because he had any ulterior purpose in writing the Diary
is highly improbable; that, considered in the strictest sense,
it merely had significance for himself personally is obvious;
and the whole production as well as the individual parts
forbids the assumption that I have before me a poetical
work, one perhaps intended for publication. He did not
need to fear anything personally in publishing it, for most
of the names are so unusual that there is absolutely no
probability of their being authentic, except that I have suspected that the Christian name was historically correct, so
that he might always be sure of identifying the actual
person, while every outsider would be misled by the surname. Such at least was the case with Cordelia, the girl I
knew, around whom the chief interest centers; she was
rightfully called Cordelia, but not, however, Wahl.

Still, how can we account for the fact that the Diary has
acquired such a poetic coloring? The answer to this is not
difficult; it is explained by the fact of his poetic temperament, which, we might say, is not rich enough, or, perhaps,
not poor enough, to distinguish poetry and reality from
one another. The poetical was the *more* he himself brought
with him. This *more* was the poetical he enjoyed in the
poetic situation of reality; he withdrew this again in the
form of poetic reflection. This afforded him a second enjoyment, and his whole life was motivated by enjoyment. In
the first instance he enjoyed the aesthetic personally, in
the second instance he enjoyed his own aesthetic personality. In the first instance the point was that he enjoyed
egoistically and personally what in part was reality's gift
to him and in part was that with which he himself had
impregnated reality; in the second instance his personality
was effaced, and he enjoyed the situation, and himself in
the situation. In the first instance he constantly needed reality as occasion, as factor; in the second instance, reality
was submerged in the poetic. The fruit of the first stage
is thus the mood from which the Diary emerges as the
fruit of the second stage, this word being used in the latter
instance in a somewhat different sense from that in the

first. Thus the poetic was constantly present in the ambiguity in which he passed his life.

Back of the world in which we live, far in the background, lies another world. The relation between the two is not unlike the relation we sometimes see in the theater between the forestage scene in the regular acting area and a scrim scene projected behind it. Through a thin gauze we see, as it were, a world of gauze, lighter, more ethereal, qualitatively different from the actual world. Many people who appear bodily in the actual world do not belong in it but in that other. But the fact that a man can thus dwindle away, aye, almost vanish from reality, may be a symptom of health or of sickness. The latter was the case with this man I had once known without knowing him. He did not belong to reality, and yet he had much to do with it. He was constantly rushing around, but even when he most completely devoted himself to it, he was already beyond it. But it was not the good which beckoned him away, nor was it precisely the bad; even at this moment I dare not say that about him. He had suffered from an *exacerbatio cerebri,* for which reality did not afford a sufficient stimulus, at most only a temporary one. He was not unequal to the pressure of reality; he was not too weak to bear it, not at all, he was too strong; but this strength was really a sickness. As soon as reality had lost its significance as a stimulus, he was disarmed, and this constituted the evil in him. He was conscious of this even in the moment of stimulation, and the evil lay in this consciousness.

I had known the girl whose story makes up the principal part of the Diary. Whether he had seduced others I do not know; it would seem so from his papers. He seems also to have been expert in another kind of practice wholly characteristic of him, for he was far too intellectually inclined to be a seducer in the ordinary sense of the word. One learns too from the Diary, that it was sometimes something altogether arbitrary that he sought, a mere greeting for example, and under no circumstances would he accept more, because this was the most beautiful thing about the person concerned. By the aid of his intellectual endowments he had known how to tempt a young girl and attract her to himself, without really caring to possess her. I can imagine that he knew how to excite a girl to the highest pitch, so that he was certain that she was ready to sacrifice everything. When the affair reached this point, he broke it off without himself having made the slightest advances and without having let fall a single word of love, let alone a declaration, a promise. And still it had happened, and the consciousness of it was doubly bitter for the unhappy girl because there was not the slightest thing to which she could appeal, because she was constantly tossed about by her varying moods in a terrible witches' dance, in which she alternately reproached herself and forgave him, then presently reproached him, and then, since the relationship had had reality only in a figurative sense, she must constantly struggle with the doubt as to whether the whole affair was not a figment of the imagination. She could not confide in anyone, for she had nothing definite to confide. When one has had a dream one can tell it to another person, but this which she had to tell was no dream, it was real, and yet when she wished to speak of it and relieve her troubled mind, there was nothing to tell. She felt it very keenly. No one could grasp it. Scarcely could she herself do so, and yet it rested upon her with an alarming weight.

Such victims were of a quite distinct nature. They were not the unfortunate girls who, cast out, or believing that they would be cast out of society, wailed loudly and wholeheartedly, who now and then, when the heart became overcharged, found relief in hate or forgiveness. There was no visible change in their appearance; they maintained their customary relationships, as respected as ever, and yet they were changed, almost inexplicably to themselves, incomprehensibly to others. Their lives were not like those snapped off or broken, but they had become introspective; lost to others, they vainly sought to find themselves. In the same way as one might say that his way through life was untraceable (for his feet were so formed that he left no footprints, thus I best picture to myself his infinite self-reflection), in that same sense one might say that no victim surrendered to him. He lived far too intellectually to be a seducer in the common understanding of the word. Sometimes, however, he assumed a parastatic body, and was then sheer sensuality.[3] Even his affair with Cordelia is so complicated that it was possible for him to appear as the one seduced; indeed, even the unfortunate girl herself was sometimes bewildered about it; here, too, his footprints are so indistinct that any certainty is impossible. The individuals were merely a stimulus to him; he cast them off as a tree sheds its leaves—he bourgeons again, the leaves wither.

But how, I wonder, does he regard himself? As he has led others astray, so he ends, I think, by going astray himself. The others he perverted not outwardly, but in their inward natures. There is something revolting when a man directs a traveler, perplexed about his way, to the wrong road, and then leaves him alone in his error; but what is that compared with causing a man to go astray inwardly? The lost wayfarer always has the consolation that the scene is constantly changing before him, and with every change there is born the hope of finding a way out. He who goes astray inwardly has not so great a range; he soons discovers that he is going about in a circle from which he cannot escape. I think it will be this way with him later, to a still more terrible extent. I can imagine nothing more excruciating than an intriguing mind, which has lost the thread of its continuity and now turns its whole acumen against itself, when conscience awakens and compels the schemer to extricate himself from this confusion. It is in vain that he has many exits from his foxhole; at the moment his anxious soul believes that it already sees daylight breaking through, it turns out to be a new entrance, and like a startled deer, pursued by despair, he constantly seeks a way out, and finds only a way in, through which he goes back into himself. Such a man is not always what we might call a criminal, he is even frequently disappointed by his intrigues, and yet a more terrible punishment overtakes him than befalls a criminal; for what is even the pain of remorse in comparison with this conscious madness? His punishment has a purely aesthetic character; for even to say that his conscience awakens is too ethical an expression to use about him. Conscience exists for him only as a higher degree of consciousness, which expresses itself in a disquietude that does not, in a more profound sense, accuse him, but which keeps him awake, and gives him no rest in his barren activity. Nor is he mad; for the multitude of finite thoughts are not petrified in the eternity of madness.

Poor Cordelia! For her too it will be difficult to find peace. She forgives him from the bottom of her heart, but she finds no rest, for then doubt awakens: it was she who broke the engagement, she who was the cause of the disaster, it was her pride which craved the uncommon. Then she repents, but she finds no rest; for then the accusing thoughts acquit her: it was he who so subtly put this plan in her mind. Then she hates, her heart finds relief in curses, but she finds no rest; she again reproaches herself, reproaches herself because she has hated when she herself is a sinner, reproaches herself because, however crafty he has been, she always remains guilty. It is hard for her that he has deceived her, even harder, one might almost be tempted to say, that he has developed the many-tongued reflection within her, that he has developed her aesthetically so far that she no longer listens humbly to one voice but is able to hear many voices at one time. Then memory awakens within her, she forgets the fault and the guilt, she remembers the beautiful moments, and she is stimulated to an unnatural exaltation. In such moments she not only remembers him, she understands him with a clairvoyance which only shows how greatly she has developed. Then she sees him neither as criminal nor as a high-minded person, she feels him only aesthetically. She had once written me a letter in which she expressed her feeling about him. "Sometimes he was so intellectual that I felt myself annihilated as woman. At other times he was so wild and passionate, so filled with desire, that I almost trembled before him. Sometimes he was like a stranger to me, sometimes he was devotion itself; when I then flung my arms about him, sometimes everything was suddenly changed, and I embraced the cloud.[4] I knew this expression before I knew him, but he taught me to understand it. When I use it, I always think of him, just as I think all my thoughts in connection with him. I have always loved music; he was a matchless instrument, always responsive; he had a range such as no musical instrument has; he was the epitome of all feelings and moods, no thoughts were too lofty for him, none too despairing, he could roar like an autumn gale, he could whisper soundlessly. No word of mine was without effect, and yet I cannot say that my word did not fail of its effect; for it was impossible for me to know what effect it would have. With an indescribable but mysterious, blissful, inexpressible dread I listened to this music I had myself evoked, and yet did not evoke; always there was harmony, always I was carried away by him."

Terrible as this is for her, it will be more terrible for him; this I can infer from the fact that even I am never quite able to control the anxiety that grips me every time I think about the case. I, too, am carried away into that nebulous realm, that dream world, where every moment one is afraid of his own shadow. Often I seek in vain to tear myself away; I follow along like a menacing shadow, an accuser who is mute. How strange! He has spread the deepest secrecy over everything, and yet there is an even deeper secret, and that is the fact that I am privy to it and that I became such in a reprehensible manner. To forget the whole affair would not be possible. I have sometimes thought of speaking to him about it. Still, how would that help? He would either deny everything, insist that the Diary was a poetic experiment, or he would impose silence upon me, something I could not refuse to promise, considering the manner in which I became aware of his secret. There is really nothing else which involves so much seduction and so great a curse as a secret.

I have received from Cordelia a collection of letters. Whether it includes all of them I do not know, although it seems to me she once intimated that she had confiscated some of them. I have made a copy of them, and will now introduce them into my manuscript. It is true that the dates are lacking, but even if I had them it would not help much, since the Diary as it progresses becomes more and more sparing of dates, until at last it is a marked exception when one is given, as if the story in its progress becomes qualitatively significant to such a degree that, although historically real, it comes nearer to being idea, and for this reason the time-designations become a matter of indifference. What did help me, however, is the fact that at different places in the Diary is found a word or two, whose significance I did not at first understand. By comparing them with the letters, I finally realized that they furnish the motive for the letters. It will therefore be a simple matter to insert them in the right places, as I shall always introduce them where the motives seem to suggest them. Had I not found these suggestive leads, I should have been guilty of a misunderstanding; for it would not have occurred to me, as now from the Diary seems probable, that at times the letters followed one another so frequently that she seems to have received several in one day. Had I followed my original intention, I should have distributed them more evenly, not suspecting what an effect he had produced by the passionate energy with which he had employed this, like all other means, to keep Cordelia at the highest point of passion.

In addition to the complete revelation of his relationship to Cordelia, the Diary also contained, interspersed here and there, several little occasional sketches. Wherever these were found, there appeared the marginal notation, N.B. These sketches have absolutely nothing to do with Cordelia's story, but they have given me a vivid conception of the meaning of an expression he often used, which I formerly understood in a different way: "One ought always to have a little extra line out." Had an earlier volume of the Diary fallen into my hands, I should probably have come across a number of these, which he somewhere on the margin characterized as *actiones in distans*;[5] for he himself says that Cordelia occupied him too much for him really to have time to look around.

Shortly after he had deserted Cordelia, he received from her two letters which he returned unopened. These were among the letters Cordelia turned over to me. She had herself broken the seal, and so I ventured to copy them. She has never mentioned their content to me; on the other hand, when she referred to her relationship to Johannes, she usually recited a little verse, which, of course, I recognized as Goethe's, which seemed to mean something different according to the diversity of her moods and the different expressions conditioned by these:

> Gehe,
> Verschmähe
> Die Treue,
> Die Reue
> Kommt nach.[6]

The letters run as follows:

Johannes!

I do not call you mine, I realize very well that you have never been mine, and I am severely enough punished in that this thought once delighted my soul; and yet I call you mine; my seducer, my deceiver, my enemy, my murderer, the cause of my unhappiness, the grave of my joy, the abyss of my destruction. I call you mine, and I call myself yours, and as it once flattered your ear which proudly bent to receive my adoration, so shall it now sound like a curse upon you, a curse to all eternity. Rejoice not at the thought that it might be my intention to pursue you, or to arm myself with a dagger to incite your ridicule! Flee where you will, I am still yours; go to the uttermost parts of the earth, I am still yours; love a hundred others, I am still yours; aye, even in the hour of death I am yours. The very language I use against you must prove that I am yours. You have presumed to deceive a human being so that you became everything to me, so now will I find all my pleasure in being your slave—I am *thine,* thine, thine, thy curse.

Thy Cordelia.

Johannes!

There was a rich man, he had great herds, and many cattle, small and great; there was a poor little maiden, she had only a single lamb, which ate from her hand and drank of her cup.[7] You were the rich man, rich in all the glories of the earth; I was the poor maiden who had only her love. You took it; you rejoiced in it; then passion beckoned you, and you did sacrifice the little I possessed; of your own would you sacrifice nothing. There was a rich man who owned great herds, and many cattle great and small; there was a poor little maiden who had only her love.

Thy Cordelia.

Johannes!

Is there then no hope at all? Will your love never awaken again? For I well know that you did love me, even if I do not know what it is that assures me of it. I will wait, however long the time may be, I will wait, wait till you are weary of the other loves, then shall your love for me rise up from its grave, then will I love you as before, thank you as before, as before, O Johannes, as before! Johannes! is your heartless coldness against me, is it your true nature? Was your love, your rich love, base and untruthful? Are you now again your true self? Have patience with my love, forgive me for continuing to love you. I well know that my love is a burden to you, but there will come a day when you will return to your Cordelia. Your Cordelia! Hear that pleading word! Your Cordelia! Your Cordelia!

Thy Cordelia.

If Cordelia did not possess the compass she admired in her Johannes, one still sees clearly that she was not without modulation. Her mood is plainly stamped upon each of her letters, even though she lacked a certain clearness in the presentation. This is especially the case with the second letter, where one rather suspects than understands her meaning, but to me this imperfection makes it very touching.

April 4.

Caution, my beautiful unknown! Caution! To step out of a carriage is not so simple a matter. Sometimes it is a decisive step. I might lend you a novel of Tieck's in which you would read about a lady who in dismounting from her horse involved herself in an entanglement such that this step became definitive for her whole life.[8] The steps on carriages, too, are usually so badly arranged that one almost has to forget about being graceful and risk a desperate spring into the arms of coachman and footman. Really, coachmen and footmen have the best of it. I really believe I shall look for a job as footman in some house where there are young girls; a servant easily becomes acquainted with the secrets of a little maid like that.—But for heaven's sake, don't jump, I beg of you! To be sure, it is dark; I shall not disturb you; I only pause under this street lamp where it is impossible for you to see me, and one is never embarrassed unless one is seen, and of course if one cannot see, one cannot be seen.—So out of regard for the servant who might not be strong enough to catch you, out of regard for the silk dress with its lacy fringes, out of regard for me, let this dainty little foot, whose slenderness I have already admired, let it venture forth into the world, dare to trust that it will find a footing. Should you tremble lest it should not find it, or should you tremble after it has done so, then follow it quickly with the other foot, for who would be so cruel as to leave you in that position, who so ungracious, so slow in appreciating the revelation of beauty? Or do you fear some intruder? Not the servant of course, nor me, for I have already seen the little foot, and since I am a natural scientist, I have learned from Cuvier how to draw definite conclusions from such details.[9] Therefore, hurry! How this anxiety enhances your beauty! Still anxiety in itself is not beautiful; it is so only when one sees at the same time the energy which overcomes it. Now! How firmly this little foot stands. I have noticed that girls with small feet generally stand more firmly than the more pedestrian large-footed ones.

Now who would have thought it? It is contrary to all experience; one does not run nearly so much risk of one's dress catching when one steps out of a carriage as when one jumps out. But then it is always risky for young girls to go riding in a carriage, lest they finally have to stay in it. The lace and ribbons got caught and are torn in shreds, and that's the end of the matter. No one has seen anything. To be sure a dark figure appears, wrapped to the eyes in a cloak. The light from the street lamp shines directly in your eyes so you cannot see whence he came. He passes you just as your are entering the door. Just at the critical second, a side glance falls upon its object. You blush, your bosom becomes too full to relieve itself in a single sigh; there is exasperation in your glance, a proud contempt; there is a prayer, a tear in your eye, both are equally beautiful, and I accept both as my due; for I can just as well be the one thing as the other.

But I am malicious—what is the number of the house? What do I see? A window display of trinkets; my beautiful unknown, perhaps it may be outrageous in me, but I follow the gleam. . . . She has forgotten the incident. Ah, yes, when one is seventeen years old, when at that happy age one goes shopping, when every object large or small that one handles gives one unspeakable pleasure, then one easily forgets. She has not even seen me. I am standing at the far end of the counter by myself. A mirror hangs on the opposite wall; she does not reflect on it, but the mirror reflects her. How faithfully it has caught her picture, like a humble slave who shows his devotion by his faithfulness, a slave for whom she indeed has significance, but who means nothing to her, who indeed dares to catch her, but not to embrace her. Unhappy mirror, that can indeed seize her image, but not herself! Unhappy mirror, which cannot hide her image in its secret depths, hide it from the whole world, but on the contrary must betray it to others, as now to me. What agony, if men were made like that! And are there not many people who are like that, who own nothing except in the moment when they show it to others, who grasp only the surface, not the essence, who lose everything if this appears, just as this mirror would lose her image, were she by a single breath to betray her heart to it?

And if a man were not able to hold a picture in memory even when he is present, then he must always wish to be at a distance from beauty, not so near that the earthly eye cannot see how beautiful that is which he holds, and which is lost to sight in his embrace. This beauty he can regain for the outward sight by putting it at a distance, but he may also keep it before the eyes of his soul, when he cannot see the object itself because it is too near, when lips are closed on lips. . . . Still, how beautiful she is! Poor mirror, it must be agony! It is well that you know no jealousy. Her head is a perfect oval, and she bends it a little forward, which makes her forehead seem higher, as it rises pure and proud, with no external evidence of intellectual faculties. Her dark hair wreathes itself softly and gently about her temples. Her face is like a fruit, every plane fully rounded. Her skin is transparent, like velvet to the touch, I can feel that with my eyes. Her eyes—well, I have not even seen them, they are hidden behind lids armed with silken fringes which curve up like hooks, dangerous to whoever meets her glance. Her head is a Madonna head, pure and innocent in cast; like a Madonna she is bending forward, but she is not lost in contemplation of the One. A variety of emotions finds expression in her countenance. What she considers is the manifold, the multitude of things over which worldly pomp and splendor cast their glamor. She pulls off her glove to show the mirror and myself a right hand, white and shapely as an antique, without adornment, and with no plain gold ring on her fourth finger. Good!—She looks up, and how changed everything is, and yet the same; the forehead seems lower, the oval of her face a little less regular, but more alive. She is talking now with the salesman, she is merry, joyous, chatty. She has already chosen two or three things, she picks up a fourth and holds it in her hand, again she looks down, she asks what it costs. She lays it to one side under her glove, it must be a secret, intended for —a lover? But she is not engaged. Alas, there are many who are not engaged and yet have a lover; many who are engaged, and who still do not have a lover.

Ought I to give her up? Ought I to leave her undisturbed in her happiness? . . . She is about to pay, but she has lost her purse. . . . She probably mentions her address, I will not listen to it, for I do not wish to deprive myself of surprise; I shall certainly meet her again in life, I shall recognize her, and perhaps she will recognize me; one does not forget my side glance so easily. Her turn will come when I am surprised at meeting her in circles where I did not expect to. If she does not recognize me, if her glance does not immediately convince me of that, then I shall surely find an opportunity to look at her from the side. I promise that she will remember the situation. No impatience, no greediness, everything should be enjoyed in leisurely draughts; she is marked out, she shall be run down.

5th day.

I like that! Alone in the evening on Eastern Street! Yes, I see the footman is following you. Do not believe I think so ill of you as to think you would go out quite alone; do not believe that I am so inexperienced that in my survey of the situation, I did not notice this sober figure. But why in such a hurry? You are still a little anxious, you can feel your heart beating; this is not because of an impatient longing to get home, but because of an impatient fear streaming through your entire body with its sweet unrest, and hence the swift rhythm of your feet. But still it is a splendid, priceless experience to go out alone—with the footman behind. . . . You are sixteen years old, you are a reader, that is to say, you read novels. You have accidentally, in going through your brothers' room, caught a word or two of a conversation between them and an acquaintance, something about Eastern Street. Later you whisked through several times, in order, if possible, to get a little more information. All in vain. One ought, it would seem, if one is a grown-up girl, to know a little something about the world. If without saying anything, one could only go out with the servant following. No, thank you. What kind of face would Father and Mother make, and, too, what excuse could one give? If one were going to a party, it would afford no opportunity, it would be a little too early, for I heard August say, between nine and ten o'clock. Going home it would be too late, and then one must usually have an escort to drag along with one. Thursday evening when we return from the theater would seem to offer a splendid opportunity, but then we always go in the carriage and have Mrs. Thomsen and her worthy cousins packed in with us. If one ever had a chance to drive alone, then one could let down the window and look around a bit. Still, it is always the unexpected that happens. Today my mother said to me: "You have not yet finished your father's birthday present; to give you time to work undisturbed, you may go to your Aunt Jette's and

stay until tea time, and I'll send Jens to fetch you!" It was
really not a very pleasing suggestion, for Aunt Jette is very
tiresome; but this way I shall be going home alone with the
servant at nine o'clock. Then when Jens comes he will have
to wait till a quarter of ten before leaving. Only I might
meet my brother or August—that wouldn't be so good, for
then I should probably be escorted home—Thanks, but I
prefer to be free—but if I could get my eye on them, so
that they did not see me. . . .

Now, my little lady, what do you see, and what do you
think I see? In the first place, the little cap you have on is
very becoming, and quite harmonizes with the haste in
your appearance. It is not a hat, neither is it a bonnet, but
rather a kind of hood. But you cannot possibly have worn
that when you went out this morning. Could the servant
have brought it, or could you have borrowed it from your
Aunt Jette?—Perhaps you are incognito.—You should not
lower the veil completely if you are going to make observations. Or perhaps it is not a veil, but only a piece of lace.
It is impossible to tell in the dark. Whatever it is, it conceals the upper part of your face. Your chin is really pretty,
a little too pointed; your mouth is small, open a trifle; that
is because you have gone so fast. Your teeth—white as snow.
That is the way it should be, teeth are of the utmost importance; they are a life-guard, hiding behind the seductive
softness of the lips. The cheeks glow with health. If one
tips one's head a little to the side, it might be possible to
get a glimpse under the veil or lace.

Look out! An upward glance like that is more dangerous
than a direct one. It is as in fencing; and what weapon is
so sharp, so penetrating, so flashing in action, and hence so
deceptive, as the eye? You feint a high quart, as fencers say,
and attack in second; the swifter the attack follows the feint,
the better. The moment of the feint is indescribable. The
opponent, as it were, feels the slash, he is touched! Aye,
that is true, but in quite a different place from where he
thought. . . . Indefatigable she goes on, without fear and
without reproach. Look out! Yonder comes a man; lower
your veil, let not his profane glance besmirch you. You
have no idea—it will perhaps be impossible for you for a

long time to forget the disgusting fear with which it touched you—you did not notice, as I did, that he had sized up the situation. Your servant is set upon as the nearest objective.—There, now you see the consequences of going out alone with a servant. The servant has fallen down. At bottom it is laughable, but what will you do now? That you should turn back and assist him in getting to his feet is impossible, to go on with a mud-stained servant is disagreeable, to go alone is dangerous. Look out! the monster approaches. . . . You do not answer me. Just look at me, is there anything about me to frighten you? I simply make no impression at all upon you. I seem to be a good-natured person from quite a different world. There is nothing in my speech to disturb you, nothing to remind you of the situation, no movement that in the least approaches too near you. You are still a little frightened, you have not yet forgotten the attempt of that sinister figure against you. You feel a certain kindliness toward me, the embarrassment that keeps me from looking directly at you makes you feel superior. It pleases you and makes you feel safe. You are almost tempted to poke a little fun at me. I wager that at this moment you would have the courage to take my arm, if it occurred to you. . . . So you live on Storm Street. You curtsy to me coldly and indifferently. Have I deserved this, I who rescued you from the whole unpleasantness? You regret your coldness, you turn back, thank me for my courtesy, offer me your hand—why do you turn pale? Is not my voice unchanged, my bearing the same, my glance as quiet and controlled? This handclasp? Can then a handclasp mean anything? Aye, much, very much, my little lady; within a fortnight I shall explain it all to you, until then you must rest in the contradiction that I am a good-natured man who, like a knight of old, came to the assistance of a young girl, and that I can also press her hand in a no less good-natured manner.

April 7.

"All right! Monday at one o'clock at the Exhibition." Very well, I shall have the honor of appearing at a quarter of one. A little rendezvous. Last Saturday I finally put business aside and decided to call upon my much-traveled friend, Adolph Bruun. Accordingly I set out about seven o'clock for Western Street where someone had told me he was living. However, I did not find him, not even on the fourth floor after I had puffed my way up. When I turned to go downstairs, my ear caught the sound of a melodious feminine voice saying, "All right! Monday at one o'clock at the Exhibition, when everybody is out, for you know I never dare to see you at home." The invitation was not for me, but for a young man who was out of the door in a jiffy, so fast that my eyes could not even follow him, to say nothing of my feet. Why do they not have light on stairways? Then I might perhaps have found out whether it would be worth while to be so punctual. Still, if there had been a light, I probably should not have heard anything. What is is rational, and I am and remain an optimist. . . . Now which one is she? The place swarms with girls, to use Donna Anna's expression.[10] It is exactly a quarter of one. My beautiful unknown! I wish your intended were as punctual as I am, or perhaps you would rather not have him come fifteen minutes too early. As you will, I am at your service in every way. . . . "Charming enchantress, witch or fairy, let your cloud vanish," reveal yourself; you are probably already here but invisible to me; betray yourself, for otherwise I dare not expect a revelation. Could there perhaps be several here on a similar errand? Possibly so, for who knows the way of a man, even when he goes to an exhibition?—There comes a young girl through the front room, hurrying faster than a bad conscience after a sinner. She forgets to give up her ticket, the doorkeeper detains her. Heaven preserve us! Why is she in such a hurry? It must be she. Why such unseemly impetuosity? It is not yet one o'clock. Do but remember that you are to meet your beloved. Are you on such occasions entirely indifferent as to how you look, or is this not a time for putting your best foot forward? When such an innocent young damsel goes to a rendezvous, she goes about the matter like a madwoman. She is all of a flutter. Meanwhile I sit here comfortably in my chair and contemplate a delightful bucolic landscape.

She is the child of the devil, the way she storms through

all the rooms. You must learn to conceal your eagerness a little. Remember the advice given to the young Lisbeth: "Is it becoming for a young girl to let it be seen how eager she is to be mated?"[11] But of course your meeting is one of the innocent ones. . . . A rendezvous is generally regarded by lovers as a most beautiful moment. I myself still remember as clearly as if it were yesterday the first time I hastened to the appointed place, with a heart as full as it was ignorant of the joy that awaited me, the first time I knocked three times, the first time a window opened, the first time a little wicket gate was unfastened by the unseen hand of a girl who hid herself as she opened it, the first time I hid a girl under my cloak in the light summer night. But there is much illusion blended in this judgment. The dispassionate third party does not always find the lovers most beautiful at this moment. I have witnessed rendezvous where, although the girl was charming and the man handsome, the total impression was almost disgusting and the meeting itself was far from being beautiful, although I supposed it seemed so to the lovers. As one becomes more experienced, he gains in a way; for though one loses the sweet unrest of impatient longing, he gains ability in making the moment really beautiful. I am vexed when I see a man with such an opportunity so upset that mere love gives him delirium tremens. It is caviar to the general. Instead of having enough discretion to enjoy her disquiet, to allow it to enhance and inflame her beauty, he only produces a wretched confusion, and yet he goes home joyously imagining it to have been a glorious experience.

But where the devil is the fellow? It is nearly two o'clock. He surely is a fine fellow, this lover! Such a scoundrel, to keep a lady waiting for him! Now I, on the contrary, am a very trustworthy man! It might indeed be best to speak to her as she now passes me for the fifth time. "Pardon my boldness, fair lady. You doubtless are looking for your family. You have hurried past me several times, and as my eyes followed you, I noticed that you always stop in the next room; perhaps you do not know that there is still another room beyond that. Possibly you might find your friends there." She curtsied to me, a very becoming gesture. The occasion is favorable. I am glad the man has not come; one always fishes best in troubled waters. When a young girl is emotionally disturbed, one can successfully venture much which would otherwise be ill-advised. I bow to her as politely and distantly as possible; I sit back again in my chair, look at my landscape, and watch her out of the corner of my eye. To follow her immediately would be too risky; it might seem intrusive to her and put her on her guard. At present she believes that I addressed her out of sympathy, and I am in her good graces.—I know very well that there is not a soul in that inner room. Solitude will be beneficial to her. As long as she sees many people about, she is disturbed; when she is alone, she will relax. Quite right that she should stay in there. After a little I shall stroll by; I have earned a right to speak to her, she owes me at least a greeting.

She has sat down. Poor girl, she looks so sad, I believe she has been crying, at least she has tears in her eyes. It is outrageous—to make such a girl cry. But be calm, you shall be avenged, I will avenge you, he shall learn what it means to wait.—How beautiful she is, now that her conflicting emotions have subsided and her mood is relaxed. Her being is a harmony of sadness and pain. She is really captivating. She sits there in a traveling dress, and yet she was not going to travel; she wandered out in search of joy, and it is now an indication of her pain, for she is like one from whom gladness flees. She looks like one who had forever said farewell to the beloved. Let him go! The situation is favorable, the moment beckons. The important thing now is to express myself so that it will seem as if I think she is looking for her family, or a party of friends, and yet warmly enough to make every word significant to her feelings. Thus I get a chance to insinuate myself into her thoughts. . . . Now may the devil take the scoundrel! There is a man approaching, who undoubtedly is he. Now write me down as a bungler if I cannot shape the situation as I want it. Yes, indeed, a little finesse brings one well out of it. I must find out their relationship, bring myself into the situation. When she sees me she will involuntarily have to smile at my believing that she was looking for someone quite different. That smile makes me an accomplice, which is always something.—A thousand thanks, my child, that smile is worth much more to me than you realize; it is the beginning, and the beginning is always the hardest. Now we are acquainted, and our acquaintance is based on a piquant situation; it is enough for me until later. You will hardly remain here more than an hour; in two hours I shall know who you are, why else do you think the police maintain a directory?

9th day.

Have I gone blind? Has the inner eye of my soul lost its power? I have seen her, but it is as if I had seen a heavenly vision, so absolutely has her image again vanished from me. Vainly have I exerted all the power of my soul to recall this image. If I were to meet her again, then I should recognize her instantly, even among a hundred other girls. Now she has fled away, and my soul's eye vainly seeks to overtake her with its longing.—I was walking along the esplanade, apparently unconcerned and indifferent to my surroundings, although my roving eye let nothing pass unnoticed, when I saw her. My eye fixed itself steadfastly upon her, it paid no attention to its master's will. It was impossible for me to direct its attention to the object I wished to look at, so I did not look, I stared. Like a fencer who becomes frozen in his pass, so was my eye fixed, petrified in the one appointed direction. It was impossible for me to look away, to withdraw my glance, impossible for me to see because I saw too much. The only thing I have retained is that she wore a green cloak; that is all, that is what one may call catching the cloud instead of Juno; she slipped away from me as Joseph did from Potiphar's wife, and left only her cloak behind. She was accompanied by a middle-aged lady, presumably her mother. I can describe her from top to toe, and that although I glanced at her only *en passant*. So it goes. The girl made an impression upon me, and I have forgotten her; the other made no impression upon me, and I can remember her.

11th day.

My soul is still ensnared in the same contradiction. I know that I have seen her, but I also know that I have forgotten her again, so that what memory retains carries no refreshment with it. With a violent unrest, as if my welfare were at stake, my soul demands that picture, and yet it does not appear; I could tear out my eyes to punish them for their forgetfulness. Then when I have raged in impatience and have at length recovered my calm, it is as if anticipation and memory wove a picture; but it will not take on definite form, because I cannot fix it in its proper context. It is like a pattern in a fine loom; the pattern is lighter than the ground; by itself it cannot be seen because it is too light. This is a peculiar state for me to be in, and yet it is not altogether unpleasant because it proves to me that I am still young. This is also to be learned from the consideration that I constantly seek my prey among young girls, not among young women. A woman is less natural, more coquettish; an affair with her is not beautiful, not interesting; it is piquant, and the piquant is always the last stage—I had never expected to be able again to taste the first fruits of infatuation; I am submerged in love, I have been given what swimmers call a ducking; no wonder that I am a little dazed. So much the better, so much the more I promise myself from this affair.

14th day.

I scarcely recognize myself. My mind is like a turbulent sea, swept by the storms of passion. If another could see my soul in this condition, it would seem to him like a boat that buried its prow deep in the sea, as if in its terrible speed it would rush down into the depths of the abyss. He does not see that high on the mast a lookout sits on watch. Roar on, ye wild forces, ye powers of passion! Let your dashing waves hurl their foam against the sky. You shall not engulf me. Serene I sit like the king of the cliff.

I can hardly find a footing. Like a water-bird I seek in vain to alight on my mind's turbulent sea. And yet such turbulence is my element; I build upon it as *Alcedo ispida* builds its nest on the sea.[12]

Turkey gobblers flare up when they see red; so it is with me when I see green, every time I see a green cloak; and since my eyes often deceive me, sometimes all my hopes are frustrated by the livery of a porter from Frederik's Hospital.[13]

20th day.

I must have more restraint, it is the chief requisite for all enjoyment. It does not look as if I shall very soon get any information about the girl who fills my soul and my thoughts so completely that the want is kept alive. I shall now keep very quiet, for this condition, this vague, indefinite, but still strong disquiet, has a sweetness of its own. I have always loved to lie in a boat on a moonlit night, out on one or another of our beautiful lakes. I haul in the sails, take in the oars and the rudder, stretch myself out full length, and gaze up at the blue vault of the heavens. When the waves rock the boat on their bosom, when the clouds scud fast before the wind so that the moon constantly vanishes and reappears, then I find rest in this unrest. The motion of the waves lulls me, their lapping against the boat is a monotonous cradle song; the swift flight of the clouds, the shifting lights and shadows all intoxicate me, so that I am in a waking dream. So now I lie here with sails furled and rudder up, longing and impatient expectation toss me about in their arms; longing and expectation become more and more quiet, more and more blissful: they fondle me like a child, the heaven of hope arches over me, and her image floats across my vision like the moon's, indistinct, now dazzling me with its light, now with its shadow. How much enjoyment in thus drifting on moving water—how much enjoyment in being moved within oneself.

21st day.

The days go by, and yet I am no nearer. Young girls please me more than ever, and still I have no desire to enjoy them. I seek her everywhere. It often makes me unreasonable, dims my vision, enervates my pleasure. That beautiful season is now approaching when in the public life on the streets and in the lanes one buys up those petty claims which in the social life of winter cost dearly enough; for a young girl may forget many things, but not a situation. Social intercourse, it is true, brings one into contact with the fair sex, but there is no artistry in beginning an affair in such surroundings. In society every young girl is armed, the occasion is poor and, encountering it repeatedly, she gets no sensuous thrill. On the street she is on the open sea, everything acts more strongly upon her, everything seems more mysterious. I would give a hundred dollars for a smile from a girl I met on the street, not ten dollars for a pressure of the hand at a party; that is an entirely different kind of currency. When the affair is under way, then you may openly seek out in society the person involved. You carry on a cryptic conversation with her which excites her pleasantly; it is the most effective incitement I know. She does not dare to talk about it, and yet she keeps thinking about it; she does not know whether you have forgotten it or not; now you delude her in one way, now in another. This year I shall probably not collect much; this girl absorbs too much of my attention. In a certain sense my returns are poor, but then I have the prospect of the grand prize.

5th day.

Accursed Chance! Never have I cursed you because you have appeared; I curse you because you do not appear at all. Or is this perhaps a new invention of yours, unfathomable being, barren mother of all, sole remnant of the past, when necessity gave birth to freedom,[14] when freedom was again lured back into its mother's womb? Accursed Chance! You, my only confidante, the only being whom I consider worthy of being my ally and my enemy, always the same by forever being different, always incomprehensible, always a riddle! You whom I love with all my soul, in whose image I mold myself, why do you not show yourself? I do not beg you, I do not humbly entreat you to show yourself in this manner or that; such worship would be idolatry, not acceptable unto you. I challenge you to battle, why do you not appear? Or has the pendulum of the world system stopped, is your riddle solved, so that you too have hurled yourself into the sea of eternity? Terrible thought, for thus the world comes to a standstill from boredom! Accursed Chance! I await you. I shall not overcome you with principles nor with what foolish people call character; no, I will be your poet! I will not be a poet for others; show yourself! I will be your poet. I consume my own verse, and that will sustain me. Or do you think I am not worthy? Like a Bayadère dancing to the honor of her gods, so have I devoted myself to your service. Nimble, thinly clad, agile, unarmed, I renounce everything for you. I own nothing, I desire to own nothing, I love nothing, I have nothing to lose, but I am not therefore more worthy of you, you who long ago must have wearied of tearing human beings away from what they love, tired of their cowardly sighs and cowardly petitions. Take me by surprise, I am ready. No stakes, let us fight for honor. Show her to me, show me a possibility which seems an impossibility; show her to me among the shades of the underworld, I shall fetch her up;[15] let her hate me, despise me, be indifferent to me, love another, I am not afraid; only let the waters be troubled, the silence be broken. To starve me in this way is paltry of you, you who imagine that you are stronger than I am.

May 6th.

Spring is at hand. Everything is in bloom, including the young girls. Coats are laid aside, probably my green one too is put away. This is what comes of making a girl's acquaintance on the street instead of in society where one may learn immediately what her name is, who her family is, where she lives, whether she is betrothed. This last is very important information for all sedate and constant suitors who would never think of falling in love with an engaged girl. Such a slow-poke would be fatally embarrassed if he were in my place; he would be entirely devastated if he succeeded in getting information and learned in addition that she was engaged. This, however, would not worry me very much. An engagement is only a comic difficulty. I fear neither comic nor tragic difficulties; the only one I fear is the tedious one. Not yet have I obtained a single bit of information, despite the fact that I have left nothing untried, and have often felt the truth of the poet's words:

> *Nox et hiems longaeque viae, saevique dolores*
> *mollibus his castris, et labor omnis inest.*[16]

Perhaps after all she does not live here in town, perhaps she is from the country, perhaps, perhaps—I could become furious over all these perhapses, and the more furious I become, the more perhapses. I always have money in readiness for a journey. I seek her in vain at the theater, at concerts, balls, and on the promenades. In a certain way it pleases me; a young girl who participates too much in such recreations is usually not worth making a conquest of. She very often lacks the primitiveness which for me is always *conditio sine qua non.* It is less inconceivable to think of finding a Preciosa among the gypsies than in the assembly halls where young girls are offered for sale—in all innocence, of course, the Lord preserve us, who says otherwise![17]

12th day.

Really, my child, why do you not stand quietly in the doorway? There is nothing to criticize about a young girl's stopping in a doorway out of the rain. I do the same myself when I have no umbrella, sometimes even when I have one, as now, for instance. Besides, I could mention a number of married ladies who have not hesitated to do so. One has only to stand quietly, turn her back to the street, so that passers-by may not know whether she is standing there or is about to enter the house. On the other hand, it is incautious to hide behind the half-opened door, principally on account of the consequences, for the more you conceal yourself, the more unpleasant it is to be surprised. If, however, you do try to hide, you should stand quite still, committing yourself to the care of your good genius and guardian angel; especially should you refrain from peeping out—to see if it has stopped raining. If you really want to

know, then you should step boldly out and look earnestly
up at the sky. But if you poke your head out a little curiously, bashfully, anxiously, uncertainly, and then hur-
riedly draw it back—then every child understands it, they
call it playing hide-and-seek. And I who am never absent
from a game, should I hold back and not answer when you
call! . . . Don't think for a moment that I'm getting ideas.
You had no ulterior motive in sticking your head out. It
was the most innocent action in the world. In return you
mustn't get ideas about me; my good name and reputation
couldn't stand it. After all it was you who started this. I
advise you never to tell anyone about this affair; you were
really in the wrong. What have I proposed to do other
than any gentleman would—to offer you my umbrella?—
Now where has she gone? Excellent, she has hidden herself
in the porter's doorway.—She is a most charming little girl,
merry and happy. "Perhaps you could tell me about a
young lady who just this blessed moment was looking out
of the door, evidently in need of an umbrella. I am looking
for her, I and my umbrella."—You laugh.—Perhaps you allow me to send my servant in the morning to fetch it, or
you suggest that I should call a cab.—Nothing to thank me
for, it is only a simple courtesy.—She is certainly the most
pleasing little maiden I have seen in a long time, her glance
is so childlike and yet so fearless, her personality is charming, so pure, and yet she is curious.—Go in peace, my child;
if it were not for a certain green cloak, I might have desired to establish a closer acquaintance.—She starts down
Market Street. How guileless and confident she was, not a
trace of prudery. See how lightly she walks, how gaily she
tosses her head. The green cloak certainly demands self-
denial.

15th day.

Thank you, kind Chance, accept my gratitude! Straight
was she and proud, mysterious and thought-provoking as a
spruce tree, a shoot, a thought, which from the depths of
earth shoots up toward heaven, unexplained and inexplicable, an undivided unity. The beech tree forms a crown; its
leaves whisper about what is taking place down beneath

it. The spruce has no crown, no story, itself mysterious—
as she was. She was hidden in herself, she rose up out of
herself, a serene pride was hers, like the daring spirit of the
spruce, even though rooted to earth. A sadness enveloped
her like the mournful cooing of the stock-dove, a profound
longing which wanted nothing. A riddle she was, mysteriously possessed of her own solution, a secret mystery, and
what are all the secrets of the diplomats in comparison with
this enigma, and what in all the world is so beautiful as the
word which solves it? How significant, how pregnant, our
Danish language is: *to solve* [*at løse*], what an ambiguity
it implies, how beautiful and how strong are all the combinations where this word appears. As the wealth of the soul
is a riddle as long as the string of the tongue is not loosed
[*løst*], by which the riddle would be solved [*løst*], so, too, a
young girl is a riddle. - - - Thanks, kind Chance, accept
my gratitude! If I had seen her in winter, she would have
been enveloped in the green cloak, cold perhaps, and the
inclemency of the weather might have made her less beautiful. Now, however, what luck! I get to see her first in the
most beautiful time of the year, in the spring, in the light
of late afternoon. True, winter also has its advantages. A
brilliantly lighted ballroom can indeed be a flattering setting
for a young lady in evening dress; but she seldom appears
to the best advantage here, partly because so much is required of her, and this requirement acts disturbingly upon
her whether she gives way to it or resists it; partly because
everything suggests vanity and the transitory, and produces an impatience which makes the enjoyment less refreshing. There are certain times when I should not wish
to dispense with the ballroom, to dispense with its costly
luxury, its priceless abundance of youth and beauty, its
manifold play of forces. But I do not so much enjoy as I
revel in its possibilities. It is not a single beauty who captivates me, but a totality; a vision floats past me in which
all these feminine natures blend into one another, and all
these emotions seek something, seek rest in one composite
picture which is not seen.

It was on the path between the north and east gates,
about half past six. The sun had lost its intensity, only the

memory of it remained in a mild radiance spreading over the landscape. Nature breathed more freely. The lake was calm, smooth as a mirror, the comfortable houses on Bleachers' Green were reflected in the water, which farther out was dark as metal. The path and buildings on the other side were lighted up by the faint rays of the setting sun. The sky was clear and bright, only a single fleecy cloud floated unnoticed across it, best seen by looking at the lake, beyond whose shining surface it was lost to view. Not a leaf moved.—It was she! My eye had not deceived me, even if the green coat had done so. Although I had long been prepared for this moment, it was still impossible for me to control a certain excitement, a rising and falling, like the song of the lark soaring above the adjacent fields. She was alone. Again have I forgotten how she was dressed, and yet now I have a picture of her. She was alone, preoccupied, manifestly not with herself but with her thoughts. She was not thinking, but the quiet play of her thoughts wove a picture of longing before her soul, a picture which held a certain foreboding, unclarified as a young girl's many sighs. She was at her most adorable age. A young girl does not develop in the sense that a boy does; she does not grow, she is born. A boy begins to develop at once, and takes a long time for the process; a young girl takes a long time in being born, and is born full-grown. Therein lies her infinite richness; at the moment she is born she is full-grown, but this moment of birth comes late. Hence she is twice born, the second time when she marries, or, rather, at this moment she ceases being born, at that moment she *is* born. It is not only Minerva who sprang full-grown from the head of Jupiter, not only Venus who rose in all her beauty from the depths of the sea; every young girl is like this if her womanliness has not been destroyed by what men call development. She does not awaken by degrees, but all at once; meantime she dreams all the longer, provided that people are not so inconsiderate as to arouse her too early. But her dream has infinite richness.

She was preoccupied not with herself, but in herself, and this preoccupation afforded infinite rest and peace to her soul. Thus is a young girl rich; to encompass this richness makes one rich. She is rich although she does not know that she possesses anything; she is rich, she is a treasure! Quiet peace broods over her, and a little melancholy. She was light to look upon, as light as Psyche who was carried away by Zephyr, even lighter, for she carried herself away. Let the theologians dispute about the assumption of the Madonna; that does not seem inconceivable to me, for she no longer belonged to the world; but a young girl's lightness is incomprehensible and makes sport of the law of gravity. —She noticed nothing, and for that reason believed herself unnoticed. I kept my distance from her, and absorbed her image. She walked slowly, no precipitancy disturbed her peace or the quiet of her surroundings. A boy sat by the lake fishing. She stood still and watched the cork floating on the water. She had not walked very fast, but she wanted to cool off. She loosened a little scarf that was fastened about her neck under her shawl; a soft breeze from the water fanned her bosom, white as snow, and yet warm and full. The boy did not seem to like to have anyone watch his catch, he turned around and regarded her with a rather phlegmatic glance. He really cut a ridiculous figure, and I did not wonder that she began to laugh at him. How youthfully she laughed! If she had been alone with the boy, I do not believe she would have been afraid to fight with him. Her eyes were large and radiant; when one looked into them they had a dark luster which suggested an infinite depth, impossible to fathom; pure and innocent it was, gentle and quiet, full of mischief when she smiled. Her nose was finely arched; when I saw her profile, her nose seemed to merge into her forehead, which made it look a little shorter, a little more spirited.

She walked on, I followed. Fortunately there were many strollers on the path. While I exchanged a word or two with one and another of my acquaintance, I let her gain a little on me, and then soon overtook her again, thus relieving myself of the necessity of walking as slowly as she did, while keeping my distance. She went toward Eastgate. I was anxious to get a nearer view without being seen. On the corner stood a house from which I might be able to do so. I knew the family, and consequently needed only to call upon them. I hurried past her at a rapid pace as if I had not noticed her in any way. I got a long way ahead of her, greeted the family right and left, and then took possession of the window that looked out upon the path. She came, I looked and looked, while at the same time I carried on a conversation with the tea party in the drawing-room. Her walk readily convinced me that she had not taken many dancing lessons, and yet there was a pride in it, a natural nobility, but a lack of self-consciousness. I got to see her one more time than I had counted on. From the window I could not see very far along the path, but I could see a pier extending out into the lake, and to my great surprise I caught sight of her again out there. It occurred to me that perhaps she lives out here in the country, that maybe her family has a summer home here.

I was on the point of regretting my call, for fear that she might turn back and I thus lose sight of her, indeed the fact that she was already at the far end of the pier indicated that she would soon turn back and disappear, when she reappeared close by. She was walking past the house. In great haste I seized my hat and stick in order, if possible, to pass her and then again fall behind as many times as might be necessary, until I found out where she lived—when in my haste I happened to jostle the arm of a lady who was just about to serve tea. A frightful screaming arose. I stood there with my hat and stick, anxious only to get away. To turn the incident off and motivate my retreat, I exclaimed pathetically: "Like Cain, I shall be banished from the place where this tea was spilled!" But as if everything had conspired against me, my host conceived the preposterous idea of continuing my remarks, and declared loudly and solemnly that I should not be allowed to go a single step until I had enjoyed a cup of tea, and had also served the ladies with tea in place of that which was spilled, thus setting everything right again. Since I was perfectly certain that my host under the circumstances would consider it courteous to detain me by force, there was nothing I could do except to stay.—She had vanished!

How beautiful it is to be in love, how interesting to know that one is in love. Lo, that is the difference. I could become embittered at the thought that for a second time I have lost sight of her, and yet in a certain sense it pleases me. The image I now have of her shifts uncertainly between being her actual and her ideal form. This picture I now summon before me; but precisely because it either is reality, or the reality is the occasion, it has a peculiar fascination. I am not impatient, for she certainly lives in the town, and that is enough for me at present. This possibility is the condition of her image appearing so clearly—everything should be savored in slow draughts. And should I not be content, I who regard myself as a favorite of the gods, I who had the rare good fortune to fall in love again? That is something that no art, no study can effect, it is a gift. But having been fortunate enough to start a new love affair, I wish to see how long it can be sustained. I coddle this love as I never did my first. The opportunity falls to one's lot seldom enough, so if it does appear, then it is in truth worth seizing; for the fact is enough to drive one to despair, that it requires no art to seduce a girl but good fortune to find one worth seducing.—Love has many mysteries, and this first falling in love is also a mystery, even though a minor one —most people who rush into it become engaged or commit some other foolishness, and in the twist of a wrist it is all over, and they neither know what they have gained nor what they have lost. Twice now has she appeared before me and vanished; that signifies that she will soon appear again. When Joseph interpreted Pharaoh's dream, he added: "And the fact that thou didst dream this twice, signifies that it will soon be fulfilled."[18]

Still, it would be interesting if one could see a little in advance the forces whose coming makes up life's content. She lives now in her quiet peace; she does not even suspect that I exist, even less what goes on in my inner consciousness, still less the certainty with which I peer into her future; for my soul demands more and more reality, it becomes stronger and stronger. When a girl at first sight does not produce a deep enough impression upon one to arouse the ideal, then the reality is generally not particularly desirable; on the other hand, if she does arouse the ideal, then however experienced one may be, he is usually a little overwhelmed. I always advise anyone who is not certain of his hand, his eye, his victory, to risk the attack at this first stage, just because he is so overwhelmed that it gives him supernatural powers; for this excessive emotion is a curious blending of love and egoism. He will, however, miss some of the enjoyment; for he is too much involved in the situation to enjoy it. Which is the more attractive choice is difficult to decide, which the more interesting, is easy. However, it is always well to come as near the dividing line as possible. This affords me the real enjoyment, but what others may enjoy, I do not know with certainty. Mere possession is not worth much, and the means which such lovers employ are generally wretched enough. They do not disdain the use of money, power, influence, soporifics, and so on. But what enjoyment can there be in love if there is not the most absolute self-surrender, at least on one side? But such submission as a rule requires spirit, and such lovers are usually destitute of spirit.

19th day.

So her name is Cordelia. Cordelia! That is a lovely name, and that, too, is of importance, since it is often very disconcerting to have to use an ugly name in connection with the tenderest predicates. I recognized her a long way off; she was walking with two other girls on the left side. Their pace seemed to indicate that they would soon stop. I stood on a street corner and read a poster, while constantly keeping an eye on my unknown. They took leave of each other. The two had evidently gone a little out of their way, for they took an opposite direction. She came on toward my corner. When she had taken a few steps, one of the other girls came running after her, calling loudly enough for me to hear: Cordelia! Cordelia! Then the third girl came up, and they stood with their heads together for a secret conference, which I tried in vain to hear. Then all three laughed and went away somewhat more hastily in the direction the two had taken before. I followed them. They went into a house on the Strand. I waited a long time since it seemed probable that Cordelia might soon return alone. However that did not happen.

Cordelia! That is a really excellent name, and it was also the name of King Lear's third daughter, that remarkable girl who did not carry her heart on her lips, whose lips were silent while her heart beat warmly.[19] So it is with my Cordelia. She resembles her, I am certain of that. But in another way she does wear her heart on her lips, not in the form of words, but more cordially in the form of a kiss. How healthily full her lips were! Never have I seen prettier ones.

That I am really in love I can tell among other things by the reticence with which I deal with this matter, even to myself. All love is secretive, even faithless love, when it has the proper aesthetic factor in it. It never occurred to me to desire a confidant or to boast of my affairs. So I am almost glad that I did not find out where her home is, but only a place where she often comes. Perhaps on account of this I have also come a little nearer to my goal. I can, without attracting her attention, start my investigations, and from this fixed point it will not be difficult to secure an approach to her family. Should this circumstance, however, appear to be a difficulty—*eh bien!* It is all in the day's work; everything I do, I do *con amore;* and so too I love *con amore.*

20th day.

Today I got some information about the house into which she disappeared. It belongs to a widow by the name of Jansen, who is blessed with three daughters. I can get an abundance of information there, that is to say, in so far as they have any. The only difficulty is in understanding this information when raised to the third power, for all three talk at once. Her name is Cordelia Wahl, and she is the daughter of a Navy captain. He died some years ago, and her mother also. He was a very hard and austere man. She now lives with an aunt, her father's sister, who resembles her brother, but who otherwise is a very respectable woman. This is good as far as it goes, but for the rest, they know nothing about the house. They never go there, but Cordelia often visits them. She and the two girls are taking a course in cooking at the Royal Kitchen. For this reason she usually comes there early in the afternoon, sometimes in the morning, but never in the evening. They live a very secluded life.

Thus her story ends. There appears to be no bridge by which I can slip over into Cordelia's house.

She has then some understanding of the sorrows and of the dark side of life. Who would have suspected it? Still, these recollections belong to her earlier years; they are a shadow on her horizon, under which she has lived, but which she has never really noticed. It really is a very good thing; it has saved her womanliness, she is not spoiled. On the other hand, it will be important in raising her to a higher level, if one really understands how to bring it out. All such circumstances usually develop pride if they do not crush, and she is certainly far from being crushed.

21st day.

She lives near the ramparts. The location is not of the best for me, no neighbors whose acquaintance I might make, no public places where I might make my observations unnoticed. The ramparts themselves are little suitable, one is too conspicuous. If one descends to the street, one can hardly cross over to the side which extends along the base of the ramparts, for no one goes there and it would be very noticeable; if one walks along the side on which the houses front, one can see nothing. It is a corner house. From the street one can also see the windows overlooking the courtyard, there being no house next door. That is probably where her bedroom is.

22nd day.

Today I saw her for the first time at Mrs. Jansen's. I was introduced to her. She did not seem to care much about it, or to pay any attention to me. I made myself as inconspicuous as possible in order to observe her the better. She stayed only a moment, she had merely called for the daugh-

ters on the way to cooking school. While the two Jansen
girls were getting their wraps, we two were alone in the
room. With a cold, almost supercilious indifference, I made
some remark to her, to which she replied with a courtesy
altogether undeserved. Then they left. I could have offered
to accompany them, but that might have set me down as
a ladies' man, and I am convinced that she is not to be won
that way.—On the contrary, I preferred to leave a moment
after they had gone, but to go more rapidly than they, and
by another street, but likewise in the direction of the cooking school, so that just as they turned into Great Kingstreet,
I passed them in the greatest hurry, without even a greeting or other recognition, to their great astonishment.

23rd day.

It is necessary for me to gain entrance to her home, and,
in military parlance, I am ready. It promises to be, however, a rather complicated and difficult problem. I have
never known a family so isolated. There are only herself
and her aunt. No brothers, no cousins, not a thread to get
hold of, no relatives however distant that one might lock
arms with. I constantly go about with one arm hanging free.
Not for anything in the world would I at this time go arm
in arm with anyone; my arm is a grappling-hook always
in readiness; it is designed for the uncertain returns, on the
chance that there might appear in the distance, a long lost
relative or friend from far away, from whom I might get a
helping hand—and so clamber aboard. Anyway it is entirely
wrong for a family to live so isolated; it deprives the poor
girl of every opportunity of getting to know the world, to
say nothing of other dangerous consequences. It always defeats itself. It is true about suitors also. By such isolation
one may guard against petty thievery. In a very hospitable
house the opportunities for theft are greater. That, however, doesn't amount to much, for with girls from such
homes there is not much to steal; when they are sixteen
years old, their hearts are already completely filled sam-
plers, and I never care about writing my name where
many have already written. It never occurs to me to scratch

my name on a windowpane or in an inn or upon a tree or a bench in Frederiksberg Park.

27th day.

The more I see of her the more I am convinced that she is a very isolated figure. A man ought never to be so, not even a young man; for since his development essentially depends upon reflection, he must therefore be in touch with others. A young girl should never try to be interesting, for the interesting always implies a reflection upon itself, just as in art the interesting always reflects the artist. A young girl who wishes to please by being interesting usually succeeds only in pleasing herself. From the aesthetic side this is the objection to all forms of coquetry. The case is quite different when it comes to the incidental coquetry, supplied by nature's own movement, as for instance, the feminine blush of modesty, which is always coquetry in its most lovely form.

It may indeed happen that an interesting girl is also pleasing, but just as she herself has renounced her femininity, so also the men she pleases are usually the effeminate ones. Such a young girl really first becomes interesting through her relationship to men. Woman is the weaker sex, and yet she needs far more essentially to be alone in her youth than a man does; she must be self-contained, but that in which and through which she is self-contained is an illusion; this illusion is the dowry Nature has bestowed upon her, like that of a king's daughter. But this resting in illusion is just what isolates her. I have often wondered how it happens that there is nothing more demoralizing for a young girl than constant association with other young girls. This is evidently due to the fact that this companionship is neither the one thing nor the other; it disturbs the illusion, but it does not clarify it. Woman's most profound destiny is to be a companion to man, but through association with her own sex her reflection becomes centered on this association, and instead of becoming a companion, she becomes a lady's companion. The language itself is significant in this respect. Man is called master, but woman is not called maidservant or the like; no, the category of the essential is used; she is companion, not "companioness."

If I were to imagine my ideal girl, she would always be alone in the world, and thereby be self-contained, and especially she would not have girl friends. It is indeed true that there were three Graces, but it certainly has never occurred to anyone to imagine them talking together; they formed in their silent trinity a beautiful feminine unity. In this respect I would almost be tempted to recommend reviving the lady's bower, if this restraint were not also injurious. It is always highly desirable that a young girl be permitted liberty, but that no opportunities be offered her. Thus she becomes beautiful, but she is saved from becoming interesting. It is in vain that one would give a bridal veil to a young girl who has been much in the company of other young girls; but a man with true aesthetic appreciation always finds that a girl who is innocent in the deepest and truest sense is brought to him veiled, even if bridal veils are not in fashion.

She has been strictly brought up, for which I honor her parents even in their graves; she lives a very secluded existence, for which I could fall on her aunt's neck in gratitude. She has not learned to know the pleasures of the world, she has not a surfeit of small talk. She is proud, she disregards that which other young girls enjoy, and this is as it should be. That is a contradiction that I shall know how to profit by. Pomp and ceremony do not please her in the same sense that they please other girls; she is a little polemic, but this is necessary for a young girl with her enthusiasm. She lives in a world of fantasy. If she fell into the wrong hands, it might bring out something very unfeminine in her, precisely because she is so very feminine.

30th day.

Everywhere our paths cross. Today I met her three times. I am conscious of her slightest movement, when and where I shall meet her; but this knowledge is not used to secure a meeting with her; on the contrary, I squander my opportunities on a frightful scale. A meeting which has cost me many hours of waiting is thrown away like a mere bagatelle. I do not meet her, I touch only the periphery of her existence. If I know that she is going to Mrs. Jansen's, then my arrival does not coincide with hers, unless I have some important observation to make. I prefer to arrive a little early at Mrs. Jansen's, and then to meet her, if possible, at the door or upon the steps, as she is coming and I am leaving, when I pass her by indifferently. This is the first net in which she must be entangled. I never stop her on the street; I may bow to her, but I never come close to her, but always keep my distance. Our continual encounters are certainly noticeable to her; she does indeed perceive that a new body has appeared on her horizon, whose orbit in a strangely imperturbable manner affects her own disturbingly, but she has no conception of the law governing this movement; she is rather inclined to look about to see if she can discover the point controlling it, but she is as ignorant of being herself this focus as if she were a Chinaman. It is with her as with my associates in general: they believe that I have a multiplicity of affairs, that I am always on the move, and that I say with Figaro, "one, two, three, four intrigues at the same time, that is my delight." I must first know her and her entire intellectual background before beginning my assault. Most men enjoy a young girl as they do a glass of champagne in a single frothing moment. Oh, yes, that is all right, and in the case of many young girls it is really the most one can manage to get; but here there is more. If the individual is too frail to endure clearness and transparency, O well, then one enjoys the obscurity, but she can evidently endure it. The more one can sacrifice to love, the more interesting. This momentary enjoyment is, if not in a physical yet in a spiritual sense, a rape, and a rape is only an imagined enjoyment; it is like a stolen kiss, a thing which requires no art. No, when one can so arrange it that a girl's only desire is to give herself freely, when she feels that her whole happiness depends on this, when she almost begs to make this free submission, then for the first time there is true enjoyment, but this always requires spiritual influence.

Cordelia! What a glorious name! I sit at home and practice repeating it parrot-like. I say: Cordelia, Cordelia, my Cordelia, my own Cordelia. I can hardly keep from smiling at the thought of how I, by means of this routine, shall be able to say these words when the decisive moment comes. One should always make preliminary studies, everything must be properly planned. It is no wonder that poets always describe as the most beautiful moment the one when the lovers first call each other by their first names, when the lovers, not by sprinkling (although many never come any further than that), but by immersing themselves in the waters of love, rise from that baptism and now for the first time know each other as old friends, although they are but a minute old. To a young girl that moment is always the most beautiful, and in order to enjoy it rightly, one ought always to transcend it a little, so as to be not only baptismal candidate but also priest. A little irony makes the next moment the interesting one, it is a spiritual disrobing. One must be poet enough not to disturb the ceremony, and yet rogue enough to be on the lookout.

                                                    June 2nd.
She is proud, I have seen that for a long time. When she is in the company of the three Jansens she talks very little, their chatter evidently bores her, and certainly the smile on her lips seems to indicate it. I am relying on that smile. At other times she can let herself go in almost boyish wildness, to the great surprise of the Jansens. It is not inexplicable to me when I consider her childhood. She had only one brother, who was a year older. She knew only her father and brother, had been a witness to very serious scenes, which gave her a distaste for gossip in general. Her father and mother had not lived happily together; that which usually appeals to a young girl more or less clearly or vaguely has no attraction for her. It may possibly be that she is puzzled about what it means to be a woman. Perhaps she may wish that she had been a boy instead of a girl.

She has imagination, spirit, passion, in short, all the substantialities, but is unaware of possessing them. I learned that by chance today. I know from Jansen & Company that she does not play, that it is against her aunt's principles.

I regret this, for music is always a good means of communicating with a girl, when one, mark this well, is prudent enough not to pose as a connoisseur. Today I went to Mrs. Jansen's. I had half opened the door without knocking, an effrontery that has often served me well, and which, when necessary, I turn into a jest by knocking on the open door. She sat alone at the piano—she seemed to be playing by stealth—it was a little Swedish melody; she did not play it very well, she became impatient, and then again, she played more softly. I closed the door and stood outside, listening to the change in her moods; there was sometimes a passion in her playing which reminded one of the maiden *Mettelil,* who smote the golden harp so passionately that milk gushed from her breasts. There was some sadness but also something dithyrambic in her execution.—I might have rushed in, seized the moment—that would have been foolish.—Memory is not only a means of preserving but also of enhancing; what is permeated by memory has a two-fold effect.—One often finds in books, especially in psalters, a little flower—there had been a beautiful moment which had furnished the occasion for keeping this, and yet the memory is even more beautiful. She is evidently concealing the fact that she plays, or perhaps she plays only this little Swedish melody—has it perhaps a special interest for her? All this I do not know, but therefore this incident is very important to me. When sometime I can talk more confidentially with her, I shall slyly lead her to this point and let her fall into the trap.

June 3rd.

Even yet I cannot decide how she is to be understood. Therefore I wait very quietly, very inconspicuously—aye, like a soldier on vidette duty who throws himself on the ground and listens for the faintest sound of an approaching enemy. I really do not exist for her in any real sense, not only not in a negative relationship, but simply not at all. Even yet I have not dared to experiment.—To see her was to love her, that is the way it is described in novels—aye, it is true enough, if love had no dialectic; but what does one really learn about love from novels? Sheer lies, which help to shorten the task.

When now after what I have learned, I think back upon the impression that first meeting made upon me, I find my ideas about her are considerably modified, to her advantage as well as to my own. It is not quite usual for a young girl to go out alone or for a young girl to be so introspective. I subjected her to my strict criterion: charming. But charm is a very fleeting factor, which is as yesterday when it is past. I had not imagined her in the environment in which she lives; least of all had I pictured her so unreflectingly familiar with the stormy side of life.

I wonder how it is with her emotions. She has certainly never been in love, for her spirit is too free-soaring for that, nor is she by any means one of those theoretically experienced maidens, who, long before their time, are so familiar with the thought of being in the arms of the loved one. The figures she has met in real life have hardly been able to bring her to confusion about the relation of dreams to reality. Her soul is still nourished by the divine ambrosia of ideals. But the ideal which hovers before her is not exactly a shepherdess or a heroine of romance, a mistress, it is someone like a Jeanne d'Arc.

The question is always whether her femininity is strong enough to make her reflective, or whether it is only to be enjoyed as beauty and charm; the question is whether one dares to tense the bow more strongly. Certainly it is a wonderful thing to find a pure immediate femininity, but if one dares to attempt a change, then one gets the interesting. In such a case it is best simply to provide her with a suitor. Some people are superstitious enough to believe that this would be injurious for a young girl.—Indeed, if she is a very fine and delicate plant whose charm is her one outstanding quality, it would always be best for her never to have heard of love; but if this is not the case, it is an advantage, and I should never hesitate to bring forward a suitor, were none at hand. This suitor must not be a mere caricature either, for then nothing is gained; he must be a respectable young man, even attractive if possible, but not a man big enough for her passion. She looks down on such a man, she gets a distaste for love, she almost doubts her own reality when she feels what her destiny might be and sees what reality offers. If this is love, she says, it is nothing to get excited about. Her love makes her proud, this pride makes her interesting, it penetrates her being with a higher incarnation; but she is also approaching her downfall—all of which only makes her increasingly more interesting. However, it is best to find out about her acquaintances first, to see whether or not there might be such a suitor. Her own home furnishes no opportunity, or as good as none, but still she does go out, and so such a one might be found. To provide a suitor before knowing this is altogether inadvisable. To allow her to compare two equally insignificant suitors would be bad for her. I must find out whether there may not be such a lover in the offing, one who lacks the courage to storm the citadel, a chicken thief, who sees no opportunity in such a cloistered house.

Consequently, the strategic principle, the law governing every move in this campaign, is always to work her into an interesting situation. The interesting is the field on which the battle must be waged; the potentialities of the interesting must be exhausted. Unless I am mistaken, her whole nature is designed for this, so that what I require is exactly what she gives, indeed, what she herself requires. Everything depends on finding out what the individual can give and therefore what she must demand in return. For this reason my love affairs always have a reality for myself, they mark a factor in my life, a creative period, of which I am fully aware; often they are bound up with one or another acquired skill. For the sake of the first girl I loved, I learned to dance; I learned to speak French for the sake of a little dancer. At that time, like all simpletons, I went to the public market, and I often made a fool of myself. Now I go in for the black market.[20] Perhaps, however, she has exhausted one phase of the interesting; her secluded life seems to indicate that. It is now wise to find another phase, which at first sight may not seem so interesting to her, but which, just on account of this resistance, may become so to her. For this purpose I do not select the poetic but the prosaic. This is just the beginning. First her femininity is neutralized by prosaic reason and ridicule, not directly but indirectly, and at the same time by an absolutely colorless intellectuality. She almost loses her sense of the feminine, but in this condition she cannot stand by herself, she throws herself into my arms, not as if I were a lover, no, still quite neutrally. Then her femininity awakens, one arouses her to the highest pitch, one allows her to offend against one or another validity, she vents her rage upon it, her femininity reaches almost supernatural heights, she belongs to me with the force of a world-passion.

5th day.

I did not have to go far after all. She visits at the home of a wholesale merchant, Baxter by name. Here I found not only Cordelia, but also a man who appears very opportunely. Edward, the son of the house, is dead in love with her. To see that, one needs only half an eye, when one looks at his two eyes. He is in business with his father; a good-looking young man, quite pleasant, somewhat bashful, which last I think does not hurt him in her eyes.

Poor Edward! He simply does not know how to go about his courtship. When he knows that she is to be there in the evening, then he dresses for her sake alone, puts on his new dark suit with collar and cuffs, just for her sake, and cuts an almost ridiculous figure among the quite commonplace company in the drawing-room. His embarrassment is almost incredible. If it were a pose, Edward would become a very dangerous rival to me. Embarrassment needs to be used very artistically, but it can be used to great advantage. How often have I not used it to fool some little maiden. Girls generally speak very harshly about bashful men, and yet they secretly like them. A little embarrassment always flatters a young girl's vanity, she feels her superiority, it is earnest money. When you have lulled them to sleep, when they believe that you are ready to die from embarrassment, then you have an opportunity to show that you are very far from that, that you are very well able to shift for yourself. By means of bashfulness, you lose your masculine significance, and therefore it is a relatively good means of neutralizing sexuality. Then when they notice that this shyness was only assumed, they are ashamed, they blush inwardly, and feel very strongly that they have certainly gone too far. It is the same as when people continue too long to treat a boy as a child.

7th day.

We are fast friends now, Edward and I; a true friendship, a beautiful relationship, exists between us, such as has not been seen since the palmiest days of Greece. We soon became intimates when, after having lured him into many conversations about Cordelia, I got him to confess his secret. It goes without saying that when all secrets are being revealed, this one is included with the others. Poor fellow, he has already sighed a long time. He dresses up every time she comes, then accompanies her home in the evening; his heart beats fast at the thought of her arm resting on his, they walk home, gaze at the stars, he rings her bell, she disappears, he despairs, but hopes for better luck next time. He has not yet had the courage to set foot over her threshold, he who has had such excellent opportunities. Although inwardly I cannot refrain from making fun of Edward, there is still something really beautiful in his childishness. Although I ordinarily imagine myself to be fairly familiar with the very quintessence of the erotic, I have never observed this condition in myself, this fear and trembling, that is, to the degree that it takes away my self-possession, for otherwise I know it well enough, but only as tending to make me stronger. Perhaps someone will say that I have never been in love. Perhaps. I have told Edward a few home truths; I have encouraged him to rely on my friendship. Tomorrow he is going to take a decisive step: go in person and invite her out. I have led him to the desperate idea of inviting me to go with him; I have promised to do so. He regards this as an extraordinary display of friendship. The occasion is exactly as I would have it: we burst in and blurt it all out. Should she have the slightest doubt as to the meaning of my appearing on the scene, my appearance itself will confuse everything.

I have never before been accustomed to prepare myself for my part in a conversation; now this becomes necessary in order to entertain the aunt. I have shouldered the disinterested task of a tête-à-tête with her, thereby covering Edward's amorous advances toward Cordelia. The aunt formerly lived in the country, and by my own prodigious studies of agronomic literature, coupled with the aunt's sententious comments based on experience, I am making definite progress in insight and efficiency.

I have made myself very acceptable to the aunt; she regards me as a steady, reliable man whom it is a pleasure to entertain, not like some of our fashionable young gentlemen. I do not seem to be particularly in Cordelia's favor. She is indeed too innocent and unspoiled to expect every man to dance attendance upon her, but still she is very conscious of the rebel in my nature.

When I sit thus in the comfortable living room, while she like a good angel diffuses her charm everywhere, over everyone with whom she comes in contact, over good and evil alike, then I sometimes get out of patience with myself; I am tempted to rush forth from my hiding place; for though I sit there, visible to everyone in the living room, still I am really lying in ambush. I am tempted to grasp her hand, to take her in my arms, to hide her in myself, for fear someone else should take her away from me. Or when Edward and I leave in the evening, when in taking leave she offers me her hand, when I hold it in mine, it sometimes becomes very difficult to let the bird slip out of my hand. Patience—*quod antea fuit impetus, nunc ratio est*[21]—she must be quite otherwise ensnared in my web, and then suddenly I let the whole power of my love rush forth. We have not spoiled that moment for ourselves by billing and cooing, by unseemly anticipation, for which you must thank me, my Cordelia. I work to develop the contrast, I tense the bow of love to wound the deeper. Like an archer, I release the string, tighten it again, listen to its song, my battle ode, but I do not aim it yet, I do not even lay the arrow on the string.

When a small number of people are frequently together in the same room, a sort of easy pattern soon develops, in which each one has his own place and chair; thus a picture of the room is formed which one can easily reproduce for himself at will, a chart of the terrain. It was that way with us in the Wahl home; we united to form a picture. In the evening we drink tea there. Generally the aunt who previously has been sitting on the sofa, moves over to the little worktable, which place Cordelia in turn vacates. She goes over to the tea table in front of the sofa, Edward follows her, I follow the aunt. Edward tries to be secretive, he talks in a whisper; usually he does it so well that he becomes entirely mute. I am not at all secretive in my outpourings to the aunt—market prices, a calculation of the quantity of milk needed to produce a pound of butter; through the medium of cream and the dialectic of buttermaking, there comes a reality which any young girl can listen to without embarrassment, but, what is far rarer, it is a solid, reasonable, and edifying conversation, equally improving for mind and heart. I generally sit with my back to the tea table and to the ravings of Edward and Cordelia. Meanwhile, I rave with the aunt. And is not Nature great and wise in her productivity, is not butter a precious gift, the glorious result of Nature and art! I had promised Edward that I would certainly prevent the aunt from overhearing the conversation between him and Cordelia, providing anything was really said, and I always keep my word. On the other hand, I can easily overhear every word exchanged between them, hear every movement. This is very important to me, for one cannot always know how far a desperate man will venture to go. The most cautious and faint-hearted men sometimes do the most desperate things. Although I have nothing at all to do with these two people, it is readily apparent that Cordelia constantly feels that I am invisibly present between her and Edward.

We four together make a peculiar picture. If I wished to find an analogy in a familiar picture, I might think of myself as Mephistopheles; but the difficulty is, however, that Edward is no Faust. If I were to be Faust, there again arises the difficulty, that Edward is certainly no Mephistopheles. Neither am I a Mephistopheles, least of all in Edward's eyes. He regards me as the guardian angel of his love, and he is right in that, for at least he can be certain that no one watches more solicitously over his love than I. I have promised him that I would talk with the aunt, and I discharge this honorable task with all seriousness. The aunt vanishes, almost before our eyes, in pure agricultural economics. We go into the kitchen and cellars, we go up into the attic, we look at the chickens, ducks, and geese, and so on. All this offends Cordelia. She naturally cannot understand what it really is that I am after. I am a riddle to her, a riddle she has no temptation to solve, but which provokes her, and almost makes her indignant. She feels very strongly that her aunt is making herself ridiculous, and yet her aunt is a very respectable lady who certainly does not deserve to be made fun of. But I do this so skillfully that she knows very well that it would be useless for her to try to stop me. Sometimes I carry it so far that Cordelia almost has to smile secretly at her aunt. These are studies that must be made. Not as if I did this in cooperation with Cordelia; far from it, I would never make her smile at her aunt. My expression does not change, I am profoundly earnest, but Cordelia cannot keep from smiling. It is the first lesson in deception: she must learn to smile ironically; but this smile is aimed almost as much at me as at her aunt, for she simply does not know what to think of me. It is barely possible that I am one of those prematurely-old young men, it is possible; there might also be a second possibility, or even a third, and so on. When she becomes indignant with herself for having smiled at her aunt, then I turn around, and without interrupting my conversation with the aunt, I look at her very seriously, then she smiles at me and at the situation.

Our relationship is not the tender and loyal embrace of understanding, not attraction, it is the repulsion of misunderstanding. My relationship to her is simply nil; it is purely intellectual, which means it is simply nothing to a young girl. The method I am following has extraordinary advantages. A man who approaches as a gallant awakens mistrust and encounters resistance. I escape all such suspicions. She is not on guard against me; instead she regards me as a trustworthy man who is fit to watch over a young girl. The method has but one drawback, namely, it is tedious, but it can, therefore, only advantageously be used against an individual when the interesting is to be the reward.

What a rejuvenating power a young girl has! Not the cooling freshness of a morning breeze, not the sigh of the wind, not the cooling breath of the sea, not the fragrance of wine with its delicious bouquet—nothing else in all the world has this rejuvenating power.

Soon I hope that I shall have brought her to the point of hating me. I have presented a perfect picture of a confirmed bachelor. All I talk about is sitting at my ease, being comfortably lodged, having a competent servant, friends of good standing whom I can rely upon as intimates. Now if I can induce the aunt to abandon her agronomic interests, then I can interest her in these, in order to get a more direct occasion for irony. One can laugh at a bachelor, even have sympathy for him, but a young man, who has any spirit at all, shocks a young girl by such conduct; the entire significance of sex, its beauty, and its poetry, are destroyed.

So the days go on, I see her, but I do not talk with her, I talk with the aunt in her presence. Occasionally at night it occurs to me to give my love air. Then wrapped in my cloak, with my hat pulled down over my eyes, I go and stand outside her window. Her bedroom looks out over the yard, but since it is a corner house, it can be seen from the street. At times she stands a moment at the window, or she opens it, looks up at the stars, unseen by anyone except the one she would least of all believe was watching her. In these hours of the night I steal about like a wraith, like a wraith I haunt the place where she lives. Then I forget everything, I have no plans, no calculations, I throw reason overboard, I expand and strengthen my chest by deep sighs, an exercise which I need in order not to suffer from the systematized routine of my life. Some are virtuous by day, sinful at night; I dissemble by day, at night I am sheer desire. If she could see me here, if she could look into my soul—if!

If this girl would only understand herself, she would have to admit that I am the man for her. She is too intense, too deeply emotional to be happy in marriage; it would not be enough for her to yield to an ordinary seducer; if she yields to me, then she will save the interesting out of the shipwreck. In relation to me, she must *zu Grunde gehn*, as the philosophers say with a play on words.[22]

She is really tired of listening to Edward. So it always is; where narrow limits are set for the interesting, one discovers all the more. Sometimes she listens to my conversation with her aunt. When I notice this, there comes a flash on the distant horizon, intimations of a very different world, to the amazement of her aunt as well as of Cordelia. The aunt sees the flash, but hears nothing, Cordelia hears the voice, but sees nothing. Suddenly everything is again as before. The conversation between the aunt and myself pursues its monotonous way, like the hoofs of post horses in the stillness of the night. It is accompanied by the melancholy singing of the samovar. At such times there sometimes seems to be something uncanny in the atmosphere of the living room, especially to Cordelia. She has no one she can talk with or listen to. If she turns to Edward, she faces the danger of his doing something foolish, just because of his embarrassment. If she turns to the other side, to her aunt and me, then the certainty which here prevails, the monotonous hammerblows of our steady conversation, makes a very disagreeable contrast to Edward's uncertainty. I can well understand that Cordelia must consider her aunt bewitched, so completely does she follow the tempo of my thought. Nor can she take part in our conversation; for this, too, is one of the ways I have used to provoke her, that is, by always treating her like a child. Not that I would permit myself any liberties with her, far from it. I know too well how disturbingly such things can work, and it is especially worth while that her womanliness should rise up again pure and lovely. On account of the intimate footing I maintain with the aunt, it is easy for me to treat her like a child who is ignorant of the world. Thereby her femininity is not offended, but only neutralized; for it cannot offend her femininity that she is ignorant of market prices, but it can irritate her that such things should be regarded as of chief importance in life. By means of my cunning assistance, her aunt overbids herself in this direction. She becomes almost fanatical on the subject, something for which she has to thank me. The only thing about me that she cannot stand is that I am nothing. Accordingly I have formed the habit, every time something is said about a position which is vacant, of exclaiming, "That is the job for me!" and then I discuss it very seriously with her. Cordelia always notices the irony, which is exactly as I wish.

Poor Edward! Too bad he is not called Fritz. Whenever I think of him in my quiet deliberations, I am reminded of Fritz and his sweetheart.[23] Edward, like his prototype, is also a corporal in the militia. To tell the truth, Edward is also very boring. He does not go about the matter in the right way, and he is always too well dressed. Just between ourselves, as a favor to him, I always go dressed as carelessly as possible. Poor Edward! The only thing that almost makes me sorry for him is that he is so everlastingly grateful to me that he hardly knows how to thank me. To allow him to thank me, that is really too much!

Why can you not be quiet and well behaved? You have done nothing the entire morning except to shake my awning, pull at my window mirror and the string by which it

hangs, play with the bell-rope from the third story, rattle
the windowpanes, in short, in every possible way impress
me with your existence, as if you would beckon me to come
out with you. Yes, it is a fine day, but I have no inclination,
let me stay at home. . . . Ye merry, wanton zephyrs, ye
happy children, go ye alone; have your pastime as always
with the young maidens. Yes, I know no one can embrace
a maiden so seductively as you; in vain would she try to
slip away from you, she cannot twist herself out of your
arms—nor does she wish to; for you are cool and refreshing,
you do not inflame. . . . Go your own way, leave me out.
. . . But then you take no satisfaction in it, you say, you
do not do it for your own sake . . . very well, then, I go
with you; but on two conditions. In the first place. There
lives on King's Newmarket a young maiden; she is very
pretty, but she has the impudence to refuse to love me, and
what is worse still, she loves another, and it has come to
such a pass that they go out walking together arm in arm.
At one o'clock I know that he goes to fetch her. Now promise me that the strongest blowers among you will conceal
yourselves somewhere in the neighborhood until the moment when he steps out of the door with her. That moment,
just as he is about to turn down Great Kingstreet, let
this detachment rush forward, take his hat from his head
in the politest manner possible, and carry it at an even
speed at precisely a yard's distance in front of him; not
faster than that, for then he might turn back home again.
Let him always believe that he is on the point of catching
it the next second, so that he does not even let go of her
arm. In that manner you will bring them through Great
Kingstreet, along the wall as far as Northport, as far as
Highbridge Place. . . . Let me see, how long will that
take? I think about half an hour. At half-past one exactly,
I approach from Eastern Street. When the detachment in
question has brought the lovers out into the middle of the
Place, let a violent attack be made upon them, during
which you will also tear her hat from her head, tangle her
curls, carry away her shawl, while all the time his hat floats
jubilantly higher and higher into the air; in short, you will
bring about a confusion so that not I alone, but the entire

public will break out in a roar of laughter, the dogs begin
to bark, and the watchman clang his bell in the tower.
You will arrange it so that her hat flies over to me, and
thus I become the happy individual privileged to restore it
to her. In the second place. The section that follows me
must obey my every hint, must keep within the bounds of
seemliness, offer no affront to any pretty maiden, permit
itself to take no liberty greater than will allow her to preserve her joy in the jest, her lips their smile, her eye its tranquillity, and her to remain without anxiety. If a single one
of you dares to behave differently, let your name be accursed.—And now away to life and joy, to youth and
beauty; show me what I have often seen, and what I never
weary of seeing, show me a beautiful young woman, unfold her beauty for me in such a way that she becomes
herself more beautiful; subject her to an examination of
such a kind that she derives happiness from that examination! . . . I choose Broad Street, but, as you know, I can
only dispose of my time until half-past one. . . .

There comes a young woman, all stiff and starched; of
course, it is Sunday today. . . . Fan her a little, waft over
her the cool air, glide in a gentle stream about her, embrace
her with your innocent contact! How I sense the heightened
color of the cheek, the reddening of the lips, the bosom's
lifting. . . . Is it not so, my dear, it is indescribable, it is a
blessed delight to breathe this refreshing air? The little collar quivers like a leaf. How full and sound her breathing!
Her pace slackens, she is almost carried along by the gentle breeze, like a cloud, like a dream. . . . Blow a little
stronger, with a longer sweep! . . . She draws herself together; she folds her arms a little closer to her bosom,
which she covers more carefully, lest a gust of wind should
prove too forward, and insinuate itself softly and coolingly
under the light covering. . . . Her color is heightened, her
cheeks become fuller, her eye clearer, her step firmer. A
little opposition tends to make a person more beautiful.
Every young woman ought to fall in love with the zephyrs;
for no man can rival them in enhancing her beauty, as they
struggle against her. . . . Her body bends a little forward,
she looks down toward the tips of her shoes. . . . Stop a

little! It is too much, her body broadens, loses its pretty slenderness. . . . Cool her a little! . . . Is it not true, my dear, it is refreshing after being warm, to feel those invigorating shivers; it is enough to make one fling open his arms in gratitude, in joy over existence. . . . She turns her side to the breeze. . . . Now quick! a powerful gust, so that I can guess the beauty of her form! . . . A little stronger! to bring the draperies more closely about her. . . . It is too much. Her posture becomes awkward, the lightness of her step is interfered with. . . . She turns again. . . . Blow, now, blow, let her try her strength! . . . Enough, it is too much! One of her curls has fallen down . . . will you be so good as to keep yourselves in check!— There comes a whole regiment on the march:

> *Die eine ist verliebt gar sehr;*
> *Die andre wäre es gerne.*[24]

Yes, it cannot be denied, it is a very poor engagement in life to have to walk with one's future brother-in-law, on his left arm. For a woman this is about the same as for a man to be an extra clerk on the waiting list. . . . But the clerk may be advanced: he has, too, his place in the office, and is called in on extraordinary occasions, which do not fall to the sister-in-law's lot; but then, on the other hand, her advancement is not so slow—when she is advanced and is moved over into another office. . . . Blow now a little briskly! When you have something firm to hold fast to, it is easy enough to offer resistance. . . . The center advances vigorously, the wings are unable to follow. . . . He stands firm enough, the winds cannot move him for he is too heavy—but also too heavy for the wings to lift from the earth. He hurls himself forward in order to show—that he is a heavy body; but the more unmoved he stands, the more do the lassies suffer under it. . . . My beautiful young ladies, may I not offer a piece of good advice: leave the future husband and brother-in-law out of it, try to walk alone, and you will find that it will be much more satisfactory. . . . Now blow a little more softly! . . . How they are tumbled about by the billowing breezes; soon they will be striking attitudes before one another down the street—

could any dance music produce a more frolicsome gaiety? And yet the wind does not exhaust, it strengthens. . . . Now they sweep along side by side, in full sail down the street—could any waltz carry a young woman away more seductively? And yet the wind does not weary, it supports. . . . Now they turn around to face the husband and brother-in-law. . . . Is it not so, a little opposition is pleasant, one is glad to struggle for possession of what one loves; and the struggle will doubtless be successful; there is a Providence which comes to the aid of love, that is why the man has the wind in his favor. . . . Have I not arranged it well: when you have the wind at your back, it can easily happen that you pass the beloved, but when it blows against you, you are pleasantly excited, then you seek refuge near him, and the gust of wind makes you sounder and more tempting, and more fascinating, and it cools the fruit of your lips which should preferably be enjoyed cold, because it is so hot, just as champagne heats when it is icy cold. . . . How they laugh and talk—and the wind carries the words away—and is there anything here to talk about?—and they laugh again and bend before the wind, and hold on to their hats, and watch their feet. . . . Stop now, lest the young women become impatient and angry at us, or afraid of us!—Just so, resolutely and vigorously, the right foot before the left. . . .

How bravely and challengingly she looks about in the world. . . . Can I be mistaken? She hangs on a man's arm, hence she must be engaged. Let me see, my child, what kind of a present you have received on life's Christmas tree. . . . Oh, so! he seems to be a very substantial fellow. She is in the first stage of the engagement, she loves him—possibly so, but yet her love flutters wide and spacious, loose about him; she still has the cloak of chastity, which suffices to cover many. . . . Blow up a little! . . . When one walks so fast, it is no wonder the ribbons on her hat stiffen in the wind, so that it looks as if they were wings bearing this light body—and her love—that too follows like a fairy veil that the wind plays with. When you look at love in this manner, it seems so spacious; but when you are about to put it on, when the veil must be made into an everyday dress—then there is not cloth enough for many puffs. . . . Heaven preserve us! When one has courage enough to dare to take a step decisive for one's entire life, one surely has the courage to walk straight against the wind. Who doubts it? Not I; but no temper, my little miss, no temper. Time is a hard schoolmaster, and the wind is not so bad either. . . . Tease her a little! . . . What became of the handkerchief? . . . Oh, you recovered it all right. . . . There went one of the hat ribbons . . . it is really quite embarrassing, in the presence of the intended. . . . There comes a girl friend who must be greeted. It is the first time she has seen you since the engagement; of course it is for the sake of showing yourself as an engaged girl that you are here on Broad Street, and are intending furthermore to go on the esplanade. As far as I know it is the custom for a newly wedded couple to go to church the first Sunday after the wedding; engaged couples, on the other hand, show themselves on the esplanade. . . . And an engagement really has something in common with the esplanade. . . . Be careful now, the wind takes hold of your hat, hold on to it a little, bend your head down. . . . How unfortunate that you did not get a chance to greet your girl friend at all, it was not calm enough to greet her with the superior air that an engaged girl ought always to assume before the unengaged. . . . Blow now a little more softly! . . . and now come the better days . . . how she clings to the beloved; she is far enough ahead of him so that she can turn her head back and look up into his face, and be glad in him, her wealth, her happiness, her hope, her future. . . . O my girl, you make too much of him. . . . Or does he not owe it to me and the wind that he looks so strong? And do you yourself not owe it to me and to the soft breezes that now bring you healing, and turn the pain into forgetfulness, that you look so full of vitality, so full of longing, so expectant?

> And I will not have a student
> Who lies and reads all night,
> But I will have an officer
> With feathers on his hat.[25]

That is evident at once, my girl, there is something in your look. . . . No, you are by no means satisfied with a student. . . . But just why an officer? A graduate now, one who has finished his studies, would he not do just as well? . . . At the moment, however, I cannot furnish you with an officer or with a graduate either. But I can serve you some cool and tempering breezes. . . . Now blow a little! . . . That's right, throw the silk shawl back over your shoulder; walk very slowly, that will make the cheek a little paler, and the eyes to shine not quite so brightly. . . . So. A little exercise, especially on a fine day like this, and then a little patience, and you will doubtless get your officer. . . . There is a couple who seem predestined for one another. What firmness in the step, what sureness in the entire bearing, based upon mutual confidence; what a pre-established harmony in all their movements, what sufficing thoroughness. Their attitudes are not light and graceful, they do not dance together, no, there is a permanency in them, a boldness, which awakens a hope that cannot be betrayed, which commands mutual respect. I will wager that their view of life is this: life is a way. And they seem destined to walk with one another, arm in arm, through the joys and sorrows of life. They harmonize to such a degree that the lady has even given up the privilege of walking on the flagstones. . . . But, my dear zephyrs, why so busy with that couple? They hardly seem to be worth so much attention. Can there be anything special to take note of? . . . But it is half-past one, off to Highbridge Place.

One would not believe it possible to calculate the developmental history of a soul so accurately. It shows how wholesome Cordelia is. She is in truth a remarkable girl. She is quiet and modest, unpretentious, but unconsciously there is in her a prodigious demand. This was evident to me today when I saw her enter the house. The slight resistance that a gust of wind can offer awakens, as it were, all the energy within her, without arousing any internal conflict. She is not a little insignificant girl who slips between your fingers, so fragile that you almost fear that she will go to pieces if you look at her; but neither is she a showy ornamental flower. Like a physician, I can therefore take pleasure in observing all the symptoms in her case history.

Gradually I am beginning to approach her in my attack, to go over to more direct action. Were I to indicate this change on my military map of the family, I should say that I have turned my chair so that my side is toward her. I have more to do with her, I address remarks to her, and elicit an answer from her. Her soul has passion, intensity, and without being foolish or vain, her reflections are remarkably pointed, she has a craving for the unusual. My irony over the foolishness of human beings, my ridicule of their cowardice, of their lukewarm indolence, fascinate her. She likes well enough to drive the chariot of the sun across the arch of heaven, to come near enough to earth to scorch people a little.[26] However, she does not trust me; hitherto I have discouraged every approach on her part, even intellectually. She must be strong in herself before I let her take rest in me. By glimpses it may indeed look as if it were she whom I would make my confidante in my freemasonry, but this is only by glimpses. She must be developed inwardly, she must feel an elasticity of soul, she must learn to evaluate the world. What progress she is making, her conversation and her eyes easily show me. I have only once seen a devastating anger in her. She must owe me nothing; for she must be free; love exists only in freedom, only in freedom is there enjoyment and everlasting delight. Although I am aiming at her falling into my arms, as it were, by a natural necessity, yet I am striving to bring it about so that as she gravitates toward me, it will still not be like the falling of a heavy body, but as spirit seeking spirit. Although she must belong to me, it must not be in the unlovely sense of resting upon me like a burden. She must neither hang on me in the physical sense, nor be an obligation in a moral sense. Between the two of us only the proper play of freedom must prevail. She must be mine so freely that I can take her in my arms.

Cordelia occupies me almost too much. I lose my balance again, not in her presence, but when in the strictest sense

I am alone with her. I long after her, not in order to talk
with her, but only to let her picture float past me. I steal
after her when I know that she is out walking, not to be
seen, but to see. The other evening we all left the Baxter
house together; Edward accompanied her. I parted from
them in greatest haste, hurried off to another street where
my servant was waiting for me. In a trice I had changed
my clothes, and I met her once more without her suspecting it. Edward was silent as usual. I am certainly in love,
but not in the ordinary sense, and for that reason I must
be very cautious, since it may always have some dangerous
consequences; and one is that way only once. Still, the god
of love is blind; if one is clever, one can fool him easily
enough. The trick, as regards an impression, consists in being as sensitive as possible, both in knowing what impression one makes upon the girl, and what impression each
girl makes upon one. In this way one can be in love with
many girls at once, because one loves each girl differently.
To love only one is too little; to love all of them is a surfeit;
to know one's self and to love as many as possible, to let
one's soul conceal all the power of love in itself, so that each
girl gets her own proper nourishment, while the consciousness embraces the whole—that is enjoyment, that is really
living.

July 3rd.

Edward cannot really complain of me. Indeed I wish
Cordelia would fall in love with him, so that through him
she might get a distaste for ordinary love, and thereby go
beyond her own limitations; but just for this reason it is
necessary that Edward should not be a caricature, for that
would not help. Now Edward is a good match, not only in
the usual sense of the word, which is of no importance in
her eyes, since a seventeen-year-old girl does not consider
such things; but personally he has a number of attractive
qualities which I try to help him exhibit in the most advantageous light. Like a lady's-maid or a decorator, I fit
him out as well as possible, according to the resources of
the house. Indeed, I sometimes hang a little borrowed finery

on him. Then when we go to Cordelia's, I, strange to say, go with him. He is, as it were, my brother, my son, and yet he is my friend, my contemporary, my rival. He can never become dangerous to me. The higher I raise him, since he is bound to fall, the better; the more it arouses a consciousness in Cordelia of what she dislikes, the more intense become her ideas of what she desires. I help him in this direction, I commend him, in short I do everything a friend can do for a friend. In order to make up for my own coldness, I almost rave about Edward. I describe him as a visionary. Since Edward does not know how to help himself, I must push him forward.

Cordelia both hates and fears me. What does a young girl fear? Intellectuality. Why? Because it constitutes a negation of her whole feminine existence. Masculine good looks and a pleasing personality and so forth are good mediators. One can make a conquest by their aid, but can never win a complete victory. Why? Because one is making war upon a girl within her own potentialities, and in these she is always the stronger. Through these methods one can make a girl blush, can put her out of countenance, but can never call forth the indescribable, fascinating anxiety which makes her beauty interesting.

Non formosus erat, sed erat facundus Ulixes,
et tamen aequoreas torsit amore Deas.[27]

Everyone ought to know his own powers. But this is something that has often disturbed me, that even those who have natural endowments behave so awkwardly. Really a man ought to be able to see in any young girl, who has become the victim of another's, or rather of her own love, just how she has been deceived. The confirmed murderer uses a definite technique, and the experienced policeman knows the perpetrator as soon as he sees the wound. But where does one meet such a systematic seducer, such a trained psychologist? The seduction of a girl means to most men the seduction of a girl, and that is the end of it. And there is a whole language concealed in this thought.

As a woman, she hates me; as an intelligent woman, she fears me; as having a good mind, she loves me. Now for the first time I have produced this conflict in her soul. My pride, my defiance, my cold ridicule, my heartless irony, all tempt her, not as if she might wish to love me; no, there is certainly not a trace of such feeling in her, least of all toward me. She would emulate me. What tempts her is a proud independence in the face of men, a freedom like that of the Arabs of the desert. My laughter and singularity neutralize every erotic impulse. She is fairly at ease with me, and in so far as there is any reserve, it is more intellectual than feminine. She is so far from regarding me as a lover, that our relation to each other is that of two able minds. She takes my hand, presses it a little, laughs, pays some attention to me in a purely Platonic sense. Then when irony and ridicule have duped her long enough, I shall follow that suggestion found in an old verse: "The knight spreads out his cape so red, and begs the beautiful maiden to sit thereon."[28] However, I do not spread out my cape in order to sit with her on the greensward, but to vanish with her into the air in a flight of thought. Or I do not take her with me, but set myself astride a thought, wave farewell to her, blow her a kiss, and vanish from her sight, audible to her only in the whistling of the winged words, not, like Jehovah, becoming more and more manifest through the voice, but ever less so, because the more I speak, the higher I mount. Then she wishes to go with me on the venturesome flight of thought. Still, this lasts only a single instant; the next moment I am cold and prosaic.

There are different kinds of feminine blushes. There is the coarse brick-red blush which romantic writers always use so freely when they let their heroines blush all over. There is the delicate blush; it is the blush of the spirit's dawn. In a young girl it is priceless. The passing blush produced by a happy idea is beautiful in a man, more beautiful in a young man, charming in a woman. It is a gleam of lightning, the heat lightning of the spirit. It is most beautiful in the young, charming in a girl because it appears in

her girlishness, and therefore it has also the modesty of surprise. The older one becomes, the more rarely one blushes.

Sometimes I read aloud to Cordelia something important;
usually, something very inconsequential. Edward must as
usual hold the spotlight. I have accordingly called his attention to the fact that a very good way to get into a young
girl's good graces is to lend her books. He has made good
headway thereby, for it puts her under obligations to him.
I am the chief gainer; for I dictate the choice of books but
otherwise keep out of it. This gives me a wide arena for
my observations. I can give Edward whatever books I wish,
since he is no judge of literature. Hence I dare go to any
extreme I wish. Then when I visit her in the evening, I
casually pick up a book, turn over a few pages in it, read
half aloud, commend Edward for his attentiveness. Last
night I wished to test the vigor of her mind by an experiment. I was puzzled whether to let Edward lend her
Schiller's *Poems,* so that I might accidentally open it to
Thekla's song,[29] which I would recite, or Bürger's *Poems.*
I chose the latter, particularly because his "Lenore" is a little extravagant, however beautiful it otherwise is. I opened
it at "Lenore," read this poem solemnly, with all the
pathos of which I was capable. Cordelia was moved; she
sewed with a nervous energy, as if it were she William
had come to fetch.[30] I paused. The aunt had listened without any apparent sympathy. She feared no Williams living
or dead; nor, in addition, is her knowledge of German very
good. However, she found herself quite in her element
when I showed her the beautiful example of bookbinding,
and began a conversation with her about the bookbinding
profession. My purpose was to destroy in Cordelia the impression of the pathetic in the very moment of its inception.
She became a little anxious, but it was clear to me that
this anxiety did not tempt her, but made her uncomfortable.

Today my eyes have for the first time rested upon her.
Someone has said that sleep can make the eyelids so heavy
that they close of themselves; perhaps my glance has a
similar effect upon Cordelia. Her eyes close, and yet an ob-

scure force stirs within her. She does not see that I am looking at her, she feels it, feels it through her whole body. Her eyes close, and it is night; but within her it is luminous day.

Edward must go; he has reached the very end. At any moment I may expect him to go to her, and make a declaration of love. There is no one who knows this better than myself, who am his confidant, and who assiduously keep him over-excited so that he can have a greater effect upon Cordelia. To allow him to confess his love is still too risky. I know very well that she will refuse him, but that will not end the affair. He will certainly take it very much to heart. This would perhaps move and touch Cordelia. Although in such a case I do not need to fear the worst, that she might start over again, still her self-esteem would possibly suffer out of pure sympathy. If this should happen, it frustrates my whole plan concerning Edward.

My relation to Cordelia is beginning to run dramatically. Something must happen, whatever it may be; I can no longer remain a mere observer without letting the moment slip. She must be taken by surprise, that is necessary; but if one would surprise her, one must be on the alert. That which might surprise someone in general would perhaps have no such effect on her. She must really be surprised in such a way that that which first causes her surprise is something that happens quite commonly. Then it must gradually appear that this something surprising was implied in this. This is always the law for the interesting, and this law again controls all my actions with regard to Cordelia. If you always know how to surprise, you always win the game. You suspend for an instant the energy of the one concerned, make it impossible for her to act, and that, whether one uses the ordinary or the extraordinary as means. I recollect with a certain degree of self-satisfaction a foolhardy experiment upon a lady of distinguished family. For some time I had been hanging around her in order to find an interesting contact, but in vain; then one day I met her on the street. I was certain that she did not know me, nor know that I belonged here in town. She was walking alone. I stole past her so that I could meet her face to face. Approaching her, I stepped aside; she kept to the narrow sidewalk. At this moment I cast a sorrowful glance at her, I almost had tears in my eyes. I took off my hat. She paused. In a voice shaken with emotion, and with a dreamy look, I said: "Do not be angry, gracious lady; there is such an extraordinary resemblance between you and a person I love with all my soul, but who lives far away from me, that you must forgive my strange behavior." She thought I was quixotic, and a young girl can well endure a little extravagance, especially when she feels superior and dares to smile at one. Just as I expected, she smiled, and this smile was indescribably becoming to her. With aristocratic condescension she bowed to me and smiled. She resumed her walk, I walked a few steps by her side. A few days later, I met her, I presumed to bow. She laughed at me. . . . Patience is still an excellent virtue, and he who laughs last, laughs best.

One could think of several methods by which to surprise Cordelia. I might attempt to raise an erotic storm, powerful enough to tear up trees by the roots. By its aid I might try, if possible, to sweep her off her feet, snatch her out of her historic continuity; attempt, in this agitation, by stealthy advances to arouse her passion. It is not inconceivable that I could do this. A man could make a girl with her passion do anything he wished. However, that would be all wrong from the aesthetic standpoint. I do not enjoy giddiness, and this condition is to be recommended only when one has to do with girls who can acquire poetic glamor in no other way. Besides, one misses some of the essential enjoyment, for too much confusion is also bad. Its effect upon Cordelia would utterly fail. In a couple of draughts I should have swallowed what I might have had the good of for a long time, indeed, even worse, what with discretion I might have enjoyed more fully and richly. Cordelia is not to be enjoyed in over-excitement. I might perhaps take her by surprise at first, if I went about it right, but she would soon be surfeited, precisely because this surprise lay too close to her daring soul.

A simple engagement is the best of all the methods, the most expedient. If she hears me make a prosaic declaration of love, *item* asking for her hand, she will perhaps believe her ears even less than if she listened to my heated eloquence, absorbed my poisonous intoxicants, heard her heart beat fast at the thought of an elopement.

The curse of an engagement is always on its ethical side. The ethical is just as tiresome in philosophy as in life. What a difference! Under the heaven of the aesthetic, everything is light, beautiful, transitory; when the ethical comes along, then everything becomes harsh, angular, infinitely boring. An engagement, however, does not have ethical reality in the stricter sense, as marriage does; it has validity only *ex consensu gentium*.[31] This ambiguity can be very serviceable to me. It has enough of the ethical in it so that in time Cordelia will get the impression that she has exceeded the ordinary bounds; however, the ethical in it is not so serious that I need fear a more critical agitation. I have always had a certain respect for the ethical. I have never given any girl a marriage promise, not even in jest. In so far as it might seem that I have done it here, that is only a fictitious move. I shall certainly manage it so that she will be the one who breaks the engagement. My chivalrous pride scorns to give a promise. I despise a judge who by the promise of liberty lures an offender into a confession. Such a judge belittles his own power and ability.

Practically, I have reached the point where I desire nothing which is not, in the strictest sense, freely given. Let common seducers use such methods. What do they gain? He who does not know how to compass a girl about so that she loses sight of everything which he does not wish her to see, he who does not know how to poetize himself in a girl's feelings so that it is from her that everything issues as he wishes it, he is and remains a bungler; I do not begrudge him his enjoyment. A bungler he is and remains, a seducer, something one can by no means call me. I am an aesthete, an eroticist, one who has understood the nature and meaning of love, who believes in love and knows it from the ground up, and only makes the private reservation that no love affair should last more than six months at the most, and that every erotic relationship should cease as soon as one has had the ultimate enjoyment. I know all this, I know, too, that the highest conceivable enjoyment lies in being loved; to be loved is higher than anything else in the world. To poetize oneself into a young girl is an art, to poetize oneself out of her is a masterpiece. Still, the latter depends essentially upon the first.

There is another method possible. I might arrange everything so as to have her become engaged to Edward. I become, thus, a friend of the family. Edward would trust me unconditionally—for I'm the one, after all, to whom he owes much of his happiness. In this way I have won the advantage of being better concealed.—No, that is no good. She cannot become engaged to Edward without more or less belittling herself. That would make my relation to her more piquant than interesting. The everlasting prosaism that lies in an engagement is precisely the sounding-board of the interesting.

Everything is assuming greater significance in the Wahl household. One clearly notes that a mysterious animation is stirring beneath the daily routine, which must soon proclaim itself in a corresponding revelation. The Wahl household is preparing for an engagement. One who was only a superficial observer might perhaps anticipate a match between the aunt and myself. What an extension of agricultural knowledge in the following generation might not come of such a match! Thus I would become Cordelia's uncle. I am a friend of freedom of thought, and no idea is too preposterous for me to lack courage to entertain it. Cordelia fears a declaration of love from Edward, Edward hopes that such a proposal will decide everything. And of that he may be sure. However, in order to spare him the unpleasant consequences of such a step, I shall try to forestall him. I am hoping soon now to be rid of him; he is very much in my way. I really felt it today. He looks so dreamy, so drunk with love, that one almost fears that he will suddenly arise like a somnambulist and, in the presence of the whole congregation, confess his love with such objective detachment that he does not even approach Cordelia. I looked daggers at him today. As an elephant catches an object with his trunk, so I caught Edward with my eyes, big as he is, and threw him over backward. Although he remained seated in his chair, I still believe that he had a corresponding sensation through his whole body.

Cordelia is not so assured in her manner toward me as she has been. She always approached me with a womanly assurance, now she vacillates a little. It has, however, no great significance, and I should not find it hard to bring everything back to the old footing. Still, I shall not do so. Only one more investigation, and then the engagement. There can be no difficulties about this. Cordelia in her surprise says yes, the aunt gives a hearty Amen. She will be beside herself with joy over such an agriculturally inclined son-in-law. Son-in-law! How we all become thick as thieves when we enter into this territory. I do not really become her son-in-law, but only her nephew, or, rather, *volente deo,* neither.

23rd day.

Today I harvested the fruit of a rumor I had caused to circulate, that I was in love with a young girl. By the aid of Edward it had also reached Cordelia's ears. She is curious, she watches me, but she does not, however, dare to question me; and yet it is not unimportant to her to make certain, partly because it seems incredible to her, partly because she might see in this a precedent for herself; for if such a cold-blooded scoffer as myself could fall in love, then there could be no disgrace in her doing the same. Today I introduced the subject. I believe I can tell a story so that the point is not lost, *item,* so that it is not revealed too soon. To keep those who listen in suspense, by means of small incidents of an episodic character, to ascertain what they wish the outcome to be, to trick them in the course of the narration—that is my delight; to make use of ambiguities, so that the listeners understand one thing in the saying, and then suddenly notice that the words could also be interpreted otherwise—that is my art. If one desires an opportunity to make certain investigations, one should always make a speech. In conversation, the one concerned can better escape from one, can, by means of questions and answers, better conceal the impression the words produce.

I began my speech to the aunt with intense seriousness: "Am I to impute this rumor to the good will of my friends, or to the malice of my enemies, and who is there among us who does not have too many of both?" Here the aunt made a remark which I helped her with all my might to spin out, so as to keep Cordelia, who was listening, in suspense, a suspense she could not put an end to, since I was talking with her aunt, and my mood was serious. I continued: "Or shall I ascribe it to an accident, a rumor's *generatio aequivoca*"[32] (Cordelia evidently did not understand this word; it only confused her, all the more because I laid a false emphasis upon it, winking at the aunt significantly as I did so, as if the point lay here), "that I who am accustomed to live in seclusion from the world, am become the object of gossip, in that they insist that I am engaged." Cordelia now quite openly wanted to hear my explanation. I continued: "It might be attributed to my friends, since it must be regarded as good fortune to fall in love (she started); to my enemies, since it would be considered very ridiculous if this happiness should fall to my lot (movement in the opposite direction); or to accident, since there is not the slightest foundation for it; or to rumor's *generatio aequivoca,* since the whole thing must have originated in an empty head's thoughtless intercourse with itself." The aunt with true feminine curiosity was quick to try to find out who the lady might be to whom gossip had been pleased to link me. Every question in this direction was waved aside. The whole story made quite an impression upon Cordelia; I almost believe Edward's stock rose a few points.

The decisive moment is approaching. I might address myself to the aunt in writing, asking for Cordelia's hand. This is indeed the customary procedure in affairs of the heart, as if it were more natural for the heart to write than to speak. What might decide me to choose this method is just the philistinism in it. But if I choose this, then I lose the essential surprise, and that I cannot give up.—If I had a friend, he might perhaps say to me: "Have you considered well this most serious step you are taking, a step which is decisive for all the rest of your life, and for another being's happiness?" Now that is the advantage that comes from having a friend. I have no friend; whether that is an advantage, I shall leave undecided; but I consider being free from his advice an absolute advantage. As to the rest, I have certainly considered the whole matter, in the strictest sense of the word.

On my side there is nothing now to obstruct the engagement. Consequently, I go ahead with my wooing, though no one realizes it but myself. Soon will my humble person be seen from a higher standpoint. I cease to be a person and become—a match; yes, a good match, the aunt will say. She is the one I am most sorry for; she loves me with such a pure and sincere agricultural love, she almost worships me as her ideal.

It is true that in my time I have made many declarations of love, and yet all my experience does not help me in the least here; for this declaration must be made in a very peculiar manner. What I must principally impress upon my mind is that the whole affair is only a fictitious move. I have held several rehearsals in order to discover which one would be the best approach. To make the moment erotic would be hazardous, since it would really anticipate that which will come later and unfold itself gradually. To make it very serious is dangerous; such a moment has great significance for a young girl, so that her soul can become as fixed in it as a dying man's in his last will. To make it frankly low-comic would be out of character with the mask I have hitherto used, and with the one I intend to assume. To make it witty and ironic is risking too much. If it were with me as with people in general on such occasions, so that the chief thing is to elicit a little yes, then it would be as easy as falling off a log. This is indeed important, but not of supreme importance; for although I have picked out this girl, although I have centered much attention, indeed my whole interest upon her, yet there are certain conditions under which I would not accept her yes. I simply do not care to possess a girl in the mere external sense, but to enjoy her in an artistic sense. Therefore my approach must be as artistic as possible. The beginning must be as vague as possible and open to every possibility. If she immediately looks on me as a deceiver, then she misunderstands me; for I am not a deceiver in the ordinary sense; if she sees me as a faithful lover, then she is also mistaken in me. The point is, that in this scene her soul should be as little predetermined as possible. A girl's soul at such a moment is as prophetic as a dying man's.[33] This must be prevented. My beloved Cordelia! I cheat you out of something beautiful, but it cannot be otherwise, and I shall compensate you as best I can. The whole episode must be kept as insignificant as possible, so that when she has accepted me, she will not be able to throw the least light upon what may be concealed in this relationship. The infinite possibility is precisely the interesting. If she is able to predict anything, then I have failed very badly, and the whole relationship loses its meaning. That she might say yes because she loves me is inconceivable, for she does not love me at all. The best thing is for me to transform the engagement from an act to an event, from something she does to something which happens to her, concerning which she must say: "God only knows how it really happened."

31st day.

Today I have written a love-letter for a third party. This I am always delighted to do. In the first place it is always interesting to enter into a situation so vividly, and yet in all possible comfort. I fill my pipe, hear about the relationship, and the letters from the intended are brought out. The way in which a young lady writes is always an important study to me. The lover sits there like a fathead, he reads her letters aloud, interrupted by my laconic comments: She writes well, she has feeling, taste, caution, she has certainly been in love before, and so on. In the second place I am doing a good deed. I am helping to bring a couple of young people together; after that I balance accounts. For every pair I make happy, I select one victim for myself; I make two happy, at the most only one unhappy. I am honorable and trustworthy. I have never deceived anyone who has taken me into his confidence. This entails always a few high jinks—but these, after all, are lawful perquisites. And why do I enjoy this confidence? Because I know Latin and attend to my studies, and because I always keep my little affairs to myself. And do I not deserve this confidence? Indeed I never misuse it.

August 2.

The moment came. I caught a glimpse of the aunt on the street, and so I knew she was not at home. Edward was at the custom-house. Consequently there was every likelihood of Cordelia's being at home alone. And so it was. She sat by her worktable occupied with some sewing. I have very rarely visited the family in the forenoon, and she was therefore a little disturbed at seeing me. The situation became almost emotional. She was not to blame for this, for she controlled herself fairly well; but I was the one, for in spite of my armor, she made an uncommonly strong impression upon me. How charming she was in a simple, blue-striped calico house-dress, with a fresh-picked rose at her bosom—a fresh-picked rose, nay the girl herself was like a freshly picked blossom, so fresh she was, so recently arrived; and, too, who knows where a young girl spends the night? In the land of illusions, I believe, but every morning she comes back, and hence her youthful freshness. She looked so young, and yet so fully developed, as if Nature, like a tender and opulent mother, had just now let go her hand. It was as if I had witnessed the farewell scene. I saw how the loving mother embraced her in farewell. I heard her saying: "Go out into the world, my child, I have made everything ready for you. Take this kiss as a seal upon your lips, it is a seal which guards the sanctuary; no one can break it, unless you yourself will it, but when the right one comes, then you will know him." And she pressed a kiss upon her lips, a kiss unlike a human kiss which always takes something, but a sacred kiss which gives everything, which gives the girl the power of the kiss.

Wonderful Nature, how profound and mysterious thou art; thou givest words to a man, and to a woman the eloquence of the kiss! This kiss was upon her lips, and the farewell blessing on her forehead, and the joyous salutation in her eyes; therefore she looked at once so much at home, for she was indeed the child of the house, and so much a stranger, for she did not know the world, but only the loving mother who unseen watched over her. She was really charming, childlike, and yet adorned with a noble maidenly dignity that inspired respect.—However, I was soon again dispassionate and solemnly stolid, as is proper when one would do the significant as if it were the insignificant. After a few general remarks, I moved a little nearer to her and began my petition. A man who talks like a book is exceedingly tiresome to listen to; sometimes, however, it is quite appropriate to speak in that way. For a book has the remarkable quality that you may interpret it as you wish. One's conversation also acquires the same quality, if one talks like a book. I kept quite soberly to general formulas. It cannot be denied that she was as surprised as I had expected. To describe how she looked is difficult. Her expressions were so variable, indeed much like the still unpublished but announced commentary to my book, a commentary which has the possibility of any interpretation. One word, and she would have laughed at me, one word, and she would have been moved, one word, and she would have fled from me; but no word crossed my lips, I remained stolidly serious, and kept exactly to the ritual.—"She had known me so short a time." Good heavens! such difficulties are encountered only in the narrow path of an engagement, not in the primrose path of love.

Curiously enough. When in the days preceding I surveyed the affair, I was rash enough and confident enough to believe that taken by surprise, she would say yes. That shows how much thorough preparation amounts to. The matter is not settled, for she said neither yes nor no, but referred me to her aunt. I should have foreseen this. However, I am still lucky, for this outcome is even better than the other.

The aunt gives her consent, about that I never had the slightest doubt. Cordelia accepts her advice. As regards my engagement, I do not boast that it is poetic, it is in every way philistine and bourgeois. The girl doesn't know whether to say yes or no; the aunt says yes, the girl also says yes, I take the girl, she takes me—and now the story begins.

3rd day.

So now I am engaged; so is Cordelia, and that is about all she knows about the whole matter. If she had a girl friend she could talk freely with, she might perhaps say: "I don't really understand what it all means. There is something about him that attracts me, but I can't really make out what it is. He has a strange power over me, but I do not love him, and perhaps I never shall; on the other hand, I can stand it to live with him, and can therefore be very happy with him; for he certainly will not demand so much if one only bears with him." My dear Cordelia! Perhaps he may demand more—and to make up for that, require less forbearance.—Of all ridiculous things imaginable, an engagement is the most ridiculous. Marriage, after all, has a meaning, even if this meaning does not please me. An engagement is a purely human invention which by no means reflects credit upon its inventor. It is neither one thing nor the other, and it has as much to do with love as the scarf which hangs down a beadle's back has to do with a professor's hood. Now I am a member of this honorable company. That is not without significance, for, as Trop says, it is only by first being an artist that one acquires the right to judge other artists. And is not a fiancé also a carnival artist?[34]

Edward is beside himself with rage. He is letting his beard grow, he has hung away his dark suit, which is very significant. He insists on talking with Cordelia in order to describe my craftiness to her. It will be an affecting scene: Edward unshaven, carelessly dressed, shouting at Cordelia.

Only he cannot cut me out with his long beard. Vainly I try to bring him to reason. I explain that it is the aunt who has brought about the match, that Cordelia perhaps still cherishes him, that I am willing to step back if he can win her. For a moment he wavers, wonders whether he should not shave his beard in a new way, buy a new black suit, then the next instant he abuses me. I do everything to keep on good terms with him; however angry he is with me, I am certain he will take no step without consulting me; he does not forget how helpful I have been to him in my role as mentor. And why should I wrest his last hope from him, why break with him? He is a good man; who knows what may happen in the future?

What I now have to do is, on the one hand, to get everything in order for getting the engagement broken, thus assuring myself of a more beautiful and significant relation to Cordelia; on the other hand, I must improve the time to the uttermost by enjoying all the charm, all the loveliness with which nature has so abundantly endowed her, enjoying myself in it, still with the self-limitation and circumspection that prevents any violation of it. When I have brought her to the point where she has learned what it is to love, and what it is to love me, then the engagement breaks like an imperfect mold, and she belongs to me. This is the point at which others become engaged, and have a good prospect of a boring marriage for all eternity. Well, let others have it.

As yet everything is *in statu quo;* but how can any fiancé be luckier than I? No miser who has found a piece of gold is happier than I am. I am intoxicated with the thought that she is in my power. A pure, innocent femininity, transparent as the sea and as profound, with no clear idea of what love is! Now she is to learn its power. Like a king's daughter who has been raised from the dust to the throne of her forefathers, so shall she be installed in the kingdom where she belongs. But this must happen through me; and when she learns to love, she learns to love me; and as she extends her domain, the paradigm by which she herself is governed increasingly grows in power, and this is myself.

When through love she becomes aware of her full significance, she expends this in loving me; and when she suspects that she has learned this from me, then her love for me is doubled. The thought of my joy so overwhelms me that I almost lose my senses.

Her soul is not dissipated nor relaxed by the undefined emotions of love, a thing which keeps many young girls from ever learning to love, that is to say, to love decisively, energetically, totally. They hold in their consciousness an indefinite, nebulous image which is supposed to be an ideal, according to which the actual is to be tested. From such half-measures something emerges wherewith one may manage one's Christian way through the world.—Now as love awakens in Cordelia's soul, I scrutinize it, listen to it as it issues from her in all its varied moods. I ascertain how it has taken shape in her, and fashion myself into likeness with it. And though I am even now immediately engrossed with the story of the love pulsing through her heart, yet outwardly I comply with her wishes, as deceptively as possible. After all, a girl loves only once.

Now I am in lawful possession of Cordelia, I have the aunt's consent and blessing, the congratulations of friends and relatives; that ought to be enough. So now all the hardships of war are over, the blessings of peace begin. How silly! As if the aunt's blessing and the congratulations of friends could put me in possession of Cordelia in the more profound sense; as if love made such a difference between war and peace, and did not rather, as long as it lasts, itself proclaim a combat, even if the weapons are different. The difference really depends on whether it is fought *cominus* or *eminus*.[35] The more a love affair has been fought *eminus*, the more regrettable; for it makes the hand to hand contest less important. A hand-clasp, a touch of the foot, belongs to the close combat, something which it is well known Ovid both warmly commends and jealously disparages—to say nothing of a kiss, an embrace. He who fights *eminus* generally must rely on his eye alone, and yet if he is an artist, he will know how to use this weapon with such virtuosity that he achieves almost the same results. He can let his eye rest upon a girl with a desultory tenderness which affects her as if he had accidentally touched her; he will be able to hold her as firmly with his eye as if he held her fast in his embrace. However, it is a fault or a misfortune for one to fight too long *eminus,* for such a struggle is constantly only a symbol, not the enjoyment. Only when the struggle is fought *cominus* does everything attain its true importance. When love no longer fights, then it has ceased. I have virtually never fought *eminus* and therefore I am not at the end, but at the beginning; I am bringing out my weapons. It is true I am in possession of her, that is, in a legal and bourgeois sense; but that means nothing at all to me, I have far higher ideals. It is true that she is engaged to me; but if I were to infer from this that she loved me, it would be a deception, for after all she is not in love. I am in lawful possession of her, and yet I do not possess her, just as I can possess a girl without being in lawful possession of her.

> *Auf heinlich erröthender Wange*
> *Leuchtet des Herzens Glühen.*[36]

She sits on the sofa by the tea table, I in a chair by her side. This position has the advantage of being intimate and yet detached. So tremendously much depends upon the position, that is, for one who has an eye for it. Love has many positions, this is the first. How regally Nature has endowed this girl; her pure soft form, her deep feminine innocence, her clear eyes—all these intoxicate me. I pay her my respects. She cheerfully greets me as usual, still a little embarrassed, a little uncertain; the engagement, after all, ought to make our relationship somewhat different, just how she does not know. She shook hands with me, but not with her usual smile. I returned the greeting with a slight, almost imperceptible pressure. I was gentle and friendly without being erotic.—She sits on the sofa by the tea table. I sit in a chair by her side. A glorified solemnity diffuses itself over the situation, a soft morning radiance. She is silent; nothing disturbs the stillness. My eyes steal softly over her, not with desire, in truth that would be shameless. A delicate fleeting blush passes over her, like a cloud over the meadow, rising and receding. What does this blush mean? Is it love? Is it longing, hope, fear; for is not the heart's color red? By no means. She wonders, she is surprised—not at me, that would be too little to offer her; she is surprised, not at herself, but in herself, she is transformed within. This moment demands stillness, therefore, no reflection shall disturb it, no intimation of passion interrupt it. It is as if I were not present, and yet it is just my presence that furnishes the condition for her contemplative wonder. My being is in harmony with hers. When she is in this condition, a young girl is to be worshipped and adored in silence, like some deities.

It is indeed fortunate that I have my uncle's house. If I wished to give a young man a distaste for tobacco, I should take him to a smoker. If I wish to give a girl a distaste for being engaged, I need only bring her here. As in a tailors' guildhall one looks only for tailors, so here one looks only for engaged couples. It is a terrible company to fall into, and I cannot blame Cordelia for becoming impatient with it. When we are assembled *en masse,* I believe we muster ten couples, besides the extra battalions which great festival days bring to the capital. Then we engaged couples can thoroughly enjoy the pleasures of engagements. I meet with Cordelia at the alarm post in order to disgust her with this love-smitten obviousness, this love-sick awkwardness of tradesmen. Incessantly throughout the evening one hears a sound as if someone were going around with a fly-swatter— it is the lovers kissing. There is a genial unrestraint in this house; no one even seeks a dark corner. No, they all sit about a big round table. I make as if to treat Cordelia the same way. To do this, I must do violence to my own feelings. It would really be outrageous of me if I were to allow myself to offend her innate femininity in this way. I would more reproach myself for doing this than I would when deceiving her. Generally I can assure any girl who entrusts herself to me a perfect aesthetic conduct: only it ends with her being deceived; but this is consistent with my aesthetics, for either the girl deceives the man, or the man deceives the girl. It would certainly be interesting if we might get some literary hack to tabulate in fairy stories, sagas, ballads, and mythologies whether it is the man or the girl who is more frequently faithless.

I cannot regret the time that Cordelia has cost me, although it is considerable. Every meeting has demanded long preparation. I am watching the birth of love within her. I am even almost invisibly present when I visibly sit by her side. My relation to her is that of an unseen partner in a dance which is danced by only one, when it should really be danced by two. She moves as in a dream, and yet she dances with another, and this other is myself, who, in so far as I am visibly present, am invisible, in so far as I am invisible, am visible. The movements of the dance require a partner, she bows to him, she takes his hand, she flees, she draws near him again. I take her hand, I complete her thought as if it were completed in herself. She moves to the inner melody of her own soul; I am only the occasion for her movement. I am not amorous, that would only awaken her; I am easy, yielding, impersonal, almost like a mood.

What does an engaged couple usually talk about? So far as I know they busy themselves in getting mutually acquainted with the tiresome family connections of their respective families. What wonder then that the erotic is lost to sight. If one does not understand making love the absolute, in comparison with which all other topics are lost sight of, one should never get involved with love even if one gets married ten times. Even if I do have an aunt called Marion, an uncle named Christopher, a father who was a major, and so forth, all such information is irrelevant to the mysteries of love. Aye, even one's own past life is nothing. A young girl usually does not have much of importance to reveal in this respect; if she has, then it may perhaps be worth while to listen to her, but, as a rule, not to love her. Personally I want no histories; I have seen enough of them; I seek the immediate. It is the eternal element in love that the individuals first exist for one another in the moment of love.

A little confidence must be aroused in her, or, rather, a doubt must be removed. I do not really belong to the class of lovers who love one another out of respect, marry each other out of respect, bear children out of respect, and so on; but yet I well understand that love, especially as long as passion is not aroused, demands that the one who is its object should not aesthetically offend against the moral sense. In this respect love has its own dialectic. Thus, while from the moral standpoint my relation to Edward was far more reprehensible than my behavior toward the aunt, I should find it far easier to justify the former to Cordelia than the latter. She has as yet said nothing, but still I have found it best to explain to her the necessity for my having approached her in this manner. The circumspection I used flatters her pride, the secretiveness with which I managed everything fascinates her. It might seem that I have here betrayed too much erotic knowledge, so that I contradict myself when later I find it necessary to imply that I have never been in love before. However, that is nothing. I am not afraid to contradict myself as long as she does not notice it, and I gain what I want. Let scholarly disputants take pride in avoiding every contradiction; a young girl's life is too exuberant not to have contradictions in it, and consequently it makes contradiction necessary.

She is proud, and at the same time she has no real conception of the erotic. Whereas she now, to a certain degree, defers to me intellectually, yet it is conceivable that when the erotic begins to assert itself, she may take it into her head to turn her pride against me. So far as I can make out, she is uncertain about her own significance as woman. That is why it was easy to arouse her pride against Edward. This pride, however, was entirely eccentric because she had no conception of love. If she acquires this, then she will have acquired true pride; but a residue of this eccentric pride might easily disturb her. It is then conceivable that she might turn against me. Although this might not make her regret having assented to our engagement, she would readily see that I had made a fairly good bargain; she would realize that it was not a proper beginning on her part.

Should this dawn upon her, she might venture to defy me. That is the way it should be. That proves to me how deeply she is moved.

Sure enough. Even from far down the street I see this charming, attractive, little head stretching as far as possible out of the window. It is the third day that I have noticed it. . . . A young girl certainly does not stand at the window for nothing, she probably has her own good reasons. . . . But, for heaven's sake, I beg you not to stretch so far out of the window; I bet you are standing on a chair round; I infer that from your position. Think how terrible it would be if you fell down on your head, not for me, of course, for I hold myself outside the case, but for him, him, for there certainly must be a him. . . . Well, of all things! Away down there comes my friend, Licentiate Hansen, walking in the middle of the street. There is something unusual in his appearance, an uncommon haste; if I am right he is being borne on the wings of longing. Can he be coming to this house, and I not know it? . . . My pretty maiden, you have disappeared. I imagine that you have gone to open the door for him. . . . You might as well come back again, for he really is not coming into the house. . . . How do I know that? I can tell you how. . . . He said so himself. If the wagon that drove past had not been so noisy, you could have heard him yourself. I said to him just *en passant:* "Are you going in here?" He replied plainly: "No." . . . Now you can really say farewell, for the licentiate and I are going for a walk. He is embarrassed, and embarrassed people are usually garrulous. Now I shall talk with him about the ecclesiastical preferment he is seeking. . . . Farewell, my pretty maiden, we are going to the custom-house. When we have reached it, I shall say to him: "Confound you, you have taken me out of my way. I ought to be up on Western Street."—Well look, here we are again. . . . What constancy! she is still standing by the window. Such a girl ought to make a man happy. . . . And why am I doing all this? you ask. Because I am a black-hearted fellow who takes pleasure in teasing others? By no means. I do it out of regard for you, my worthy maiden. In the first place. You have waited for the licentiate, longed for him, and so when he finally comes he is doubly welcome. In the second place. When the licentiate now comes into the house, he will say: "We were almost caught that time by that accursed fellow standing by the door when I wanted to come in. But I was clever, I lured him into a long talk about the living I am trying to get, and I walked him up and down, here and there, and finally clear out to the custom-house. I can promise you he noticed nothing." So what? So you think more of the licentiate than ever. For you have always thought that he had a remarkable mind, but that he was clever . . . aye, now you see it yourself. And you have me to thank for it.—But now something else occurs to me. Their engagement cannot yet have been announced, otherwise I should have heard of it. The girl is beautiful and pleasing to look at, but she is young. Perhaps her insight is not yet mature. Is it not conceivable that she is thoughtlessly planning to take a very serious step? It must be prevented; I must talk with her. I owe her that, for she is certainly a very attractive girl. I owe it to the licentiate, for he is my friend. So far as that goes, I owe it to her, for she is my friend's intended. I owe it to her family, for it is certainly a very respectable one. I owe it to the whole human race, for it is a good deed. The whole human race! Great thought, inspiring deed, to act in the name of the whole human race, to possess such general authority! Now for Cordelia. I can always make use of a mood, and the girl's beautiful yearning has really affected me.

So now the first war with Cordelia begins, in which I flee, and thereby teach her to triumph in pursuing me. I constantly retreat before her, and in this retreat, I teach her through myself to know all the power of love, its unquiet thoughts, its passion, what longing is, and hope, and impatient expectation. As I thus set all this before her in my own person, the same power develops correspondingly in her. It is a triumphal procession in which I lead her, and I myself am just as much the one who dithyrambically sings praises for her victory as the one who shows the way. She will gain courage to believe in love, to believe that it is an eternal power, when she sees its mastery over me, sees my emotions. She will believe me, partly because I have confidence in my art, and partly because fundamentally there is truth in what I am doing. If this were not the case, then she would not believe me. With every movement of mine, she becomes stronger and stronger; love is awakening in her soul, she is becoming initiated into her significance as a woman. Hitherto I have not set her free in the ordinary meaning of the word. I do it now, I set her free, for only thus will I love her. She must never suspect that she owes this freedom to me, for that would destroy her self-confidence. When she at last feels free, so free that she is almost tempted to break with me, then the second war begins. Now she has power and passion, and the struggle becomes worth while to me. It matters little what the immediate consequences may be. Suppose she becomes dizzy with pride, suppose she should break with me, oh, well, she is free; but she shall yet be mine. That the engagement should bind her is foolishness; I will have her only in her freedom. Let her forsake me, the second war is just beginning, and in this second war I shall be the victor, just as certainly as it was an illusion that she was the victor in the first. The more abundant strength she has, the more interesting for me. The first war was a war of liberation, it was only a game; the second is a war of conquest, it is for life and death.

Do I love Cordelia? Yes. Sincerely? Yes. Faithfully? Yes —in an aesthetic sense, and this also indicates something important. What good would it do this girl to fall into the hands of some numbskull, even if he were a faithful husband? What would she then become? Nothing. Someone has said that it takes a little more than honesty to get through life. I should say that it takes something more than honesty to love such a girl. That more I have—it is duplicity. And yet I really love her faithfully. Rigidly and abstemiously I watch over myself, so that everything there is in her, the whole divinely rich nature, may come to its unfolding. I am one of the few who can do this, she is one of the few who is fitted for this; are we not then suited to one another?

Is it sinful of me that instead of looking at the preacher, I fix my eye on the beautiful embroidered handkerchief you hold in your hand? Is it sinful for you to hold it thus? . . . It has a name in the corner. . . . Your name is Charlotte Hahn? It is so fascinating to learn a lady's name in such an accidental manner. It is as if there were a helpful spirit who mysteriously made me acquainted with you. . . . Or is it perhaps not accidental that the handkerchief was folded just right for me to see your name? . . . You are disturbed, you wipe a tear from your eye, the handkerchief again hangs carelessly down. . . . It is evident to you that I am looking at you, not at the preacher. You look at the handkerchief, you notice that it has betrayed your name. . . . It is really a very innocent matter. It is easy to get to know a girl's name. . . . Why do you take it out on the handkerchief, why do you crumple it up? Why are you angry at it? Why angry at me? Listen to what the preacher says: "No one should lead a man into temptation; even one who does so unwittingly, has a responsibility, he is even in debt to the other, a debt which he can discharge only by increased benevolence." . . . Now he says Amen. Outside the church door you'll probably dare to let the handkerchief flutter loosely in the wind . . . or have you become afraid of me? What have I done? . . . Have I done more than you can forgive, more than you dare remember—in order to forgive?

A two-fold movement becomes necessary in relation to Cordelia. If I constantly flee before her superior force, it makes it possible for the erotic in her to become too diffused and vague for the deeper womanliness to hypostatize itself. Then, when the second war began, she would not be able to offer resistance. She may be asleep to her victory, —that's as it should be; but, on the other side, she must constantly be awakened. Then, when for an instant it seems to her that her victory has been wrested from her, she must learn to hold it fast. In this conflict her womanhood is matured. I might either use conversation to inflame or letters to cool, or vice versa. The latter is by all means to be preferred. I then enjoy her most intense moments. When she has received a letter, when she has absorbed its sweet poison in her blood, then a word is enough to make her love break forth. The next moment irony and coldness awaken doubt, but yet not sufficiently to nullify her sense of victory, rather she feels it increased through the reception of the next letter. Irony does not lend itself well to expression in a letter, for one runs the risk of her not understanding it. Glimpses only of one's ardent feelings may be allowed to enter into conversation. My personal presence prevents extravagance of mood. When I am only present in a letter, she can easily endure me, to a certain extent she confuses me with a universal being who lives in her love. In a letter, too, one can better let oneself go; in a letter I can throw myself at her feet beautifully, a thing that would certainly make me look like a fool if I were actually to do it, and would destroy all the illusion. The contradiction in these movements will evoke and develop, strengthen and consolidate her love, in one word, tempt it.

These letters must not assume a strongly erotic coloring too early. In the beginning it is best for them to have a general character, contain a single suggestion, remove a single doubt. Occasionally they may also suggest the advantage an engagement gives in keeping people away by some trickery. What imperfections an engagement otherwise has, she shall have plenty of opportunities to discover. In my uncle's house all the travesties necessary can always be found. The intimate erotic she cannot develop without my assistance. When I refuse this, and let its caricature worry her, then she will soon become tired of being engaged, still without realizing that I am the one who made her tired of it.

A little note today describing the condition of my soul will give her an insight into how it stands with herself. It is the correct method, and I always have method. I have you to thank for that, you dear girls, whom I formerly have loved. I owe it to you that my soul is so attuned that I can be whatever I wish to Cordelia. I remember you with gratitude, the honor belongs to you. I shall always acknowledge that a young girl is a born teacher, from whom one can always learn, if nothing else, how to deceive her—for one learns this best from the girls themselves; no matter how old I may become, I shall never forget that everything is first really over for a man when he has got so old that he can learn nothing from a young girl.

My Cordelia!

You say that you had not imagined that I was like this, but neither had I imagined that I could become like this. Does not the change lie in yourself? For it is conceivable that I am not really changed, but that the eye with which you look at me is changed. Or does that change lie in me? It lies in me, for I love you; it lies in you, for it is you I love. Proudly and inexorably I considered everything by the calm, cold light of reason, nothing terrified me, nothing surprised me; even if a spirit had knocked at my door, I should calmly have taken the candelabrum and opened the door.[37] But lo, it was not wraiths I opened to, not pale, nerveless forms, it was to you, my Cordelia; it was life and youth and health and beauty who entered in. My arm trembled, I could hardly hold the light steady. I retreat before you, and cannot refrain from fixing my eyes upon you, cannot refrain from wishing I might hold the light steady. I am changed; but how, why, in what does this change consist? I do not know. I know no better definition, no richer predicate to use than this, when I very mysteriously say about myself: I am changed.

                                                    Thy Johannes.

My Cordelia!

Love loves secrecy—an engagement is a revelation; it loves silence—an engagement is a public notice; it loves a whisper, an engagement is a proclamation from the house-tops; and yet an engagement, with my Cordelia's help, may be an excellent trick for deceiving the enemies. On a dark night there is nothing more dangerous to other ships than hanging out a lantern, which is more deceptive than the darkness.

                                                    Thy Johannes.

She sits on the sofa by the tea table. I sit by her side; she holds my arm, her head weighed down by many thoughts rests on my shoulder; she is so near me, and yet so far away. She resigns herself to me, and yet she does not belong to me. Even yet she resists me, but this is not subjectively reflective, it is the ordinary feminine resistance, for woman's nature is submission in the form of resistance.— She sits on the sofa by the tea table, I sit by her side. Her heart is beating, yet without passion; her bosom moves, yet not in disquiet; sometimes she changes color, yet in an easy transition. Is that love? By no means. She listens, she understands. She listens to the winged word, she understands it; she listens to another's speech, she understands it as her own; she hears the voice of another as it echoes through her; she understands this echo also, as if it were her own voice, which is manifest to her and to another.

What am I doing? Do I fool her? Not at all; that would be of no use to me. Am I stealing her heart? By no means; I really prefer that the girl I love should retain her heart. Then what am I doing? I am creating for myself a heart in the likeness of her own. An artist paints his beloved; that gives him pleasure; a sculptor fashions his. I do this, too, but in a spiritual sense. She does not know that I possess this picture, and therein lies my real deception. Mysteriously have I secured it, and in this sense I have stolen her heart, just as Rebecca stole Laban's heart when she craftily took away from him his household gods.[38]

Environment and setting still have a great influence upon one; there is something about them which stamps itself firmly and deeply in memory, or rather upon the whole soul, and which is therefore never forgotten. However old I may become, it will always be impossible for me to think of Cordelia amid surroundings different from this little room. When I come to visit her, the maid admits me to the hall; Cordelia herself comes in from her room, and, just as I open the door to enter the living room, she opens her door, so that our eyes meet exactly in the doorway. The living room is small, comfortable, little more than a cabinet. Although

I have now seen it from many different viewpoints, the one dearest to me is the view from the sofa. She sits there by my side; in front of us stands a round tea table, over which is draped a rich tablecloth. On the table stands a lamp shaped like a flower, which shoots up vigorously to bear its crown, over which a delicately cut paper shade hangs down so lightly that it is never still. The form of the lamp reminds one of oriental lands, the movement of the shade of the mild oriental breezes. The floor is concealed by a carpet woven from a certain kind of osier, which immediately betrays its foreign origin. For the moment I let the lamp become the keynote of my landscape. I am sitting there with her outstretched on the ground, under the lamp's flowering. At other times I let the osier rug evoke ideas about a ship, about an officer's cabin—we sail out into the middle of the great ocean. When we sit at a distance from the window, we gaze directly into heaven's vast horizon. This adds to the illusion. When I sit by her side, then I describe these things as pictures which pass as lightly over reality as death walks over one's grave.

Environment is always of great importance, especially for the sake of memory. Every erotic relation should always be lived so that one can easily reproduce a picture of it, in all the beauty of the original scene. To make this successful one must be especially observant of the surroundings. If one does not find them as one wants them, then one must make them so. In the case of Cordelia and her love, the environment was entirely suitable. What a different picture appears to me when I think about my little Emily, and yet, again, how suitable was the environment. I cannot imagine her, or rather, I only remember her in the little garden room. The door stood open, a little garden in front of the house cut off the view, forcing the eye to stop there, to pause at the boldly inviting highway that vanished in the distance. Emily was charming, but more insignificant than Cordelia. Her environment, too, suited her. The eye was held to earth, it did not rush boldly and impatiently forward, it rested in this little foreground. Even the highway which romantically lost itself in the distance only emphasized this, so that the eye traversing the stretches lying before it turned back again into this garden in order to traverse the same stretches again. The apartment was of the earth. Cordelia's environment must have no foreground, but only the infinite boldness of far horizons. She must not be of the earth, but ethereal, not walking but flying, not forward and back, but everlastingly forward.

When a man is himself engaged, he is straightway initiated with a vengeance into all the foolishness of the engaged. Some days ago Licentiate Hansen turned up with the attractive young girl he has become engaged to. He confided to me that she was charming, which I knew before, that she was very young, which I also knew; finally he confided to me that this was exactly the reason he had chosen her, so that he might shape her according to the ideal which was ever floating before his mind. Ye gods, what a silly licentiate,—and a healthy, blooming, joyous girl! Now I am a fairly old practitioner, yet I should never approach a young girl otherwise than as Nature's *Venerabile*,[39] and learn first from her. In so far as I can have any formative influence upon her, it is by repeatedly teaching her what I have learned from her.

Her soul must be set in motion, agitated in every possible direction; not, however, piecemeal and by sudden gusts, but totally. She must discover the infinite, experience what it is that lies nearest to man. This must she discover, not by the way of thought, which for her is the wrong way, but in imagination, which is the real mode of communication between her and me; for what is but a part with man, is the whole with woman. Not by the toilsome labor of thought should she work toward the infinite, for woman is not born for intellectual work, but she should grasp it through imagination and the easy way of the heart. The infinite is just as naturally a part of a young girl as is the conception she holds that all love must be happy. A young girl has above all, wherever she turns, the infinite about her, and the transition is a leap, but, it is well to note, a feminine not a masculine leap. Why are men generally so clumsy? When a man would leap, he first takes a run, makes lengthy preparations, measures the distance with his eye, takes several running starts, becomes afraid, and turns back again. At last he jumps and falls in. A young girl leaps in a different fashion. In mountainous regions one often sees twin peaks towering above the mountain range. A yawning chasm separates them, terrible to gaze down into. No man would dare this leap. A young girl, however, so the mountain folk say, did venture it, and for this reason it is called the Maiden's Leap. I can readily believe it, as I believe everything remarkable about a young girl, and it is intoxicating to me to hear the simple mountain folk talk about it. I believe everything, believe the miraculous, am amazed at it only in order to believe, as the only thing in the world which has astonished me is a young girl, the first and the last. And yet, such a leap is for a young girl only a hop, while a man's leap always becomes ridiculous, because however far he straddles, his exertion at once becomes nothing, compared with the distance between the peaks, and yet it acts as a sort of measuring stick.

But who could be so foolish as to imagine a young girl's taking a running start? One can indeed imagine her running, but then the running is itself a game, a pleasure, an unfolding of charm, whereas the conception of a preliminary run separates those things which belong together in a woman. A run, in fact, has its own dialectic, which is contrary to woman's nature. And now the leap; who here dares again to be so ungracious as to separate what there belongs together? Her leap is a floating through the air. And when she has reached the other side, she stands there, not exhausted by the exertion, but more beautiful than ever, instinct with feeling, she wafts a kiss over to us who stand on this side. Young, new-born like a flower which has shot up from the root of the mountain, she swings out over the abyss, so that it almost turns us dizzy. . . . What she must learn is to go through all the movements of infinity, to sway, to lull herself in her moods, to confuse poetry and reality, truth and romance, to be tossed about in the infinite. When she becomes familiar with this confusion, then I set the erotic in motion, then she becomes what I wish and desire. Then is my duty ended, my labor; then I take in my sail, then I sit by her side, and under her sail we travel forward. And in truth, when this girl is first erotically intoxicated, I shall have enough to do in sitting by the rudder to moderate the speed, so that nothing comes too early, nor in an unlovely manner. Sometimes I may take in a little sail, but in the next moment we rush forward again.

Cordelia becomes more and more indignant whenever we go to my uncle's house. She has several times requested that we should not go there again; there is no help for her, I always know how to find an excuse. Last night when we left she pressed my hand with unusual passion. She had probably felt tortured at being there, and it was no wonder. If I did not always get some amusement out of watching the artificiality of these artistic performances, it would be impossible for me to stand it. This morning I received a letter from her in which she, with more wit than I had expected from her, ridiculed the engagements. I have kissed that letter; it is the dearest one I have received from her. Rightly so, my Cordelia, this is the way I wish it.

It happens quite curiously that on Eastern Street there are two confectioners whose places are exactly opposite one another. On the first floor to the left lives a little maiden or matron. She is usually hidden behind a curtain which screens the windowpane where she sits. The curtain is made of very thin material, and if anyone knows the girl, or has seen her often, he will, if he has good eyesight, easily be able to recognize every feature, while to one who does not know her, or does not see well, she will appear only as a dark shadow. The latter is to a certain degree the case with me; the former the case with a young officer who appears in the offing every day precisely at noon, and looks up at this window. I really first noticed this beautiful telegraphic relation because of the curtain. There are no curtains for the rest of the windows, and such a single curtain covering only one pane is usually a sign that some very retiring person sits behind it. One forenoon I stood at the window of the confectionery across the street. It was exactly twelve o'clock. Without paying any attention to the passers-by, I stood looking fixedly at this curtain, when suddenly the dark shadow behind it began to move. A feminine head appeared in profile at the next pane, so that it curiously turned toward the curtain. Thereupon the fair owner of the head nodded in a very friendly way, and again hid herself behind the curtain.

First and foremost, I decided that the person she greeted was a man, for her greeting was too passionate to be occasioned by the sight of a girl friend; in the second place, I decided that he whom she greeted must be coming from the other direction. Thus she had placed herself exactly right to be able to see him a long distance away, aye, she could even greet him while concealed by the curtain. . . . Very well, at precisely twelve o'clock, the hero in this little love scene appears, our gallant lieutenant. I am sitting in the shop of the confectioner who lives on the ground floor of the building whose first floor is occupied by the young lady. The lieutenant already had his eyes fixed upon her. Take care now, my friend, it is not so easy a matter to bow gracefully to the first floor. On the whole, he is not so bad —well developed, erect, a handsome figure, hooked nose, dark hair, the tricorn is very becoming to him. Now for the difficulties! The knees gradually begin to knock together a little from standing too long in one position. It makes an impression on the eyes comparable to the feeling a man with a toothache has when the teeth are left in the mouth too long. If a man centers his whole power in his eyes and directs it to the first floor, it soon takes too much strength from the legs. I beg your pardon, Lieutenant, for intercepting that heaven-directed glance. It was impertinent, I know that well enough. One cannot call this glance very significant, rather insignificant, and yet very promising. But these many promises evidently rise too strongly to the head; he totters, to use the poet's word about *Agnete*, he wavers, he falls.[40] That is tough, and if anyone asked me, I should say it ought never to happen. He is too good for that. It is really fatal, for when a man would impress a lady as a cavalier, he must never fall. If he would be a cavalier, he must conduct himself as such. If on the other hand, he only appears as a great intellect, then all such things are matters of indifference; he may sink into himself, he may collapse; if then he actually falls, there is nothing at all remarkable about it. . . . What impression might this incident have made upon my little miss?

It is unfortunate that I cannot be on both sides of the Dardanelles at the same time. I could, of course, post an acquaintance on the other side of the street, but, partly, I always prefer to make my own observations, partly, I never know what there might be in it for me, and in such a case it is well never to have a confidant, since then one must waste a great deal of time finding out what he knows, and confusing him about the matter. . . . I am really getting tired of my good lieutenant. Day after day he shows up in full uniform. This is a terrible constancy. Is such a quality becoming to a soldier? Dear Sir, don't you carry side arms? Ought you not to take the house by storm? and the lady by violence? Of course, if you were a student, a licentiate, a curate who lives on hope, that would be a different matter. Still, I forgive you, for the girl pleases me the more I look at her. She is pretty, her brown eyes are full of mischief. When she is awaiting your arrival her appearance is enhanced by a higher beauty, indescribably becoming to her. Therefore I infer that she must have a great deal of imagination, and imagination is the natural rouge of beautiful women.

My Cordelia!

What is longing? Language and the poets rhyme it with the word prison [*Længsel—Fængsel*]. How absurd! As if only a prisoner could know longing. As if one could not long when one is free. If I were set free, would I not long? And on the other side, I am free, yes, free as a bird, and yet do I not long? I long when I am going to you, I long when I leave you, even when I sit by your side, I am longing for you. Can one then long for what one has? Aye, when one considers that in the next moment one may not have it. My longing is an eternal impatience. Only when I had lived through all eternities and assured myself that at every moment you belonged to me, would I return to you, and with you live through all eternities, and not even have the patience to be separated from you for a single moment without longing, but with confidence enough to sit quiet by your side.

Thy Johannes.

My Cordelia!

Outside the door stands a little carriage which to me is large enough for the whole world, since it is large enough for two; hitched to it are a pair of horses, wild and unmanageable as the forces of Nature, impatient as my passion, spirited as your thoughts. If you are willing, I shall carry you away, my Cordelia! Only command it. Your command is the word which loosens the reins and spurs on the lust of flight. I carry you away, not from one person to another, but out of the world.—The horses rear, the carriage rises, the steeds in their ascent are almost directly above our heads. We ride heavenward through the clouds; the wind whistles about us. Is it we who are sitting still while all the world is moving, or is it our daring flight? Does it make you dizzy, my Cordelia? Then hold fast to me; I do not become dizzy. One never becomes giddy in a spiritual sense when one thinks only of a single thing, and I think only of you—in the physical sense one is never giddy if one fastens the eyes on a single object. I look only at you. Hold fast; if the world passes away, if our comfortable carriage vanishes beneath us, we still hold each other close, floating in the harmony of the spheres.

Thy Johannes.

It is almost too much. My servant has waited six hours, I myself have waited two, in the wind and rain, just to meet that dear child, Charlotte Hahn. She is in the habit of visiting an old aunt of hers regularly every Wednesday between two and five. Today she doesn't come, just when I was so eager to see her. And why? Because she puts me in a very definite mood. I bow to her, she curtsies to me in a manner at once indescribably worldly, and yet so divine; she almost stops, sinks nearly to the ground, looking all the time as if she might ascend to heaven. When I look at her, my mind is at once solemn and yet filled with desire.

As for the rest, the girl does not interest me in the least. All I want is this greeting, nothing more, even if she were willing to give it. Her greeting creates a mood in me, and it is this mood which I then squander on Cordelia. . . . I'll wager now that in some way she has slipped by us. It is not only in comedies but in real life as well that it is difficult to keep track of a young girl; one needs to have an eye on every finger. It was a nymph, Cardea, who devoted her life to fooling men. She lived in a wood, lured her lover to its thickest copse, and disappeared. She wished to fool Janus also, but he fooled her instead; for he had eyes in the back of his head.

My letters do not fail of their purpose. They develop her mentally, if not erotically. For that purpose I must not use letters but notes. The more the erotic is to come out, the shorter they should be, but the more positively they should stress the erotic side. However, in order not to make her sentimental or soft, irony must again stiffen her emotions, while yet giving her an appetite for the nourishment dearest to her. The notes vaguely and remotely suggest the absolute. As soon as this suspicion begins to dawn in her soul, the relation is ruptured. By my resistance the suspicion takes form in her soul, as if it were her own thought, her own heart's impulse. This is just what I want.

My Cordelia!

Somewhere in this town there lives a little family consisting of a widow and her three daughters. Two of the latter go to the Royal Kitchen to learn to cook. It was about five o'clock on an afternoon in spring, the door of the living room opened softly, a spying glance stole about the room. There was no one; only a young girl sat at the piano. The door stood ajar, so one could listen unobserved. It was no artist who was playing; had it been, the door would have been shut tight. She was playing a Swedish melody, suffused with the impermanence of youth and beauty. The words mocked the girl's own youth and beauty; her youth and beauty mocked the words. Which was right: the girl or the words? The tones were so quiet, so melancholy, as if sad-

ness were the arbitrator who should decide the question.—
But it is wrong, this sadness. What connection is there between youth and these reflections? What fellowship between morning and evening! The tones quiver and tremble;
the spirits of the sounding-board rise in confusion and do
not understand one another—my Cordelia, why so violent!
to what end this passion!

How far remote in time must an event be for us to remember it? How far must it be so that memory's longing
can no longer seize upon it? Most people have a limit in
this respect: the things which lie too near them in time,
they cannot remember, nor can they remember the more
remote. I know no limit. What was experienced yesterday,
I push back a thousand years in time, and remember it as
if it had happened yesterday.

Thy Johannes.

My Cordelia!

I have a secret to confide to you, my confidante. To
whom should I confide it? Echo? It would betray it. The
stars? They are cold. People? They do not understand it.
Only to you can I confide it; for you know how to keep a
secret. There is a girl more beautiful than my soul's dream,
purer than the light of the sun, deeper than the depth of
the sea, prouder than the flight of eagles—there is a girl—
O! incline your head to my ear and to my words, that my
secret may slip into it—I love this girl more dearly than my
life, for she is my life; more than all my desires, for she is
my sole desire; more than all my thoughts, for she is my
sole thought; more warmly than the sun loves the flowers;
more fervently than sorrow loves the secrecy of the troubled
heart; more wistfully than the burning sands of the desert
love the rain—I cling to her more tenderly than the mother's
eye fastens itself upon the child; more worshipfully than
the pleading soul to God; more inseparably than the plant
to its root.—Your head becomes heavy and thoughtful, it
sinks down on your breast, your bosom rises to support it
—my Cordelia! You have understood me, you have understood me exactly, to the letter, no jot has been ignored.
Shall I attune my ears and let your voice assure me of

this? Could I doubt? Will you keep this secret? Dare I depend on you? Someone tells about men who in terrible crimes dedicate themselves to mutual silence. I have confided to you a secret which is my life, and my life's content; have you nothing to confide in me, nothing which is so beautiful, so significant, so chaste, that supernatural forces would be set in motion if I betrayed it?

Thy Johannes.

My Cordelia!

The heaven is overcast—dark rain clouds hang over it like dark brows above a passionate countenance; the trees of the forest move restlessly, tossed about by unquiet dreams. You are hidden from me in the forest. Behind every tree I perceive a feminine being who resembles you; if I come nearer, then it hides behind the next tree. Will you not reveal yourself to me? Unify yourself? Everything is in confusion before me; a solitary part of the woods loses its isolated outline, I see everything as a foggy sea, where everywhere feminine beings resembling you appear and disappear. I do not see you, you constantly move in the waves of intuition, and yet I am made happy by every single resemblance to you. Wherein does it lie—is it in the rich unity of your being or in the poor manifold of my own?—Is not loving you to love the world?

Thy Johannes.

It would really be interesting, if it were possible, to record exactly the conversations between Cordelia and myself. However it is easy to see that this is an impossibility; for if I were fortunate enough to remember every single word exchanged between us, still it would always be impossible to express the contemporaneity which really forms the nerve center of the conversation, the surprised outbreak, the passionateness which is the life-principle of conversation. In general, I have naturally not prepared myself, since this would militate against the essential nature of conversation, especially erotic conversation. Only I always have the contents of my letters well in mind, the moods which these might possibly evoke in her, always before my eyes. Naturally it would never occur to me to ask her whether she had read my letter. I can easily prove for myself that she has read it. I never talk with her directly about it, but I make mysterious allusions to it in the course of my conversation, partly to fix one or another impression more firmly in her soul, partly to wrest it from her and make her irresolute. Then she can reread the letter and get a new impression of it, and so on.

A change is taking place, and it is taking place in her. Should I try to characterize the condition of her soul at this moment, then I should say that it is pantheistically daring. Her glance betrays this immediately. It is daring, almost rash in expectancy, as if it demanded and at every moment was prepared to view the extraordinary. Like an eye that sees beyond itself, so her glance travels beyond that which appears immediately before it, and sees the marvelous. It is daring, almost rash in its expectancy, but not in self-confidence; it is therefore dreamy and prayerful, not proud and commanding. She seeks the marvelous outside herself, she prays for it to appear, as if it was not in her own power to evoke it. This must be prevented, otherwise I get predominance over her too early. She said yesterday that there was something regal in my nature. Perhaps she will submit; that will not do at all. Certainly, my dear Cordelia, there is something kingly in my nature, but you do not suspect what it is I rule over as a kingdom. It is over stormy moods. Like Aeolus I hold them shut up in the mountain of my personality, and let now one, now another, go forth.[41] Flattery will give her self-esteem; the difference between me and thee will be made valid; everything throws the responsibility on her. Great caution is needed in using flattery. Sometimes one must value himself very highly, yet so that there remains something still higher; sometimes one must set one's self very low. The first is more correct when one is moving toward the spiritual, the second, when one moves toward the erotic.—Does she owe me anything? Nothing at all. Could I wish that she did? Not at all. I am too much a connoisseur—I have too much understanding of the erotic for any such foolishness. If this were actually the case I should endeavor with all my might to make her forget it, and hush my own thoughts about it to sleep. Every young girl is, in relation to the labyrinth of her heart, an Ariadne; she holds the thread by which one can find his way through it, but she has it, without herself knowing how to use it.[42]

My Cordelia!

Speak—I obey. Your wish is a command. Your prayer is an all-powerful invocation, every fleeting wish of yours is a benefaction to me; for I obey you not like a servile spirit, as if I stood outside of you. When you command, then your will increases, and with it I myself; for I am a confusion of the soul which only awaits your word.

Thy Johannes.

My Cordelia!

You know that I am very fond of talking to myself. I have found that the most interesting person of my acquaintance is myself. Sometimes I have feared that I might finally lack subjects for these conversations; now I no longer fear, now I have you. I talk, then, now and to all eternity about you with myself, about the most interesting subject with the most interesting man.—Alas, I am only an interesting man, you the most interesting subject.

Thy Johannes.

My Cordelia!

Because I have loved you so short a time you almost seem to fear that I may have loved someone before. There are manuscripts on which the trained eye immediately suspects an older writing, which in the course of time has been superseded by insignificant foolishness. By means of chemicals, this later writing may be erased, and then the original stands out plain and clear. So your eye has taught me to find myself in myself. I let forgetfulness consume everything which does not concern you, and then I discover an exceedingly old, a divinely young, original writing, then I discover that my love for you is as old as myself.

Thy Johannes.

My Cordelia!

How can a kingdom stand which is at strife with itself?[43] How shall I be able to survive, when I strive with myself? What about? About you, in order, if possible, to find rest in the thought that I am in love with you. But how shall I find this rest? One of the striving powers will constantly persuade the other that he is most deeply and heartily in love; the next moment the other will do the same. It would not trouble me greatly if my war were external, if there were someone who dared to be in love with you, or dared to refrain from loving you, the crime is equally great; but this struggle in my own being consumes me, this one passion in its ambiguity.

                                        Thy Johannes.

Just make yourself scarce, my little fisher-maiden; just hide yourself among the trees; just take up your burden, it is becoming to you to bend over, aye, even as you are now doing, with a natural grace, under the load of fagots you have collected—that such a creature should bear such burdens! Like a dancer you reveal your beautiful form—slender waist, lovely bosom, not yet fully mature, that every registry clerk must admit. You perhaps believe that your beauty is not worth mentioning, you think that fashionable ladies are far more beautiful. Ah, my child! You do not know how much deception there is in the world. But start your journey with your burden on your shoulders, into the great forest, which probably stretches many, many miles into the country, up to the very foot of the blue mountains. You are perhaps not a real fisher-maiden, but an enchanted princess; you are the slave of a troll; he is cruel enough to make you fetch fagots from the forest. It is always this way in fairy stories; otherwise why should you go deeper into the forest? If you are really a fisher-maiden, you should go down to your lodgings with your firewood, past me, as I stand on the other side of the road.—If you just follow the foot-path which winds invitingly through the trees, my eyes will find you; just look around at me, my eyes are following you; move me you cannot; no desire pulls me hence.

I sit calmly on the railing and smoke my cigar.—Some other time—perhaps. Yes, your glance is roguish enough, when you half turn your head back that way; your graceful walk is inviting—yes, I know it, I understand where this path leads,—to the solitude of the forest, to the murmur of the trees, to the manifold stillness. Look, even heaven encourages you, it hides itself in the clouds, it darkens the background of the forest, it is as if it pulled down the curtain for us.—Farewell, my pretty fisher-maiden, live well. Thanks for your favor, it was a beautiful moment, a mood, not strong enough to move me from my firm place on the railing, but still rich in inward emotion.

When Jacob had bargained with Laban about the pay for his services, they agreed that Jacob should watch the white sheep, and as a reward for his work, should have the ringstraked and piebald lambs which were born in his flock. Then he laid mottled sticks in the water, and let the sheep look at them.[44]—So I place myself everywhere before Cordelia, she sees me constantly. It seems to her sheer attentiveness on my part; personally I know, however, that her soul is losing interest in everything else, that there is developing within her a spiritual concupiscence which sees me everywhere.

My Cordelia!

How could I forget you? Is my love then a work of memory? Even if time expunged everything else from its tablets, even expunged memory itself, my relation to you would continue to live, you would still not be forgotten. As if I could forget you! What should I then remember? I have even forgotten myself to remember you; if I then forgot you, I would come to remember myself; but at the moment I remembered myself, I would have to remember you again. As if I could forget you! What would happen then? There is a picture dating from antiquity.[45] It represents Ariadne. She is leaping up from her couch and gazing earnestly toward a ship which is departing under full sail. By her side stands Cupid with unstrung bow, and dries his

eyes. Behind her stands a winged and helmeted female figure. It is usually assumed that this figure represents Nemesis. Imagine this picture. Imagine it a little changed. Cupid
does not weep, and his bow is strung; or were you then become less beautiful, less victorious, because I had become
mad? Cupid smiles and bends his bow. Nemesis does not
stand inactive by your side, she also draws her bow. In that
picture we see in the ship a manly figure who is busily occupied. We assume that it is Theseus. Not so in my picture.
He stands on the stern, he looks longingly back, he stretches
out his arms, he has repented, or, rather, his madness has
left him, but the ship bears him away. Cupid and Nemesis
both aim at him, and arrows fly from both bows; their aim
is true; one sees, one understands, that they have both hit
the same place in his heart, as a sign that his love was the
Nemesis which avenged.

Thy Johannes.

My Cordelia!

People say that I am in love with myself; I don't wonder;
for how could they notice that I am in love, since I love
only you; how could anyone suspect it, since I love only
you? I am in love with myself, why? Because I am in love
with you; for I love you truly, you alone, and everything
which belongs to you, and so I love myself because this
myself belongs to you, so if I cease to love you, I cease to
love myself. What is, then, in the profane eyes of the world
an expression of the greatest egotism is for your initiated
eyes an expression of purest sympathy; what is for the
profane eyes of the world an expression of the most prosaic
self-preservation is in your sacred sight an expression for
the most enthusiastic self-annihilation.

Thy Johannes.

What I had most feared was that her whole process of
development might take too long a time. I see, however,
that Cordelia is making such great strides forward that it
becomes necessary, in order to keep her attention properly,
to set everything in movement. Not for all the world must

she become faint too early, that is to say, before the time
when time is past for her.

When people are in love, they do not follow the public
highway. It is only marriage which plods along the middle
of the king's highway; when lovers walk from Nøddebo,
they do not stroll along the path by Esrom Lake, even
though that is really only a hunting road, for it is blazed,
and love prefers to blaze its own way. They penetrate
deeper into Grib's Forest. And when they thus wander arm
in arm, each one understands the other, and that becomes
clear which before was obscurely amusing and painful. The
lovers do not suspect that anyone is present.—Consequently,
this beautiful beech tree becomes a witness to your love;
under its crown you first confessed your love. You remembered everything so clearly: the first time you saw each
other, the first time you clasped each other's hand in the
dance, the first time you separated from each other in the
morning hour, when neither of you would admit anything
to yourself, to say nothing of making an admission to the
other.—It is sufficiently entertaining to listen to the repertory
of love.—They fell on their knees under the tree, they
pledged each other inviolable love, they sealed the pact
with the first kiss.—These are fruitful moods which must be
squandered on Cordelia. . . . Consequently this beech became a witness. O well, a tree is a proper witness, but still
it is not enough. Well, you think, heaven was also a witness,
but heaven without something else is a very abstract idea.
Behold, therefore, there was nevertheless a witness.—Ought
I to stand up, let them know that I am here? No, perhaps
they would know me, and that would spoil the game.
Should I, when they leave, stand up and let them know
someone was present? No, that is inexpedient. Silence shall
rest over their secret—as long as I wish. They are in my
power, I can separate them when I will. I am privy to their
secret; only from him or from her, can I have learned it—
from her, that would be impossible—consequently, from
him—that is abominable! Bravo! And yet it is almost malicious. Well, we'll see. If I can get a definite impression of

her, which I cannot otherwise get normally, as I would prefer, then there is nothing else for it.

My Cordelia!

I am poor—you are my riches; dark—you are my light; I own nothing, want nothing. And how could I own anything? It is a contradiction to say that he can own something who does not own himself. I am as happy as a child, who can and should own nothing. I own nothing; for I belong only to you; I am not, I have ceased to be, in order to be yours.

Thy Johannes.

My Cordelia!

Mine, what does this word signify? Not what belongs to me, but what I belong to, what contains my whole being, which is mine in so far as I belong to it. My God is not the God who belongs to me, but the God to whom I belong, and so again, when I say my native land, my home, my calling, my longing, my hope. If hitherto there had been no immortality, then would this thought that I am thine break through Nature's accustomed course.

Thy Johannes.

My Cordelia!

What am I? The unassuming herald who attends upon your triumph; the dancer who supports you when you lightly and gracefully leap into the air; the greensward on which you rest for a moment when you are tired of flying; the bass voice which is heard under the soprano ecstasy, helping it to rise ever higher.—What am I? I am the force of gravity which holds you to the earth. What am I then? Body, mass, earth, dust and ashes—you, my Cordelia, you are soul and spirit.

Thy Johannes.

My Cordelia!

Love is everything. For this reason, to one who loves, everything ceases to have significance in and of itself, and has it only in the interpretation that love puts upon it. If there was some fiancé who found that he cared about another girl, he would probably stand there like a criminal, and she would be highly incensed. You, on the contrary, would, I know, see in such a confession an act of homage, for you know it would be impossible for me to love another; it is my love for you that casts its splendor over the whole of life. When then I concern myself with someone else, it is not for the purpose of convincing myself that I don't love her but only you—that would be presumptuous; but since my whole soul is filled with you, life takes on another significance for me. It becomes a myth about you.

Thy Johannes.

My Cordelia!

My love consumes me. Only my voice is left, a voice which is in love with you everywhere whispers to you that I love you.[46] O! does it tire you to listen to this voice? Everywhere it encompasses you; like a manifold, inconstant compassing, my thoroughly reflective soul enfolds your pure deep being.

Thy Johannes.

My Cordelia!

One reads in ancient tales that a river fell in love with a maiden. So my soul is like a river that loves you. Sometimes it is peaceful and reflects your image deeply and quietly; sometimes it imagines that it has captured your image; then its waves rise up to prevent your escaping; sometimes the surface ripples softly, playing with your image; sometimes it has lost it, then its floods are black with despair.—Such is my soul: like a river which has fallen in love with you.

Thy Johannes.

To tell the truth: without having an unusually vivid imagination, one could conceive of a more convenient, comfortable, and above all, a more suitable conveyance; to ride with a peat-cutter really creates a sensation.—In a pinch, however, one accepts it with thanks. One goes out for a walk on the highway; one seats one's self in the cart; one rides a mile and meets no one; two miles, all goes well; one feels quiet and secure; really one can take in the scenery better from this point of view than when one is walking; one has gone almost three miles—now who would have expected to meet anyone from Copenhagen so far out here on the highway? And it is someone from Copenhagen, you are sure, not a man from the countryside; he has quite a distinguished manner, so decisive, so observant, so appraising, and so little derisive. Yes, my dear girl, you are in an uncomfortable position, you look as if you were sitting on a tray, the wagon-box is so shallow there is no room for your feet.—But it is your own fault; my carriage is entirely at your service; I venture to offer you a much less inconvenient place, if it would not embarrass you to sit by my side. If it does, I will turn over the whole carriage to you, sit in the driver's seat myself, pleased at being permitted to convey you to your destination.—The straw hat does not adequately protect you against a side glance. It is useless for you to bend your head down, I can still admire your lovely profile.—Is it not annoying that the peasant bows to me? But it is indeed quite proper for a peasant to bow to a distinguished man.—You do not get off with that; here is a tavern, yes, a station, and a peat-cutter is in his way too pious to neglect his devotions. Now I shall see to him. I have an unusual gift for pleasing peat-cutters. O! may I also be fortunate enough to please you. He cannot resist my offer, and when he has accepted it, then he cannot resist the effect of it. If I cannot, then my servant can.—He has gone into the taproom, leaving you alone on the wagon in the shelter.—Heaven only knows what the girl is. Could she be a little middle-class girl, perhaps the daughter of a parish clerk? If so, she is uncommonly pretty, and dressed in unusual taste. The clerk must have a good living. It has just occurred to me that she may be a little aristocrat who is tired of riding in her carriage, and perhaps went for a little hike in the country, and now has embarked on a little adventure. It is possible, such things are not unheard of.— The peasant does not know anything; he is an oaf who only knows how to drink. Aye, aye, let him drink, the numbskull, he is welcome to it.

But what do I see? It is neither more nor less than Miss Jespersen, the daughter of the wholesaler. Heaven preserve me, we two know each other. I met her once on Broad Street; she was riding backwards, she could not get the carriage window up; I put on my glasses, and then had the satisfaction of following her with my eyes. It was a very cramped position; there were so many in the carriage she could not move, and she probably did not dare to make an outcry. Her present situation is just as embarrassing. It is clear that we two are predestined for each other. She is a very romantic little girl, and definitely she is out on her own. —There comes my servant with the peat-cutter. He is dead drunk. It is disgusting. They are an abominably depraved lot, these peat-cutters. Alas, yes! And yet there are worse men than peat-cutters.—See, now you will just have to ride in the carriage. Now that it becomes necessary for you to drive the horses, it is quite romantic.—You refuse my invitation. You insist that you are a very good driver. You do not deceive me. I can see well enough how cunning you are. When you have gone a little way, then you will jump out, you can easily find a hiding place in the woods.—My horse must be saddled. I follow you on horseback.—There, see! Now I am ready, now you can feel safe against any attack.—Don't be so terribly afraid, or I'll turn back immediately. I only want to frighten you enough to furnish the occasion for enhancing your natural beauty. You don't know that I was responsible for your peasant getting drunk, and I have not allowed myself to make a single offensive remark. Even yet everything can be all right; I shall certainly give the affair such a comic turn that you will laugh at the whole story. I only desire a little settling of accounts with you. Never believe that I would take any young girl off her guard. I am a friend of freedom, and whatever does not come to me freely, I never trouble myself about.—"You will certainly see yourself that you cannot continue your journey in this manner. I myself am going hunting, that is why I am on horseback. My carriage is ready at the tavern. If you are willing, it shall instantly overtake you and take you where you want to go. Unfortunately, I cannot have the pleasure of attending upon you, for I am bound by a hunting promise, and that is sacred."—You accept, on the contrary, and instantly everything is all right. Now you see you do not need to be embarrassed at the thought of seeing me again, or, at least, not more so than is becoming to you. You can be amused at the whole affair, laugh a little, and think a little about me. More I do not ask. This may not seem very much, but it is enough for me. It is the beginning, and I am especially strong on beginnings.

Last evening the aunt had a little party. I knew Cordelia would have her knitting-bag with her, so I had hidden a little note in it. She dropped it, picked it up, read it, and showed both embarrassment and wistfulness. One should never fail to take advantage of such opportunities. It is incredible how much it can help. The note had nothing of importance in it, but it became infinitely significant to her when she read it under such circumstances. She had no chance to talk with me; I had arranged it so that I had to escort a lady home. Consequently Cordelia had to wait until today. It is always best to give an impression time to sink into her soul. It always looks as if I were very attentive. This gives me the advantage of everywhere being in her thoughts, of everywhere surprising her.

Love still has its own dialectic. I was once in love with a young girl. Last summer in the theater in Dresden, I saw an actress who strikingly resembled her. Because of that I desired the pleasure of her acquaintance; then I discovered that there was really not a very great resemblance. Today I met a lady on the street who reminded me of that actress. This story can go on as long as you like.

Everywhere my thoughts encompass Cordelia, I dispose them like guardian angels about her. Like Venus riding in her chariot drawn by doves, so Cordelia sits in her triumphal chariot, and I harness my thoughts like winged creatures. She sits there joyous, rich as a child, powerful as a goddess; I walk by her side. Truly a young girl is still and remains *Venerabile* of Nature and the whole of existence. No one knows this better than myself. The only pity is that this glory is so short-lived. She smiles at me, she greets me, she beckons to me as if she were my sister. A single glance reminds her that she is my beloved.

Love has many positions. Cordelia makes good progress. She is sitting on my knee, her arm, soft and warm, encircles my neck; she rests upon my breast, light, without bodily weight; her soft form hardly touches me; like a flower her graceful figure twines about me, freely as a ribbon. Her eyes are hidden behind her lashes, her bosom is of a dazzling whiteness like snow, so smooth that my eye cannot rest upon it, would glance off, if her bosom did not move. What does this agitation mean? Is it love? Perhaps. It may be its anticipation, its dream. It still lacks energy. She embraces me elaborately, as the cloud the transfigured one, casually as a breeze, softly as one caresses a flower; she kisses me as dispassionately as heaven kisses the sea, softly and quietly as the dew kisses a flower, solemnly as the sea kisses the image of the moon.

So far I should call her passion a naïve passion. When the change comes, and I begin to draw back in earnest, then she will really muster all her resources in order to captivate me. She has no way to accomplish this except by means of the erotic, but this will now appear on a very different scale. It then becomes the weapon in her hand which she swings against me. Then I have the reflected passion. She fights for her own sake because she knows that I possess the erotic; she fights for her own sake in order to overcome me. She develops in herself a higher form of the erotic. What I taught her to suspect by inflaming her, my coldness now teaches her to understand, but in such a way that she believes she discovered it herself. Through this she will try to take me by surprise; she will believe that her boldness has outstripped me, and that she has thereby caught me. Then her passion becomes definite, energetic, conclusive, logical; her kiss total, her embrace firm.—In me she seeks her freedom, the more firmly I encompass her, the better she finds it. The engagement is broken. When this happens, then she needs a little rest, so that this wild tumult may not bring out something unseemly. Then her passion gathers itself again, and she is mine.

As formerly in the time of Edward of blessed memory I supervised her reading indirectly, so now I do it directly. That which I furnish her I regard as the best food for thought: myths and fairy stories. Still, she is free in this as in everything. I draw everything out of her. If it was not there to begin with, I manage to implant it.

When the servant girls go to the Deer Park in the summer time, it generally affords them but a meager pleasure. They go only once a year, and feel, accordingly, that they ought to celebrate. So they put on hat and shawl, and disfigure themselves in every way. Their gaiety is wild, unseemly and lascivious. No, then I prefer Frederiksberg Park. They go there on Sunday afternoon, and I, too. Everything here is seemly and decent, the jollity itself has a quieter and finer stamp. In general, the man who has no appreciation of servant girls loses more thereby than they do. Their multitudinous host is really the most beautiful civil guard we have in Denmark. If I were king I know what I would do— I would not review the troops of the line. If I were one of the city's aldermen, I should immediately move to have a committee appointed whose business it would be, in every possible way, by insight, by advice and admonition, and by suitable rewards, to encourage the girls of the servant class to make a beautiful and meticulous toilet. Why should beauty go to waste, why should it go through life unnoticed? Let it at least once a week show itself in the most favorable light! But above all let us have taste, restriction. A servant girl ought not to be dressed like a lady, so far I agree with *Politievennen*, but the reasons assigned by this respectable sheet are altogether fallacious.[47] Could we look forward to so desirable a flowering of the servant class, would not this in turn have a beneficial effect upon our own daughters? or am I too daring, when I descry a future for Denmark which may truly be called matchless?[48] If I were only so fortunate as to be living when this golden age comes, I could employ the whole day in the highways and byways with a good conscience, just to rejoice in the pleasures of the eye. How enthusiastic my thought has become, so bold, so daring, so patriotic! But it must be remembered that I am here in Frederiksberg Park, where the servant girls come on Sunday afternoon, and I, too.

First come the country lassies, hand in hand with their sweethearts; or in another pattern, all the girls hand in hand in front, all the men behind; or in still another pattern, two girls and one man. This host constitutes the setting; they usually stand or sit under the trees in the great square in front of the pavilion. They are sound, full of health; only the color contrasts are a little too strong, both in their dress and in their complexions. Now come the girls from Jutland and Funen: tall, rank, a little too stalwart of build, their dress a little careless. Here there would be much for the committee to do. There is not wanting a representative for the Bornholm division: clever cooks, but not very approachable, either in the kitchen or in Frederiksberg; there is something proud and restrained about them. Their presence here has a certain contrast value, and I should regret missing them here, but I rarely have anything to do with them.

Now come the troops of the center, the girls from Nyboder. Of moderate height, plump, a rounded figure, a delicate complexion, gay, happy, nimble, gossipy, a little given to coquetry, and above all, bareheaded. Their dress may readily approximate a lady's, but two things are to be noted: they do not wear a shawl but a kerchief, and no hat—at most, a smart little cap; preferably they are bareheaded - - - Why, how do you do, Marie; to think that I should meet you here. It is a long time since I saw you last. I suppose you are still in service at the Counsellor's?—"Yes"—It is a very good place, is it not?—"Yes"—But you are so alone out here, have you no one to keep you company . . . no sweetheart . . . perhaps he hasn't the time today, or perhaps you are waiting for him?—What, you are not engaged? Impossible! The prettiest girl in Copenhagen, a girl who is in service at the Counsellor's, a girl who is an ornament and an example to all servant girls, who knows how to dress so neatly and . . . so richly. What a dainty little handkerchief you have in your hand, of the finest cambric . . .

and look, with embroidery around the edge; I'll wager it cost ten marks . . . and you may be sure that there is many a fine lady who does not own its equal . . . French gloves . . . a silk parasol. . . . And such a girl not engaged. . . . Why, it is absurd. If I remember rightly, was it not Jens who thought quite a little of you, you know whom I mean, Jens, the wholesaler's Jens, who lived on the second floor . . . I see I struck it right. . . . Why, then, didn't you become engaged? Jens was a handsome fellow, he had a good situation, and in course of time the Counsellor's influence would have made him a policeman or a fireman, it wouldn't have been at all a bad match . . . I am afraid you must have been at fault, you have been too hard on him. . . . "No, but I found out that Jens had been engaged to a girl before, and that he had not treated her right at all." - - - Well, well, who could have believed that Jens was such a rascal . . . those guardsmen . . . ah, those guardsmen, they are not to be depended on. . . . You did just right, a girl like you is really too good to be thrown at everyone. . . . You will make a better match some day, I will guarantee that. - - - How is Miss Juliana? I have not seen her for a long time. My pretty Marie might be so kind as to help me with a little information . . . because one has been unhappy in love oneself, one need not be without sympathy for others. . . . There are so many people here. . . . I dare not talk with you about it; I am afraid that someone might spy on me. . . . Listen just for a moment, my pretty Marie. . . . Ah, here is the place, here in this shaded walk, where the trees entwine themselves so as to hide us from others, where we see nobody, hear no human voice, only a soft echo of the music . . . here I dare speak of my secret. . . . Is it not so, if Jens had not been a bad man, you would have walked here with him arm in arm, and listened to the happy music, and yourself have enjoyed a still higher happiness. . . . Why so moved? Just forget Jens. . . . Will you then be unjust to me. . . . Why do you suppose I came out here? . . . I came to meet you . . . it was to see you that I came to the Counsellor's . . . you must have noticed . . . every time I could, I always passed by the kitchen door. . . . You must be mine. . . . The banns shall be published from the pulpit. . . . Tomorrow evening I will explain everything to you . . . up the backstairs, the door to the left, right across from the kitchen. . . . Goodbye, my pretty Marie, let no one know that you have seen me out here, or spoken with me, you know my secret. - - - She is really a beautiful girl; it is possible that something might be made of her.—If I once get a foothold in her chamber, I will take care of the banns myself. I have always sought to develop the beautiful Greek self-sufficiency, and especially to make a priest superfluous.

If it were possible for me to stand behind Cordelia when she receives a letter from me, it might be very interesting. Then I could easily find out how far she has, in the most essential sense, appropriated the erotic to herself. On the whole, a letter is always an invaluable means of making an impression upon a girl; the dead letter often has greater influence than the living word.[49] A letter is a mysterious communication; you are master of the situation, you feel no pressure from anyone's presence, and I believe a young girl would really rather be alone with her ideal, that is, at a given moment, and particularly at the moment when it exerts the strongest influence upon her mind. Even if her ideal has found a sufficiently complete expression in a definite beloved object, there are still moments when she feels that there is an immensity in the ideal which reality lacks. These great feasts of the atonement must be granted to her; only one must take care that they are used rightly, so that she does not turn away from them back to reality weakened, but strengthened. For that reason a letter is helpful, since through it, although invisible, one may be spiritually present in these sacred moments of consecration, while the idea that the real person is the author of the letter creates a natural and easy transition back to reality.

Could I become jealous of Cordelia? Damnation, yes! And yet, in another sense, no! For if I saw, for instance, that even though I won in my fight against the other, her nature would be disturbed and not what I desired—then I would give her up.

An ancient philosopher has said that, if a man were to record accurately all of his experiences, then he would be, without knowing a word of the subject, a philosopher. I have now for a long time lived in close association with the community of the betrothed. Such a relationship ought then to bear some fruit. I have considered gathering all the material into a book, entitled: *Contribution to the Theory of the Kiss,* dedicated to all tender lovers. It is quite remarkable that no such work on this subject exists. If, then, I succeed in completing it, I will also be supplying a long-felt want. Could this lack in literature be due to the fact that philosophers do not consider such matters, or that they do not understand them?—I am able to offer several suggestions immediately. The perfect kiss requires a man and a girl as the participants. A kiss between men is tasteless, or —what is worse is distasteful.—Next, I believe a kiss comes nearer the idea when a man kisses a girl than when a girl kisses a man. When in the course of years there has come about an indifference in this relation, then the kiss has lost its significance. This is true about the domestic kiss of marriage with which married people, apparently in lieu of a napkin, dab each other's lips as the man mutters the ceremonial thanks, "That was swell, Mother."—If the difference in age is very great, then the kiss is without idea. I remember in a girl's school in one of the provinces, the senior class had a peculiar byword, "to kiss the judge," an expression connoting anything but an agreeable idea. It had originated in this way: The schoolmistress had a brother-in-law who lived in her house. He was an elderly man, had been a judge, and took advantage of his age to kiss the young girls. —The kiss ought to be the expression of a definite passion. When a brother and sister who are twins kiss each other, it is not a true kiss. This also holds true of kisses given during Christmas games, as well as of the stolen kiss. A kiss is a symbolic action which is unimportant when the feeling it should indicate is not present, and this feeling can only be present under certain conditions.

If one wishes to classify the kiss, then one must consider several principles of classification. One may classify kissing with respect to the sound. Here the language is not sufficiently elastic to record all my observations. I do not believe that all the languages in the world have an adequate supply of onomatopoeia to denote the different sounds I have learned to know at my uncle's house. Sometimes it was smacking, sometimes hissing, sometimes crackling, sometimes explosive, sometimes booming, sometimes sonorous, sometimes hollow, sometimes squeaky, and so on forever. One may also classify kissing with regard to contact, as in the close kiss, or the kiss *en passant*, and the clinging kiss. One may classify them with reference to the time element, as the brief and the prolonged. With reference to time, there is still another classification, and this is the only one I really care about. One makes a difference between the first kiss and all others. That which is the subject of this reflection is incommensurable with everything which is included in the other classifications; it is indifferent to sound, touch, time in general. The first kiss is, however, qualitatively different from all others. There are only a few people who consider this; it would really be a pity if there was but one who had thought about it.

My Cordelia!

A good answer is like a sweet kiss, says Solomon.[50] You know I am bad about asking questions, I am almost taken to task for it. That happens because people do not understand what I ask; for you and you alone understand what I ask, and you and you alone understand how to answer, and you and you alone understand how to give a good answer; for a good answer is like a sweet kiss, says Solomon.

Thy Johannes.

There is a difference between spiritual love and physical. Hitherto I have chiefly tried to develop the spiritual in Cordelia. My physical presence must now be something different, not only an accompanying mood, it must be a temptation. I have in these days been constantly preparing myself by reading the celebrated passages in *Phaedrus* concerning love. It electrifies my whole being, and is an excellent prelude. Plato really understood about love.[51]

My Cordelia!

A Roman says of an attentive disciple that he hangs on his master's lips. To love, everything is symbol, and in turn symbol is reality. Am I not a diligent, an attentive disciple? But you, after all, aren't saying a word!

Thy Johannes.

If someone other than myself were guiding this development, he would probably be too clever to allow himself to be guided. If I were to consult an initiate among the engaged, he would probably declare with a haughty gesture of erotic boldness: "I seek in vain in these positions of love for the sonorous figures in which the lovers talk about their love." I should answer: "I am glad that you do seek in vain; for figures of speech simply do not belong within the intrinsic limits of the erotic, not even if one includes the interesting. Love is far too substantial to be satisfied with chitchat; the erotic situations far too important to be filled up with chitchat. They are silent, still, in definite outlines, and yet eloquent as the music of Memnon's statue.[52] Eros gestures, he does not speak; or, in so far as he does, it is a mysterious hint, a symbolic music. Erotic situations are always either plastic or picturesque; but for two people to talk together about their love is neither plastic nor picturesque. The substantial engagement, however, always begins with such small talk, which later becomes the connecting thread in their garrulous marriage. This small talk also furnishes assurance that their marriage will not lack the dowry Ovid speaks about: *dos est uxoria lites*.[53]

If there is talking to be done, it is sufficient for one to do it. The man ought to do the talking, and therefore he ought to be in possession of some of the powers that lay in the girdle of Venus, with which she beguiled men: conversation and sweet insinuating flattery.

It by no means follows that Eros is silent, or that it would be erotically incorrect to converse, but the conversation itself should be erotic, not lost in edifying observations about the prospects for life, and so on, and it should be regarded essentially as a respite from the erotic act, a pastime, not as the highest. Such a conversation, such a *confabulatio*, is quite divine in its nature, and I never weary of talking with a young girl. That is to say, I can get tired of talking with a particular young girl, but never of talking with a young girl. That is just as impossible for me as to get tired of breathing. That which is the essential characteristic of such a conversation is its vegetative flowering. The conversation is held down to earth, it has no essential objective, and the accidental is the law for its movement—but as charming and profuse as the daisy (*Bellis perennis*), a source of perpetual delight.

My Cordelia!

"My—Thy" these words enclose like a parenthesis the impoverished content of my letters. Have you noticed that the distance between its arms is growing shorter? Oh, my Cordelia! It is beautiful that the emptier the parenthesis becomes, the more significant it becomes.

Thy Johannes.

My Cordelia!

Is an embrace an appeal to arms?

Thy Johannes.

Generally Cordelia keeps silent. This has always pleased me. She has too deep a feminine nature to worry one with hiatuses, a fashion of speech particularly characteristic of women, and one which is inevitable when the man who should provide the preceding or the following limiting consonant, is equally feminine. Sometimes, however, a single brief utterance betrays how much there is in her, and then I can help her. It is as if behind a man who with an unsteady hand roughly sketched an outline drawing, there was standing another who constantly brought something bold and well rounded out of this. Even she is surprised, and yet it seems to be her own. So I watch over her, over every casual remark, every loosely dropped word, and when I give it back to her, it always becomes something more significant, something she both knows and does not know.

Today we were at a party. We had not exchanged a word with each other. We were leaving the table; a servant came in and informed Cordelia that a messenger wished to speak with her. This messenger was from me, he brought a letter which alluded to a remark I had made at the table. I had managed to introduce it into the general table conversation so that Cordelia, although she sat at a distance from me, must necessarily overhear it and misunderstand it. The letter was calculated with this in mind. Had I not been fortunate enough to give the conversation this turn, then I should have been ready at the right time to confiscate the letter. When she returned to the room, she had to tell a little fib. Such things consolidate the erotic mystery, without which she cannot progress on her appointed way.

My Cordelia!

Do you believe that he who lays his head on a fairy hillock sees the image of a fairy in his dreams? I do not know, but I do know this, that when I rest my head upon your breast, and then do not close my eyes, but peep up through my eyelids, then I see an angel's face. Do you believe that he whose head reclined on a fairy hillock cannot lie quiet? I do not believe it; but I know that when my head rests on your bosom, I am moved too strongly for sleep to close my eyes.

Thy Johannes.

Jacta est alea.[54] Now the change begins. I was with her today, quite carried away by an idea that has always engaged my thought. I had neither eyes nor ears for her. The idea was interesting in itself, and it fascinated her. Besides, it would have been wrong to begin this new plan of action by treating her coldly. Now when I have left her and the idea no longer interests her, she will readily discover that I was different from what I used to be. That she should come to realize this change when she is by herself makes it more painful to her; it acts more slowly but more earnestly upon her. She cannot immediately flare up, and so when the opportunity does come, she has already imagined so much that she cannot find expression for it all at once, but will retain a residuum of doubt. Unrest increases, the letters cease, the erotic nourishment is diminished, love is ridiculed as laughable. Perhaps she goes along with it for a short time, but in the long run, she cannot endure it. Then she wishes to captivate me by the same means I had used with her, by means of the erotic.

In the matter of breaking off an engagement, every little maiden is a born casuist; and although the schools offer no courses in it, every girl is ready with an excellent answer when the question is, under what circumstances an engagement ought to be broken. This really ought to be a routine question in the school examinations of the senior year; and, while I know that the themes one usually gets in girls' schools are very monotonous, yet I am certain that here one would not lack variety, since the problem itself offers a wide range for a girl's acumen. And why should not a girl be given an opportunity to sharpen her wits in the best manner possible? And does not this afford her an opportunity to show that she is mature enough—to be engaged? I once had an experience which interested me very much. In a family where I sometimes visited, the elders were away one day, and the two young daughters had invited a group of their girl friends for a forenoon coffee party. There were eight in all, ranging from sixteen to twenty years old. They had probably not expected any visitors; indeed, the maid had orders to say they were not at home. However, I went in, and realized clearly that they were a little surprised. Heaven only knows what eight young girls like that really talk about in such a solemn synodical meeting. Married women, too, sometimes assemble in similar meetings. They of course discuss pastoral theology; especially the important question as to whether it is proper to let the maid go alone to the market; whether it is better to have an account with the butcher, or to pay cash; whether it is probable that the cook has a sweetheart, and how best to discourage his coming so that he won't interfere with her duties.

I took my place in this beautiful circle. It was very early in spring. The sun sent a few scattered rays as harbingers of its coming. Inside everything was still wintry, and this made the sunbeams so welcome. The coffee on the table gave forth its rich aroma—and the young girls themselves were happy, healthy, blooming, frolicsome; for their anxiety was soon allayed, and besides, what was there to be afraid of? After all, they had the strength of numbers. I succeeded in turning their attention and their talk to the question of the conditions under which an engagement ought to be broken. While my eye amused itself by flitting from one flower to another in this garland of girls, amused itself by resting now on one, now on another beauty, while my outer ear reveled in the enjoyment of their musical voices, my inner ear listened to their observations on the question. A single word often enabled me to get a deep insight into a girl's heart and its history. How seductive is the way of love, and how interesting to investigate how far along this way the individual has come. I constantly stimulated them; cleverness, wit, aesthetic objectivity combined to make the relationship freer, and yet everything was kept within the bounds of strictest decorum. While we thus jested in the easy give and take of conversation, there slumbered the possibility of causing these good children an unfortunate embarrassment. This possibility lay in my power. The girls themselves neither knew nor suspected it. Through the easy play of the conversation, this possibility was at every moment held in abeyance, just as Scheherezade held the death warrant away by her storytelling.[55]

Sometimes I carried the conversation to the verge of sadness; sometimes I let wantonness run wild; sometimes I tried them in a dialectical game. And what other subject contains so many possibilities in itself, however one looks at it? I constantly suggested new themes. I told about a girl who was forced by the cruelty of her parents to break her engagement. The unhappy collision almost brought tears to their eyes. I told them about a man who had broken his engagement, and who had given two reasons for doing so, first, that the girl was too tall, and, second, that he had not gone on his knees to her when he proposed. When I objected that these were insufficient reasons, he answered that they were sufficient to accomplish what he wanted; certainly no one can give a logical answer to that. I presented for the consideration of the assembly a very difficult case. A young girl broke her engagement because she felt convinced that she and her sweetheart were not suited to each other. The lover tried to bring her to reason by assuring her of how much he loved her; then she would answer him: "Either we are suited to each other, and there is a real sympathy between us, so that you will realize that we are not suited to each other; or we are not suited to each other, and then you will realize that we are not suited to each other." It was quite gratifying to see how the girls racked their brains over this puzzling story, and I could clearly see that a couple of them really understood it; for on the question of whether to break an engagement or not, every girl is a born casuist. I really believe it would be easier for me to dispute with the devil himself than with a young girl, when the question is under what circumstances one ought to break an engagement.

Today I was with Cordelia. With the speed of thought, I adroitly directed the conversation to the same subject we had considered yesterday, in a renewed effort to arouse ecstasy within her. "There is something I really should have said yesterday; it occurred to me after I had gone." That succeeded. As long as I am with her she enjoys listening to me; when I have gone, she realizes that she has been cheated, and that I am changed. In this way one extends his credit. This method is underhanded, but entirely expedient, like all indirect methods. She can very well argue to herself that the things I talk about can really engross me, that they even interest her for the moment, and yet I defraud her of the real erotic.

Oderint, dum metuant[56]—as if only fear and hate belong together, while fear and love have nothing to do with one another! As if it were not fear that makes love interesting! With what kind of love do we embrace nature? Is there not a secret fear and terror in it, because this beautiful harmony stems from lawlessness and wild confusion, its security from insecurity? But just this anxiety is most fascinating. So, too, with love, if it is to claim our interest. At the bottom of this, there ought to brood the deep fearful night from which the flower of love springs forth. So the chalice of *nymphæa alba*, the white water lily, rests on the surface of the water, while thought fears to plunge down into the profound blackness where it has its root.—I have noticed that she always calls me *mine* when she writes to me; but she lacks the courage to say it to me. Today I begged her to do it, with all the insinuating and erotic warmth possible. She started to do so; an ironic glance, indescribably swift and brief, was enough to make it impossible for her, although my lips urged her with all their might. This mood is entirely normal.

She is mine. I do not confide this to the stars, as use and custom prescribe. I do not really see how this information can interest those distant spheres. Neither do I confide it to any human being, not even to Cordelia. This secret I keep for myself alone, whisper it to myself, as it were, even in my most secret conversations with myself. The attempted resistance on her part was not particularly strong; on the other hand, the erotic energy she is developing is admirable. How interesting she is in this deep passionateness, how great she becomes, almost supernaturally so! How supple she is in evasion, how pliant in insinuating herself wherever she discovers a vulnerable point. Everything is in movement, but in these elemental storms I find myself precisely in my element. And yet she is by no means unbeautiful even in this commotion, not distracted in her moods, nor dissipated in the elements. She is always an Aphrodite, except that she does not rise up in naïve charm, nor in immaculate serenity, but is influenced by the strong heart throbs of love, while she retains unity and poise. Erotically she is completely equipped for the struggle, she fights with the darts of her eyes, with the command of her brows, with the secretiveness of her forehead, with the eloquence of her bosom, with the dangerous allurement of the embrace, with the prayer on her lips, with the smile on her face, with all the sweet longing of her entire being. There is a power in her, an energy, as if she were a valkyrie; but this erotic force is in turn tempered by a certain languishing weakness which is breathed out over her.—She must not be held too long at this peak, where only anxiety and unrest can hold her steady, and prevent her from falling. With such emotions she will soon feel that the engagement is too narrow, too confining. She herself will become the tempter who seduces me to go beyond the usual limitation. She will do this consciously, and for me that is the principal consideration.

Now she lets drop numerous remarks which clearly indicate that for her part she is tired of our engagement. They do not pass my ear unheeded, they are the scouts of my operation in the domain of her soul, who give me enlightening hints; they are the ends of the thread by which I weave her into my plan.

My Cordelia!
You complain about the engagement. You think our love does not need an external bond which exists only to hinder. In that I immediately recognize my wonderful Cordelia! In truth, I admire you. Our external union is only a separation. There is still a wall between us that separates us like Pyramus and Thisbe. That people should share our secret is disturbing. Only in opposition is there liberty. Only when no outsider suspects the love does it become significant. When every stranger believes that the lovers hate each other, only then is love happy.

Thy Johannes.

Soon the engagement will be broken. She herself is the one who breaks it, in order, if possible, by releasing me to bind me more strongly, as flowing locks entangle more than those which are bound up. If I were the one to break the engagement, then I should miss this erotic *salto mortale* which is so seductive to look at, and so certain an indication of the daring of her spirit. This is the main thing to me. Add to this the fact that the whole incident might cause me a great many unpleasant consequences, because of its effect upon other people. I should be blamed, hated, detested, although unjustly so. For might it not be very advantageous to many? There are many little maidens, who, in default of an engagement, would be quite satisfied with having been mighty close to it. That is always something, even though, to tell the truth, it be painfully little; for when one has pushed oneself forward to get a place on the waiting list, then precisely one has nothing to await; the higher one rises on the list and the more one gets advanced, the less there is to expect. In the world of love, the principle of seniority with respect to advancement is not in force. So it happens that such a little maiden is tired of retaining undivided possession of the estate; she wants her life to be stirred by an event. But what is there comparable to an unhappy love affair, especially when one can take the matter so lightly? Consequently, she deludes herself and her neighbor into thinking that she has been deceived, and since she is not eligible for admission to a Magdalen hospital, she takes lodgings by the side of it, in the tear-jerking press. I get hated, as a matter of duty.

In addition, there is still another division of those who have been wholly, or half, or three-quarters deceived. In this class there are many degrees, ranging from those who have a ring to appeal to, to those who pin their hopes on the squeezing of the hand at a country-dance. Their wounds are torn open again by this new pain. I accept their hate as a bonus. But all these hates are naturally like so many secret loves to my poor heart. A king without a country is a laughable figure; but a war of succession between a crowd of pretenders to a kingdom without a country—this outstrips itself as the most laughable of all. Consequently, I ought to be loved and taken care of by the fair sex as a pawnshop. A real fiancé can only take care of one, but such a diffuse possibility as I am can tolerably well provide for as many as may be. All this finite nonsense I become free from, and I also have the advantage of afterwards being able to appear in an entirely new role. The girls will pity me, sympathize with me, sigh for me; I strike in in exactly the same key; also in this way one may catch something.

Strangely enough, I notice now with dismay that I am getting the indicative sign which Horace wished on all faithless girls—a black tooth, and a front tooth at that! How superstitious we still can be. The tooth disturbs me extraor-

dinarily. I can't really stand any allusion to it; that is a weak
side I have. While in other respects I am fully armed, here
even the veriest bungler can give me a shock, which goes
deeper than he thinks, when he touches on the tooth. I do
everything possible to make it white, but in vain. I say
with Palnatoke:

> I rub it by day and night,
> But I cannot erase this dark shadow.[57]

Life still holds an extraordinary amount of mystery. Such
a little circumstance can disturb me more than the most
dangerous attack, the most painful situation. I would let
them extract it, but that would interfere with my speech
and its effectiveness. Still, if I let them take it out, I will
have a false one set in; it will be false to the world; the
black one was false to me.

It is capital that Cordelia is so set against an engagement.
Marriage will always be an honorable estate, even though
it has the tedium of enjoying in the early years part of the
honor which should belong to the later years. A betrothal,
on the other hand, is a purely human invention, and, as
such, so remarkable and ridiculous that it is quite natural
that on one side, a young girl in the whirl of passion should
disregard it, and still, on the other side, feel its significance,
feel her soul's energy, like a higher circulatory system, present everywhere in herself. What is necessary here is to direct her, so that in her bold flight she loses sight of marriage, and of the mainland of reality in general, so that
her soul, just as much in her pride as in her fear of losing
me, destroys an imperfect human form, in order to hasten
to something which is higher than humanity in general. As
regards this, however, I do not greatly fear, for Cordelia's
way of life is already so ethereal and light that reality is
to a large degree lost sight of. Besides I am always on board,
and can always break out the sails.

Woman will always offer an inexhaustible fund of material for reflection, an eternal abundance for observation.
The man who feels no impulse toward the study of woman

may, as far as I am concerned, be what he will; one thing he certainly is not, he is no aesthetician. This is the glory and divinity of aesthetics, that it enters into relation only with the beautiful: it has to do essentially only with fiction and the fair sex. It makes me glad and causes my heart to rejoice when I represent to myself how the sun of feminine loveliness diffuses its rays into an infinite manifold, refracting itself in a confusion of tongues, where each individual woman has her little part of the whole wealth of femininity, yet so that her other characteristics harmoniously center about this point. In this sense feminine beauty is infinitely divisible. But the particular share of beauty which each one has must be present in a harmonious blending, for otherwise the effect will be disturbing, and it will seem as if Nature had intended something by this woman, but nothing ever came of it.

My eyes can never weary of surveying this peripheral manifold, these scattered emanations of feminine beauty. Each particular has its little share, and yet is complete in itself, happy, glad, beautiful. Every woman has her share: the merry smile, the roguish glance, the wistful eye, the pensive head, the exuberant spirits, the quiet sadness, the deep foreboding, the brooding melancholy, the earthly homesickness, the unbaptized movements, the beckoning brows, the questioning lips, the mysterious forehead, the ensnaring curls, the concealing lashes, the heavenly pride, the earthly modesty, the angelic purity, the secret blush, the light step, the airy grace, the languishing posture, the dreamy yearning, the inexplicable sighs, the willowy form, the soft outlines, the luxuriant bosom, the swelling hips, the tiny foot, the dainty hand.—Each woman has her own traits, and the one does not merely repeat the other. And when I have gazed and gazed again, considered and again considered this multitudinous variety, when I have smiled, sighed, flattered, threatened, desired, tempted, laughed, wept, hoped, feared, won, lost—then I shut up my fan, and gather the fragments into a unity, the parts into a whole. Then my soul is glad, my heart beats, my passion is aflame. This one woman, the only woman in all the world, she must belong to me, she must be mine. Let God keep His heaven, if only I can keep her. I know full well what I choose; it is something so great that heaven itself must be the loser by such a division, for what would be left to heaven if I keep her? The faithful Mohammedans will be disappointed in their hopes when in their Paradise they embrace pale, weak shadows; for warm hearts they cannot find, since all the warmth of the heart is concentrated in her breast; they will yield themselves to a comfortless despair when they find pale lips, lustreless eyes, a lifeless bosom, a limp pressure of the hand; for all the redness of the lips and the fire of the eye and the heaving of the bosom and the promise of the hand and the foreboding of the sigh and the seal of the kiss and the trembling of the touch and the passion of the embrace—all, all are concentrated in her, who lavishes on me a wealth sufficient for a whole world, both for time and eternity.

Thus I have often reflected upon this matter; but every time I conceive woman thus, I become warm, because I think of her as warm. And though in general, warmth is accounted a good sign, it does not follow that my mode of thinking will be granted the respectable predicate that it is solid. Hence I shall now for variety's sake attempt, myself being cold, to think coldly of woman. I shall attempt to think of woman in terms of her category. Under what category must she be conceived? Under the category of being for another. But this must not be understood in the bad sense, as if the woman who is for me is also for another. Here as always in abstract thinking, it is essential to refrain from every reference to experience; for otherwise, as in the present case, I should find, in the most curious manner, that experience is both for me and against me. Here as always, experience is a most curious thing, because its nature is always to be both for and against. Woman is therefore being for another. Here again, but from another side, it will be necessary not to let oneself be disturbed by experience, which teaches that it is a rare thing to find a woman who is in truth a being for another, since a great many are in general absolutely nothing, either for themselves or for others. Woman shares this category with Nature, and, in general, with everything feminine. Nature as a whole exists only for another; not in the teleological sense, so that one part of Nature exists for another part, but so that the whole of Nature is for an Other—for the Spirit. In the same way with the particulars. The life of the plant, for example, unfolds in all naïveté its hidden charms and exists only for another. In the same way a mystery, a charade, a secret, a vowel, and so on, has being only for another. And from this it can be explained why, when God created Eve, He caused a deep sleep to fall upon Adam; for woman is the dream of man. In still another way the story teaches that woman is a being for another. It tells, namely, that Jehovah created Eve from a rib taken from the side of man. Had she been taken from man's brain, for example, woman would indeed still have been a being for another; but it was not the intention to make her a figment of the brain, but something quite different. She became flesh and blood, but this causes her to be included under the category of Nature, which is essentially being for another. She awakens first at the touch of love; before that time she is a dream. Yet in her dream life we can distinguish two stages: in the first, love dreams about her; in the second, she dreams about love.

As being for another, woman is characterized by pure virginity. Virginity is, namely, a form of being, which, in so far as it is a being for itself, is really an abstraction, and only reveals itself to another. The same characterization also lies in the concept of female innocence. It is therefore possible to say that woman in this condition is invisible. As is well known, there existed no image of Vesta, the goddess who most nearly represented feminine virginity. This form of existence is, namely, jealous for itself aesthetically, just as Jehovah is ethically, and does not desire that there should be any image or even any notion of one. This is the contradiction, that the being which is for another *is* not, and only becomes visible, as it were, by the interposition of another. Logically, this contradiction will be found to be quite in order, and he who knows how to think logically will not be disturbed by it, but will be glad in it. But whoever thinks illogically will imagine that whatever is a being for another *is,* in the finite sense in which one can say about a particular thing: that is something for me.

This being of woman (for the word *existence* is too rich in meaning, since woman does not persist in and through herself[58]) is rightly described as charm, an expression which suggests plant life; she is a flower, as the poets like to say, and even the spiritual in her is present in a vegetative manner. She is wholly subject to Nature, and hence only aesthetically free. In a deeper sense she first becomes free by her relation to man, and when man courts her properly, there can be no question of a choice.[59] Woman chooses, it is true, but if this choice is thought of as the result of a long deliberation, then this choice is unfeminine. Hence it is, that it is a humiliation to receive a refusal, because the individual in question has rated himself too high, has desired to make another free without having the power.—In this situation there is deep irony. That which merely exists for another has the appearance of being predominant: man sues, woman chooses. The very concept of woman requires that she be the vanquished; the concept of man, that he be the victor; and yet the victor bows before the vanquished. And yet this is quite natural, and it is only boorishness, stupidity, and lack of erotic sensibility to take no notice of that which immediately yields in this fashion. It has also a deeper ground. Woman is, namely, substance, man is reflection. She does not therefore choose independently; man sues, she chooses. But man's courtship is a question, and her choice only an answer to a question. In a certain sense man is more than woman, in another sense he is infinitely less.

This being for another is the true virginity. If it makes an attempt to be a being for itself, in relation to another being which is being for it, then the opposition reveals itself in an absolute coyness; but this opposition shows at the same time that woman's essential being is being for another. The diametrical opposite to absolute devotion is absolute coyness, which in a converse sense is invisible as the abstraction against which everything breaks, without the abstraction itself coming to life. Femininity now takes on the character of an abstract cruelty, the caricature in its extreme form of the intrinsic feminine brittleness. A man can never be so cruel as a woman. Consult mythologies, fables, folk-tales, and you will find this view confirmed. If there is a description of a natural force whose mercilessness knows no limits, it will always be a feminine nature. Or one is horrified at reading about a young woman who callously allows all her suitors to lose their lives, as so often happens in the folk-tales of all nations. A Bluebeard slays all the women he has loved on their bridal night, but he does not find his happiness in slaying them; on the contrary, his happiness has preceded, and in this lies the concreteness; it is not cruelty for the sake of cruelty. A Don Juan seduces them and runs away, but he finds no happiness at all in running away from them, but rather in seducing them; consequently, it is by no means this abstract cruelty.

Thus, the more I reflect on this matter, I see that my practice is in perfect harmony with my theory. My practice has always been impregnated with the theory that woman is essentially a being for another. Hence it is that the moment has here such infinite significance; for a being for another is always the matter of a moment. It may take a longer, it may take a shorter time before the moment comes, but as soon as it has come, then that which was originally a being for another assumes the character of relative being, and then all is over. I know very well that husbands say that the woman is also in another sense a being for another, that she is everything to her husband through life. One must make allowance for husbands. I really believe that it is something which they mutually delude one another into thinking. Every class in society generally has certain conventional customs, and especially certain conventional lies. Among these must be reckoned this sailor's yarn. To be a good judge of the moment is not so easy a matter, and he who misjudges it is in for boredom for the rest of his life. The moment is everything, and in the moment, woman is everything; the consequences I do not understand. Among these consequences is the begetting of children. Now I fancy that I am a fairly consistent thinker, but if I were to think until I became crazy, I am not a man who could think this consequence; I simply do not understand it; to understand it requires a husband.

Yesterday Cordelia and I visited a family at their summer home. The party spent most of the day in the garden, where we passed the time in all sorts of physical exercises. Among other things, we played Ring. I took the opportunity, when another swain who had been playing with Cordelia had gone away, to take his place. What a wealth of charm she revealed, even more seductive than usual, as a result of the beautifying exercise! What graceful harmony in the self-contradiction of her movements. How light she was—like a dance over the meadows! How vigorous, yet without needing opposition, deceptive, until her poise explained everything. How dithyrambic her appearance, how challenging her glance. The game itself had naturally a special interest for me. Cordelia appeared not to notice it. A remark I made to one of the spectators about the beautiful custom of exchanging the rings struck like a bolt of lightning into her soul. From that moment a higher radiance rested over the entire situation, a deeper significance impregnated it, a higher energy pulsed through her being. I held both rings on my stick. I paused a moment, I exchanged a few words with the bystanders. She understood this pause. I again tossed the rings to her. Soon after she caught both of them on her stick. As if inadvertently she tossed them both straight up into the air at once, so high that it was impossible for me to catch them. This toss was accompanied by a glance full of boundless audacity. Someone tells the story of a French soldier who had taken part in the Russian campaign, whose leg was amputated because of gangrene. As soon as the painful operation was finished, he grabbed the leg by the foot, threw it in the air, and shouted: *Vive l'empereur!* With the same kind of look, she threw both rings into the air, even more gracefully than before, and said as if to herself: Long live love! I found it inadvisable to let her run away in this mood, or to leave her alone in it, for fear of the exhaustion that so often follows it. I therefore remained quite calm and, abetted by the presence of the spectators, I obliged her to continue playing, as if I had noticed nothing. Such a procedure gives her more elasticity.

If, in our time, one could expect any support in such an investigation, then I should pose the prize question: aesthetically considered, which is the more modest, a young girl or a young matron, the ignorant or the informed; to which does one dare grant more freedom? But such things do not interest our serious age. In Greece such an inquiry would have aroused general attention; the whole state would have been set in ferment, especially the young maids and matrons. No one in our age would believe this, but neither will anyone now believe, if one were to tell them, about the well-known contest between two Greek girls, and the extremely thoroughgoing investigation it occasioned, for in Greece people did not treat such problems carelessly. And yet everyone knows that Venus bears a surname as a result of this contest, and everyone admires the statue of Venus which has immortalized her.[60] A married woman has two periods in her life when she is interesting: first of all, her youth, and then again, long after, when she has become much older. But she has also—one must not deny her this—a moment when she is even more charming than a young girl, inspires even more respect; but it is a moment which is rarely met with in life, it is rather a picture for the imagination which need not be seen in life, and which perhaps never is seen. I think of her then, healthy, vigorous, well developed; she holds a child on her arm, on whom her whole attention is focused, in whose contemplation she is lost. It is a picture which one might call the most charming that human life has to offer, it is a myth of Nature which must therefore be seen artistically, not in actuality. There should never be additional figures in the picture, no setting, which is only disturbing. If one goes into our churches one often has an opportunity to see a mother approaching with a child in her arms. Disregarding now the disconcerting wail of the child and apart from the anxious thoughts in the expectation of the parents for the future of the little one, occasioned by this childish cry, all the surroundings are already so confusing that, even if everything else were perfect, the effect is lost. One sees the father, which is a great fault, since it destroys the myth, the enchantment; one sees—*horrenda refero*[61]—the sponsors' earnest chorus, and one sees—simply nothing. The conception, as a picture of fantasy, is the most charming of all. I do not lack boldness and briskness, nor rashness enough to venture an assault—but if I saw such a picture in reality, I would be defenseless.

How Cordelia engrosses me! And yet the time is soon over; always my soul requires rejuvenescence. I can already hear, as it were, the far distant crowing of the cock. Perhaps she hears it too, but she believes it heralds the morning.— Why is a young girl so pretty, and why does it last so short a time? I could become quite melancholy over this thought, and yet it is no concern of mine. Enjoy, do not talk. The people who make a business of such deliberations, do not generally enjoy. However, it can do no harm to think about it; for this sadness, not for one's self but for others, makes one a little more attractive in a masculine way. A sadness which darkens like a veil of mist deceptively over the manly strength is one of the things contributing to the masculine erotic. This corresponds to a certain melancholy in women.—When a girl has first given herself entirely, then everything is over. Always I approach a young girl with a certain anxiety, with a rapid pulse, because I feel the eternal power that lies in her nature. In the presence of a married woman I have never experienced it. The slight resistance she tries to offer with the help of art is nothing. It is as if one should say that a married woman's cap is more becoming than a young girl's uncovered head. For that reason Diana has always been my ideal. Her pure virginity, her absolute independence, has greatly engaged my attention. But while she has indeed occupied me, I have always kept a suspicious eye upon her. I imagine that she has not really deserved all the praise for her virginity that she has received. She knew that her role in life depended on her preserving her virginity. It happens that in a philological corner of the world, I have heard mumblings that she had an idea of the terrible birth pains her mother had gone through, and this had frightened her. I cannot blame Diana. I only say with Euripides: I would rather go to war three times than to bear one child. I could not really fall in love with Diana, but I do not deny that I would give much for a conversation with her, for what I might call a heart to heart talk with her. She must be well versed in various kinds of tricks. Obviously my good Diana in one way or another possesses a knowledge which makes her far less naïve even than Venus. I am not interested in spying on her in her bath,[62] not at all, but I would like to spy on her with my questions. If I were stealing off to a rendezvous where I feared for my victory, then I would prepare myself, arm myself, set all the spirits of love in motion, by conversing with her.

A frequent subject of reflection with me has been what situation, what moment should be regarded as the most seductive. The answer to this naturally depends upon what one desires, how one desires it, and how one is developed. I consider it the wedding day, and especially a definite moment on that day. When she then stands decked out as bride, and all the magnificence of her attire pales before her beauty, and she herself turns pale, when the blood almost stops, when her bosom rests, when the glance falters, when the foot gives way, when the maiden trembles, when the fruit ripens; when heaven exalts her, when earnestness strengthens her, when the promise sustains her, when prayers bless her, when the myrtle wreath crowns her; when the heart throbs, when the eyes are downcast, when she hides herself in herself, when she belongs not to the world, but wholly to one; when her bosom swells, when creation sighs, when the voice fails, when the tear trembles, before the riddle is explained, when the torch is lighted, when the bridegroom waits—then has the moment come. Soon it will be too late. There is only one step left, but this is exactly enough for a false step. This moment makes even an insignificant girl significant, even a little Zerlina becomes a significant object. Everything must be unified, the greatest contrasts be united in the moment; if there is something lacking, especially one of the chief contrasts, the situation immediately loses a part of its seductiveness. There is a well-known engraving. It represents a penitent. She looks so young and innocent, that on account of her and her confessor, one is almost embarrassed at wondering what she can really have to confess. She raises her veil a little, she looks out into the world as if seeking something she might perhaps later have an opportunity to confess, and of course one understands that it is nothing more than duty, out of respect for—the father confessor. The situation is really seductive, and since she is the only figure in the piece, there is nothing to prevent one's thinking that the church wherein all this takes place is so spacious that a great many preachers could all preach here at the same time. The situation is highly seductive, and I have no objections to disposing myself in the background, especially if the girl does not object. However, it remains a highly subordinate position, for the girl seems in both senses to be only a child, and consequently there must be time before her moment comes.

Have I been constantly faithful to my pact in my relation to Cordelia? That is to say, my pact with the aesthetic. For it is this which makes me strong, that I always have the idea on my side. This is a secret, like Samson's hair, which no Delilah shall wrest from me. Simply and directly to betray a young girl, that I certainly could not endure; but that the idea is set in motion, that it is in its service that I act, to its service that I dedicate myself, that gives me self-discipline, abstemiousness from every forbidden enjoyment. Has the interesting always been preserved? Yes, I dare say it freely and openly in this secret conversation with myself. Even the engagement was interesting, precisely because it did not offer that which one generally understands by the interesting. It preserved the interesting by the fact of the outward appearance being in contradiction to the inner life. Had I been secretly bound to her, then it would have been interesting only in the first degree. This, however, is interesting in the second degree, and therefore for the first time becomes interesting for her. The engagement is broken, but in such a way that she herself breaks it, in order to raise herself to a higher sphere. So it should be; this is, in fact, the form of the interesting which will occupy her most.

Sept. 16.

The bond burst; longing, strong, daring, divine, she flies like a bird which now for the first time gets the right to stretch its wings. Fly, bird, fly! In truth if this royal flight were a withdrawal from me, then my pain would be in finitely deep. As if Pygmalion's beloved were again turned to stone, so would this be for me.[63] Light have I made her, light as a thought, and why should not this, my thought, belong to me! That would be a cause for despair. A moment earlier it would not have mattered, a moment later it will not trouble me, but now—now—this now, which is an eternity to me! But she does not fly away from me. Fly, then, bird, fly; soar proudly on your wings, glide through the soft realms of the air, soon I shall be with you, soon I shall hide myself with you in a profound solitude!

The aunt was somewhat taken aback by the news. However, she is too liberal to wish to coerce Cordelia, although I, partly to lull her to a sounder sleep, partly to fool Cordelia a little, have made some attempt to get her to interest herself in my behalf. As for the rest, she shows me much sympathy; she does not suspect how much reason I have for deprecating all sympathy.

She has received permission from her aunt to spend some time in the country; she will visit a family. It happens very fortunately that she cannot immediately give herself up to excessive moods. She will still, for some time, be kept tense by all kinds of external criticism. I maintain a desultory communication with her by means of letters, so our relationship is sustained. She must now be strengthened in every way; especially, it is best to permit her to make a few eccentric flights to show her contempt for mankind in general. Then when the day for her departure arrives, a trustworthy man will appear as coachman. Outside the gate my confidential servant will join them. He will accompany her to her destination, and remain with her to render attention and assistance in case of need. Next to myself I know no one who is better fitted for this than John. I have myself arranged everything out there as tastefully as possible.

Nothing is lacking which can in any way serve to delude her soul, and to soothe it with a sense of well-being.

My Cordelia!

Not yet have the cries of "Fire!" rising from individual households merged into a city-wide hubbub, a capitoline cackle of alarm.[64] Individual solos you have probably already had to endure. Consider the whole assembly of tea and coffee dowagers; consider the lady president who furnishes a worthy counterpart to that immortal President Lars in *Claudius,* and you have a picture of and a conception about and a measure for what you have lost and with whom: the esteem of good people.

With this letter I enclose the celebrated copper print which represents President Lars.[65] I could not purchase it separately, and so I bought the whole of *Claudius,* tore it out, and threw the rest away; for how could I dare to trouble you with a gift which would have no significance for you at this time; how should I not do my utmost to procure something which might be acceptable to you, if only for a moment; how could I permit more to be mingled in a situation than belongs to it? Nature has such a prolixity, and so does the man who is enslaved by all the finite relationships of life; but you, my Cordelia, you, in your freedom, would hate it.

Thy Johannes.

Spring is the most beautiful time of the year to fall in love; autumn the most beautiful to reach the goal of one's desires. There is a sadness in the autumn which entirely corresponds to the emotion evoked by the thought of the fulfillment of one's desires. Today I was out at the country place where soon Cordelia will find surroundings that are attuned to her soul. For myself I do not desire to participate in her surprise and pleasure over this; such erotic conditions would only enervate her soul. If she is alone there, she will pass her time in reverie. Everywhere she will see allusions, hints, an enchanted world, but all this would lose its significance if I were with her; it would cause her to forget that for us the period of time when such things enjoyed in fellowship had significance is past. This environment must not like a narcotic ensnare her soul, but constantly incite it to rise up, because she sees it as a game, which has no significance in comparison with that which is to come. I myself intend in these days which still remain to visit this place more often in order to retain my mood.

My Cordelia!

Now I call you *mine* in truth. No external sign reminds me of my possession.—Soon I call you mine in truth. And when I hold you fast in my arms, when you entwine me in your embrace, then we need no ring to remind us that we belong to each other, for is not this embrace a ring which is more than a sign. And the more firmly this ring encloses us, the more inseparably it knits us together, the greater the freedom, for your freedom consists in being mine, as mine in being yours.

Thy Johannes.

My Cordelia!

While hunting, Alpheus fell in love with the nymph Arethusa. She would not grant his prayer, but always fled before him, until on the island of Ortygia she was changed into a spring. Alpheus sorrowed over this so bitterly that he was changed into a river in Elis in the Peloponnesus. However, he did not forget his love, but united himself under the sea with this spring. Is the time of changes past? Answer: Is the time of love over? With what can I compare your pure deep soul, which has no connection with the world, except with a spring? And have I not said to you that I am like a river which has fallen in love? And since we are separated, am I not plunging under the sea to be united with you? There under the sea we meet again, for first in this depth do we really belong together.

Thy Johannes.

My Cordelia!

Soon, soon, you are mine. When the sun closes its spying eye, when history is over and the myths begin, then I not only fling my cloak about me, but I fling the night about

me like a cloak, and hasten to you, and hearken to find
you, not by the sound of footfalls, but by the beating of
your heart.

Thy Johannes.

In these days when I cannot be with her personally
whenever I wish, I have been disturbed by the thought
that it may occur to her to consider the future. So far it
has not happened, for I have known how to drug her aesthetically. Nothing less erotic can be imagined than this talk
about the future, which is usually the result of one's having
nothing with which to fill the present. If only I am present,
then I have no such fear, for I can make her forget both
time and eternity. If a man does not understand how to
put himself in rapport with a girl, he should never attempt
to deceive, for then it will be impossible to escape the two
rocks: questions about the future, and a catechizing about
faith. Hence it is quite proper that Gretchen should conduct
such an examination of Faust, since he had been imprudent
enough to display his chivalry; and against such an attack,
a girl is always armed.

Now I believe everything is in order for her reception;
she must not lack occasion to admire my memory, or,
rather, she must get no time to admire it. Nothing is forgotten which could have any significance for her, and, on
the other hand, nothing is included which might directly
remind her of me, while still I am everywhere invisibly
present. The effect will, however, largely depend on the
circumstances under which she sees it for the first time.
With regard to this my servant has received most particular
instructions, and he is in his way a perfect virtuoso. He
knows how to drop a remark accidentally and casually
when so ordered; he knows how to be ignorant, in short,
he is invaluable to me.—The arrangement is everything she
might wish. If she sits in the center of the room, she can
look out in both directions with nothing to obstruct the
view; on both sides it stretches away to an infinite horizon,
she is alone in a wide sea of air. If she comes nearer a
broad bank of windows on the one side, there, far on the

horizon is a forest curving like a wreath, limiting and enclosing. That is the way it should be. What does love love?
—An enclosure; was not Paradise itself an enclosed place, a
garden toward the east? But it closes itself too tightly about
one, this ring—she comes nearer the window, a placid lake
lies humbly concealed between its higher shores, a boat
lies at the water's edge. A sigh from the fullness of the
heart, a gust from the thought's unrest—it loosens itself from
its moorings, it glides over the surface of the lake, softly
moved by the gentle breezes of inexpressible longing; one
disappears into the mysterious solitude of the forest, cradled
on the surface of the lake which dreams of the deep shadow
of the woods.

One turns to the other side, where the sea spreads out
before the sight with nothing to limit it, filled with thoughts
which nothing restrains.—What does love love? Infinitude.
What does love fear? Limitation.—Beyond this large room
there is a smaller one, or rather a cabinet, for whatever
that room in the Wahl house purported to be, this is it.
The likeness is delusive. A carpet woven of osiers covers
the floor; before the sofa stands a little tea table, a lamp
upon it which matches the one at home. Everything is the
same, only richer. This difference I allow myself in the
room. In the salon stands a piano, a very simple one, but
reminiscent of the one found at the Jansens. It is open; on
the music-rest a little Swedish melody stands open. The
door into the entry stands ajar. She comes in at the door at
the back of the room, as John has been instructed. Her eye
takes in at once the cabinet and the piano. Memory awakens
in her; at that moment John opens the door. The illusion
is perfect. She goes into the cabinet. She is pleased, I am
sure of that. As she glances at the table, she sees a book.
Just then John picks it up as if to lay it to one side, as he
casually adds: "The master must have forgotten this, when
he was out here this morning." Thus she learns for the first
time that I had already been out there in the morning.
Next she looks at the book. It is a German translation of
the well-known work by Apuleius: *Amor and Psyche*. It is
not poetry, nor should it be; for it is always an insult to
a young girl to offer her a poetical work, as if in such a

moment she were not poetical enough to absorb the poetry which lies immediately concealed in the situation, and which has not been predigested in another's thought. People generally do not consider this, but it is true. She will read the book, and thereby its purpose is attained. When she opens to the place where it was last read, there she will find a little sprig of myrtle; she will also find that this signifies a little more than being a mere bookmark.[66]

My Cordelia!

What, frightened? When we keep together, then are we strong, stronger than the world, stronger even than the gods themselves. You know there once lived a race of people on the earth who were indeed men, but who were each self-sufficient, not knowing the inner union of love.[67] Yet they were mighty, so mighty that they could storm heaven. Jupiter feared them, and divided them so that from one came two, a man and a woman. Now, if it sometimes happens that what had once been united is united again in love, then is such a union stronger than Jupiter. They are not only as strong as the individuals were, but even stronger, for love's union is an even higher union.

Thy Johannes.

Sept. 24.

The night is still—the clock strikes a quarter before twelve. The watchman by the gate blows his benediction out over the countryside. It echoes back from Bleacher's Green—he goes inside the gate—he blows again, it echoes even farther.—Everything sleeps in peace, everything except love. So rise up, ye mysterious powers of love, gather yourselves together in this breast! The night is silent—only a lonely bird breaks this silence with its cry and the beat of its wings, as it skims over the dewy field down the glacial slope to its rendezvous—*accipio omen!*[68] How portentous all Nature is! I read the omen in the flight of birds, in their cries, in the playful flap of the fish against the surface of the water, in their vanishing into its depth, in the distant baying of the hounds, in a wagon's faraway rumble, in footfalls which echo in the distance. I do not see specters in this night hour; I do not see that which has been, but that which will be, in the bosom of the sea, in the kiss of the dew, in the mist that spreads out over the earth, and hides its fertile embrace. Everything is symbol; I myself am a myth about myself, for is it not as a myth that I hasten to this meeting? Who I am has nothing to do with it. Everything finite and temporal is forgotten, only the eternal remains, the power of love, its longing, its happiness. Now my soul is attuned like a bent bow, now my thoughts lie ready like arrows in my quiver, not poisoned, and yet able to blend themselves with the blood. How vigorous is my soul, sound, happy, omnipresent like a god.—Her beauty was a gift of Nature. I give thee thanks, O wonderful Nature! Like a mother hast thou watched over her. Accept my gratitude for thy care. Unsophisticated was she. I thank you, you human beings, to whom she was indebted for this. Her development was my handiwork—soon I shall enjoy my reward.—How much I have gathered into this one moment which now draws nigh. Damnation—if I should fail!

I do not yet see my carriage.—I hear the crack of the whip, it is my coachman.—Drive now for dear life, even if the horses drop dead, only not a single second before we reach the place.

Sept. 25.

Why cannot such a night be longer? If Alectryon could forget himself, why cannot the sun be equally sympathetic?[69] Still, it is over now, and I hope never to see her again. When a girl has given away everything, then she is weak, then she has lost everything. For a man guilt is a negative moment; for a woman it is the value of her being. Now all resistance is impossible, and only as long as that is present is it beautiful to love; when it is ended there is only weakness and habit. I do not wish to be reminded of my relation to her; she has lost the fragrance, and the time is past when a girl suffering the pain of a faithless love can be changed into a sunflower.[70] I will have no farewell scene with her; nothing is more disgusting to me than a woman's tears and a woman's prayers, which alter everything, and yet really mean nothing. I have loved her, but from now on she can no longer engross my soul. If I were a god, I would do for her what Neptune did for a nymph: I would change her into a man.

It would, however, really be worth while to know whether or not one might be able to poetize himself out of a girl, so that one could make her so proud that she would imagine that it was she who tired of the relationship. It could become a very interesting epilogue, which, in its own right, might have psychological interest, and along with that enrich one with many erotic observations.

NOTES AND INDEX

NOTES

1. The motto for A's Papers is from Edward Young, the eighteenth-century English poet, who published sensitive, philosophical poems under the title *The Complaint, or Night-Thoughts on Life, Death and Immortality*. The quotation can be found in "The Fourth Night," verses 629–30. It expresses a demand that the passions be recognized as legitimate and sacred. Compare the motto for B's Papers in the second volume of *Either/Or*.

2. The familiar philosophical maxim in the Hegelian philosophy.

3. Xerxes had the Hellespont whipped when his first bridge over it was destroyed by a storm (Herodotus, vii, 35).

4. *Diapsalmata* is the Greek plural for the Hebrew *selah*, a word occurring frequently in the Psalms of David at the end of a verse. The exact meaning of the word is in doubt. It could be a liturgical direction, perhaps indicating a pause for the playing of a musical interlude. But in *Either/Or*, Kierkegaard has availed himself of another possible meaning. Coming each time at the end of a verse, *diapsalm* might be taken to mean *refrain*, and it is clear from his Journals (*Papirer*, III B 175) that he understands the term in this second sense. As refrains the *Diapsalmata* are always saying the same thing, the same thing over and over again, *idem per idem*, as we read in one of them. "They are variations on the theme of world-weariness: boredom, indolence, malice, contempt, cynicism, desperation" (Billeskov Jansen). At the same time, we must not be surprised to find in the *Diapsalmata* many contradictions, for S.K. tells us that the moods of the romanticist are contradictory and without essential continuity.

5. *Ad se ipsum:* to himself; Latin version of the Greek title to the *Meditations* of Marcus Aurelius.

6. April 7, 1834, actually did fall on Monday.

7. Diogenes Laertius was the author of *Lives of Eminent Philosophers*. Cf. I, 13.

8. Jøcher was the author of *Allgemeines Gelehrten-Lexicon* (Leipzig, 1750); Morèri, the author of *Le grand Dictionnaire historique* (Basel, 1731).

9. *The White Lady* was a Danish opera based on Scott's *The Monastery*.

10. With no attempt at writing poetry, we may give the meaning of these lines by saying:

High rank, knowledge, renown,
Friendship, pleasure, and possessions
—Everything is nought but wind, vapor:
To say it better, everything is nothing.

The verse is by the French writer, Paul Pelisson (1624–93). Kierkegaard probably got it from Lessing's *Zerstreute Anmerkungen über das Epigramm*.

11. According to Lucian (*Phalaris*, I, 11), Phalaris, tyrant of Agrigentum, roasted his prisoners in a brazen bull; reeds had been placed in the nostrils of the bull in such wise that the shrieks of the prisoners were transmuted into music.

12. Jonathan Swift, English satirist, died insane, 1745.

13. David Hartley was an English philosopher and physician, 1705–57.

14. Cornelius Nepos was a Roman historian of the first century B.C.; cf. his biography of Eumenes (V, 4–5).

15. A *shewa*, in Hebrew grammar, is a sign consisting of two dots placed under a consonant at the beginning of a syllable to indicate a quick, unaccented vowel sound. A *daghesh lene*, in Hebrew grammar, is a point placed in a consonant to indicate its degree of hardness.

16. "Their reward taken away" was said (incorrectly) of "the hypocrites" in the authorized Danish version of the Bible used by S.K. Cf. Matthew 6:16. In subsequent versions the mistake, which misled Kierkegaard by totally missing the irony of the New Testament passage, has been corrected.

17. The mythological hero, Lynceus, was reputed to have had unusually sharp eyes. Mythology tells us that the giants, overcome by the gods, were imprisoned under volcanic mountains, whence came outbreaks, noises, sighs.

18. The Greek word here translated "whipped top" is

memastigomenos, which means flogged or whipped. The word is used in the Greek translation of the Old Testament, Job 15:11. Older readers will remember that tops spun by whipping were once popular.

19. During the Middle Ages the Roman poet, Virgil, was regarded as a sorcerer.

20. The Reverend Jesper Morten is an echo of Baggesen's *Jeppe,* the tenth song.

21. Apis was the sacred bull of Memphis.

22. "The same in the same."

23. The "immortal overture" is, of course, the overture to Mozart's *Don Giovanni.*

24. According to Apuleius, Cupid told Psyche their child would be immortal if she kept the secret of its paternity, only human if she betrayed it. The verses cited are from Joseph Kehrein's metrical translation of *Amor und Psyche.*

25. The story about Parmeniscus, the Pythagorean, to which Kierkegaard alludes, was related by Athenaeus, xiv, 614.

26. "Thou art fulfilled, thou nightwatch of my life."

27. The speakers in this dialogue are Demosthenes, Athenian general, and Nicias, a statesman. In the play Aristophanes represents them as slaves of Demos, who personifies the Athenian people. Kierkegaard cites the original Greek; the translation used here is that of J. H. Frere.

28. To "die the death" is reminiscent of Genesis 2:17.

29. Here Kierkegaard ascribes to A the teaching of the philosopher Stilpon, who denied the possibility of asserting anything about anything else.

30. In *Wissenschaft der Logik,* Hegel speaks of the *positive-infinite judgment* which is, in fact, no judgment at all, for subject and predicate are identical. Such a judgment is a *tautology,* i.e., attributing to a concept or an object several designations, all of which mean the same thing. When S.K. here calls these tautologies *paradoxical* and *transcendent,* he is following Hegel's description of them as "repugnant to common-sense" (*widersinnig*). Obviously Kierkegaard means to distinguish between good and bad tautologies. The first are paradoxical and playful, with the help of which the aesthete holds at bay reality and its de-

mand that one choose and thus would seek to avoid ethics and its either/or. We shall have an example of this in the "ecstatic lecture" entitled "Either/Or" which follows presently. The others are the serious tautologies, the empty repetitions so dear to orators and preachers.

31. Diogenes Laertius ascribes a similar utterance to Socrates (ii, 33), a fact which S.K. notes in the margin of his own copy of *Either/Or*.

32. Kierkegaard uses *aeterno modo* in the sense of Spinoza's *sub specie aeternitatis:* from the viewpoint of eternity.

33. Sintenis, German author of a book of devotions called *Stunden für die Ewigkeit gelebt,* Berlin, 1791.

34. *Nyboder* is the name given to a series of row houses built in Copenhagen for occupancy by the families of sailors permanently attached to the Royal Navy. Within this quarter there was an orphanage. In 1817 the orphanage was destroyed by a fire in which several children perished. It was this occurrence, presumably, which gives point and pathos to the present passage.

35. Infants weeping in Elysium, as described in Virgil's *Aeneid*, VI, 426 ff.

36. "The angel of death" is an allusion to Exodus 12:23 ff.

"THE IMMEDIATE STAGES OF THE EROTIC"

1. In Rome the "optimate" was the political designation for the aristocratic party; here the term is used metaphorically for the sake of the play on words with "optimism."

2. The phrase "kingdom of the gods" is reminiscent of what Kineas, the emissary of King Pyrrhus to Rome, said about the Roman senate, "an assembly of many kings" (Plutarch, *Pyrrhus,* 19).

3. The school of aestheticians here accused of one-sidedness is represented by, for instance, C. H. Weisse, *System der Aesthetic,* 1830.

4. *The Battle between the Frogs and Mice,* mock epic, formerly attributed to Homer.

5. "Reception-piece" was a term applied to the painting

an artist must produce to secure admission to the Academy of Arts.

6. Here we encounter two Danish words, both of which we shall meet many times again in this book and both of which present difficulties for the translator.

In Danish, the word *sandselig* (here translated as "sensuous") has to do double duty and serve to mean both *sensuous* and *sensual*. In English, of course, the former word is free of implied moral censure, which is not true of the latter word; but Danish does not make this distinction.

Sometimes it would seem from the context that we must render *det Sandselige* and *Sandselighed* by *the sensuous* and *sensuousness;* other times, by *the sensual* and *sensuality;* but there are still other times when the translator hasn't known *which* to use, for it is difficult to be precise when the Danish to be translated is not itself precise on this point.

In this essay the English ear expects to hear Don Juan accused of *sensuality*. It comes as a jolt, therefore, to find (in this translation) that to Don Juan nothing more serious is attributed than *sensuousness*. Yet the arguments of several scholars, T. H. Croxall among them, have availed to convince most students of Kierkegaard that A, the "young man" who writes this essay on Don Juan, has no intention of introducing a moral issue; his Don Juan is not guilty of sensuality but simply represents sensuousness—an amoral wild impulse following its purely natural urge. *Sandselighed* is no more than an obscure, elemental force of nature.

The second difficult word, here translated as *genius,* is *Genialitet*. It means not a person (as when we say, "That man is a genius"), but a quality or capacity (as when we say, "It is the genius of the German language that it can . . ."). Unfortunately, we lack in English a word corresponding to *Genialitet,* as distinct from *genius*. It should have been *geniality*—but of course that word means something else! In this chapter, therefore, the reader is to understand by "the sensuous genius" the quality or inmost essence of sensuousness.

To make Kierkegaard speak English, we must make him

say that "the most abstract idea conceivable is sensuousness in its innermost essential character." (Cf., e.g., Croxall's *Kierkegaard Studies* and *Kierkegaard Commentary.*)

7. "Poor is the house where there are not goods in superabundance." (Horace, *Letters*, I, 6, 45.)

8. The one exception was his love for Psyche. Her name means *soul*, and it is to this that reference is made a few sentences later when it is remarked that his love is based on the psychical.

9. "In addition I vote for . . ." The words with which Cato invariably introduced his oft-reiterated demand for the destruction of Carthage.

10. *Karikaturen des Heiligsten* (Leipzig, 1819–21, II, pp. 82 ff.) treats of the relations of sight and hearing to the other senses.

11. The story is told in *Owen Tudor*.

12. As good as any (i.e., one represents them all).

13. *The Irish March of the Elves* treats of a changeling, the little bagpiper, who bewitched everything, animate and inanimate, by his playing. See *Der kleine Sackpfeifer* by the Grimms.

14. Grand opera.

15. "And appears to be floating in the air." (Virgil's *Georgics,* i, 404.)

16. Cf. Thor's contest with Utgard-Loki in Norse mythology.

17. The particular speech is in Mozart's *Marriage of Figaro,* Act I, Sc. 5: "She is a woman," spoken by Cherubino to Susanne.

18. In Leporello's list.

19. "I came, I saw, I conquered." Caesar's laconic report of his victory over Pharnaces.

20. The Latin means: "The farmer stands and waits for the river to flow by." (Horace, *Letters,* i, 2, 42.)

21. I Samuel 16:14 ff.

22. This is perhaps a reference to the Danish poet Hauch's poem, *The Mountain Maiden*.

23. H. G. Hotho, German art historian, 1802–73.

24. *Sub una specie* means "under one form"; *sub utraque specie,* "under both forms."

25. By "aesthetic indifference" S.K. means an undifferentiated (immediate, unreflective) aesthetic condition or stage.

26. The folk-book mentioned was actually found among S.K.'s papers.—A *privatdocent*, in German and Scandinavian universities, is an unsalaried lecturer or tutor, who receives only the students' fees. Kierkegaard is here making an ironical gibe against the scholars who consult secondary rather than original sources.—"Tribler's Widow" refers to the firm of E. M. Tribler, bookbinder of Copenhagen, which was carried on by his widow.

27. The few stanzas are:
"Der Mond der scheint so helle, die Todten reiten schnelle"
    and
"Graut Liebchen auch?
Wie sollte mir grauen?
Ich bin ja bei dir."
See *Gedichte* of Gottfried Bürger (Titmann's edition), Leipzig, 1869, p. 319.

28. "If she only wears a petticoat, you know well what he does." See "The List," *Don Juan.*

29. An arrangement of *Don Juan,* adapted to Mozart's music by L. Kruse.

30. *Armuth, Reichtum, Schuld und Busse der Gräfin Dolores* (*Werke,* VIII, p. 25).

31. The lesser mysteries were a preparatory celebration in Athens, before the celebration of the great festival of the mysteries at Eleusis.

32. A puppet show, Copenhagen, 1814.

33. Professor Hauch was the author of two dramas, *Gregory the Seventh* and *Don Juan,* published in Copenhagen in 1829.

34. Elvira's servant.

35. In Heiberg's adaptation Herr Paaske (Mr. Easter) corresponds to Molière's M. Dimanche.

36. See Note 9 to *Preface* and *Diapsalmata.*

37. In a higher sense.

38. "He will be inside with the fair sex," from the servant's aria.

39. Jeronimus is a character in Holberg's *Barselstuen,*

who put in an appearance when he was most needed.
40. Act I, Sc. 15.

"THE ANCIENT TRAGICAL MOTIF AS REFLECTED IN THE MODERN"

1. From the standpoint of Greek, Kierkegaard has produced what Professor Eduard Geismar of the University of Copenhagen calls an "impossible word." Yet it is easy enough to see what Kierkegaard meant by it, and Geismar freely translates it as "the fellowship of buried lives." Kierkegaard imagines himself addressing a society composed of people "who, for one cause or another, are living lives which are spiritually or mentally entombed and isolated" (Croxall).

2. Cf. Aristotle's *Poetics*.

3. I Chronicles 21.

4. It was about the Etruscan prophets and soothsayers, not the Roman augurs, that Cato said that he could not understand how they could look at each other without laughing. Cf. Cicero, *De divinatione*, ii, 51; *De natura deorum*, i, 71.

5. Thiers was the statesman in question.

6. Aristotle's words, here translated as "thought and character," are *dianoia kai ethos*. Cf. *Poetics*, Chap. 6. In the same place, action or plot, not character, is indicated as the aim (*telos*) of tragedy. "The actions do not therefore take place to depict character, but one uses characters for the sake of the action."

7. Aristotle's word is *hamartia*, which means "error," "guilt." Cf. *Poetics*, Chap. 13.

8. Pelagius, the opponent of Augustine, denied the doctrine of original (i.e., hereditary) sin.

9. Chr. D. Grabbe, *Don Juan und Faust*, Frankfort, 1829.

10. For example, the Latin *partim*, an adverb meaning "partly" or "partially," was an old accusative of the substantive *pars*, or "part."

11. See Aristotle's *Poetics*, Chap. 6, and Hegel's *Aesthetik* III, 531–32, 1838. A few lines later S.K. quotes Hegel's definition of true compassion; the sentence may be para-

phrased as follows: true compassion involves the gift or ability to enter sympathetically into the situation of a sufferer because one understands the external circumstances which provide an ethical justification for him.

12. Hebrews 10:31.

13. *Philoctetes* is a tragedy by Sophocles.

14. *Philoctetes*, ver. 732 ff.

15. The force or law of inertia.

16. "Substantiality" is here used in the sense of "immediacy," the opposite of reflection.

17. Labdakos was the grandfather of Oedipus.

18. "Whom the god would destroy he first makes mad."

19. According to a thirteenth-century French metrical romance, Robert, first Duke of Normandy, was devoted to the devil by his mother before his birth. He ran a career of cruelties and crimes unparalleled.

20. Høgne was the son of Queen Grimhild and a troll.

21. An attempt to predispose the listener or the judge favorably.

22. *Antigone*, ver. 850. The translation used in the text is that of Campbell, Oxford University Press.

23. "Which she does not meditate upon in her heart." Not an exact quotation.

24. Sophocles, *The Trachinian Maidens*, ver. 1159.

"SHADOWGRAPHS"

1. *Gestern liebt' ich* is to be found in Lessing's *Songs from the Spanish*. The two poems may be roughly translated as follows:

> Though love may ever be forsworn,
> Still, by love's magic, in this cave,
> The startled, drunken soul is lulled
> Into forgetting it has sworn.

> *   *   *

> Yesterday I loved,
> Today I suffer,
> Tomorrow I die.
> Yet, tomorrow and today,
> I think, without resisting,
> Of yesterday.

2. Cf. I Kings 19:11–12.

3. Certain Greek philosophers, called the Atomists, assumed a constant whirling motion in the atoms of the universe.

4. Veronica was a woman of Jerusalem who, according to Christian tradition, dried the face of Christ on His way to Golgotha. It is alleged that on the handkerchief was left an image of His face. The name Veronica means "true image."

5. *Odyssey,* iv, 450 ff.

6. I Samuel 28.

7. Common nouns.

8. "That ancient sage" was Simonides. Cicero, *De natura deorum,* i, 60.

9. I Peter 3:4.

10. Persecuted church.

11. In Kruse's adaptation of *Don Juan,* Elvira had been a nun.

12. Oehlenschläger's *Aladdin.*

13. Elvira does carry a dagger in Kruse's *Don Juan.*

14. Virgil, *Aeneid,* vi, 469.

15. The modern philosophy in question is Hegelianism.

16. Heraclitus used these words about the oracle at Delphi.

17. The obol was a small coin which the Greeks placed in a dead man's mouth as Charon's fee for ferrying him over the Styx.

18. Miss Swanwick translates this as follows:
"Half childish sport,
Half God in thy young heart!" (*Faust* V, 3435.)

19. *Wilhelm Meister's Lehrjahre,* Book IV, Chap. 13, toward the end.

20. Florine is a character in Swedish folklore. Cf. "The Blue Bird" in Bäckström's *Svenska Folkböcker.*

"THE UNHAPPIEST MAN"

1. The epitaph really exists in Worcester. Chateaubriand mentions this.

2. Pram, *Heroic Odes,* 1785.

3. Though pursued by the Eumenides, Orestes at length found asylum in the Temple of Delphi. Not so the "unhappiest." He finds refuge nowhere.

4. *Aphorismenoi* = *segregati*, separated, cast out.

5. Solon had warned Croesus against the dangers of success; later, falling into the hands of Cyrus, Croesus called upon Solon.

6. An instance is *Phaenomenologie des Geistes*, IV, B.

7. "The third nut is death." (Clemens Brentano, *The Three Nuts*.)

8. Ancaeus, King of Samos, just as he was about to drink of the new wine, which the oracle had warned him against tasting, was killed by a wild boar.

9. Latona was condemned to wander about the earth before she could give birth to Apollo and Diana. The Hyperboreans were supposed to live back of the north wind. See Thomas Moore's "Song of the Hyperboreans."

10. Niobe was changed into stone through grief over the death of her children.

11. Job 1:21.

12. From this statement it is evident that "the unhappiest" is the person whose condition was described in the paragraph beginning, "Let us proceed. Let us imagine a combination . . ."

"THE FIRST LOVE"

1. Augustin Eugène Scribe (1791–1861) was a French dramatist. Heiberg's translation of his comedy, *The First Love*, was published in 1832.

2. This is from *Om en Jødepige* by Johan Herman Wessel (1742–85), a satirical and witty Norwegian versifier.

3. Cf. Plato's *Phaedo*, 60 b.

4. I Corinthians 1:23.

5. Pelagius emphasized the absolute freedom of the will.

6. The Latin *vates* means both poet and prophet.

7. The quotation is from Johan Georg Hamann, *Leser und Kunstrichter*, in the Roth edition of the *Werke*, II, p. 397.

8. In the public domain.

9. Emmeline remarks to her father, who says he could not recognize the assumed Charles, "Oh, you! that is a different matter; but I, who am in sympathy with him, can never be deceived."

10. Thus Charles, in the person of Rinville, describes himself to Emmeline.

11. Wehmüller, a character in a novel by Clemens Brentano, *Die mehreren Wehmüller und ungarischen Nationalgesichter,* was a painter who attempted to produce a national face from a composite picture of many people.

12. When Philip III of Spain saw a student reading with expressions of great amusement, he said: "Either this student is a simpleton, or he is reading *Don Quixote.*"

13. A moneylender to whom Charles is in debt.

14. A thing missing and missed.

15. This appears in Scene 8 as an aside after the following dialogue:

"Rinville: If I remember correctly, the next day I stole a new kiss.

Emmeline: No, the next morning you set out on your journey."

16. One is reminded of the spirit of the lamp in *Aladdin.*

17. The worst is that Charles is married.

18. Hence these tears.

"THE ROTATION METHOD"

1. In Hegel's philosophy, "the negative" plays an important role. Every concept produces of itself its negation or opposite. It is by the mediation or reconciliation of the two opposites that a higher concept is attained, which again produces its "negation"—and so on indefinitely. The negative has, consequently, the power to set in movement, to produce motion.

2. Bread and circuses were, according to Juvenal, the Roman citizen's sole desire.

3. Saxo Grammaticus tells this in the beginning of Book 6, *Gesta Danorum.*

4. For the use of everyone.

5. Aristotle's definition, *Politics* i, 1, 9.

6. "Idleness is the devil's pillow."

7. The second form of boredom is the "acquired imme-diacy" mentioned in the first line of the paragraph.

8. To speak of boredom as a pantheistic conception is to talk in a full-blown Hegelian manner. Boredom is defined by its contrariety to pantheism: viz., as emptiness in op-position to fulness. Since every concept contains its own opposite, we may say that pantheism lies hidden in bore-dom; for this reason boredom was referred to a bit earlier as "the daemonic [i.e., hidden] side of pantheism."

9. *Europamüde,* or "tired of Europe," was a literary catchword around 1840.

10. The Emperor Marcus Aurelius (Antoninus Philoso-phus), in his *Meditations,* VII, 2, says: "To recover thy life is in thy power. Look at things again as thou didst use to look at them; for in this consists the recovery of thy life" (trans. by G. Long). In the rough draft Kierkegaard trans-lated it: "Look at things you saw before from another point of view." In this it would appear that S.K. was following the German translation of J. M. Schultz. Kierkegaard reads the translation but cites the original, apparently without taking notice of the real meaning of the latter.

11. Fire and blind hope, according to Aeschylus, *Pro-metheus,* ver. 250 ff.

12. To wonder at nothing.

13. See Holberg's comedy of that name.

14. To will the same and not to will the same makes for a firm friendship (Sallust, *Catilina,* 20).

15. Prepared, ready to march.

"DIARY OF THE SEDUCER"

1. "His ruling passion is the fresh young girl" (from the "list" aria).

2. *Commentarius perpetuus* means "running commen-tary."

3. The word "parastatic" came into currency in the struggle between the Church and the Gnostics in the sec-ond century over the nature of the body of Christ, the

Gnostics maintaining that the divine Logos had assumed an apparent or phantom body only, not an actual one, for according to the heretical view, it would be unseemly for the Logos to be manifested in the flesh. It comes as a bit of a jolt to have a word from that context applied here, but the meaning is plain enough: the author of the Diary, although a coldly intellectual type, did occasionally take upon himself the characteristics of passionate flesh and blood.

4. Ixion, who wished to seize Hera (Juno), was deceived by a cloud in her form.

5. *Actiones in distans* means "operations directed toward a distant goal." The Diary contains eleven novelistic interpolations which S.K. calls by this name. In the *Papirer* (III B 52) he remarks that "the diary ought not to begin with Cordelia's story but with the first *actio in distans* which is to be found in the blue book." This first is the one in which the seducer demonstrates the irresistible power of his "side glance."

6. Goethe, *Jery und Bätely* (Werke, XI). The words mean: "Go then—scorn fidelity. Remorse will follow."

7. I Samuel 12.

8. The novel of Ludwig Tieck's referred to is *Die wilde Engländerin in Das Zauberschloss*. A beautiful English noblewoman refused all suitors because of inhibitions about married life she had acquired as a child while reading a textbook on anatomy. So it was that she passionately devoted herself to the study of astronomy and other sciences. Even a wise and worthy lord who shared her scientific interests was unable to win her hand. One day, when they had been out riding together, they quarreled. In her agitation she dismounted so hastily that her riding habit, catching on the saddle, was torn off her. Beside herself, she hid for a week in her room, and then suddenly realized that she loved the nobleman and would marry him.

9. Georges Cuvier was a French scientist, who affirmed that from a single bone a scientist could reconstruct the whole animal.

10. "There he comes, who always swarms with girls" (*Don Juan*, Act I, Sc. 16, Kruse's adaptation).

11. Holberg's *Erasmus Montanus*, Act V, Sc. 5.

12. *Alcedo ispida*, the kingfisher, was believed by the ancients to build its nest on the water.

13. The hospital attendants wore green liveries.

14. In the thought of Kierkegaard it is only the eternal, the divine, which may be described as necessary; in the course of history no event is necessary. Necessity is thus another word for eternity.

15. Like Orpheus, who fetched Eurydice up from the underworld.

16. "Night and winter, long roads and cruel pains, and all manner of exertion there are in this unwarlike camp" (Ovid, *Ars amandi*, ii, 235).

17. *Preciosa* is a lyric drama by Wolff, with music by Weber.

18. Genesis 41:32.

19. Shakespeare, *King Lear*, Act I, Sc. 1.

20. The Danish word is *Forsprang*. It means "forbidden purchase of goods outside the market place and outside of legally permitted hours."

21. "What before was impulse is now method" (Ovid, *Remedia amoris*, ver. 10).

22. The literal meaning of *zu Grunde gehn* is "to sink, founder; go to ruin, perish." But Hegel often uses this expression (e.g., in *Wissenschaft der Logik, Werke* IV, 1834, 157) in a quite special way, the exposition of which would require a monograph. In brief, however, it may be remarked that, according to Hegel, being is in process of transition in such wise that it explicates or evolves itself in terms of its fundamental essence (*Grund*). By developing itself, by becoming that which fundamentally and essentially it *is*, being can be said to have reached its *ground*. That is, it founders or disappears but in the sense of its being taken up into a new and higher sphere.

23. In *La Fiancée*, a comedy in three acts with music by Auber and libretto by Scribe, Fritz was jilted by his "girl friend" because of his awkwardness and stupidity.

24. This couplet is from Joseph von Eichendorff's poem, *Vor der Stadt*, which says of two musicians that "the one is madly in love, the other would like to be."

25. The lines are from a Norwegian peasant ditty.

26. Like Phaeton, who received permission from his father, the sun god, to drive his chariot, and came too near the earth.

27. Odysseus was not handsome, but he was eloquent, and he caused the sea goddesses, Circe and Calypso, to be tormented by love. Cf. Ovid, *Ars amandi,* ii, 123.

28. Kierkegaard probably got this "old verse" from a musical game called "The Monk and the Nun," one line of which reads, "The monk spreads out his cloak so blue and begs the beautiful maiden to rest upon it."

29. Thekla's song is from Schiller's tragedy, *The Piccolomini.* The value of this poem for Johannes lies in the fact that in a romantic way it combines the thoughts of love and death. The same is true of *Lenore.*

30. William is the dead lover in Bürger's *Lenore.*

31. By unanimous consent of the people.

32. Spontaneous generation.

33. This is mentioned as a general belief in Plato's *Apology,* 39 c.

34. Trop is a carnival barker in Heiberg's *The Reviewer and the Beast.*

35. *Cominus* means "close at hand"; *eminus,* "at a distance."

36. "The secretly blushing cheek reflects the glow of the heart."

37. As did Don Juan when the statue of the commandant knocked.

38. Evidently S.K. was depending too much on memory. He means Rachel, not Rebecca. And when we read Genesis 31:9–34, we see that it was Jacob who "stole Laban's heart," not Rachel—who only took the household gods! The Danish Bible, unlike the King James version, reproduces literally the Hebrew idiom, "to steal the heart." The heart was regarded as the seat of the intelligence. To steal it means, accordingly, to trick or deceive.

39. Something worthy of worship.

40. "Agnete, she swayed, she drooped, she fell" (Baggesen, *Agnete fra Holmegaard*).

41. Aeolus was the god of winds, who held them imprisoned in a cave (*Odyssey* X, 1 ff.).

42. Ariadne helped Theseus escape from the Labyrinth by means of a spool of thread.

43. Mark 3:24.

44. Genesis 30:31 ff.

45. A mural picture was found in Herculaneum, showing Theseus, who had carried Ariadne away, but deserted her at Naxos.

46. The nymph Echo wasted away with unrequited love for Narcissus until only her voice remained.

47. In 1837 this newspaper published a piece satirizing the maidservants for dressing like ladies.

48. "Matchless" and "golden age" were words greatly beloved of Bishop Grundtvig. They are used here as an ironic dig at Grundtvig, who (to quote Kierkegaard in another place) "with falcon eye" often espied an approaching matchless golden age.

49. This is probably another gibe at Grundtvig, whose teaching about the power of the living word (i.e., the oral transmission of the Apostle's Creed as distinct from the written word of the Bible) Kierkegaard criticizes with serious intent at some length in his papers.

50. Proverbs 24:26. Kierkegaard is here following Luther's translation: *"Eine richtige Antwort ist wie ein lieblicher Kuss."*

51. *Phaedrus,* Chap. 31 ff.

52. This was a colossal statue on the banks of the Nile, which gave out a musical sound when the rays of the morning sun fell on it.

53. "The wife's dowry is quarrels."

54. "The die is cast." These words were ascribed to Caesar when he crossed the Rubicon.

55. In *The Arabian Nights*, Queen Scheherezade, by relating a series of tales from night to night, so excited the Sultan's curiosity that he spared her life for a thousand and one nights, in spite of his having resolved to espouse a new sultana every evening and to strangle her in the morning. Grateful to Scheherezade for her stories, he finally repented of his vow and revoked it.

56. "Let them hate, if only they fear" (a line often quoted by Caligula).

57. Oehlenschläger's *Palnatoke*.

58. S.K. is playing on the original meaning of *ex-sisto*, "appear, come forth." Woman does *not* come forth of herself but of man, from whose rib she was formed.

59. In Danish the verb "to court" is *at frie;* "to set free" is *at befri*. In this whole section about suitors and freedom Kierkegaard is availing himself of a pleasant play on words.

60. The well-known contest, which was won by Venus, was to determine who had the more beautiful back. By reason of her victory a temple was built in her honor and called "Kallipygos" (with beautiful back).

61. Horrible to relate.

62. Actaeon spied on Diana in her bath and was punished by being changed into a stag and devoured by hounds.

63. Pygmalion was a Greek sculptor who fell in love with a statue he had made of a beautiful woman. In answer to his prayers, Venus brought her to life.

64. When the Gauls, who had besieged Rome, attempted one night to storm the Capitoline Hill, the cackling of geese alerted the guards and the attack was repulsed.

65. A German writer, Matthias Claudius (1741–1815), collected some of his critical contributions to magazines in a volume entitled *Asmus omnia sua secum portans* ["Asmus who carries with him everything that belongs to him"]. In the Vienna edition of 1844, a parody of an erudite squabble is accompanied by a comic picture of the leader of the disputation, President Lars.

66. Myrtle was a plant sacred to Venus.

67. This refers to the speech of Aristophanes in Plato's *Symposium*, Chaps. 14, 15.

68. "I accept the omen" (Cicero, *De divinatione*, I, 103).

69. Alectryon was Mars' friend who stood guard at the rendezvous of Mars and Venus, but fell asleep, so that they were surprised by Apollo and Vulcan.

70. Clytie was turned into a sunflower when Apollo became untrue to her.

INDEX